Physical Anthropology 10/11

Nineteenth Edition

EDITOR

Elvio Angeloni
Pasadena City College

Elvio Angeloni received his BA from UCLA in 1963, his MA in anthropology from UCLA in 1965, and his MA in communication arts from Loyola Marymount University in 1976. He has produced several films, including *Little Warrior,* winner of the Cinemedia VI Best Bicentennial Theme, and *Broken Bottles,* shown on PBS. He served as an academic adviser on the instructional television series *Faces of Culture.* He received the Pasadena City College Outstanding Teacher Award in 2006. He is also the academic editor of *Annual Editions: Anthropology, Classic Edition Sources: Anthropology,* co-editor of *Rountable Viewpoints Physical Anthropology,* and co-editor of *Annual Editions: Archaeology.* His primary area of interest has been indigenous peoples of the American Southwest.

ANNUAL EDITIONS: PHYSICAL ANTHROPOLOGY, NINETEENTH EDITION

Published by McGraw-Hill, a business unit of The McGraw-Hill Companies, Inc., 1221 Avenue
of the Americas, New York, NY 10020. Copyright © 2010 by The McGraw-Hill Companies, Inc.
All rights reserved. Previous edition(s) 1990–2009. No part of this publication may be reproduced
or distributed in any form or by any means, or stored in a database or retrieval system, without the
prior written consent of The McGraw-Hill Companies, Inc., including, but not limited to, in any
network or other electronic storage or transmission, or broadcast for distance learning.

Some ancillaries, including electronic and print components, may not be available to customers outside the United States.

Annual Editions® is a registered trademark of the McGraw-Hill Companies, Inc.

Annual Editions is published by the **Contemporary Learning Series** group within the McGraw-
Hill Higher Education division.

1 2 3 4 5 6 7 8 9 0 QPD/QPD 0 9

ISBN 978–0–07–812780–9
MHID 0–07–812780–7
ISSN 1074–1844

Managing Editor: *Larry Loeppke*
Senior Managing Editor: *Faye Schilling*
Developmental Editor: *Debra Henricks*
Editorial Coordinator: *Mary Foust*
Editorial Assistant: *Cindy Hedley*
Production Service Assistant: *Rita Hingtgen*
Permissions Coordinator: *Lenny J. Behnke*
Senior Marketing Manager: *Julie Keck*
Senior Marketing Communications Specialist: *Mary Klein*
Marketing Coordinator: *Alice Link*
Project Manager: *Joyce Watters*
Design Specialist: *Tara McDermott*
Production Supervisor: *Sue Culbertson*
Cover Graphics: *Kristine Jubeck*

Compositor: Laserwords Private Limited
Cover Image: © Digital Vision/Getty Images/RF (inset top), © Ingram Publishing/AGE Fotostock
(inset bottom), © Getty Images/RF (background)

Library in Congress Cataloging-in-Publication Data
Main entry under title: Annual Editions: Physical Anthropology. 2010/2011.
    1. Physical Anthropology—Periodicals. I. Angeloni, Elvio, *comp.* II. Title: Physical Anthropology.
658'.05

www.mhhe.com

Editors/Academic Advisory Board

Members of the Academic Advisory Board are instrumental in the final selection of articles for each edition of ANNUAL EDITIONS. Their review of articles for content, level, and appropriateness provides critical direction to the editors and staff. We think that you will find their careful consideration well reflected in this volume.

ANNUAL EDITIONS: Physical Anthropology 10/11
19th Edition

EDITOR

Elvio Angeloni
Pasadena City College

ACADEMIC ADVISORY BOARD MEMBERS

Preface

In publishing ANNUAL EDITIONS we recognize the enormous role played by the magazines, newspapers, and journals of the public press in providing current, first-rate educational information in a broad spectrum of interest areas. Many of these articles are appropriate for students, researchers, and professionals seeking accurate, current material to help bridge the gap between principles and theories and the real world. These articles, however, become more useful for study when those of lasting value are carefully collected, organized, indexed, and reproduced in a low-cost format, which provides easy and permanent access when the material is needed. That is the role played by ANNUAL EDITIONS.

This nineteenth *Annual Editions: Physical Anthropology* contains a variety of articles relating to human evolution. The writings were selected for their timeliness, relevance to issues not easily treated in the standard physical anthropology textbooks, and clarity of presentation.

Whereas textbooks tend to reflect the consensus within the field, *Annual Editions: Physical Anthropology 10/11* provides a forum for the controversial. We do this in order to convey to the student that the study of human development is an evolving entity in which each discovery encourages further research and each added piece of the puzzle raises new questions about the total picture.

Our final criterion for selecting articles is readability. All too often, the excitement of a new discovery or a fresh idea is deadened by the weight of a ponderous presentation. We seek to avoid that by incorporating essays written with enthusiasm and with the desire to communicate some very special ideas to the general public.

Included in this volume are a number of features that are designed to be useful for students, researchers, and professionals in the field of anthropology. While the articles are arranged along the lines of broadly unifying subject areas, the *topic guide* can be used to establish specific reading assignments that tailor to the needs of a particular course of study. Other useful features include the *table of contents* abstracts, which summarize each article and present key concepts in bold italics.

In addition, each unit is preceded by an *overview* that provides a background for informed reading of the articles, emphasizes critical issues, and presents *key points* to consider in the form of questions. Also included are websites that are coordinated to follow the volume's units.

In contrast to the usual textbooks, which by their nature cannot be easily revised, this book will be continually updated to reflect the dynamic, changing character of its subject. Those involved in producing *Annual Editions: Physical Anthropology 10/11* wish to make the next one as useful and effective as possible. Your criticism and advice are welcomed. Please complete and return the postage-paid *article rating form* on the last page of the book and let us know your opinions. Any anthology can be improved, and this one will continue to be.

Elvio Angeloni

Elvio Angeloni
Editor
evangeloni@gmail.com

Contents

UNIT 1
Evolutionary Perspectives

The concepts in bold italics are developed in the article. For further expansion, please refer to the Topic Guide.

UNIT 2
Primates

UNIT 3
Sex and Gender

The concepts in bold italics are developed in the article. For further expansion, please refer to the Topic Guide.

UNIT 4
The Fossil Evidence

The concepts in bold italics are developed in the article. For further expansion, please refer to the Topic Guide.

UNIT 5
Late Hominid Evolution

UNIT 6
Human Diversity

The concepts in bold italics are developed in the article. For further expansion, please refer to the Topic Guide.

UNIT 7
Living with the Past

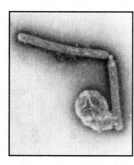

The concepts in bold italics are developed in the article. For further expansion, please refer to the Topic Guide.

The concepts in bold italics are developed in the article. For further expansion, please refer to the Topic Guide.

Correlation Guide

The *Annual Editions* series provides students with convenient, inexpensive access to current, carefully selected articles from the public press. **Annual Editions: Physical Anthropology 10/11** is an easy-to-use reader that presents articles on important topics such as *evolution, natural selection, taxonomy,* and many more. For more information on *Annual Editions* and other *McGraw-Hill Contemporary Learning Series* titles, visit www.mhhe.com/cls.

This convenient guide matches the units in **Annual Editions: Physical Anthropology 10/11** with the corresponding chapters in two of our best-selling McGraw-Hill Anthropology textbooks by Relethford and Park.

Annual Editions: Physical Anthropology 10/11	The Human Species: An Introduction to Biological Anthropology, 8/e by Relethford	Biological Anthropology, 6/e by Park
Unit 1: Evolutionary Perspectives	**Chapter 1:** Biological Anthropology and Evolution **Chapter 2:** Human Genetics **Chapter 3:** Microevolution **Chapter 4:** The Evolution and Classification of Species	**Chapter 1:** Biological Anthropology **Chapter 2:** The Evolution of Evolution **Chapter 3:** Evolutionary Genetics **Chapter 4:** The Processes of Evolution **Chapter 5:** The Origin of Species and the Shape of Evolution **Chapter 6:** A Brief Evolutionary Timetable
Unit 2: Primates	**Chapter 4:** The Evolution and Classification of Species **Chapter 5:** The Primates **Chapter 6:** Primate Behavior and Ecology **Chapter 9:** Primate Origins and Evolution	**Chapter 5:** The Origin of Species and the Shape of Evolution **Chapter 7:** The Primates **Chapter 8:** Primate Behavior and Human Evolution **Chapter 10:** Evolution of the Early Hominins
Unit 3: Sex and Gender	**Chapter 7:** The Human Species	**Chapter 14:** Human Biological Diversity
Unit 4: The Fossil Evidence	**Chapter 1:** Biological Anthropology and Evolution **Chapter 8:** Paleoanthropology **Chapter 12:** The Evolution of Archaic Humans	**Chapter 9:** Studying the Human Past
Unit 5: Late Hominid Evolution	**Chapter 10:** The Beginnings of Human Evolution **Chapter 11:** The Origin of the Genus Homo **Chapter 12:** The Evolution of Archaic Humans **Chapter 13:** The Origin of Modern Humans	**Chapter 11:** The Evolution of Genus Homo **Chapter 12:** The Debate Over Modern Human Origins
Unit 6: Human Diversity	**Chapter 14:** The Study of Human Variation **Chapter 15:** Recent Microevolution of Human Populations	**Chapter 13:** Evolution and Adaptation in Human Populations **Chapter 14:** Human Biological Diversity
Unit 7: Living with the Past	**Chapter 16:** Human Adaptation **Chapter 17:** The Biological Impact of Agriculture and Civilization	**Chapter 13:** Evolution and Adaptation in Human Populations **Chapter 15:** Biological Anthropology and Today's World

Topic Guide

This topic guide suggests how the selections in this book relate to the subjects covered in your course. You may want to use the topics listed on these pages to search the Web more easily.

On the following pages a number of websites have been gathered specifically for this book. They are arranged to reflect the units of this Annual Editions reader. You can link to these sites by going to *http://www.mhcls.com*.

All the articles that relate to each topic are listed below the bold-faced term.

Aggression
11. Dim Forest, Bright Chimps
17. Face-Offs of the Female Kind
26. Hard Times among the Neanderthals

Anatomy
2. Was Darwin Wrong?
3. The Facts of Evolution
5. How the Dog Got Its Curly Tail
18. What's Love Got to Do with It?: Sex among Our Closest Relatives Is a Rather Open Affair
21. The Woman Who Shook up Man's Family Tree
22. Hunting the First Hominid
25. The Scavenging of "Peking Man"
26. Hard Times among the Neanderthals
27. Rethinking Neanderthals
28. Last of the Neanderthals: A Hunter Retreats
29. The Great Human Migration
30. The Littlest Human
31. The Gift *of* Gab
32. The Birth of Childhood
33. The Brain
36. How Real Is Race?: Using Anthropology to Make Sense of Human Diversity

Archeology
27. Rethinking Neanderthals
28. Last of the Neanderthals: A Hunter Retreats
30. The Littlest Human

Bipedalism
18. What's Love Got to Do with It?: Sex among Our Closest Relatives Is a Rather Open Affair
22. Hunting the First Hominid
24. Scavenger Hunt

Burials
27. Rethinking Neanderthals
28. Last of the Neanderthals: A Hunter Retreats

Communication
13. Why Are Some Animals So Smart?
15. A Telling Difference
31. The Gift *of* Gab
33. The Brain

Culture
10. Got Culture?
12. Thinking Like a Monkey
13. Why Are Some Animals So Smart?
15. A Telling Difference
27. Rethinking Neanderthals
29. The Great Human Migration
30. The Littlest Human
36. How Real Is Race?: Using Anthropology to Make Sense of Human Diversity
40. The Inuit Paradox

Darwin, Charles
1. Charles Darwin Was Born into a World That Today's Scientists Wouldn't Recognize
2. Was Darwin Wrong?
3. The Facts of Evolution
4. Evolution in Action
41. Dr. Darwin

Disease
7. Why Should Students Learn Evolution?
38. The Viral Superhighway
39. The Perfect Plague
41. Dr. Darwin
42. Curse and Blessing of the Ghetto
43. Ironing It Out

DNA (deoxyribonucleic acid)
7. Why Should Students Learn Evolution?
8. The 2% Difference
23. Made in Savannahstan
29. The Great Human Migration
35. Born Gay?
42. Curse and Blessing of the Ghetto

Dominance hierarchy
16. What Are Friends For?
17. Face-Offs of the Female Kind
18. What's Love Got to Do with It?: Sex among Our Closest Relatives Is a Rather Open Affair

Ethnicity
40. The Inuit Paradox
42. Curse and Blessing of the Ghetto

Evolution
1. Charles Darwin Was Born into a World That Today's Scientists Wouldn't Recognize
2. Was Darwin Wrong?
3. The Facts of Evolution
4. Evolution in Action
5. How the Dog Got Its Curly Tail
7. Why Should Students Learn Evolution?
8. The 2% Difference
20. The Salamander's Tale
23. Made in Savannahstan
34. Skin Deep
39. The Perfect Plague
43. Ironing It Out

Evolutionary perspective
1. Charles Darwin Was Born into a World That Today's Scientists Wouldn't Recognize
2. Was Darwin Wrong?
3. The Facts of Evolution
4. Evolution in Action
5. How the Dog Got Its Curly Tail
6. The Latest Face of Creationism

Internet References

The following Internet sites have been selected to support the articles found in this reader. These sites were available at the time of publication. However, because websites often change their structure and content, the information listed may no longer be available. We invite you to visit http://www.mhcls.com for easy access to these sites.

Annual Editions: Physical Anthropology 10/11

General Sources

American Anthropological Association (AAA)
http://www.aaanet.org/

Maintained by the AAA, this site provides links to AAA's publications (including tables of contents of recent issues, style guides, and others) and to other anthropology sites.

Anthropology in the News
http://www.tamu.edu/anthropology/news.html

Texas A&M provides data on news articles that relate to anthropology, including biopsychology and sociocultural anthropology news.

Anthropology on the Web
http://www.as.ua.edu/ant/lib/web1.htm

This website provides addresses and tips on acquiring links to regional studies, maps, anthropology tutorials, and other data.

Anthropology Resources on the Internet
http://www.socsciresearch.com/r7.html

Links to Internet resources of anthropological relevance, including Web servers in different fields, are available here. The Education Index rated it "one of the best education-related sites on the Web."

Anthropology Resources Page
http://www.usd.edu/anth/

Many topics can be accessed from this University of South Dakota site. South Dakota archaeology, American Indian issues, and paleopathology resources are just a few examples.

Library of Congress
http://www.loc.gov

Examine this extensive website to learn about resource tools, library services/resources, exhibitions, and databases in many different subfields of anthropology.

The New York Times
http://www.nytimes.com

Browsing through the archives of The New York Times will provide a wide array of articles and information related to the different subfields of anthropology.

Physical Anthropology Resources
http://www.killgrove.org/osteo.html

This website provides numerous links to other resources from the Web covering all aspects of physical anthropology.

Smithsonian Institution Web Home Page
http://www.si.edu/

Access to the vast anthropological and archaeological resources of the Smithsonian Institution.

UNIT 1: Evolutionary Perspectives

American Institute of Biological Sciences
http://www.actionbioscience.org/

An education resource promoting bioscience literacy.

Charles Darwin on Human Origins
http://www.literature.org/Works/Charles-Darwin/

This website contains the text of Charles Darwin's classic writing, Origin of Species, which presents his scientific theory of natural selection.

Enter Evolution: Theory and History
http://www.ucmp.berkeley.edu/history/evolution.html

Find information related to Charles Darwin and other important scientists at this website. It addresses preludes to evolution, natural selection, and more. Topics cover systematics, dinosaur discoveries, and vertebrate flight.

Harvard Dept. of MCB—Biology Links
http://mcb.harvard.edu/BioLinks.html

This site features sources on evolution and links to anthropology departments and laboratories, taxonomy, paleontology, natural history, journals, books, museums, meetings, and many other related areas.

National Center for Science Education
http://www.natcenscied.org/

A nationally-recognized clearinghouse for information on how to defend the teaching of evolution in public schools.

UNIT 2: Primates

African Primates at Home
http://www.indiana.edu/~primate/primates.html

Don't miss this unusual and compelling site describing African primates on their home turf. "See" and "Hear" features provide samples of vocalizations and beautiful photographs of various types of primates.

The Dian Fossey Gorilla Fund International
http://www.gorillafund.org

This site is dedicated to the conservation of gorillas and their habitats in Africa through anti-poaching, regular monitoring, research, education, and support of local communities. The DFGFI uniquely continues to promote the ideals and vision of Dr. Dian Fossey.

Electronic Zoo/NetVet-Primate Page
http://netvet.wustl.edu/primates.htm

This site touches on every kind of primate from A to Z and related information. The long list includes Darwinian theories and the Descent of Man, the Ebola virus, fossil hominids, the nonhuman Primate Genetics Lab, the Simian Retrovirus Laboratory, and zoonotic diseases, with many links in between.

Great Ape Survival Project: United Nations
http://www.unep.org/grasp/ABOUT_GRASP/index.asp

GRASP complements existing great ape conservation efforts by means of intergovernmental dialogue and policy making, conservation planning initiatives, technical and scientific support to great ape range state governments, flagship field projects and fund and awareness raising in donor countries.

Internet References

Jane Goodall Institute for Wildlife Research, Education and Conservation
http://www.janegoodall.org/jane/default.asp

This organization is devoted to wildlife research, education and conservation.

Laboratory Primate Newsletter
http://www.brown.edu/Research/Primate/other.html

This series of websites on primates includes links to a large number of primate sites.

Living Links
http://www.emory.edu/LIVING_LINKS/dewaal.html

An Emory University Website consisting of a compendium of Franz De Waal's research and publications along with links to other related primate Websites.

National Primate Research Center
http://pin.primate.wisc.edu/factsheets

A series of factsheets as a starting point to find information about the various primate species.

Orangutan Foundation International
http://www.orangutan.org/

This organization promotes the dissemination of information about the orangutan and its plight in order to galvanize the public and policy makers towards an appreciation of the ape's value and current dilemma so that it might be saved from extinction.

San Francisco State University
http://online.sfsu.edu/~,mgriffin/primates.html

This site provides links to a variety of primate Websites.

UNIT 3: Sex and Gender

American Anthropologist
http://www.aaanet.org/aa/index.htm

Check out this site, the home page of *American Anthropologist,* for general information about anthropology as well as articles relating to such topics as biological research.

American Scientist
http://www.amsci.org/amsci.html

Investigating this site will help students of physical anthropology to explore issues related to sex and society.

Bonobo Sex and Society
http://songweaver.com/info/bonobos.html

Accessed through Carnegie Mellon University, this site includes a *Scientific American* article discussing a primate's behavior that challenges traditional assumptions about male supremacy in human evolution.

UNIT 4: The Fossil Evidence

Fossil Hominids FAQ
http://www.talkorigins.org/faqs/homs/

Institute of Human Origins
http://iho.asu.edu/node/27

An important source for news, events, and current research into the hominid origins in Africa.

The African Emergence and Early Asian Dispersals of the Genus *Homo*
http://www.uiowa.edu/~bioanth/homo.html

Read this classic article to learn about what the Rift Valley in East Africa has to tell us about early hominid species. An excellent bibliography is included.

Long Foreground: Human Prehistory
http://www.wsu.edu/gened/learn-modules/top_longfor/lfopen-index.html

This Washington State University site presents a learning module covering three major topics in human evolution: Overview, Hominid Species Timeline, and Human Physical Characteristics. It also provides a helpful glossary of terms and links to other websites.

UNIT 5: Late Hominid Evolution

Hominid Evolution Survey
http://www.geocities.com/SoHo/Atrium/1381/index.html

This survey of the Hominid family categorizes known hominids by genus and species. Beginning with the oldest known species, data include locations and environments, physical characteristics, technology, social behaviors, charts, and citations.

Human Prehistory
http://users.hol.gr/~dilos/prehis.htm

The evolution of the human species, beginning with the *Australopithecus* and continuing with *Homo habilis, Homo erectus,* and *Homo sapiens,* is examined on this site. Also included are data on the people who lived in the Palaeolithic and Neolithic Age and are the immediate ancestors of modern man.

Max Planck Institute for Evolutionary Anthropology
http://www.eva.mpg.de/english/index.htm

This is the home page of one of the world's most important research centers for the study of human evolution. Its mission is to understand the human past through the study of genes, cultures, cognitive abilities, languages, social systems, and our closest primate relatives. You will also find publication references as well as links to other related sites.

UNIT 6: Human Diversity

Human Genome Project Information
http://www.ornl.gov/TechResources/Human_Genome/home.html

Obtain answers about the U.S. Human Genome Project from this site, which details progress, goals, support groups, ethical, legal, and social issues, and genetics information.

OMIM Home Page-Online Mendelian Inheritance in Man
http://www3.ncbi.nlm.nih.gov/omim/

This database from the National Center for Biotechnology Information is a catalog of human genes and genetic disorders. It contains text, pictures, and reference information of great interest to students of physical anthropology.

UNIT 7: Living with the Past

Evolution and Medicine Network
http://www.evolutionandmedicine.org/

A resource for scientists and medical professionals working at the interface of evolutionary biology and medicine.

Internet References

Forensic Science Reference Page
http://www.lab.fws.gov

Look over this site from the U.S. Fish and Wildlife Forensics Lab to explore topics related to forensic anthropology.

The Paleolithic Diet Page
http://www.paleodiet.com/

A good source for research results on the paleolithic diet and its implications for living in the modern world.

Zeno's Forensic Page
http://www.forensic.to/forensic.html

A complete list of resources on forensics is presented on this website. It includes general information sources, DNA/serology sources and databases, forensic medicine anthropology sites, and related areas.

UNIT 1

Evolutionary Perspectives

Unit Selections

1. **Charles Darwin Was Born into a World That Today's Scientists Wouldn't Recognize,** Tom Siegfried
2. **Was Darwin Wrong?,** David Quammen
3. **The Facts of Evolution,** Michael Shermer
4. **Evolution in Action,** Jonathan Weiner
5. **How the Dog Got Its Curly Tail,** David Sloan Wilson
6. **The Latest Face of Creationism,** Glenn Branch and Eugenie C. Scott
7. **Why Should Students Learn Evolution?,** Brian J. Alters and Sandra M. Alters

Key Points to Consider

- How did Darwin, having studied for the ministry, develop into one of the greatest scientists of all time?

- What is "natural selection?"

- How would you summarize Darwin's evidence for evolution?

- In what ways is human ecological pressure bringing about an "evolution in action" in wildlife?

- How did the dog get its curly tail?

- Why should "creationism" not be taught in the classroom?

- Why should students learn about evolution?

Student Website
www.mhcls.com

Internet References

American Institute of Biological Sciences
  http://www.actionbioscience.org/
Charles Darwin on Human Origins
  http://www.literature.org/Works/Charles-Darwin/
Enter Evolution: Theory and History
  http://www.ucmp.berkeley.edu/history/evolution.html
Harvard Dept. of MCB—Biology Links
  http://mcb.harvard.edu/BioLinks.html
National Center for Science Education
  http://www.natcenscied.org/

As we reflect upon where the biological sciences have taken us over the past 300 years, we can see that we have been swept along a path of insight into the human condition, as well as into a heightened controversy of how to handle this potentially dangerous and/or unwanted knowledge of ourselves.

Certainly, Gregor Mendel, in the late nineteenth century, could not have anticipated that his study of pea plants would ultimately lead to the better understanding of over 3,000 genetically caused diseases, such as sickle-cell anemia, Huntington's chorea, Tay-Sachs, and hemophilia. Nor could he have foreseen the present-day controversies over matters such as cloning and genetic engineering. The significance of Mendel's work, of course, was his discovery that hereditary traits are conveyed by particular units that we now call "genes," a then-revolutionary notion that was later followed by a better understanding of how and why such units change. It is the knowledge of the process of "mutation," or alteration of the chemical structure of the gene, that is now providing us with the potential to control the genetic fate of individuals. This does not mean, however, that we should not continue to look at the role the environment plays in the development of what might be better termed as "genetically influenced conditions," such as alcoholism.

The other side of the evolutionary coin, as discussed in "The Facts of Evolution" is natural selection, a concept provided by Charles Darwin and Alfred Wallace. Natural selection refers to the "weeding out" of unfavorable mutations and the perpetuation of favorable ones. (See "Charles Darwin was Born into a World that Today's Scientist Wouldn't Recognize" and "Was Darwin Wrong?")

As our understanding of evolutionary processes continues to become more refined (See "Evolution in Action" and "How the Dog Got its Curly Tail"), it also, unfortunately, continues to be badly understood by the general public. Thus, all of us too often have to confront creationists with fallacies in their thinking (as in "The Latest Face of Creationism"), as well as remind ourselves why this battle is important (See "Why Should Students Learn Evolution?").

There is something to be learned from this conflict. Consider the claim of the "intelligent design theory" that nature is too orderly to have come about by a random process. What is missing from this view is the fact that natural selection is not a theory

of chance, but is instead a process which results in the *appearance* of intentional design. In fact, what we see in nature is not the absolute perfection that one might expect from a purposeful god, but, rather, the somewhat orderly but less than ideal adaptation on the part of creatures that must make do with what they have. As we survey the articles in this section, we must keep in mind that science is not simply an established and agreed upon body of knowledge. Rather, it is a way of thinking and a method of investigation in which we seek understanding for its own sake and not for some comforting, preconceived ideas.

Charles Darwin Was Born into a World That Today's Scientists Wouldn't Recognize

TOM SIEGFRIED

When baby Darwin arrived on February 12, 1809, modern science was also in its infancy. Dalton had just recently articulated the modern theory of the chemical atom, but nobody had any idea what atoms were really like. Physicists had not yet heard of the conservation of energy or any other laws of thermodynamics. Faraday hadn't yet shown how to make electricity from magnetism, and no one had a clue about light's electromagnetic identity. Geology was trapped in an antediluvian paradigm, psychology hadn't been invented yet and biology still seemed, in several key ways, to be infused with religion, resistant to the probes of experiment and reason.

Then came Darwin. By the time he died in 1882, thermodynamics possessed two unbreakable laws, chemistry had been codified in Mendeleye's periodic table, Maxwell had discovered the math merging electricity and magnetism to explain light. Lyell had established uniformitarianism as the basis for geology, Wundt had created the first experimental psychology laboratory, and science had something substantial to say about how life itself got to be the way it was—thanks to Darwin's perspicacious curiosity, intellectual rigor, personal perseverance and power of persuasion.

Superlatives are commonplace in accounts of Darwin's life. "An intellect which had no superior, and with a character which was even nobler than the intellect," wrote Thomas Henry Huxley, Darwin's champion in the original evolution debates. More recently Stephen Jay Gould called Darwin "the Muhammad Ali of biology." But all Ali did was fight. Darwin was more like Willie Mays—he could hit, hit with power, run, field and throw. Translated to science, Darwin could read, reason, experiment, theorize and write—all as well or better than any of his contemporaries. Several scientists before Darwin had expressed the idea of evolution, some even hinting about the role of selection. But none had the wherewithal to perceive the abundance of evidence for evolution, deduce its many nuances, explain its mechanism, foresee and counter the many objections, and articulate it so convincingly to the world.

And even had Darwin never written a word about evolution, he would be remembered today as one of the 19th century's premier botanists, a superb entomologist and prominent geologist. He was a leading authority on carnivorous plants and coral reefs, pigeons and bees, earthworms and orchids, beetles and barnacles (especially barnacles). And yet he was never educated to be a scientist and held no academic position. All he brought to the scientific table was his brain. What a brain.

Woe unto the Beetles

In his youth, Darwin was an average student but an avid reader. He had an early interest in observing and collecting, mainly beetles and butterflies. ("Woe unto the beetles of South America, woe unto all tropical butterflies," a friend wrote in advance of Darwin's famous sea voyage.) When it came time for higher education, Darwin headed to Edinburgh, a few hundred kilometers north of his birthplace in Shrewsbury, England, to study medicine. Soon discovering that he couldn't stand the sight of blood, Darwin headed back south to Cambridge, to prepare for the clergy, a profession in which blood wouldn't be such a problem.

His heart was not in religion, though, and his Cambridge years exposed him to other intellectual pursuits—lectures on botany, for instance, fieldwork with geologist Adam Sedgwick and friendships cultivated with biologists like John Stevens Henslow. Darwin's interest in science was most significantly stirred while reading books by the German savant Alexander von Humboldt and the English astronomer John Herschel, which imbued in him "a burning zeal to add even the most humble contribution to the noble structure of Natural Science," Darwin wrote later.

Henslow was perhaps the first to see in Darwin the makings of an uncommon scientist, and recommended him to serve as naturalist on the exploration voyage of the Beagle. During that ship's leisurely circumnavigation of the globe,

Darwin spent five years observing the planet's diverse life, its sundry geological formations and rich fossil record of life long gone. Darwin's eye saw more than what met it. He remarked on the variations between fossils and living forms, on the similarities of animals separated by vast distances and on the subtle differences and relationships among organisms on the South American mainland and the nearby Galápagos Islands.

By the time the voyage ended in October 1836, Darwin had amassed a mental catalog of life's diversities and subtleties never before held in one head. It gave him a lot to think about.

Sick at Down

Darwin's dispatches to England during the Beagle trip made him a scientific celebrity by the time he returned, and he hobnobbed with London's elite. But soon ill health drove him southeast of London to a rural home (known as Down House) near the town of Downe.

For the rest of his life, Darwin suffered, almost daily, from a mystery illness something akin to repetitive food poisoning. Doctors of his day couldn't help him; modern diagnosticians have speculated on a variety of disorders, ranging from lactose intolerance to Crohn's disease.

Whatever it was, Darwin's illness, a curse to him, perhaps established the circumstances subserving his scientific success. Forced to live in the country, he had no job and few distractions. He could devote his time to investigating nature in his own way. He spent eight years studying every aspect of every species of barnacle, for instance. All that time he also read with a vengeance, compiling and indexing detailed notes from book after book. He read science and philosophy and history and even trashy novels (there should be a law, he said, against unhappy endings). When Darwin opined, he knew what he was talking about, and he knew what everybody else knew, too.

He knew so much that he could often see what others couldn't, and he could also reason about things without wondering whether his suspicions would be supported by observations—he knew what observations had already been made. If they were insufficient, he made his own, growing orchids, breeding pigeons, spying on earthworms.

Of all his reading, the most signal was the 1798 essay on population by Thomas Malthus, which Darwin perused "for amusement" in 1838. About 15 months earlier, Darwin had begun a systematic investigation of "the species question," an issue at biology's foundation. Conventional wisdom held that species had been created individually and were immutable. Some thinkers, though (including Darwin's grandfather, Erasmus), believed otherwise. While on the Beagle, Darwin began to suspect that immutability was not correct (though he was unimpressed by grandpa's book, judging it to have an excessively high ratio of speculation to fact). But the idea of natural selection had not yet entered the grandson's mind.

Malthus Helped

Population, unchecked, would grow uncontrollably and run out of resources, he wrote. Scarcity kept populations in check; not all who were born could survive to reproduce. Darwin recognized in this account the "struggle for existence" he had observed in all manner of plants and animals. "It at once struck me that under these circumstances favorable variations would tend to be preserved and unfavorable ones to be destroyed," he wrote in his autobiography. "The result of this would be the formation of new species. Here, then, I had at least got a theory by which to work."

By 1842 he had prepared a rough 35-page outline (in pencil) of his evolutionary ideas, expanded by 1844 to a 230-page manuscript. In a letter to his wife, he allowed that his theory would be "a considerable step in science," if it ever were to be accepted "even by one competent judge." He asked in that letter that she be sure to publish the manuscript if he died before getting around to it himself. He did show it to a couple of colleagues, but otherwise the most earthshaking ideas in the history of biological science remained unpublicized. Darwin was busy classifying barnacles.

By 1854 he had begun spending most of his time on the species question, and in 1856 the geologist Lyell warned him to publish soon, before another naturalist anticipated him. Sure enough, two years later Alfred Russel Wallace, working in Indonesia, arrived at nearly the same notion—that species developed over time as small variations accumulated, with favorable ones enhancing survival. For counsel and comment, Wallace sent his paper to—Darwin.

Dismayed, Darwin sought advice from Lyell. Wallace's idea deserved to be published. Could Darwin now dare publish himself, without appearing to be stealing Wallace's discovery?

Lyell and Henslow brokered a compromise. Wallace's paper would be read to the Linnean Society, and so would an extract of Darwin's 1844 manuscript, at one session, with Lyell and Henslow vouching that they had indeed seen Darwin's work years earlier. Wallace was acknowledged, but Darwin's claim to priority was preserved. That hardly mattered, though. It was Darwin's artful reasoning and marshaling of the evidence that established evolution by natural selection, as presented in his masterwork, *On the Origin of Species*. Published in 1859, it electrified the scientific and intellectual world, evoking the prejudicial condemnation that afflicts most great new insights, but also filling the open-minded with food for centuries' worth of future biological thought.

A Simple Solution

For so momentous a problem, Darwin's solution seems elegantly simple, although also so subtle that its exposition is often badly mangled. Offspring differ slightly from their parents and each other (descent with modification), making some "fitter" than others in the struggle for existence (survival of the fittest). Over periods of time unimaginably long, the small changes from generation to generation accumulate, mutating one species into others. On smaller scales, over shorter times, such accumulated changes can be seen in various breeds of dogs or pigeons or plants, often induced by the artificial selection of particular traits by human breeders. On evolutionary scales of millions of years, the selection driving the appearance of new species is natural.

Some scientists (such as Huxley) saw the truth in Darwin's views immediately; others came to agree gradually. Many, of course, disagreed bitterly. But most of the "rebuttals" of evolution, even today, merely raise points that Darwin anticipated and countered. Gaps in the fossil record? To be expected, Darwin explained, because the geological record was so imperfect, as if only a few pages remained from only the most recent volume in the entire encyclopedia of the Earth's history.

Today Darwin's original idea has been borrowed by investigators in diverse disciplines, from psychologists to computer science. Even in physics, the word "Darwinian" appears in papers on thermodynamics, quantum physics and black holes. Within biology, Darwin's ideas have themselves evolved. Speciation isn't always gradual, change isn't always the result of selection, organisms are not the only units of selection, evolutionists now believe. Darwin foresaw some of these views, and he would have embraced them all—as a man of science willing "to give up any hypothesis, however much beloved . . . as soon as facts are shown to be opposed to it," in his words. "If I know myself, I work from a sort of instinct to try to make out truth."

And in the battle to wrest truth from nature, none fought better than Darwin. "He found a great truth," Huxley wrote in Darwin's obituary, "trodden under foot, reviled by bigots, and ridiculed by all the world; he lived long enough to see it, chiefly by his own efforts, irrefragably established in science, inseparably incorporated with the common thoughts of men."

Was Darwin Wrong?

DAVID QUAMMEN

Evolution by natural selection, the central concept of the life's work of Charles Darwin, is a theory. It's a theory about the origin of adaptation, complexity, and diversity among Earth's living creatures. If you are skeptical by nature, unfamiliar with the terminology of science, and unaware of the overwhelming evidence, you might even be tempted to say that it's "just" a theory. In the same sense, relativity as described by Albert Einstein is "just" a theory. The notion that Earth orbits around the sun rather than vice versa, offered by Copernicus in 1543, is a theory. Continental drift is a theory. The existence, structure, and dynamics of atoms? Atomic theory. Even electricity is a theoretical construct, involving electrons, which are tiny units of charged mass that no one has ever seen. Each of these theories is an explanation that has been confirmed to such a degree, by observation and experiment, that knowledgeable experts accept it as fact. That's what scientists mean when they talk about a theory: not a dreamy and unreliable speculation, but an explanatory statement that fits the evidence. They embrace such an explanation confidently but provisionally—taking it as their best available view of reality, at least until some severely conflicting data or some better explanation might come along.

The rest of us generally agree. We plug our televisions into little wall sockets, measure a year by the length of Earth's orbit, and in many other ways live our lives based on the trusted reality of those theories.

Evolutionary theory, though, is a bit different. It's such a dangerously wonderful and far-reaching view of life that some people find it unacceptable, despite the vast body of supporting evidence. As applied to our own species, *Homo sapiens,* it can seem more threatening still. Many fundamentalist Christians and ultraorthodox Jews take alarm at the thought that human descent from earlier primates contradicts a strict reading of the Book of Genesis. Their discomfort is paralleled by Islamic creationists such as Harun Yahya, author of a recent volume titled *The Evolution Deceit,* who points to the six-day creation story in the Koran as literal truth and calls the theory of evolution "nothing but a deception imposed on us by the dominators of the world system." The late Srila Prabhupada, of the Hare Krishna movement, explained that God created "the 8,400,000 species of life from the very beginning," in order to establish multiple tiers of reincarnation for rising souls. Although souls ascend, the species themselves don't change, he insisted, dismissing "Darwin's nonsensical theory."

Other people too, not just scriptural literalists, remain unpersuaded about evolution. According to a Gallup poll drawn from more than a thousand telephone interviews conducted in February 2001, no less than 45 percent of responding U.S. adults agreed that "God created human beings pretty much in their present form at one time within the last 10,000 years or so." Evolution, by their lights, played no role in shaping us.

Only 37 percent of the polled Americans were satisfied with allowing room for both God and Darwin—that is, divine initiative to get things started, evolution as the creative means. (This view, according to more than one papal pronouncement, is compatible with Roman Catholic dogma.) Still fewer Americans, only 12 percent, believed that humans evolved from other lifeforms without any involvement of a god.

The most startling thing about these poll numbers is not that so many Americans reject evolution, but that the statistical breakdown hasn't changed much in two decades. Gallup interviewers posed exactly the same choices in 1982, 1993, 1997, and 1999. The creationist conviction—that God alone, and not evolution, produced humans—has never drawn less than 44 percent. In other words, nearly half the American populace prefers to believe that Charles Darwin was wrong where it mattered most.

Why are there so many antievolutionists? Scriptural literalism can only be part of the answer. The American public certainly includes a large segment of scriptural literalists—but not *that* large, not 44 percent. Creationist proselytizers and political activists, working hard to interfere with the teaching of evolutionary biology in public schools, are another part. Honest confusion and ignorance, among millions of adult Americans, must be still another. Many people have never taken a biology course that dealt with evolution nor read a book in which the theory was lucidly explained. Sure, we've all heard of Charles Darwin, and of a vague, somber notion about struggle and survival that sometimes goes by the catchall label "Darwinism." But the main sources of information from which most Americans have drawn their awareness of this subject, it seems, are haphazard ones at best: cultural osmosis, newspaper and magazine references, half-baked nature documentaries on the tube, and hearsay.

Evolution is both a beautiful concept and an important one, more crucial nowadays to human welfare, to medical science, and to our understanding of the world than ever before. It's also deeply persuasive—a theory you can take to the bank. The essential points are slightly more complicated than most people assume, but not so complicated that they can't be comprehended by any attentive person. Furthermore, the supporting evidence is abundant, various, ever increasing, solidly interconnected, and easily available in museums, popular books, textbooks, and a mountainous accumulation of peer-reviewed scientific studies. No one needs to, and no one should, accept evolution merely as a matter of faith.

Two big ideas, not just one, are at issue: the evolution of all species, as a historical phenomenon, and natural selection, as the main mechanism causing that phenomenon. The first is a question of what happened. The second is a question of how. The idea that all species are descended from common ancestors had been suggested by other thinkers, including Jean-Baptiste Lamarck, long before Darwin published *The Origin of Species* in 1859. What made Darwin's book so remarkable when it appeared, and so influential in the long run, was that it offered a rational explanation of how evolution must occur. The same insight came independently to Alfred Russel Wallace, a young naturalist doing fieldwork in the Malay Archipelago during the late 1850s. In historical annals, if not in the popular awareness, Wallace and Darwin share the kudos for having discovered natural selection.

The gist of the concept is that small, random, heritable differences among individuals result in different chances of survival and reproduction—success for some, death without offspring for others—and that this natural culling leads to significant changes in shape, size, strength, armament, color, biochemistry, and behavior among the descendants. Excess population growth drives the competitive struggle. Because less successful competitors produce fewer surviving offspring, the useless or negative variations tend to disappear, whereas the useful variations tend to be perpetuated and gradually magnified throughout a population.

So much for one part of the evolutionary process, known as anagenesis, during which a single species is transformed. But there's also a second part, known as speciation. Genetic changes sometimes accumulate within an isolated segment of a species, but not throughout the whole, as that isolated population adapts to its local conditions. Gradually it goes its own way, seizing a new ecological niche. At a certain point it becomes irreversibly distinct—that is, so different that its members can't interbreed with the rest. Two species now exist where formerly there was one. Darwin called that splitting-and-specializing phenomenon the "principle of divergence." It was an important part of his theory, explaining the overall diversity of life as well as the adaptation of individual species.

This thrilling and radical assemblage of concepts came from an unlikely source. Charles Darwin was shy and meticulous, a wealthy landowner with close friends among the Anglican clergy. He had a gentle, unassuming manner, a strong need for privacy, and an extraordinary commitment to intellectual honesty. As an undergraduate at Cambridge, he had studied halfheartedly toward becoming a clergyman himself, before he discovered his real vocation as a scientist. Later, having established a good but conventional reputation in natural history, he spent 22 years secretly gathering evidence and pondering arguments—both

for and against his theory—because he didn't want to flame out in a burst of unpersuasive notoriety. He may have delayed, too, because of his anxiety about announcing a theory that seemed to challenge conventional religious beliefs—in particular, the Christian beliefs of his wife, Emma. Darwin himself quietly renounced Christianity during his middle age, and later described himself as an agnostic. He continued to believe in a distant, impersonal deity of some sort, a greater entity that had set the universe and its laws into motion, but not in a personal God who had chosen humanity as a specially favored species. Darwin avoided flaunting his lack of religious faith, at least partly in deference to Emma. And she prayed for his soul.

In 1859 he finally delivered his revolutionary book. Although it was hefty and substantive at 490 pages, he considered *The Origin of Species* just a quick-and-dirty "abstract" of the huge volume he had been working on until interrupted by an alarming event. (In fact, he'd wanted to title it *An Abstract of an Essay on the Origin of Species and Varieties Through Natural Selection,* but his publisher found that insufficiently catchy.) The alarming event was his receiving a letter and an enclosed manuscript from Alfred Wallace, whom he knew only as a distant pen pal. Wallace's manuscript sketched out the same great idea—evolution by natural selection—that Darwin considered his own. Wallace had scribbled this paper and (unaware of Darwin's own evolutionary thinking, which so far had been kept private) mailed it to him from the Malay Archipelago, along with a request for reaction and help. Darwin was horrified. After two decades of painstaking effort, now he'd be scooped. Or maybe not quite. He forwarded Wallace's paper toward publication, though managing also to assert his own prior claim by releasing two excerpts from his unpublished work. Then he dashed off *The Origin,* his "abstract" on the subject. Unlike Wallace, who was younger and less meticulous, Darwin recognized the importance of providing an edifice of supporting evidence and logic.

The evidence, as he presented it, mostly fell within four categories: biogeography, paleontology, embryology, and morphology. Biogeography is the study of the geographical distribution of living creatures—that is, which species inhabit which parts of the planet and why. Paleontology investigates extinct life-forms, as revealed in the fossil record. Embryology examines the revealing stages of development (echoing earlier stages of evolutionary history) that embryos pass through before birth or hatching; at a stretch, embryology also concerns the immature forms of animals that metamorphose, such as the larvae of insects. Morphology is the science of anatomical shape and design. Darwin devoted sizable sections of *The Origin of Species* to these categories.

Biogeography, for instance, offered a great pageant of peculiar facts and patterns. Anyone who considers the biogeographical data, Darwin wrote, must be struck by the mysterious clustering pattern among what he called "closely allied" species—that is, similar creatures sharing roughly the same body plan. Such closely allied species tend to be found on the same continent (several species of zebras in Africa) or within the same group of oceanic islands (dozens of species of honeycreepers in Hawaii, 13 species of Galápagos finch), despite their species-by-species preferences for different habitats, food sources, or conditions of climate. Adjacent areas of South America, Darwin noted, are occupied by two similar species of large, flightless birds (the rheas, *Rhea americana* and *Pterocnemia pennata),* not by ostriches as in Africa or emus as in Australia. South America also has agoutis and viscachas (small rodents) in terrestrial habitats, plus coypus and capybaras in the wetlands, not—as Darwin wrote—hares and rabbits in terrestrial habitats or beavers and muskrats in the wetlands. During his own youthful visit to the Galápagos, aboard the survey ship *Beagle,* Darwin himself had discovered three very similar forms of mockingbird, each on a different island.

Why should "closely allied" species inhabit neighboring patches of habitat? And why should similar habitat on different continents be occupied by species that aren't so closely allied? "We see in these facts some deep organic bond, prevailing throughout space and time," Darwin wrote. "This bond, on my theory, is simply inheritance." Similar species occur nearby in space because they have descended from common ancestors.

Paleontology reveals a similar clustering pattern in the dimension of time. The vertical column of geologic strata, laid down by sedimentary processes over the eons, lightly peppered with fossils, represents a tangible record showing which species lived when. Less ancient layers of rock lie atop more ancient ones (except where geologic forces have tipped or shuffled them), and likewise with the animal and plant fossils that the strata contain. What Darwin noticed about this record is that closely allied species tend to be found adjacent to one another in successive strata. One species endures for millions of years and then makes its last appearance in, say, the middle Eocene epoch; just above, a similar but not identical species replaces it. In North America, for example, a vaguely horselike creature known as *Hyracotherium* was succeeded by *Orohippus,* then *Epihippus,* then *Mesohippus,* which in turn were succeeded by a variety of horsey American critters. Some of them even galloped across the Bering land bridge into Asia, then onward to Europe and Africa. By five million years ago they had nearly all disappeared, leaving behind *Dinohippus,* which was succeeded by *Equus,* the modern genus of horse. Not all these fossil links had been unearthed in Darwin's day, but he captured the essence of the matter anyway. Again, were such sequences just coincidental? No, Darwin argued. Closely allied species succeed one another in time, as well as living nearby in space, because they're related through evolutionary descent.

Embryology too involved patterns that couldn't be explained by coincidence. Why does the embryo of a mammal pass through stages resembling stages of the embryo of a reptile? Why is one of the larval forms of a barnacle, before metamorphosis, so similar to the larval form of a shrimp? Why do the larvae of moths, flies, and beetles resemble one another more than any of them resemble their respective adults? Because, Darwin wrote, "the embryo is the animal in its less modified state" and that state "reveals the structure of its progenitor."

Morphology, his fourth category of evidence, was the "very soul" of natural history, according to Darwin. Even today it's on display in the layout and organization of any zoo. Here are the monkeys, there are the big cats, and in that building are the alligators and crocodiles. Birds in the aviary, fish in the aquarium. Living creatures can be easily sorted into a hierarchy of categories—not just species but genera, families, orders, whole kingdoms—based on which anatomical characters they share and which they don't.

All vertebrate animals have backbones. Among vertebrates, birds have feathers, whereas reptiles have scales. Mammals have fur and mammary glands, not feathers or scales. Among mammals, some have pouches in which they nurse their tiny young. Among these species, the marsupials, some have huge rear legs and strong tails by which they go hopping across miles of arid outback; we call them kangaroos. Bring in modern microscopic and molecular evidence, and you can trace the similarities still further back. All plants and fungi, as well as animals, have nuclei within their cells. All living organisms contain DNA and RNA (except some viruses with RNA only), two related forms of information-coding molecules.

Such a pattern of tiered resemblances—groups of similar species nested within broader groupings, and all descending from a single source—isn't naturally present among other collections of items. You won't find anything equivalent if you try to categorize rocks, or musical instruments, or jewelry. Why not? Because rock types and styles of jewelry don't reflect unbroken descent from common ancestors. Biological diversity does. The number of shared characteristics between any one species and another indicates how recently those two species have diverged from a shared lineage.

That insight gave new meaning to the task of taxonomic classification, which had been founded in its modern form back in 1735 by the Swedish naturalist Carolus Linnaeus. Linnaeus showed how species could be systematically classified, according to their shared similarities, but he worked from creationist assumptions that offered no material explanation for the nested pattern he found. In the early and middle 19th century, morphologists such as Georges Cuvier and Étienne Geoffroy Saint-Hilaire in France and Richard Owen in England improved classification with their meticulous studies of internal as well as external anatomies, and tried to make sense of what the ultimate source of these patterned similarities could be. Not even Owen, a contemporary and onetime friend of Darwin's (later in life they had a bitter falling out), took the full step to an evolutionary vision before *The Origin of Species* was published. Owen made a major contribution, though, by advancing the concept of homologues—that is, superficially different but fundamentally similar versions of a single organ or trait, shared by dissimilar species.

For instance, the five-digit skeletal structure of the vertebrate hand appears not just in humans and apes and raccoons and bears but also, variously modified, in cats and bats and porpoises and lizards and turtles. The paired bones of our lower leg, the tibia and the fibula, are also represented by homologous bones in other mammals and in reptiles, and even in the long-extinct bird-reptile *Archaeopteryx.* What's the reason behind such varied recurrence of a few basic designs? Darwin, with a nod to Owen's "most interesting work," supplied the answer: common descent, as shaped by natural selection, modifying the inherited basics for different circumstances.

Vestigial characteristics are still another form of morphological evidence, illuminating to contemplate because they show that the living world is full of small, tolerable imperfections. Why do male mammals (including human males) have nipples? Why do some snakes (notably boa constrictors) carry the rudiments of a pelvis and tiny legs buried inside their sleek profiles? Why do certain species of flightless beetles have wings, sealed beneath wing covers that never open? Darwin raised all these questions, and answered them, in *The Origin of Species*. Vestigial structures stand as remnants of the evolutionary history of a lineage.

Today the same four branches of biological science from which Darwin drew—biogeography, paleontology, embryology, morphology—embrace an ever growing body of supporting data. In addition to those categories we now have others: population genetics, biochemistry, molecular biology, and, most recently, the whiz-bang field of machine-driven genetic sequencing known as genomics. These new forms of knowledge overlap one another seamlessly and intersect with the older forms, strengthening the whole edifice, contributing further to the certainty that Darwin was right.

He was right about evolution, that is. He wasn't right about *everything*. Being a restless explainer, Darwin floated a number of theoretical notions during his long working life, some of which were mistaken and illusory. He was wrong about what causes variation within a species. He was wrong about a famous geologic mystery, the parallel shelves along a Scottish valley called Glen Roy. Most notably, his theory of inheritance—which he labeled pangenesis and cherished despite its poor reception among his biologist colleagues—turned out to be dead wrong. Fortunately for Darwin, the correctness of his most famous good idea stood independent of that particular bad idea. Evolution by natural selection represented Darwin at his best—which is to say, scientific observation and careful thinking at its best.

Douglas Futuyma is a highly respected evolutionary biologist, author of textbooks as well as influential research papers. His office, at the University of Michigan, is a long narrow room in the natural sciences building, well stocked with journals and books, including volumes about the conflict between creationism and evolution. I arrived carrying a well-thumbed copy of his own book on that subject, *Science on Trial: The Case for Evolution*. Killing time in the corridor before our appointment, I noticed a blue flyer on a departmental bulletin board, seeming oddly placed there amid the announcements of career opportunities for graduate students. "Creation vs. evolution," it said. "A series of messages challenging popular thought with Biblical truth and scientific evidences." A traveling lecturer from something called the Origins Research Association would deliver these messages at a local Baptist church. Beside the lecturer's photo was a drawing of a dinosaur. "Free pizza following the evening service," said a small line at the bottom. Dinosaurs, biblical truth, and pizza: something for everybody.

In response to my questions about evidence, Dr. Futuyma moved quickly through the traditional categories—paleontology, biogeography—and talked mostly about modern genetics. He pulled out his heavily marked copy of the journal *Nature* for February 15, 2001, a historic issue, fat with articles reporting and analyzing the results of the Human Genome Project. Beside it he slapped down a more recent issue of *Nature,* this one devoted to the sequenced genome of the house mouse, *Mus musculus.* The headline of the lead editorial announced: "HUMAN BIOLOGY BY PROXY." The mouse genome effort, according to *Nature's* editors, had revealed "about 30,000 genes, with 99% having direct counterparts in humans."

The resemblance between our 30,000 human genes and those 30,000 mousy counterparts, Futuyma explained, represents another form of homology, like the resemblance between a five-fingered hand and a five-toed paw. Such genetic homology is what gives meaning to biomedical research using mice and other animals, including chimpanzees, which (to their sad misfortune) are our closest living relatives.

No aspect of biomedical research seems more urgent today than the study of microbial diseases. And the dynamics of those microbes within human bodies, within human populations, can only be understood in terms of evolution.

Nightmarish illnesses caused by microbes include both the infectious sort (AIDS, Ebola, SARS) that spread directly from person to person and the sort (malaria, West Nile fever) delivered to us by biting insects or other intermediaries. The capacity for quick change among disease-causing microbes is what makes them so dangerous to large numbers of people and so difficult and expensive to treat. They leap from wildlife or domestic animals into humans, adapting to new circumstances as they go. Their inherent variability allows them to find new ways of evading and defeating human immune systems. By natural selection they acquire resistance to drugs that should kill them. They evolve. There's no better or more immediate evidence supporting the Darwinian theory than this process of forced transformation among our inimical germs.

Take the common bacterium *Staphylococcus aureus,* which lurks in hospitals and causes serious infections, especially among surgery patients. Penicillin, becoming available in 1943, proved almost miraculously effective in fighting staphylococcus infections. Its deployment marked a new phase in the old war between humans and disease microbes, a phase in which humans invent new killer drugs and microbes find new ways to be unkillable. The supreme potency of penicillin didn't last long. The first resistant strains of *Staphylococcus aureus* were reported in 1947. A newer staph-killing drug, methicillin, came into use during the 1960s, but methicillin-resistant strains appeared soon, and by the 1980s those strains were widespread. Vancomycin became the next great weapon against staph, and the first vancomycin-resistant strain emerged in 2002. These antibiotic-resistant strains represent an evolutionary series, not much different in principle from the fossil series tracing horse evolution from *Hyracotherium* to *Equus.* They make evolution a very practical problem by adding expense, as well as misery and danger, to the challenge of coping with staph.

The biologist Stephen Palumbi has calculated the cost of treating penicillin-resistant and methicillin-resistant staph infections, just in the United States, at 30 billion dollars a year. "Antibiotics exert a powerful evolutionary force," he wrote last year, "driving infectious bacteria to evolve powerful defenses against all but the most recently invented drugs." As reflected in their DNA, which uses the same genetic code found in humans

8

and horses and hagfish and honeysuckle, bacteria are part of the continuum of life, all shaped and diversified by evolutionary forces.

Even viruses belong to that continuum. Some viruses evolve quickly, some slowly. Among the fastest is HIV, because its method of replicating itself involves a high rate of mutation, and those mutations allow the virus to assume new forms. After just a few years of infection and drug treatment, each HIV patient carries a unique version of the virus. Isolation within one infected person, plus differing conditions and the struggle to survive, forces each version of HIV to evolve independently. It's nothing but a speeded up and microscopic case of what Darwin saw in the Galápagos—except that each human body is an island, and the newly evolved forms aren't so charming as finches or mockingbirds.

Understanding how quickly HIV acquires resistance to antiviral drugs, such as AZT, has been crucial to improving treatment by way of multiple drug cocktails. "This approach has reduced deaths due to HIV by severalfold since 1996," according to Palumbi, "and it has greatly slowed the evolution of this disease within patients."

Insects and weeds acquire resistance to our insecticides and herbicides through the same process. As we humans try to poison them, evolution by natural selection transforms the population of a mosquito or thistle into a new sort of creature, less vulnerable to that particular poison. So we invent another poison, then another. It's a futile effort. Even DDT, with its ferocious and long-lasting effects throughout ecosystems, produced resistant house flies within a decade of its discovery in 1939. By 1990 more than 500 species (including 114 kinds of mosquitoes) had acquired resistance to at least one pesticide. Based on these undesired results, Stephen Palumbi has commented glumly, "humans may be the world's dominant evolutionary force."

Among most forms of living creatures, evolution proceeds slowly—too slowly to be observed by a single scientist within a research lifetime. But science functions by inference, not just by direct observation, and the inferential sorts of evidence such as paleontology and biogeography are no less cogent simply because they're indirect. Still, skeptics of evolutionary theory ask: Can we see evolution in action? Can it be observed in the wild? Can it be measured in the laboratory?

The answer is yes. Peter and Rosemary Grant, two British-born researchers who have spent decades where Charles Darwin spent weeks, have captured a glimpse of evolution with their long-term studies of beak size among Galápagos finches. William R. Rice and George W. Salt achieved something similar in their lab, through an experiment involving 35 generations of the fruit fly *Drosophila melanogaster.* Richard E. Lenski and his colleagues at Michigan State University have done it too, tracking 20,000 generations of evolution in the bacterium *Escherichia coli.* Such field studies and lab experiments document anagenesis—that is, slow evolutionary change within a single, unsplit lineage. With patience it can be seen, like the movement of a minute hand on a clock.

Speciation, when a lineage splits into two species, is the other major phase of evolutionary change, making possible the

divergence between lineages about which Darwin wrote. It's rarer and more elusive even than anagenesis. Many individual mutations must accumulate (in most cases, anyway, with certain exceptions among plants) before two populations become irrevocabldy separated. The process is spread across thousands of generations, yet it may finish abruptly—like a door going slam!—when the last critical changes occur. Therefore it's much harder to witness. Despite the difficulties, Rice and Salt seem to have recorded a speciation event, or very nearly so, in their extended experiment on fruit flies. From a small stock of mated females they eventually produced two distinct fly populations adapted to different habitat conditions, which the researchers judged "incipient species."

After my visit with Douglas Futuyma in Ann Arbor, I spent two hours at the university museum there with Philip D. Gingerich, a paleontologist well-known for his work on the ancestry of whales. As we talked, Gingerich guided me through an exhibit of ancient cetaceans on the museum's second floor. Amid weird skeletal shapes that seemed almost chimerical (some hanging overhead, some in glass cases) he pointed out significant features and described the progress of thinking about whale evolution. A burly man with a broad open face and the gentle manner of a scoutmaster, Gingerich combines intellectual passion and solid expertise with one other trait that's valuable in a scientist: a willingness to admit when he's wrong.

Since the late 1970s Gingerich has collected fossil specimens of early whales from remote digs in Egypt and Pakistan. Working with Pakistani colleagues, he discovered *Pakicetus,* a terrestrial mammal dating from 50 million years ago, whose ear bones reflect its membership in the whale lineage but whose skull looks almost doglike. A former student of Gingerich's, Hans Thewissen, found a slightly more recent form with webbed feet, legs suitable for either walking or swimming, and a long toothy snout. Thewissen called it *Ambulocetus natans,* or the "walking-and-swimming whale." Gingerich and his team turned up several more, including *Rodhocetus balochistanensis,* which was fully a sea creature, its legs more like flippers, its nostrils shifted backward on the snout, halfway to the blowhole position on a modern whale. The sequence of known forms was becoming more and more complete. And all along, Gingerich told me, he leaned toward believing that whales had descended from a group of carnivorous Eocene mammals known as mesonychids, with cheek teeth useful for chewing meat and bone. Just a bit more evidence, he thought, would confirm that relationship. By the end of the 1990s most paleontologists agreed.

Meanwhile, molecular biologists had explored the same question and arrived at a different answer. No, the match to those Eocene carnivores might be close, but not close enough. DNA hybridization and other tests suggested that whales had descended from artiodactyls (that is, even-toed herbivores, such as antelopes and hippos), not from meat-eating mesonychids.

In the year 2000 Gingerich chose a new field site in Pakistan, where one of his students found a single piece of fossil that changed the prevailing view in paleontology. It was half of a pulley-shaped anklebone, known as an astragalus, belonging to another new species of whale.

A Pakistani colleague found the fragment's other half. When Gingerich fitted the two pieces together, he had a moment of humbling recognition: The molecular biologists were right. Here was an anklebone, from a four-legged whale dating back 47 million years, that closely resembled the homologus anklebone in an artiodactyl. Suddenly he realized how closely whales are related to antelopes.

This is how science is supposed to work. Ideas come and go, but the fittest survive. Downstairs in his office Phil Gingerich opened a specimen drawer, showing me some of the actual fossils from which the display skeletons upstairs were modeled. He put a small lump of petrified bone, no longer than a lug nut, into my hand. It was the famous astragalus, from the species he had eventually named *Artiocetus clavis*. It felt solid and heavy as truth.

Seeing me to the door, Gingerich volunteered something personal: "I grew up in a conservative church in the Midwest and was not taught anything about evolution. The subject was clearly skirted. That helps me understand the people who are skeptical about it. Because I come from that tradition myself." He shares the same skeptical instinct. Tell him that there's an ancestral connection between land animals and whales, and his reaction is: Fine, maybe. But show me the intermediate stages. Like Charles Darwin, the onetime divinity student, who joined that round-the-world voyage aboard the *Beagle* instead of becoming a country parson, and whose grand view of life on Earth was shaped by attention to small facts, Phil Gingerich is a reverant empiricist. He's not satisfied until he sees solid data. That's what excites him so much about pulling shale fossils out of the ground. In 30 years he has seen enough to be satisfied. For him, Gingerich said, it's "a spiritual experience."

"The evidence is there," he added. "It's buried in the rocks of ages."

The Facts of Evolution

Michael Shermer

The affinities of all the beings of the same class have sometimes been represented by a great tree. I believe this simile largely speaks the truth. As buds give rise by growth to fresh buds, and these, if vigorous, branch out and overtop on all sides many a feebler branch, so by generation I believe it has been with the great Tree of Life, which fills with its dead and broken branches the crust of the earth, and covers the surface with its ever branching and beautiful ramifications.

—Charles Darwin,
On the Origin of Species, 1859

The theory of evolution has been under attack since Charles Darwin first published *On the Origin of Species* in 1859. From the start, its critics have seized on the *theory* of evolution to try to undermine its facts. But all great works of science are written in support of some particular view. In 1861, shortly after he published his new theory, Darwin wrote a letter to his colleague, Henry Fawcett, who had just attended a special meeting of the British Association for the Advancement of Science during which Darwin's book was debated. One of the naturalists had argued that *On the Origin of Species* was too theoretical, that Darwin should have just "put his facts before us and let them rest." In response, Darwin reflected that science, to be of any service, required more than list-making; it needed larger ideas that could make sense of piles of data. Otherwise, Darwin said, a geologist "might as well go into a gravelpit and count the pebbles and describe the colours." Data without generalizations are useless; facts without explanatory principles are meaningless. A "theory" is not just someone's opinion or a wild guess made by some scientist. A theory is a well-supported and well-tested generalization that explains a set of observations. Science without theory is useless.

The process of science is fueled by what I call *Darwin's Dictum,* defined by Darwin himself in his letter to Fawcett: "all observation must be for or against some view if it is to be of any service."

Darwin's casual comment nearly a hundred and fifty years ago encapsulates a serious debate about the relative roles of data and theory, or observations and conclusions, in science. In a science like evolution, in which inferences about the past must be made from scant data in the present, this debate has been exploded to encompass a fight between religion and science.

Prediction and Observation

Most essentially, *evolution is a historical science.* Darwin valued above all else prediction and verification by subsequent observation. In an act of brilliant historical science, for example, Darwin correctly developed a theory of coral reef evolution years before he developed his theory of biological evolution. He had never seen a coral reef, but during the *Beagle*'s famous voyage to the Galápagos, he had studied the types of coral reefs Charles Lyell described in *Principles of Geology.* Darwin reasoned that the different examples of coral reefs did not represent different types, each of which needed a different causal explanation; rather, the different examples represented different stages of development of coral reefs, for which only a single cause was needed. Darwin considered this a triumph of theory in driving scientific investigation: Theoretical prediction was followed by observational verification, whereby "I had therefore only to verify and extend my views by a careful examination of coral reefs." In this case, the theory came first, then the data.

The publication of the *Origin of Species* triggered a roaring debate about the relative roles of data and theory in science. Darwin's "bulldog" defender, Thomas Henry Huxley, erupted in a paroxysm against those who pontificated on science but had never practiced it themselves: "There cannot be a doubt that the method of inquiry which Mr. Darwin has adopted is not only rigorously in accord with the canons of scientific logic, but that it is the only adequate method," Huxley wrote. Those "critics exclusively trained in classics or in mathematics, who have never determined a scientific fact in their lives by induction from experiment or observation, prate learnedly about Mr. Darwin's method," he bellowed, "which is not inductive enough, not Baconian enough, forsooth for them."

Darwin insisted that theory comes to and from the facts, not from political or philosophical beliefs, whether from God or the godfather of scientific empiricism. It is a point he voiced succinctly in his cautions to a young scientist. The facts speak for themselves, he said, advising "the advantage, at present, of being very sparing in introducing theory in your papers; let theory guide your observations, but till your reputation is well established, be sparing of publishing theory. It makes persons doubt your observations." Once Darwin's reputation was well established, he published his book that so well demonstrated the power of theory. As he noted in his autobiography, "some of my critics have said, 'Oh, he is a good observer, but has no power of reasoning.' I do not think that this can be true, for the *Origin of Species* is one long argument from the beginning to the end, and it has convinced not a few able men."

Against Some View

Darwin's "one long argument" was with the theologian William Paley and the theory Paley posited in his 1802 book, *Natural Theology: or, Evidences of the Existence and Attributes of the Deity, Collected from the Appearances of Nature.* Sound eerily familiar? The scholarly agenda of this first brand of Intelligent Design was to correlate the works of God (nature) with the words of God (the Bible). Natural theology kicked off with John Ray's 1691 *Wisdom of God Manifested in Works of the Creation,* which itself was inspired by Psalms 19:11: "The Heavens declare the Glory of the Lord and the Firmament sheweth his handy work." John Ray, in what still stands as a playbook for creationism, explains the analogy between human and divine creations: If a "curious Edifice or machine" leads us to "infer the being and operation of some intelligent Architect or Engineer," shouldn't the same be said of "the Works of nature, that Grandeur and magnificence, that excellent contrivance for Beauty, Order, use, &c. which is observable in them, wherein they do as much transcend the Efforts of human Art and infinite Power and Wisdom exceeds finite" to make us "infer the existence and efficiency of an Omnipotent and All-wise Creator?"

Paley advanced Ray's work through the accumulated knowledge of a century of scientific exploration. The opening passage of Paley's *Natural Theology* has become annealed into our culture as the winningly accessible and thus appealing "watchmaker" argument:

> In crossing a heath, suppose I pitched my foot against a stone, and were asked how the stone came to be there. I might possibly answer, that, for any thing I knew to the contrary, it had lain there forever. But suppose I had found a watch upon the ground, and it should be enquired how the watch happened to be in that place. The inference, we think, is inevitable; that the watch must have had a maker; that there must have existed, at some time and in some place or other, an artificer or artificers who formed it for the purpose which we find it actually to answer; who comprehended its construction, and designed its use.

But life is far more complex than a watch—so the design inference is even stronger!

> There cannot be design without a designer; contrivance without a contriver . . . The marks of design are too strong to be got over. Design must have had a designer. That designer must have been a person. That person is GOD.

For longer than we have had the theory of evolution, we have had theologians arguing for Intelligent Design.

From Natural Theology to Natural Selection

After abandoning medical studies at Edinburgh University, Charles Darwin entered the University of Cambridge to study theology with the goal of becoming a Church of England cleric. Natural theology provided him with a socially acceptable excuse to study natural history, his true passion. It also educated Darwin in the arguments on design popularized by Paley and others. His intimacy with their ideas was respectful, not combative. For example, in November 1859, the same month that the *Origin of Species* was published, Darwin wrote his friend John Lubbock, "I do not think I hardly ever admired a book more than Paley's 'Natural Theology.' I could almost formerly have said it by heart." Both Paley and Darwin addressed a problem in nature: the origin of the design of life. Paley's answer was to posit a top-down designer—God. Darwin's answer was to posit a bottom-up designer—natural selection. Natural theologians took this to mean that evolution was an attack on God, without giving much thought to what evolution is.

Ever since Darwin, much has been written about what, exactly, evolution is. Ernst Mayr, arguably the greatest evolutionary theorist since Darwin, offers a subtly technical definition: "evolution is change in the adaptation and in the diversity of populations of organisms." He notes that evolution has a dual nature, a "'vertical' phenomenon of adaptive change," which describes how a species responds to its environment over time, and a "'horizontal' phenomenon of populations, incipient species, and new species," which describes adaptations that break through the genetic divide. And I'll never forget Mayr's definition of a species, because I had to memorize it in my first course on evolutionary biology: "A species is a group of actually or potentially interbreeding natural populations reproductively isolated from other such populations."

Mayr outlines five general tenets of evolutionary theory that have been discovered in the years since Darwin published his revolutionary book:

1. *Evolution:* Organisms change through time. Both the fossil record of life's history and nature today document and reveal this change.
2. *Descent with modification:* Evolution proceeds through the branching of common descent. As every parent and child knows, offspring are similar to but not exact replicas of their parents, producing the necessary variation that allows adaptation to the ever-changing environment.
3. *Gradualism:* All this change is slow, steady, and stately. Given enough time, small changes within a species can accumulate into large changes that create new species; that is, macro-evolution is the cumulative effect of microevolution.
4. *Multiplication:* Evolution does not just produce new species; it produces an increasing number of new species.

And, of course,

5. *Natural selection:* Evolutionary change is not haphazard and random; it follows a selective process. Codiscovered

by Darwin and the naturalist Alfred Russel Wallace, natural selection operates under five rules:

A. Populations tend to increase indefinitely in a geometric ratio: 2, 4, 8, 16, 32, 64, 128, 256, 512, 1024 . . .
B. In a natural environment, however, population numbers must stabilize at a certain level. The population cannot increase to infinity—the earth is just not big enough.
C. Therefore, there must be a "struggle for existence." Not all of the organisms produced can survive.
D. There is variation in every species.
E. Therefore, in the struggle for existence, those individuals with variations that are better adapted to the environment leave behind more offspring than individuals that are less well adapted. This is known as *differential reproductive success.*

As Darwin said, "as more individuals are produced than can possibly survive, there must in every case be a struggle for existence, either one individual with another of the same species, or with the individuals of distinct species, or with the physical conditions of life."

The process of natural selection, when carried out over countless generations, gradually leads varieties of species to develop into new species. Darwin explained:

It may be said that natural selection is daily and hourly scrutinising, throughout the world, every variation, even the slightest; rejecting that which is bad, preserving and adding up all that is good; silently and insensibly working, whenever and wherever opportunity offers, at the improvement of each organic being in relation to its organic and inorganic conditions of life. We see nothing of these slow changes in progress, until the hand of time has marked the long lapses of ages, and then so imperfect is our view into long past geological ages, that we only see that the forms of life are now different from what they formerly were.

The time frame is long and the changes from generation to generation are subtle. This may be one of the most important and difficult points to grasp about the theory of evolution. It is tempting to see species as they exist today as a living monument to evolution, to condense evolution into the incorrect but provocative shorthand that humans descended from chimpanzees—a shorthand that undercuts the facts of evolution.

Natural selection is the process of organisms struggling to survive and reproduce, with the result of propagating their genes into the next generation. As such, it operates primarily at the local level. The Oxford evolutionary biologist Richard Dawkins elegantly described the process as "random mutation plus non-random cumulative selection," emphasizing the non-random. Evolution is not the equivalent of a warehouse full of parts randomly assorting themselves into a jumbo jet, as the creationists like to argue. If evolution were truly random there would be no biological jumbo jets. Genetic mutations and the mixing of parental genes in offspring may be random, but the selection of genes through the survival of their hosts is anything but random. Out of this process of self-organized directional selection emerge complexity and diversity.

Natural selection is a description of a process, not a force. No one is "selecting" organisms for survival or extinction, in the benign sense of dog breeders selecting for desirable traits in show breeds, or in the malignant sense of Nazis selecting prisoners at Auschwitz-Birkenau. Natural selection, and thus evolution, is unconscious and nonprescient—it cannot look forward to anticipate what changes are going to be needed for survival. The evolutionary watchmaker is blind, says Dawkins, *pace* Paley.

By way of example, once when my young daughter asked how evolution works, I used the polar bear as an example of a "transitional species" between land mammals and marine mammals, because although they are land mammals they spend so much time in the water that they have acquired many adaptations to an aquatic life. But this is not correct. It implies that polar bears are *on their way* (in transition) to becoming marine mammals. They aren't. Polar bears are not "becoming" anything. Polar bears are well adapted for their lifestyle. That's all. If global warming continues, perhaps polar bears will adapt to a full-time aquatic existence, or perhaps they will move south and become smaller brown bears, or perhaps they will go extinct. Who knows? No one.

Where Are All the Fossils?

Evolution is a historical science, and historical data—fossils—are often the evidence most cited for and against it. In the creationist textbook, *Of Pandas and People*—one of the bones of contention in the 2005 Intelligent Design trial of *Kitzmiller et al. v. Dover Area School District,* in Dover, Pennsylvania—the authors state: "Design theories suggest that various forms of life began with their distinctive features already intact: fish with fins and scales, birds with feathers and wings, mammals with fur and mammary glands . . . Might not gaps exist . . . not because large numbers of transitional forms mysteriously failed to fossilize, but because they never existed?"

Darwin himself commented on this lack of transitional fossils, asking, "Why then is not every geological formation and every stratum full of such intermediate links?" In contemplating the answer, he turned to the data and noted that "geology assuredly does not reveal any such finely graduated organic chain; and this, perhaps, is the gravest objection which can be urged against my theory." So where *are* all the fossils?

One answer to Darwin's dilemma is the exceptionally low probability of any dead animal's escaping the jaws and stomachs of predators, scavengers, and detritus feeders, reaching the stage of fossilization, and then somehow finding its way back to the surface through geological forces and unpredictable events to be discovered millions of years later by the handful of paleontologists looking for its traces. Given this reality, it is remarkable that we have as many fossils as we do.

There is another explanation for the missing fossils. Ernst Mayr outlines the most common way that a species gives rise to a new species: when a small group (the "founder" population) breaks away and becomes geographically—and thus reproductively—isolated from its ancestral group. As long as it remains small and detached, the founder group can experience fairly rapid genetic changes, especially relative to large populations, which tend to sustain their genetic homogeneity through diverse interbreeding. Mayr's theory, called *allopatric speciation,* helps to explain why so few fossils would exist for these animals.

The evolutionary theorists Niles Eldredge and Stephen Jay Gould took Mayr's observations about how new species emerge and applied them to the fossil record, finding that gaps in the fossil record are not missing evidence of gradual changes; they are extant evidence of punctuated changes. They called this theory *punctuated equilibrium.* Species are so static and enduring that they leave plenty of fossils in the strata while they are in their stable state (equilibrium). The change from one species to another, however, happens relatively quickly on a geological time scale, and in these smaller, geographically isolated population groups (punctuated). In fact, species change happens so rapidly that few "transitional" carcasses create fossils to record the change. Eldredge and Gould conclude that "breaks in the fossil record are real; they express the way in which evolution occurs, not the fragments of an imperfect record." Of course, the small group will also be reproducing, following the geometric increases that are observed in all species, and will eventually form a relatively large population of individuals that retain their phenotype for a considerable time—and leave behind many well-preserved fossils. Millions of years later this process results in a fossil record that records mostly the equilibrium. The punctuation is in the blanks.

The Evidence of Evolution

In August 1996, NASA announced that it discovered life on Mars. The evidence was the Allan Hills 84001 rock, believed to have been ejected out of Mars by a meteor impact millions of years ago, which then fell into an orbit that brought it to Earth. On the panel of NASA experts was paleobiologist William Schopf, a specialist in ancient microbial life. Schopf was skeptical of NASA's claim because, he said, the four "lines of evidence" claimed to support the find did not converge toward a single conclusion. Instead, they pointed to several possible conclusions.

Schopf's analysis of "lines of evidence" reflects a method of science first described by the nineteenth-century philosopher of science William Whewell. To prove a theory, Whewell believed, one must have more than one induction, more than a single generalization drawn from specific facts. One must have multiple inductions that converge upon one another, independently but in conjunction. Whewell said that if these inductions "jump together" it strengthens the plausibility of a theory: "Accordingly the cases in which inductions from classes of facts altogether different have thus jumped together, belong only to the best established theories which the history of science contains. And, as I shall have occasion to refer to this particular feature in their evidence, I will take the liberty of describing it by a particular phrase; and will term it the Consilience of Inductions." I call it a *convergence of evidence.*

Just as detectives employ the convergence of evidence technique to deduce who most likely committed a crime, scientists employ the method to deduce the likeliest explanation for a particular phenomenon. Cosmologists reconstruct the history of the universe through a convergence of evidence from astronomy, planetary geology, and physics. Geologists reconstruct the history of the planet through a convergence of evidence from geology, physics, and chemistry. Archaeologists piece together the history of civilization through a convergence of evidence from biology (pollen grains), chemistry (kitchen middens), physics (potsherds, tools), history (works of art, written sources), and other site-specific artifacts.

As a historical science, evolution is confirmed by the fact that so many independent lines of evidence converge to its single conclusion. Independent sets of data from geology, paleontology, botany, zoology, herpetology, entomology, biogeography, comparative anatomy and physiology, genetics and population genetics, and many other sciences each point to the conclusion that life evolved. This is a convergence of evidence. Creationists can demand "just one fossil transitional form" that shows evolution. But evolution is not proved through a single fossil. It is proved through a convergence of fossils, along with a convergence of genetic comparisons between species, and a convergence of anatomical and physiological comparisons between species, and many other lines of inquiry. For creationists to disprove evolution, they need to unravel all these independent lines of evidence, as well as construct a rival theory that can explain them better than the theory of evolution. They have yet to do so.

The Tests of Evolution

Creationists like to argue that evolution is not a science because no one was there to observe it and there are no experiments to run today to test it. The inability to observe past events or set up controlled experiments is no obstacle to a sound science of cosmology, geology, or archaeology, so why should it be for a sound science of evolution? The key is the ability to test one's hypothesis. There are a number of ways to do so, starting with the broadest method of how we know evolution happened.

Consider the evolution of our best friend, the dog. With so many breeds of dogs popular for so many thousands of years, one would think that there would be an abundance of transitional fossils providing paleontologists with copious data from which to reconstruct their evolutionary ancestry. Not so. In fact, according to Jennifer A. Leonard of the National Museum of Natural History in Washington, D.C., "the fossil record from wolves to dogs is pretty sparse." Then how do we know the origin of dogs? In a 2002 issue of *Science,* Leonard and her colleagues report that mitochrondrial DNA (mtDNA) data from early dog remains "strongly support the hypothesis that ancient American and Eurasian domestic dogs share a common origin from Old World gray wolves." In the same issue of *Science,* Peter Savolainen from the Royal Institute of Technology in Stockholm and his colleagues note that the fossil record is problematic "because of the difficulty in discriminating between small wolves and domestic dogs," but their study of mtDNA sequence variation among 654 domestic dogs from around the world "points to an origin of the domestic dog in East Asia ~15,000 yr B.P." from a single gene pool of wolves. Finally, Brian Hare from Harvard and his colleagues describe the results of their study in which they found that domestic dogs are more skillful than wolves at using human communicative signals indicating the location of hidden food, but that "dogs and wolves do not perform differently in a non-social memory task, ruling out the possibility that dogs outperform wolves in all human-guided tasks." Therefore, "dogs' social-communicative skills with humans were acquired during the process of domestication." Although no single fossil proves that dogs came from wolves, the convergence of evidence from archaeological, morphological, genetic, and behavioral "fossils" reveals the ancestor of all dogs to be the East Asian wolf.

The tale of human evolution is revealed in a similar manner (although here we do have an abundance of transitional fossil riches), as it is for all ancestors in the history of life. One of the finest compilations of evolutionary convergence is Richard Dawkins's magnum opus, *The Ancestor's Tale,* 673 pages of convergent science recounted with literary elegance. Dawkins traces innumerable "transitional fossils" (what he calls "concestors"—the "point of rendezvous" of the last common ancestor shared by a set of species) from *Homo sapiens* back four billion years to the origin of replicating molecules and the emergence of evolution. No one concestor proves that evolution happened, but together they reveal a majestic story of a process over time. We know human evolution happened because innumerable bits of data from myriad fields of science conjoin to paint a rich portrait of life's pilgrimage.

But the convergence of evidence is just the start. The *comparative method* allows us to infer evolutionary relationships using data from a wide variety of fields. Luigi Luca CavalliSforza and his colleagues, for example, compared fifty years of data from population genetics, geography, ecology, archaeology, physical anthropology, and linguistics to trace the evolution of the human races. Using both the convergence and comparative methods led them to conclude that "the major stereotypes, all based on skin color, hair color and form, and facial traits, reflect superficial differences that are not confirmed by deeper analysis with more reliable genetic traits." By comparing surface (physical) traits—the phenotype of individuals—with genetic traits—the genotype—they teased out the relationship between different groups of people. Most interesting, they found that the genetic traits disclosed "recent evolution mostly under the effect of climate and perhaps sexual selection." For example, they discovered that Australian aborigines are genetically more closely related to southeast Asians than they are to African blacks, which makes sense from the perspective of the evolutionary timeline: The migration pattern of humans out of Africa would have led them first to Asia and then to Australia.

Dating techniques provide evidence of the timeline of evolution. The dating of fossils, along with the earth, moon, sun, solar system, and universe, are all tests of evolutionary theory, and so far they have passed all the tests. We know that the earth is approximately 4.6 billion years old because of the convergence of evidence from several methods of dating rocks: Uranium Lead, Rubidium Strontium, and Carbon-14. Further, the age of the earth, the age of the moon, the age of the sun, the age of the solar system, and the age of the universe are consistent, maintaining yet another consilience. If, say, the earth was dated at 4.6 billion years old but the solar system was dated at one million years old, the theory of evolution would be in trouble. But Uranium Lead, Rubidium Strontium, and Carbon-14 have not provided any good news for the so-called Young Earth creationists.

Better yet, the fossils and organisms speak for themselves. *Fossils do show intermediate stages,* despite their rarity. For example, there are now at least eight intermediate fossil stages identified in the evolution of whales. In human evolution, there are at least a dozen known intermediate fossil stages since hominids branched off from the great apes six million years ago. *And geological strata consistently reveal the same sequence of fossils.* A quick and simple way to debunk the theory of evolution would be to find a fossil horse in the same geological stratum as a trilobite. According to evolutionary theory, trilobites and mammals are separated by hundreds of millions of years. If such a fossil juxtaposition occurred, and it was not the product of some geological anomaly (such as uplifted, broken, bent, or even flipped strata—all of which occur but are traceable), it would mean that there was something seriously wrong with the theory of evolution.

Evolution also posits that *modern organisms should show a variety of structures from simple to complex, reflecting an evolutionary history rather than an instantaneous creation.* The human eye, for example, is the result of a long and complex pathway that goes back hundreds of millions of years. Initially a simple eyespot with a handful of light-sensitive cells that provided information to the organism about an important source of the light, it developed into a recessed eyespot, where a small surface indentation filled with light-sensitive cells provided additional data on the direction of light; then into a deep recession eyespot, where additional cells at greater depth provide more accurate information about the environment; then into a pinhole camera eye that is able to focus an image on the back of a deeply recessed layer of light-sensitive cells; then into a pinhole lens eye that is able to focus the image; then into a complex eye found in such modern mammals as humans. All of these structures are expressed in modern eyes.

Further, *biological structures show signs of natural design.* The anatomy of the human eye, in fact, shows anything but "intelligence" in its design. It is built upside down and backwards, requiring photons of light to travel through the cornea, lens, aqueous fluid, blood vessels, ganglion cells, amacrine cells, horizontal cells, and bipolar cells before they reach the light-sensitive rods and cones that transduce the light signal into neural impulses—which are then sent to the visual cortex at the back of the brain for processing into meaningful patterns. For optimal vision, why would an intelligent designer have built an eye upside down and backwards? This "design" makes sense only if natural selection built eyes from available materials, and in the particular configuration of the ancestral organism's preexisting organic structures. The eye shows the pathways of evolutionary history, not of intelligent design.

Additionally, *vestigial structures stand as evidence of the mistakes, the misstarts, and, especially, the leftover traces of evolutionary history.* The cretaceous snake *Pachyrhachis problematicus,* for example, had small hind limbs used for locomotion that it inherited from its quadrupedal ancestors, gone in today's snakes. Modern whales retain a tiny pelvis for hind legs that existed in their land mammal ancestors but have disappeared today. Likewise, there are wings on flightless birds, and of course humans are replete with useless vestigial structures, a distinctive sign of our evolutionary ancestry. A short list of just ten vestigial structures in humans leaves one musing: Why would an Intelligent Designer have created these?

1. *Male nipples.* Men have nipples because females need them, and the overall architecture of the human body is more efficiently developed in the uterus from a single developmental structure.

2. *Male uterus.* Men have the remnant of an undeveloped female reproductive organ that hangs off the prostate gland for the same reason.

3. *Thirteenth rib.* Most modern humans have twelve sets of ribs, but 8 percent of us have a thirteenth set, just like chimpanzees and gorillas. This is a remnant of our primate ancestry: We share common ancestors with chimps and gorillas, and the thirteenth set of ribs has been retained from when our lineage branched off six million years ago.

4. *Coccyx.* The human tailbone is all that remains from our common ancestors' tails, which were used for grasping branches and maintaining balance.

5. *Wisdom teeth.* Before stone tools, weapons, and fire, hominids were primarily vegetarians, and as such we chewed a lot of plants, requiring an extra set of grinding molars. Many people still have them, despite the smaller size of our modern jaws.

6. *Appendix.* This muscular tube connected to the large intestine was once used for digesting cellulose in our largely vegetarian diet before we became meat eaters.

7. *Body hair.* We are sometimes called "the naked ape"; however, most humans have a layer of fine body hair, again left over from our evolutionary ancestry from thick-haired apes and hominids.

8. *Goose bumps.* Our body hair ancestry can also be inferred from the fact that we retain the ability of our ancestors to puff up their fur for heat insulation, or as a threat gesture to potential predators. Erector pili— "goose bumps"—are a telltale sign of our evolutionary ancestry.

9. *Extrinsic ear muscles.* If you can wiggle your ears you can thank our primate ancestors, who evolved the ability to move their ears independently of their heads as a more efficient means of discriminating precise sound directionality and location.

10. *Third eyelid.* Many animals have a nictitating membrane that covers the eye for added protection; we retain this "third eyelid" in the corner of our eye as a tiny fold of flesh.

Evolutionary scientists can provide dozens more examples of vestigial structures—let alone examples of how we know evolution happened from all of these other various lines of historical evidence. Yet as a science, evolution depends primarily on the ability to test a hypothesis. How can we ever test an evolutionary hypothesis if we cannot go into a lab and create a new species naturally?

I once had the opportunity to help dig up a dinosaur with Jack Horner, the curator of paleontology at the Museum of the Rockies in Bozeman, Montana. As Horner explains in his book *Digging Dinosaurs,* "paleontology is not an experimental science; it's an historical science. This means that paleontologists are seldom able to test their hypotheses by laboratory experiments, but they can still test them." Horner discusses this process of historical science at the famous dig in which he exposed the first dinosaur eggs ever found in North America. The initial stage of the dig was "getting the fossils out of the ground." Unsheathing the bones from the overlying and surrounding stone is backbreaking work. As you move from jackhammers and pickaxes to dental tools and small brushes, historical interpretation accelerates as a function of the rate of bone unearthed. Then, in the second phase of a dig, he gets "to look at the fossils, study them, make hypotheses based on what we saw and try to prove or disprove them."

When I arrived at Horner's camp I expected to find the busy director of a fully sponsored dig barking out orders to his staff. I was surprised to come upon a patient historical scientist, sitting cross-legged before a cervical vertebra from a 140-million-year-old *Apatosaurus* (formerly known as *Brontosaurus*), wondering what to make of it. Soon a reporter from a local paper arrived inquiring of Horner what this discovery meant for the history of dinosaurs. Did it change any of his theories? Where was the head? Was there more than one body at this site? Horner's answers were those of a cautious scientist: "I don't know yet." "Beats me." "We need more evidence." "We'll have to wait and see." It was historical science at its best.

After two long days of exposing nothing but solid rock and my own ineptness at seeing bone within stone, one of the paleontologists pointed out that the rock I was about to toss away was a piece of bone that appeared to be part of a rib. If it was a rib, then the bone should retain its riblike shape as more of the overburden was chipped away. This it did for about a foot, until it suddenly flared to the right. Was it a rib, or something else? Horner moved in to check. "It could be part of the pelvis," he suggested. If it was part of the pelvis, then it should also flare out to the left when more was uncovered. Sure enough, Horner's prediction was verified by further digging.

In science, this process is called the *hypothetico-deductive method,* in which one forms a hypothesis based on existing data, deduces a prediction from the hypothesis, then tests the prediction against further data. For example, in 1981 Horner discovered a site in Montana that contained approximately thirty million fossil fragments of approximately ten thousand *Maiasaurs* in a bed measuring 1.25 miles by .25 miles. His hypothesizing began with a question: "What could such a deposit represent?" There was no evidence that predators had chewed the bones, yet many were broken in half lengthwise. Further, the bones were all arranged from east to west—the long dimension of the bone deposit. Small bones had been separated from bigger bones, and there were no bones of baby *Maiasaurs,* only those of individuals between nine and twenty-three feet long. What would cause the bones to splinter lengthwise? Why would the small bones be separated from the big bones? Was this one giant herd, all killed at the same time, or was it a dying ground over many years?

An early hypothesis—that a mud flow buried the herd alive—was rejected because "it didn't make sense that even the most powerful flow of mud could break bones lengthwise . . . nor did it make sense that a herd of living animals buried in mud would end up with all their skeletons disarticulated." Horner constructed another hypothesis. "It seemed that there had to be a twofold event," he reasoned, "the dinosaurs dying in one incident and the bones being swept away in another." Since there was a layer of volcanic ash 1.5 feet above the bone bed, volcanic activity was implicated in the death of the herd. Horner then deduced that only fossil bones would split lengthwise, and therefore the damage to the bones had occurred long after the dying event.

His hypothesis and deduction led to his conclusion that the herd was "killed by the gases, smoke and ash of a volcanic eruption. And if a huge eruption killed them all at once, then it might have also killed everything else around." Then perhaps there was a flood, maybe from a breached lake, carrying the rotting bodies downstream, separating the big bones from the small, lighter bones, and giving the bones a uniform orientation.

A paleontological dig is a good example of how hypothetico-deductive reasoning and historical sciences can make predictions based on initial data that are then verified or rejected by later historical evidence. Evolutionary theory is rooted in a rich array of data from the past that, while nonreplicable in a laboratory, are nevertheless valid sources of information that can be used to piece together specific events and test general hypotheses. While the specifics of evolution—how quickly it happens, what triggers species change, at which level of the organism it occurs—are still being studied and unraveled, the general theory of evolution is the most tested in science over the past century and a half. Scientists agree: Evolution happened.

Evolution in Action

Finches, monkeyflowers, sockeye salmon, and bacteria are changing before our eyes.

JONATHAN WEINER

harles Darwin's wife, Emma, was terrified that they would be separated for eternity, because she would go to heaven and he would not. Emma confessed her fears in a letter that Charles kept and treasured, with his reply to her scribbled in the margin: "When I am dead, know that many times, I have kissed and cryed over this."

Close as they were, the two could hardly bear to talk about Darwin's view of life. And today, those of us who live in the United States, by many measures the world's leading scientific nation, find ourselves in a house divided. Half of us accept Darwin's theory, half of us reject it, and many people are convinced that Darwin burns in hell. I find that old debate particularly strange, because I've spent some of the best years of my life as a science writer peering over the shoulders of biologists who actually watch Darwin's process in action. What they can see casts the whole debate in a new light—or it should.

Darwin himself never tried to watch evolution happen. "It may metaphorically be said," he wrote in the *Origin of Species,*

> that natural selection is daily and hourly scrutinizing, throughout the world, the slightest variations; rejecting those that are bad, preserving and adding up all that are good; silently and insensibly working, whenever and wherever opportunity offers. . . . We see nothing of these slow changes in progress, until the hand of time has marked the lapse of ages.

Darwin was a modest man who thought of himself as a plodder (one of his favorite mottoes was, "It's dogged as does it"). He thought evolution plodded too. If so, it would be more boring to watch evolution than to watch drying paint. As a result, for several generations after Darwin's death, almost nobody tried. For most of the twentieth century the only well-known example of evolution in action was the case of peppered moths in industrial England. The moth had its picture in all the textbooks, as a kind of special case.

Then, in 1973, a married pair of evolutionary biologists, Peter and Rosemary Grant, now at Princeton University, began a study of Darwin's process in Darwin's islands, the Galápagos,

watching Darwin's finches. At first, they assumed that they would have to infer the history of evolution in the islands from the distribution of the various finch species, varieties, and populations across the archipelago. That is pretty much what Darwin had done, in broad strokes, after the *Beagle's* five-week survey of the islands in 1835. But the Grants soon discovered that at their main study site, a tiny desert island called Daphne Major, near the center of the archipelago, the finches were evolving rapidly. Conditions on the island swung wildly back and forth from wet years to dry years, and finches on Daphne adapted to each swing, from generation to generation. With the help of a series of graduate students, the Grants began to spend a good part of every year on Daphne, watching evolution in action as it shaped and reshaped the finches' beaks.

At the same time, a few biologists began making similar discoveries elsewhere in the world. One of them was John A. Endler, an evolutionary biologist at the University of California, Santa Barbara, who studied Trinidadian guppies. In 1986 Endler published a little book called *Natural Selection in the Wild,* in which he collected and reviewed all of the studies of evolution in action that had been published to that date. Dozens of new field projects were in progress. Biologists finally began to realize that Darwin had been too modest. Evolution by natural selection can happen rapidly enough to watch.

Now the field is exploding. More than 250 people around the world are observing and documenting evolution, not only in finches and guppies, but also in aphids, flies, grayling, monkeyflowers, salmon, and sticklebacks. Some workers are even documenting pairs of species—symbiotic insects and plants—that have recently found each other, and observing the pairs as they drift off into their own world together like lovers in a novel by D.H. Lawrence.

The Grants' own study gets more sophisticated every year. A few years ago, a group of molecular biologists working with the Grants nailed down a gene that plays a key role in shaping the beaks of the finches. The gene codes for a signaling molecule called bone morphogenic protein 4 (BMP4). Finches with bigger beaks tend to have more BMP4, and finches with smaller beaks have less. In the laboratory, the biologists demonstrated that they could sculpt the beaks themselves by adding or subtracting BMP4. The same gene that shapes the beak of the finch in the egg also shapes the human face in the womb.

Some of the most dramatic stories of evolution in action result from the pressures that human beings are imposing on the planet. As Stephen Palumbi, an evolutionary biologist at Stanford University, points out, we are changing the course of evolution for virtually every living species everywhere, with consequences that are sometimes the opposite of what we might have predicted, or desired.

Take trophy hunting. Wild populations of bighorn mountain sheep are carefully managed in North America for hunters who want a chance to shoot a ram with a trophy set of horns. Hunting permits can cost well into the six figures. On Ram Mountain, in Alberta, Canada, hunters have shot the biggest of the bighorn rams for more than thirty years. And the result? Evolution has made the hunters' quarry scarce. The runts have had a better chance than the giants of passing on their genes. So on Ram Mountain the rams have gotten smaller, and their horns are proportionately smaller yet.

Or take fishing, which is economically much more consequential. The populations of Atlantic cod that swam for centuries off the coasts of Labrador and Newfoundland began a terrible crash in the late 1980s. In the years leading up to the crash, the cod had been evolving much like the sheep on Ram Mountain. Fish that matured relatively fast and reproduced relatively young had the better chance of passing on their genes; so did the fish that stayed small. So even before the population crashed, the average cod had been shrinking.

We often seem to lose out wherever we fight hardest to control nature. Antibiotics drive the evolution of drug-resistant bacteria at a frightening pace. Sulfonamides were introduced in the 1930s, and resistance to them was first observed a decade later. Penicillin was deployed in 1943, and the first penicillin resistance was observed in 1946. In the same way, pesticides and herbicides create resistant bugs and weeds.

Palumbi estimates that the annual bill for such unintended human-induced evolution runs to more than $100 billion in the U.S. alone. Worldwide, the pressure of global warming, fragmented habitats, heightened levels of carbon dioxide, acid rain, and the other myriad perturbations people impose on the chemistry and climate of the planet—all change the terms of the struggle for existence in the air, in the water, and on land. Biologists have begun to worry about those perturbations, but global change may be racing ahead of them.

To me, the most interesting news in the global evolution watch concerns what Darwin called "that mystery of mysteries, the origin of species."

The process whereby a population acquires small, inherited changes through natural selection is known as microevolution. Finches get bigger, fish gets smaller, but a finch is still a finch and a fish is still a fish. For people who reject Darwin's theory, that's the end of the story: no matter how many small, inherited changes accumulate, they believe, natural selection can never make a new kind of living thing. The kinds, the species, are eternal.

Darwin argued otherwise. He thought that many small changes could cause two lines of life to diverge. Whenever animals and plants find their way to a new home, for instance, they suffer, like emigres in new countries. Some individuals fail, others adapt and prosper. As the more successful individuals reproduce, Darwin maintained, the new population begins to differ from the ancestral one. If the two populations diverge widely enough, they become separate species. Change on that scale is known as macroevolution.

In *Origin,* Darwin estimated that a new species might take between ten thousand and fourteen thousand generations to arise. Until recently, most biologists assumed it would take at least that many, or maybe even millions of generations, before microevolutionary changes led to the origin of new species. So they assumed they could watch evolution by natural selection, but not the divergence of one species into separate, reproductively isolated species. Now that view is changing too.

Not long ago, a young evolution-watcher named Andrew Hendry, a biologist at McGill University in Montreal, reported the results of a striking study of sockeye salmon. Sockeye tend to reproduce either in streams or along lake beaches. When the glaciers of the last ice age melted and retreated, about ten thousand years ago, they left behind thousands of new lakes. Salmon from streams swam into the lakes and stayed. Today their descendants tend to breed among themselves rather than with sockeyes that live in the streams. The fish in the lakes and streams are reproductively isolated from each other. So how fast did that happen?

In the 1930s and 1940s, sockeye salmon were introduced into Lake Washington, in Washington State. Hundreds of thousands of their descendants now live and breed in Cedar River, which feeds the lake. By 1957 some of the introduced sockeye also colonized a beach along the lake called Pleasure Point, about four miles from the mouth of Cedar River.

Hendry could tell whether a full-grown, breeding salmon had been born in the river or at the beach by examining the rings on its otoliths, or ear stones. Otolith rings reflect variations in water temperature while a fish embryo is developing. Water temperatures at the beach are relatively constant compared with the river temperatures. Hendry and his colleagues checked the otoliths and collected DNA samples from the fish—and found that more than a third of the sockeye breeding at Pleasure Point had grown up in the river. They were immigrants.

With such a large number of immigrants, the two populations at Pleasure Point should have blended back together. But they hadn't. So at breeding time many of the river sockeye that swam over to the beach must have been relatively unsuccessful at passing on their genes.

Hendry could also tell the stream fish and the beach fish apart just by looking at them. Where the sockeye's breeding waters are swift-flowing, such as in Cedar River, the males tend to be slender. Their courtship ritual and competition with other males requires them to turn sideways in strong current—an awkward maneuver for a male with a deep, roundish body. So in strong current, slender males have the better chance of passing on their genes. But in still waters, males with the deepest bodies have the best chance of getting mates. So beach males tend to be rounder—their dimensions greater from the top of the back to the bottom of the belly—than river males.

What about females? In the river, where currents and floods are forever shifting and swirling the gravel, females have to dig deep nests for their eggs. So the females in the river tend to be bigger than their lake-dwelling counterparts, because bigger females can dig deeper nests. Where the water is calmer, the gravel stays put, and shallower nests will do.

So all of the beachgoers, male and female, have adapted to life at Pleasure Point. Their adaptations are strong enough that reproductive isolation has evolved. How long did the evolution take? Hendry began studying the salmon's reproductive isolation in 1992. At that time, the sockeyes in the stream and the ones at Pleasure Point had been breeding in their respective habitats for at most thirteen generations. That is so fast that, as Hendry and his colleagues point out, it may be possible someday soon to catch the next step, the origin of a new species.

And it's not just the sockeye salmon. Consider the three-spined stickleback. After the glaciers melted at the end of the last ice age, many sticklebacks swam out of the sea and into new glacial lakes—just as the salmon did. In the sea, sticklebacks wear heavy, bony body armor. In a lake they wear light armor. In a certain new pond in Bergen, Norway, during the past century, sticklebacks evolved toward the lighter armor in just thirty-one years. In Loberg Lake, Alaska, the same kind of change took only a dozen years. A generation for sticklebacks is two years. So that dramatic evolution took just six generations.

Dolph Schluter, a former finch-watcher from the Galapagos and currently a biologist at the University of British Columbia in Vancouver, has shown that, along with the evolution of new body types, sticklebacks also evolve a taste for mates with the new traits. In other words, the adaptive push of sexual selection is going hand-in-hand with natural selection. Schluter has built experimental ponds in Vancouver to observe the phenomenon under controlled conditions, and the same patterns he found in isolated lakes repeat themselves in his ponds. So adaptation can sometimes drive sexual selection and accelerate reproductive isolation.

There are other developments in the evolution watch, too, many to mention in this small space. Some of the fastest action is microscopic. Richard Lenski, a biologist at Michigan State University in East Lansing, watches the evolution of *Escherichia coli*. Because one generation takes only twenty minutes, and billions of *E. coli* can fit in a petri dish, the bacteria make ideal subjects for experimental evolution. Throw some *E. coli* into a new dish, for instance, with food they haven't

encountered before, and they will evolve and adapt—quickly at first and then more slowly, as they refine their fit with their new environment.

And then there are the controversies. Science progresses and evolves by controversy, by internal debate and revision. In the United States these days one almost hates to mention that there are arguments among evolutionists. So often, they are taken out of context and hyperamplified to suggest that nothing about Darwinism is solid—that Darwin is dead. But research is messy because nature is messy, and fieldwork is some of the messiest research of all. It is precisely here at its jagged cutting edge that Darwinism is most vigorously alive.

Not long ago, one of the most famous icons of the evolution watch toppled over: the story of the peppered moths, familiar to anyone who remembers biology 101. About half a century ago, the British evolutionist Bernard Kettlewell noted that certain moths in the British Isles had evolved into darker forms when the trunks of trees darkened with industrial pollution. When the trees lightened again, after clean air acts were passed, the moths had evolved into light forms again. Kettlewell claimed that dark moths resting on dark tree trunks were harder for birds to see; in each decade, moths of the right color were safer.

But in the past few years, workers have shown that Kettlewell's explanation was too simplistic. For one thing, the moths don't normally rest on tree trunks. In forty years of observation, only twice have moths been seen resting there. Nobody knows where they do rest. The moths did evolve rapidly, but no one can be certain why.

To me what remains most interesting is the light that studies such as Hendry's, or the Grants', may throw on the origin of species. It's extraordinary that scientists are now examining the very beginnings of the process, at the level of beaks and fins, at the level of the genes. The explosion of evolution-watchers is a remarkable development in Darwin's science. Even as the popular debate about evolution in America is reaching its most heated moment since the trial of John Scopes, evolutionary biologists are pursuing one of the most significant and surprising voyages of discovery since the young Darwin sailed into the Galápagos Archipelago aboard Her Majesty's ship *Beagle*.

Not long ago I asked Hendry if his studies have changed the way he thinks about the origin of species. "Yes," he replied without hesitation, "I think it's occurring all over the place."

JONATHAN WEINER began writing about evolution in 1990, when he met Peter and Rosemary Grant, who observe evolution firsthand in finch populations in the Galápagos. Weiner's book *The Beak of the Finch* (Alfred A. Knopf) won a Pulitzer Prize in 1994. He is a professor in the Graduate School of Journalism at Columbia University, in New York City. He is also working on a book about human longevity for Ecco Press.

From *Natural History*, November 2005, pp. 47–52. Copyright © 2005 by Natural History Magazine. Reprinted by permission.

How the Dog Got Its Curly Tail

David Sloan Wilson

Dmitry K. Belyaev was not where he wanted to be. As a Russian geneticist who refused to endorse the ideologically driven theories of his colleague Trofim Lysenko, Belyaev had been removed from a prestigious post in Moscow and sent to Siberia—not to work in the gulag, but to begin a new scientific institute. Even his old job sounds strange to American ears: head of the Department of Fur Animal Breeding at the Central Research Laboratory of Fur Breeding. Nevertheless, an experiment that Belyaev started at his new institute in 1959 revealed something fundamental about evolution in general.

The narrow purpose of the experiment was to create a tamer variety of silver fox. Wild silver foxes had been caged and bred for their fur since the beginning of the twentieth century, but they were by no means fully tame. Belyaev established a rigid protocol for measuring tameness throughout development, from pups a month old to sexual maturity. Individuals were selected for breeding purely on the basis of their tameness index without regard to any other trait. Forty years and forty-five thousand foxes later, Belyaev (who died in 1985) and his successors had produced a new breed that qualified for the exalted title of "domesticated elite." Rather than fleeing from people and biting when handled as their ancestors had, the new breed was eager for human contact, whimpering, sniffing, and licking like dogs, even as little pups less than one month old.

Such is the power of artificial selection, which partially inspired Darwin's theory of natural selection. The most amazing thing about the experiment, however, was that the foxes had become like dogs in *other* respects. Their tails had become curly. Their ears had become floppy. Their coat color had become spotted. Their legs had become shorter and their skulls more broad. These physical traits had not been selected, but they still came along for the ride, as if connected to the behavioral trait of tameness by invisible strings.

These hidden connections force me to amend my description of heritable variation as a kind of living clay that can be shaped by natural selection. That was too simple. Real clay is so malleable that you can shape one part of a sculpture without altering other parts. Living clay is more complex and interconnected, imposing a shape of its own. As a good evolutionist, you might become interested in a conspicuous trait, such as a curly tail or a floppy ear, and ask how it evolved by contributing to survival and reproduction. That's a good question, and I could provide many examples of traits that initially appear as whimsical as a

floppy ear but turn out to be important adaptations upon further study. However, the fox experiment reveals a completely different possibility, that the trait has no function whatsoever. It exists because of hidden connections with other traits that can be as obscure as the connection between a curly tail and tameness.

To learn more, we must understand the living clay of heritable variation in more detail. In Chapter 3, I described three ways of thinking based on theology, materialism, and natural selection. Theology is no longer used to explain the material world, not because it is unfairly excluded but because it proved its inadequacy many times over. I mean no disrespect by saying this and will turn my attention to theology in future chapters. For the moment, suffice it to say that the proper business of theology is to establish values, not facts about the material world.

That leaves the other two ways of thinking, based on materialism and natural selection. These are complementary and one can never substitute for the other. Complete knowledge about the physical makeup of organisms will not tell us about the shaping influence of natural selection. Complete knowledge about natural selection will not tell us about the actual mechanisms that evolve or the mysterious hidden connections such as those revealed by the fox experiment. Evolutionists use the terms "ultimate" (for explanations based on natural selection) and "proximate" (for materialist explanations) to make this distinction. Using these terms, we need to learn more about the proximate mechanisms that cause a fox to be wild or tame.

Almost all wild animals are tamer as infants than as adults. This is probably obvious from your own experience and makes good functional sense. A baby fox is incapable of defending itself and lives in a nurturing world provided by its parents. Only later will it have both the means and reasons to run or fight. This adaptive logic (the ultimate explanation) is implemented in real baby foxes by hormonal mechanisms (the proximate explanation). They are born tame, and fear falls like a curtain between two and four months of age, caused by surging levels of corticosteroids, a hormone associated with stress. Their bodies are simply programmed to do this; no experience is necessary. It's easy to imagine a fox baby that must experience a fearful event before becoming fearful, but those babies didn't survive as well as the ones who automatically became fearful at a certain age.

Individual foxes differ in the exact time that the hormonal curtain falls, and this variation is heritable. When Belyaev was selecting foxes purely for their tameness, he was selecting those with the most prolonged infant period. But hormones don't influence single behaviors; they are like conductors that influence many behaviors in a coordinated fashion. The tame foxes remained infantile in many respects, including their floppy puppy ears, short legs, and broad skulls. Another fact of mammalian development is that pigment cells (melanocytes) originate in one part of the embryo (the neural crest) and migrate to their final location on the skin. Prolonging infant development delays their migration and causes some to die, resulting in patches of unpigmented skin—spots.

These are very general rules of mammalian development, which explains a striking pattern. Have you ever noticed that all domestic mammals, including dogs, cats, cattle, horses, pigs, and guinea pigs, tend to share certain traits? They even tend to share the same star-shaped white patch on their foreheads. The ever-observant Darwin noted that "not a single domestic animal can be named which has not in some country drooping ears." Now *there's* a fact that is humble by itself but becomes great in combination with other facts! Among wild mammals, most infants have drooping ears but only the elephant has drooping ears as an adult. *All* of our domesticated animals have become tame by retaining their juvenile traits, just like the foxes in Belyaev's experiment.

Belyaev was a great evolutionist and scientist who struggled against enormous odds. His colleague Trofim Lysenko robbed him of his prestigious post and virtually outlawed the study of genetics and evolution in Russia for decades. His government didn't understand the value of basic knowledge, forcing him to justify his work in terms of the narrow benefits of the fur trade. His nation was so poor that it offered meager support for any kind of science, basic or applied. It's amazing that he could maintain his commitment to basic science under such circumstances.

Compared to Belyaev, a young American scientist named Douglas Emlen is a lucky, lucky man. He is exactly where he wants to be, which is the University of Montana at Missoula. He is doing exactly what he wants to do, which is studying evolution and development, just like Belyaev. Even better, he can concentrate entirely on advancing basic knowledge, which has led him to study a group of beetles without any economic significance but with great scientific significance.

These beetles are a bit like my burying beetles except that they bury dung rather than carrion. Most people who visit Africa marvel at the big game, but another spectacle takes place every time one of those big animals takes a poop. Almost before it hits the ground, hundreds of beetles converge from every direction. I know from experience that you can hear them coming before you can get your pants up. They include dozens of species, from the size of a golf ball to the size of a lentil, and many of them have horns like miniature flying rhinoceroses.

Doug studies a single genus of dung beetles called *Onthophagus*. A genus is the next taxonomic unit above species, so all its members are derived from a recent common ancestor. The genus *Onthophagus* includes over two thousand species, distributed worldwide, and their horn morphology is amazingly diverse. Some are hornless, while others sport huge tusks. The horns can exist on their snout, forehead, or the shield (called a pronotum)

behind their head. Molecular studies have shown that any given horn type within the genus has evolved not once but numerous times. If we could turn the evolution of the whole genus into a flipbook, we would see horns madly sprouting, shrinking, and changing position. Doug chose the genus because it affords so many comparisons and his goal is to study the evolution and development of the horns from both an ultimate and proximate perspective. Of course, the main interest is not in the beetles per se but what they can tell us about evolution and development in general.

On the ultimate side, we want to know if the horns are adaptations that evolved by natural selection. As we have seen, the answer need not be yes. Horns could be like floppy fox ears that have no function. Once you enter the lives of these wonderful creatures, however, the function of horns becomes clear enough. Females, who do not have horns in most species, pack dung into subterranean tunnels to raise their broods. Males, who do have horns, guard the entrances of the tunnels against other males. A Homeric battle among males for females and resources rages under every pile of poop.

Some males are too small to play the warrior game. The reason that they are small is because they were not provisioned with enough food. When you're a baby dung beetle, you take what you get and transform into an adult when the food runs out. It's better to be a wimpy adult than no adult at all. Wimpy males aren't strong, but they are devious, gaining access to the females by digging side tunnels of their own. Horns would be an impediment for this "sneaky" strategy, and small males don't have horns.

. . . you might be amazed that insects are capable of so many "intelligent" strategies. Not only do males and females engage in very different tasks, but males adopt different strategies as adults depending upon the amount of food they received as larvae. They change not only their behaviors but their very bodies, such as the presence and absence of horns. Dung beetles do not possess humanlike intelligence any more than burying beetles, but they do possess a system of physical mechanisms (the proximate explanation) that equips them with the bodies and behaviors that help them to survive and reproduce (the ultimate explanation).

In dung beetles, a critical period occurs when the larva transforms into an adult (the pupal stage). At this point the presence or absence of the sex chromosome determines what genes will be turned on or off to produce an adult male or female. If it's a male, then body size is assessed and compared to a threshold to determine if a horn will be produced. Other decisions are made as well. The larval body is like a single pot of money that needs to be allocated to adult body parts: how much should go to the wings, eyes, legs, antennae, ovaries, or testes? Somehow, the hormonal interactions inside the beetle function like a calculator, receiving information (such as body size) and giving sensible answers (the right body parts and proportions).

Horns are clearly adaptive for the individuals that have them (large males), but we have yet to explain the *diversity* of horns. Why are they located on the snout, forehead, or shield behind the head in different dung beetle species? It turns out that the answer to this question is based not on a diversity of functions (all horns are used for basically the same purpose) but on a quirk of beetle development. Competition occurs not only between male beetles battling with their horns but between adjacent body parts within male beetles during adult development. If the horn is located on the snout, it can become bigger only at the expense of the antennae becoming smaller. If the horn is located on the forehead, it can become bigger only at the expense of the eyes becoming smaller. If the horn is located on the shield, it can become bigger only at the expense of the wings becoming smaller. These trade-offs might seem puzzling. Shouldn't it be possible to design a system that doesn't require competition among adjacent structures? Perhaps, but that's not the system that evolved in dung beetles.

Internal competition among adjacent body parts begins to explain why horns might be located on different parts of the body in different species. For example, among the thousands of species in the genus *Onthophagus,* some are diurnal and others are nocturnal. Nocturnal species need bigger eyes to see in the dark, so their horns should be located on their snouts or shields but not on their foreheads. Sure enough, that is what Doug discovered when he compared diurnal and nocturnal species within this single genus. Similarly, species that must fly long distances should not have horns on their shields, and species that rely especially on their antennae to sense chemicals should not have horns on their snouts. Doug is in the process of testing these hypotheses by comparing the thousands of species in this single genus in the appropriate ways.

Doug's dung beetles and Belyaev's foxes tell us that natural selection thinking and mechanistic thinking—ultimate and proximate—must take place in combination to fully understand the evolutionary process. The living clay of heritable variation is not infinitely malleable and its properties can only be discovered by hard work. No one could have known beforehand that foxes selected purely for tameness would become like dogs in other respects or that adjacent body parts compete with each other during beetle development. The only way to obtain this knowledge is to roll up our sleeves and get to work using scientific methods and a good theory that asks the right questions.

Doug and I are both evolutionists, but we practice our craft in very different ways. I use evolution to study the length and breadth of creation, spending only a few years on any particular organism or subject. He is basing his entire career on a single subject (horns) and a single esoteric group of insects (dung beetles), which might seem incredibly narrow. But Doug's work is narrow the way a laser beam is narrow. He uses his detailed knowledge to ask and answer basic questions that I can't begin

to approach with my relatively superficial knowledge. Both approaches deserve to coexist for their separate insights.

Doug and I are both basic scientists, which means that our primary goal is to advance knowledge for its own sake. It might seem that basic and practical science should be fully compatible. If you can study evolution and development while breeding a better fox, why not? Alas, such happy combinations are only sometimes available. Just as there are trade-offs between adjacent body parts of a dung beetle, there are trade-offs between basic and practical science. The fox experiment could have been performed much more quickly and inexpensively using wild mice, which happen to have no economic significance. Emlen chose his dung beetles as the very best system for advancing basic knowledge about evolution and development. There is no comparable system that is economically significant. Modern life rests upon a foundation of basic knowledge, and strengthening the foundation does not need to be justified in terms of a more narrow practical goal.

The metaphor of basic science as a foundation can be taken further. Building a foundation requires a certain amount of stability and wealth. There's no point if you won't be here tomorrow or if you are worried about your next meal. Russian society lacks the stability and wealth to invest much in basic knowledge. In fact, the situation after the collapse of Communism is worse than ever, as Belyaev's successors describe in a 1999 article that amounts to a cry for help in their heroic effort to continue the fox experiment:

> For the first time in 40 years, the future of our domestication experiment is in doubt, jeopardized by the continuing crisis of the Russian economy. In 1996 the population of our breeding herd stood at 700. Last year, with no funds to feed the foxes or to pay the salaries of our staff, we had to cut the number to 100. Earlier we were able to cover most of our expenses by selling the pelts of the foxes culled from the breeding herd. Now that source of revenue has all but dried up, leaving us increasingly dependent on outside funding at a time when shrinking budgets and changes in the grant-rewarding system in Russia are making long-term experiments such as ours harder and harder to sustain. Like many other enterprises in our country, we are becoming more entrepreneurial.

It is fortunate that at least some nations on this earth have the stability, wealth, and wisdom to invest in the advancement of basic knowledge for its own sake.

The Latest Face of Creationism

Creationists who want religious ideas taught as scientific fact in public schools continue to adapt to courtroom defeats by hiding their true aims under ever changing guises.

GLENN BRANCH AND EUGENIE C. SCOTT

Professors routinely give advice to students but usually while their charges are still in school. Arthur Landy, a distinguished professor of molecular and cell biology and biochemistry at Brown University, recently decided, however, that he had to remind a former premed student of his that "without evolution, modern biology, including medicine and biotechnology, wouldn't make sense."

The sentiment was not original with Landy, of course. Thirty-six years ago geneticist Theodosius Dobzhansky, a major contributor to the foundations of modern evolutionary theory, famously told the readers of *The American Biology Teacher* that "nothing in biology makes sense, except in the light of evolution." Back then, Dobzhansky was encouraging biology teachers to present evolution to their pupils in spite of religiously motivated opposition. Now, however, Landy was addressing Bobby Jindal—the governor of the state of Louisiana—on whose desk the latest antievolution bill, the so-called Louisiana Science Education Act, was sitting, awaiting his signature.

Remembering Jindal as a good student in his genetics class, Landy hoped that the governor would recall the scientific importance of evolution to biology and medicine. Joining Landy in his opposition to the bill were the American Institute of Biological Sciences, which warned that "Louisiana will undoubtedly be thrust into the national spotlight as a state that pursues politics over science and education," and the American Association for the Advancement of Science, which told Jindal that the law would "unleash an assault against scientific integrity." Earlier, the National Association of Biology Teachers had urged the legislature to defeat the bill, pleading "that the state of Louisiana not allow its science curriculum to be weakened by encouraging the utilization of supplemental materials produced for the sole purpose of confusing students about the nature of science."

But all these protests were of no avail. On June 26, 2008, the governor's office announced that Jindal had signed the Louisiana Science Education Act into law. Why all the fuss? On its face, the law looks innocuous: it directs the state board of education to "allow and assist teachers, principals, and other school administrators to create and foster an environment within public

Key Concepts

- Creationists continue to agitate against the teaching of evolution in public schools, adapting their tactics to match the roadblocks they encounter.
- Past strategies have included portraying creationism as a credible alternative to evolution and disguising it under the name "intelligent design."
- Other tactics misrepresent evolution as scientifically controversial and pretend that advocates for teaching creationism are defending academic freedom.

—The Editors

elementary and secondary schools that promotes critical thinking skills, logical analysis, and open and objective discussion of scientific theories being studied," which includes providing "support and guidance for teachers regarding effective ways to help students understand, analyze, critique, and objectively review scientific theories being studied." What's not to like? Aren't critical thinking, logical analysis, and open and objective discussion exactly what science education aims to promote?

As always in the contentious history of evolution education in the U.S., the devil is in the details. The law explicitly targets evolution, which is unsurprising—for lurking in the background of the law is creationism, the rejection of a scientific explanation of the history of life in favor of a supernatural account involving a personal creator. Indeed, to mutate Dobzhansky's dictum, nothing about the Louisiana law makes sense except in the light of creationism.

Creationism's Evolution

Creationists have long battled against the teaching of evolution in U.S. public schools, and their strategies have evolved in reaction to legal setbacks. In the 1920s they attempted to ban the

It's Your Move

This time line notes some key events in the seesawing history of the battle between creationists and evolutionists. It high-lights the way creationist tactics have shifted in response to evolution's advances in classrooms and to court rulings that have banned religious proselytizing in public schools.

Late 1910s and Early 1920s

As high school attendance rises, more American students become exposed to evolution.

1989

Of *Pandas and People,* the first book systematically to use the term "intelligent design" is published; it touts the notion as an alternative to evolution.

1925

Butler Act in Tennessee outlaws teaching of human evolution. Teacher John T. Scopes (*above*) is prosecuted and convicted under the law, although the conviction is later overturned on a technicality.

2001

Passage of the No Child Left Behind Act cements the importance of state science standards, which have become a new battleground between creationism and evolution (because inclusion of evolution in science standards increases the likelihood that evolution will be taught).

1958

Biological Sciences Curriculum Study (BSCS) is founded with funds from a federal government concerned about science education in the wake of Sputnik. BSCS's textbooks emphasize evolution, which was largely absent from textbooks after the Scopes trial; commercial publishers follow suit.

1968

Supreme Court rules in case of *Epperson v. Arkansas* that laws barring the teaching of evolution in public schools are unconstitutional. Teacher Susan Epperson is shown at the left in 1966.

2005

Decision in *Kitzmiller v. Dover Area School District* rules that teaching intelligent design in the public schools is unconstitutional. The photograph at the right captures plaintiff Tammy Kitzmiller during a break from the trial.

1981

Louisiana passes the Balanced Treatment for Creation-Science and Evolution-Science in Public School Instruction Act. Also in the 1980s legislators in more than 25 states introduce bills calling for "creation science" to have equal time with evolution.

2008

Governor Bobby Jindal *(right)* signs the Louisiana Science Education Act into law. Marketed as supporting critical thinking in classrooms, the law threatens to open the door for the teaching of creationism and for scientifically unwarranted critiques of evolution in public school science classes.

1987

Supreme Court rules in the case of *Edwards v. Aguillard* that the Louisiana Balanced Treatment Act violates the Establishment Clause of the First Amendment.

---

teaching of evolution outright, with laws such as Tennessee's Butler Act, under which teacher John T. Scopes was prosecuted in 1925. It was not until 1968 that such laws were ruled to be unconstitutional, in the Supreme Court case *Epperson v. Arkansas.* No longer able to keep evolution out of the science classrooms of the public schools, creationists began to portray creationism as a scientifically credible alternative, dubbing it creation science or scientific creationism. By the early 1980s legislation calling for equal time for creation science had been introduced in no fewer than 27 states, including Louisiana. There, in 1981, the legislature passed the Balanced Treatment for Creation-Science and Evolution-Science in Public School Instruction Act, which required teachers to teach creation science if they taught evolution.

The Louisiana Balanced Treatment Act was based on a model bill circulated across the country by creationists working at the grassroots level. Obviously inspired by a particular literal interpretation of the book of Genesis, the model bill defined creation science as including creation ex nihilo ("from nothing"), a worldwide flood, a "relatively recent inception" of the earth, and a rejection of the common ancestry of humans and apes. In

Arkansas, such a bill was enacted earlier in 1981 and promptly challenged in court as unconstitutional. So when the Louisiana Balanced Treatment Act was still under consideration by the state legislature, supporters, anticipating a similar challenge, immediately purged the bill's definition of creation science of specifics, leaving only "the scientific evidences for creation and inferences from those scientific evidences." But this tactical vagueness failed to render the law constitutional, and in 1987 the Supreme Court ruled in *Edwards v. Aguillard* that the Balanced Treatment Act violated the Establishment Clause of the First Amendment to the Constitution, because the act "impermissibly endorses religion by advancing the religious belief that a supernatural being created humankind."

Creationism adapts quickly. Just two years later a new label for creationism—"intelligent design"—was introduced in the supplementary textbook *Of Pandas and People,* produced by the Foundation for Thought and Ethics, which styles itself a Christian think tank. Continuing the Louisiana Balanced Treatment Act's strategy of reducing overt religious content, intelligent design is advertised as not based on any sacred texts and as not requiring any appeal to the supernatural. The designer, the proponents say, might be God, but it might be space aliens or time-traveling cell biologists from the future. Mindful that teaching creationism in the public schools is unconstitutional, they vociferously reject any characterization of intelligent design as a form of creationism. Yet on careful inspection, intelligent design proves to be a rebranding of creationism—silent on a number of creation science's distinctive claims (such as the young age of the earth and the historicity of Noah's flood) but otherwise riddled with the same scientific errors and entangled with the same religious doctrines.

Such a careful inspection occurred in a federal courtroom in 2005, in the trial of *Kitzmiller v. Dover Area School District.* At issue was a policy in a local school district in Pennsylvania requiring a disclaimer to be read aloud in the classroom alleging that evolution is a "Theory . . . not a fact," that "gaps in the Theory exist for which there is no evidence," and that intelligent design as presented in *Of Pandas and People* is a credible scientific alternative to evolution. Eleven local parents filed suit in federal district court, arguing that the policy was unconstitutional. After a trial that spanned a biblical 40 days, the judge agreed, ruling that the policy violated the Establishment Clause and writing, "In making this determination, we have addressed the seminal question of whether [intelligent design] is science. We have concluded that it is not, and moreover that [intelligent design] cannot uncouple itself from its creationist; and thus religious, antecedents."

The expert witness testimony presented in the *Kitzmiller* trial was devastating for intelligent design's scientific pretensions. Intelligent design was established to be creationism lite: at the trial philosopher Barbara Forrest, co-author of *Creationism's Trojan Horse: The Wedge of Intelligent Design,* revealed that references to creationism in *Of Pandas and People* drafts were replaced with references to design shortly after the 1987 *Edwards* decision striking down Louisiana's Balanced Treatment Act was issued. She even found a transitional form, where the replacement of "creationists" by "design proponents" was incomplete—"cdesign proponentsists" was the awkward result. More important, intelligent design was also established to be scientifically bankrupt: one of the expert witnesses in the trial, biochemist Michael Behe, testified that no articles have been published in the scientific research literature that "provide detailed rigorous accounts of how intelligent design of any biological system occurred"—and he was testifying in *defense* of the school board's policy.

Donning a Fake Mustache

Failing to demonstrate the scientific credibility of their views, creationists are increasingly retreating to their standard fallback strategy for undermining the teaching of evolution: misrepresenting evolution as scientifically controversial while remaining silent about what they regard as the alternative. This move represents only a slight rhetorical shift. From the Scopes era onward, creationists have simultaneously employed three central rhetorical themes, sometimes called the three pillars of creationism, to attack evolution: that evolution is unsupported by or actually in conflict with the facts of science; that teaching evolution threatens religion, morality and society; and that fairness dictates the necessity of teaching creationism alongside evolution. The fallback strategy amounts to substituting for creationism the scientifically unwarranted claim that evolution is a theory in crisis.

Creationists are fond of asserting that evolution is a theory in crisis because they assume that there are only two alternatives: creationism (whether creation science or intelligent design) and evolution. Evidence against evolution is thus evidence for creationism; disproving evolution thus proves creationism. The judge in *McLean v. Arkansas,* the 1981 case in which Arkansas's Balanced Treatment Act was ruled to be unconstitutional, succinctly described the assumption as "a contrived dualism." Yet by criticizing evolution without mentioning creationism, proponents of the fallback strategy hope to encourage students to acquire or retain a belief in creationism without running afoul of the Establishment Clause. Creationism's latest face is just like its earlier face, only now thinly disguised with a fake mustache.

Underscoring the conscious decision to emphasize the supposed evidence against evolution, the Institute for Creation Research, which promotes creation science, candidly recommended immediately after the *Edwards* decision that "school boards and teachers should be strongly encouraged at least to stress the scientific evidences and arguments *against evolution* in their classes . . . even if they don't wish to recognize these as evidences and arguments *for creation.*" Similarly, the Discovery Institute, the de facto institutional headquarters of intelligent design, saw the writing on the wall even before the decision in the *Kitzmiller* ruling that teaching intelligent design in the public schools is unconstitutional. Although a widely discussed internal memorandum-"The Wedge Document"—had numbered among its goals the inclusion of intelligent design in the science curricula of 10 states, the Discovery Institute subsequently retreated to a strategy to undermine the teaching of evolution, introducing a flurry of labels and slogans—"teach the controversy," "critical analysis" and "academic freedom"—to promote its version of the fallback strategy.

"Academic freedom" was the creationist catchphrase of choice in 2008: the Louisiana Science Education Act was in fact born as the Louisiana Academic Freedom Act, and bills invoking the idea were introduced in Alabama, Florida, Michigan, Missouri and South Carolina, although, as of November, all were dead or stalled [*see box on Antievolution Bills of 2008*]. And academic freedom was a central theme of the first creationist movie to tarnish the silver screen: *Expelled: No Intelligence Allowed.* (Science columnist Michael Shermer eviscerated *Expelled* in his review in the June 2008 issue of *Scientific American,* and the magazine's staff added commentary on www.SciAm.com.) Portraying the scientific community as conspiring to persecute scientists for their views on creationism, *Expelled* was ostensibly concerned with academic freedom mainly at the college level, but it was used to lobby for the academic freedom legislation in Missouri and Florida aimed at the public schools. (The movie, by the way, was a critical failure and jam-packed with errors.)

The appeal of academic freedom as a slogan for the creationist fallback strategy is obvious: everybody approves of freedom, and plenty of people have a sense that academic freedom is desirable, even if they do not necessarily have a good understanding of what it is. The concept of academic freedom is primarily relevant to college teaching, and the main organization defending it, the American Association of University Professors, recently reaffirmed its opposition to antievolution laws such as Louisiana's, writing, "Such efforts run counter to the overwhelming scientific consensus regarding evolution and are inconsistent with a proper understanding of the meaning of academic freedom." In the public schools, even if there is no legal right to academic freedom, it is sound educational policy to allow teachers a degree of latitude to teach their subjects as they see fit—but there are limits. Allowing teachers to instill scientifically unwarranted doubts about evolution is clearly beyond the pale. Yet that is what the Louisiana Science Education Act was evidently created, or designed, to do.

The Worm in the Apple

The real purpose of the law—as opposed to its ostensible support for academic freedom—becomes evident on analysis. First, consider what the law seeks to accomplish. Aren't teachers in the public schools *already* exhorted to promote critical thinking, logical analysis and objective discussion of the scientific theories that they discuss? Yes, indeed: in Louisiana, policies established by the state board of education already encourage teachers to do so, as critics of the bill protested during a legislative hearing.

So what is the law's true intent? That only a handful of scientific topics—"biological evolution, the chemical origins of life, global warming, and human cloning"—are explicitly mentioned is a hint. So is the fact that the bill was introduced at the behest of the Louisiana Family Forum, which seeks to "persuasively present biblical principles in the centers of influence on issues affecting the family through research, communication and networking." And so is the fact that the group's executive director was vocally dismayed when those topics were temporarily deleted from the bill.

Second, was there in fact a special need for the Louisiana legislature to encourage teachers to promote critical thinking with respect to evolution in particular? No evidence seems to have been forthcoming. Patsye Peebles, a veteran science teacher in Baton Rouge, commented, "I was a biology teacher for 22 years, and I never needed the legislature to tell me how to present anything. This bill doesn't solve any of the problems classroom teachers face, and it will make it harder for us to keep the focus on accurate science in science classrooms." And of course, the National Association of Biology Teachers, representing more than 9,000 biology educators across the country, took a firm stand against the bill. In neighboring Florida, the sponsors of similar bills alleged that there were teachers who were prevented from or penalized for "teaching the 'holes'" in evolution. But no such teachers were ever produced, and the state department of education and local newspapers were unable to confirm that the claimed incidents of persecution ever occurred.

And, third, what are these "holes" in evolution, anyhow? The savvier supporters of bills such as Florida's and Louisiana's

Antievolution Bills of 2008

Several states aside from Louisiana entertained antievolution bills last year. Clearly, efforts to push such legislation continue unabated

State (Bill)	Ostensible Aim	Status
Alabama (HB 923)	Support academic freedom	Died May 2008
Florida (HB 1483)	Foster critic, analysis	Died May 2008
Florida (SB 2692)	Support academic freedom	Died May 2008
Michigan (SB 1361)	Support academic freedom	In committee when this issue went to press
Michigan (HB 6027)	Support academic freedom	Identical to SB 1361; in committee when this issue went to press
Missouri (HB 2554)	Promote teaching of evolution's strengths and weaknesses	Died May 2008
South Carolina (SB 1386)	Promote teaching of evolution's strengths and weaknesses	Died June 2008

realize that it is crucial to disclaim any intention to promote creationism. But because there is no scientifically credible challenge to evolution, only long-ago-debunked creationist claptrap [see "15 Answers to Creationist Nonsense," by John Rennie; *Scientific American*, June 2002], the supporters of such bills are forced to be evasive when asked about what material would be covered.

In Florida, for example, a representative of the Discovery Institute dithered when asked whether intelligent design constituted "scientific information" in the sense of the bill, saying, "In my personal opinion, I think it does. But the intent of this bill is not to settle that question," and adding, unhelpfully, "The intent of this bill is . . . it protects the 'teaching of scientific information.'" Similarly, during debate on the Senate floor, the bill's sponsor was noticeably reluctant to address the question of whether it would license the teaching of creationism, preferring instead to simply recite its text.

Thus, despite the lofty language, the ulterior intent and likely effect of these bills are evident: undermining the teaching of evolution in public schools—a consequence only creationists regard as a blessing. Unfortunately, among their numbers are teachers. A recent national survey conducted by researchers at Pennsylvania State University reveals that one in eight U.S. high school biology teachers already presents creationism as a "valid scientific alternative to Darwinian explanations for the origin of species," with about the same percentage emphasizing that "many reputable scientists" view creationism as a scientifically valid alternative to evolution.

Not all creationist teachers are as extreme as John Freshwater, a Mount Vernon, Ohio, middle school teacher who became immersed in legal troubles over his religious advocacy in the classroom, which included not only teaching creationism but also, allegedly, using a high-voltage electrical apparatus to brand his students with a cross. But even the less zealous will probably take laws such as Louisiana's as a license to miseducate. Such laws are also likely to be used to bully teachers who are not creationists: nationally, three in 10 already report pressure to present creationism or downplay evolution.

These bills will also further encourage school districts where creationists are politically powerful to adopt antievolution policies. A statement by a member of the Livingston Parish School Board who supported the Louisiana bill is instructive. After saying "both sides—the creationism side and the evolution side—should be presented," he explained that the bill was needed because "teachers are scared to talk about" creation. How plausible is it, then, that the law's provision that it is not to be "construed to promote any religious doctrine" will be honored in practice? As conservative columnist John Derbyshire commented, "the Act will encourage Louisiana local school boards to unconstitutional behavior. That's what it's *meant* to do."

The Future of Steady Misrepresentation

What are the legal prospects of the creationist fallback strategy? A case in Georgia, *Selman v. Cobb County School District,* is suggestive, if not decisive. In 2002 the Cobb County board of education, bowing to the demands of local creationists, decided to require warning labels for biology textbooks. Using a phrase employed by creationists even before the Scopes trial in 1925, the labels described evolution as "a theory, not a fact," while remaining silent about creationism. Five parents in the county filed suit in federal district court, arguing that the policy requiring the labels was unconstitutional, and the trial judge agreed, citing the abundant history linking the warning labels with creationist activity in Cobb County in particular and linking the fallback strategy with creationism in general. The case was vacated on appeal because of concerns about the evidence submitted at trial, remanded to the trial court and settled on terms favorable to the parents. It remains to be seen whether the fallback strategy will survive constitutional scrutiny elsewhere—but it is likely that it will be challenged, whether in Louisiana or elsewhere.

In the meantime, it is clear why the Louisiana Science Education Act is pernicious: it tacitly encourages teachers and local school districts to miseducate students about evolution, whether by teaching creationism as a scientifically credible alternative or merely by misrepresenting evolution as scientifically controversial. Vast areas of evolutionary science are for all intents and purposes scientifically settled; textbooks and curricula used in the public schools present precisely such basic, uncomplicated,

What to Do

If controversy over the teaching of evolution erupts in your area, here are some actions you can take:

- Resolving the controversy requires thinking politically, which means forming coalitions. Join with like-minded science educators, scientists, members of the clergy and other citizens to convince policymakers not to accede to creationist proposals.
- Keep in mind that the goal is not only to keep creationism out of the science classroom but also to ensure that evolution is taught properly—without qualifiers such as "only a theory" and unaccompanied by specious "evidence against evolution."
- Be ready to rebut assertions that evolution is a theory in crisis; that evolution is a threat to religion, morality and society; and that it is only fair to teach "both sides" of the issue.
- Arrange for defenders of evolution to write letters to the editor and op-eds, attend and speak at meetings of the board of education or legislature, and work to turn out the vote on Election Day.

Adapted from "Defending the Teaching of Evolution: Strategies and Tactics for Activists," by Glenn Branch, in *Not in Our Classrooms: Why Intelligent Design Is Wrong for Our Schools*. Edited by Eugenie C. Scott and Glenn Branch. Beacon, 2006.

uncontroversial material. Telling students that evolution is a theory in crisis is—to be blunt—a lie.

Moreover, it is a dangerous lie, because Dobzhansky was right to say that nothing in biology makes sense except in the light of evolution: without evolution, it would be impossible to explain why the living world is the way it is rather than otherwise. Students who are not given the chance to acquire a proper understanding of evolution will not achieve a basic level of scientific literacy. And scientific literacy will be indispensable for workers, consumers and policymakers in a future dominated by medical, biotechnological and environmental concerns.

In the sesquicentennial year of *On the Origin of Species,* it seems fitting to end with a reference to Charles Darwin's seminal' 1859 book. In the first edition of *Origin of Species,* Darwin was careful to acknowledge the limits to his project, writing, "I am convinced that natural selection has been the main but not the exclusive means of modification." Nevertheless, he was misinterpreted as claiming that natural selection was entirely responsible for evolution, provoking him to add a rueful comment to the sixth edition: "Great is the power of steady misrepresentation; but the history of science shows that fortunately this power does not long endure."

The enactment of the Louisiana Science Education Act, and the prospect of similar legislation in the future, confirms Darwin's assessment of the power of steady misrepresentation. But because the passage of such antievolution bills ultimately results from politics rather than science, it will not be the progress of science that ensures their failure to endure. Rather it will take the efforts of citizens who are willing to take a stand and defend the uncompromised teaching of evolution.

More to Explore

Analyzing Critical Analysis: The Fallback Antievolutionist Strategy. Nicholas J. Matzke and Paul R. Gross in *Not in Our Classrooms: Why Intelligent Design Is Wrong for Our Schools.* Edited by Eugenie C. Scott and Glenn Branch. Beacon, 2006.

Evolution: The Triumph of an Idea. Carl Zimmer. Harper Perennial, 2006.

Creationism's Trojan Horse: The Wedge of Intelligent Design. Revised edition. Barbara Forrest and Paul R. Gross. Oxford University Press, 2007.

The Devil in Dover: An Insider's Story of Dogma v. Darwin in Small-Town America. Lauri Lebo. New Press, 2008.

Evolution vs. Creationism: An introduction. Second edition. Eugenie C. Scott. Greenwood, 2009.

GLENN BRANCH AND EUGENIE C. SCOTT are deputy director and executive director, respectively,of the National Center for Science Education (NCSE) in Oakland, Calif., where they work to defend the teaching of evolution in the public schools. Together they edited *Not in Our Classrooms: Why Intelligent Design Is Wrong for Our Schools.* Branch is trained in philosophy and is a longtime observer of pseudoscience of all kinds. Scott, a physical anthropologist by training and a former university professor, is internationally known as a leading authority on the antievolution movement and has received many awards and honorary degrees for her work at NCSE.

Why Should Students Learn Evolution?

BRIAN J. ALTERS AND SANDRA M. ALTERS

"When you combine the lack of emphasis on evolution in kindergarten through 12th grade, with the immense popularity of creationism among the public, and the industry discrediting evolution, it's easy to see why half of the population believes humans were created 10,000 years ago and lived with dinosaurs. It is by far the biggest failure of science education from top to bottom."

—Randy Moore, Editor, *The American Biology Teacher*

"This is an important area of science, with particular significance for a developmental psychologist like me. Unless one has some understanding of the key notions of species, variation, natural selection, adaptation, and the like (and how these "have been discovered), unless one appreciates the perennial struggle among individuals (and populations) for survival in a particular ecological niche, one cannot understand the living world of which we are a part."

—Howard Gardner, Professor, Harvard Graduate School of Education

With all of the controversy over the teaching of evolution reported in the media, with parents confronting their children's science teachers on this issue, and with students themselves confronting their instructors in high schools and colleges, would it be best—and easiest—to just delete the teaching of evolution in the classroom? Can't students attain a well-rounded background in science without learning this controversial topic? The overwhelming consensus of biologists in the scientific community is "no." Why, then, should science students learn about evolution?

A simple answer is that evolution is the basic context of all the biological sciences. Take away this context, and all that is left is disparate facts without the thread that ties them all together. Put another way, evolution is the explanatory framework, the unifying theory. It is indispensable to the study of biology, just as the atomic theory is indispensable to the study of chemistry. The characteristics and behavior of atoms and their subatomic particles form the basis of this physical science. So, too, biology can be understood fully only in an evolutionary context. In explaining how

the organisms of today got to be the way they are, evolution helps make sense out of the history of life and explains relationships among species, It, is a useful and often essential framework within which scientists organize and interpret observations, and make predictions about the living world.

But this simple answer is not the entire reason why students should learn evolution. There are other considerations as well. Evolutionary explanations answer key questions in the biological sciences such as why organisms across species have so many striking similarities yet are tremendously diverse. These key questions are the *why* questions of biology. Much of biology explains *how* organisms work . . . how we breathe, how fish swim, or how leopard frogs produce thousands of eggs at one time . . . but it is up to evolution to explain the why behind these mechanisms. In answering the key *why* questions of biology, evolutionary explanations become an important lens through which scientists interpret data, whether they are developmental biologists, plant physiologists, or biochemists, to mention just a few of the many foci of those who study life.

Understanding evolution also has practical considerations that affect day-to-day life. Without an understanding of natural selection, students cannot recognize and understand problems based on this process, such as insect resistance to pesticides or microbial resistance to antibiotics. In a report released in June, 2000, Dr. Gro Harlem Brunddand, Director-General of the World Health Organization, stated that the world is at risk of losing drugs that control many infectious diseases because of increasing antimicrobial resistance. The report goes on to give examples, stating that 98% of strains of gonorrhea in Southeast Asia are now resistant to penicillin. Additionally, 14,000 people die each year from drug-resistant infections acquired in hospitals in the United States. And in New Delhi, India, typhoid drugs are no longer effective against this disease. Such problems face every person on our planet, and an understanding of natural selection will help students realize how important their behavior is in either contributing to or helping stem this crisis in medical progress.

Evolution not only enriches and provides a conceptual foundation for biological sciences such as ecology, genetics, developmental biology, and systematics, it provides a framework for scientific disciplines with historical aspects, such as anthropology, astronomy, geology, and paleontology. Evolution is therefore a unifying theme among many sciences, providing students with a framework by which to understand the natural world from many perspectives.

As scientists search for evolutionary explanations to the many questions of life, they develop methods and formulate concepts that are being applied in other fields, such as molecular biology, medicine, and statistics. For example, scientists studying molecular evolutionary change have developed methods to distinguish variations in gene sequences within and among species. These methods not only add to the toolbox of the molecular biologist but also will have likely applications in medicine by helping to identify variations that cause genetic diseases. In characterizing and analyzing variation, evolutionary biologists have also developed statistical methods, such as analysis of variance and path analysis, which are widely used in other fields. Thus, methods and concepts developed by evolutionary biologists have wide relevance in other fields and influence us all daily in ways we cannot realize without an understanding of this important and central idea.

Evolution is not only a powerful and wide-reaching concept among the pure and applied sciences, it also permeates other disciplines such as philosophy, psychology, literature, and the arts. Evolution by means of natural selection, articulated amidst controversy in the mid-nineteenth century, has reached the twenty-first century having had an extensive and expansive impact on human thought. An important intellectual development in the history of ideas, evolution should hold a central place in science teaching and learning.

Why is evolution the context of the biological sciences—A unifying theory?

First, how does evolution take place? A key idea is that some of the individuals within a population of organisms possess measurable changes in inheritable characteristics that favor their survival. (These characteristics can be morphological, physiological, behavioral, or biochemical.) These individuals are more likely to live to reproductive age than are individuals not possessing the favorable characteristics. These reproductively advantageous traits (called *adaptive traits* or *adaptations*) are passed on from surviving individuals to their offspring. Over time, the individuals carrying these traits will increase in numbers within the population, and the nature of the population as a whole will gradually change. This process of survival of the most reproductively fit organisms is called *natural selection.*

The process of evolutionary change explains that the organisms of today got to be the way they are, at least in part, as the result of natural selection over billions of years and even billions more generations. Organisms are related to one another, some more distantly, branching from a common ancestor long ago, and some more recently, branching from a common ancestor closer to the present day. The fact that diverse organisms have descended from common ancestors accounts for the similarities exhibited among species. Since biology is the story of life, then evolution is the story of biology and the relatedness of all life.

How do evolutionary explanations answer key questions in the biological sciences?

Evolution answers the question of the unity and similarity of life by its relatedness and shared history. But what about its diversity? And how does evolution answer other key questions in the biological sciences? What are these questions and how does evolution answer the *why* question inherent in each?

Evolution explains the diversity of life in the same way that it explains its unity. As mentioned in the preceding paragraphs, some individuals within a population of organisms possess measurable changes in inheritable characteristics that favor their survival. These adaptive traits are passed on from surviving individuals to their offspring. Over time, as populations inhabit different ecological niches, the individuals carrying adaptive traits in each population increase in numbers, and the nature of each population gradually changes. Such divergent evolution, the splitting of single species into multiple, descendant species, accounts for variation. There are different modes, or patterns, of divergence, and various reproductive isolating mechanisms that contribute to divergent evolution. However, the result is the same: Populations split from common ancestral populations and their genetic differences accumulate.

What are some other key questions in biology that are answered by evolution? One key question asks why form is adapted to function. Evolutionary theory tells us that more organisms that have parts of their anatomy (a long, slender beak, for instance) better adapted to certain functions (such as capturing food that lives deep within holes in rotting tree trunks) will live to reproductive age in greater numbers than those with less-well-adapted beaks. Therefore, the organisms with better-adapted beaks will pass on the genes for these features to greater numbers of off-spring. Eventually, after numerous generations, natural selection will result in a population that has long slender beaks adapted to procuring food. Thus, anatomical, behavioral, or biochemical traits (the "forms") fit their functions because form fitting function is adaptive. But this idea leads us to yet another important question: Why do organisms have a variety of nonadaptive features that coexist amidst those that are adaptive?

During the course of evolution, traits that no longer confer a reproductive advantage do not disappear in the population unless they are reproductively disadvantageous. A population of beige beach birds that escaped predation because of protective coloration will not change coloration if this population becomes geographically isolated to a grasslands environment, unless the now useless beige coloration allows the birds to be hunted and killed more easily. In other words, if beige coloration is not a liability in the new environment, the genes that code for this trait will be passed on by all surviving birds in this grasslands niche. Even as the population of birds changes over generations, the genes for beige feathers will be retained in the population as long as this trait confers no reproductive disadvantage (and as long as mutation and genetic drift do not result in such a change).

These preceding examples do not cover all the key questions of biology (of course), but do show that such key questions are really questions about evolution and its mechanisms. Only evolutionary theory can answer the *why* questions inherent in these themes of life.

31

How does understanding evolution help us understand processes that affect our health and our day-to-day life? and How are evolutionary methods applied to other fields?

As mentioned earlier, without an understanding of natural selection, students cannot recognize and understand problems based on this process, such as insect resistance to pesticides or microbial resistance to antibiotics. Additionally, it is only through such understanding that scientists can hope to find solutions to these serious situations. Scientists know that the underlying cause of microbial resistance to antibiotics is improper use of these drugs. As explained in the World Health Organization report *Overcoming Antimicrobial Resistance,* in poor countries antibiotics are often used in ways that encourage the development of resistance. Unable to afford the full course of treatment, patients often take antibiotics only until their symptoms go away—killing the most susceptible microbes while allowing those more resistant to survive and reproduce. When these most resistant pathogens infect another host, antibiotics are less effective against the more resistant strains. In wealthy countries such as the United States, antibiotics are overused, being prescribed for viral diseases for which they are ineffective and being used in agriculture to treat sick animals and promote the growth of those that are well. Such misuse and overuse of antibiotics speeds the process whereby less resistant strains of bacteria are wiped out and more resistant strains flourish.

In addition to developing resistance to antibiotics and other therapies, pathogens can evolve resistance to the body's natural defenses. The virulence of pathogens (the ease with which they cause disease) can also evolve rapidly. Understanding the co-evolution of the human immune system and the pathogens that attack it help scientists track and predict disease outbreaks.

Understanding evolution also helps researchers understand the frequency, nature, and distribution of genetic disease. Gene frequencies in populations are affected by selection pressures, mutation, migration, and random genetic drift. Studying genetic diseases from an evolutionary standpoint helps us see that even lethal genes can remain in a population if there is a reproductive advantage in the heterozygote, as in the case of sickle-cell anemia and malaria.

Sickle-cell anemia is one of the most common genetic disorders among African Americans, having arisen in their African ancestors. It has been observed in persons whose ancestors came from the Mediterranean basin, the Indian subcontinent, the Caribbean, and parts of Central and South America (particularly Brazil). The sickle-cell gene has persisted in these populations, even though the disease eventually kills its victims, because carriers who inherit a single defective gene are resistant to malaria. Those with the sickle-cell gene have a survival advantage in regions of the world in which malaria is prevalent, which are the regions of the ancestral populations listed previously. Although many of these peoples have since migrated from these areas, this ancestral gene still persists within their populations.

Scientists are also working to identify gene variations that cause genetic diseases. Molecular evolutionary biologists have developed methods to distinguish between variations in gene sequences that affect reproductive fitness and variations that do not. To do this, scientists analyze human DNA sequences and DNA sequences among closely related species. The Human Genome Project, a worldwide effort to map the positions of all the genes and to sequence the over 3 billion DNA base pairs of the human genome, is providing much of the data for this effort and also is allowing scientists to study the relationships between the structure of genes and the proteins they produce. (On June 26, 2000, scientists announced the completion of the "working draft", of the human genome. The working draft covers 85% of the genome's coding regions in rough form.)

Some diseases are caused by interaction between genes and environment (lifestyle) factors. Genetic factors may predispose a person to a disease. For example, America's number one killers, cardiovascular disease and cancer, have both genetic and environmental causes. However, the complex interplay between genes and environmental factors in the development of these diseases makes it difficult for scientists to study the genetics of these diseases. Nevertheless, using evolutionary principles and approaches, scientists have developed a technique called *gene tree analysis* to discover genetic markers that are predictive of certain diseases. (Genetic markers are pairs of alleles whose inheritance can be traced through a pedigree [family tree].) Analyses of gene trees can help medical researchers identify the mutations in genes that cause certain diseases. This knowledge helps medical researchers understand the cause of the diseases to which these genes are linked and can help them develop treatments for such illnesses.

How is evolution indispensable to the subdisciplines of biology and How does it enrich them?

Organizing life, for example, a process on which Linnaeus worked as he grouped organisms by morphological characteristics, continues today with processes that reflect evolutionary relationships. Systematics, the branch of biology that studies the classification of life, does so in the context of evolutionary relationships. Cladistics, the predominant method used in systematics today, classifies organisms with respect to their phylogenetic relationships—those based on their evolutionary history. Therefore, students who do not understand evolution cannot understand modern methods of classification.

Developmental biology is another example of a biological subdiscipline enriched by an evolutionary perspective. In fact, some embryological phenomena can be understood only in the light of evolutionary history. For example, why terrestrial salamanders go through a larval stage with gills and fins that are never used is a question answered by evolution. During evolution, as new species (e.g., terrestrial salamanders) evolve from ancestral forms (e.g., aquatic ancestors), their new developmental instructions are often added to developmental instructions already in place. Thus, patterns of development in groups of organisms were built over the evolutionary history of those groups, thus retaining ancestral instructions. This process results in the embryonic stages of particular vertebrates reflecting the embryonic stages of those vertebrates' ancestors.

The study of animal behavior is enriched by an evolutionary perspective as well. Behavioral traits also evolve, and like morphological traits they are often most similar among closely related species. Phylogenetic studies of behavior have provided examples of how complex behaviors such as the courtship displays of some birds have evolved from simpler ancestral behaviors. Likewise, the study of human behavior can be enhanced by an evolutionary perspective. Evolutionary psychologists seek to uncover evolutionary reasons for many human behaviors, searching through our ancestral programming to determine how natural selection has resulted in a species that behaves as it does.

There are many sciences with significant historical aspects, such as anthropology, astronomy, geology, and paleontology. Geology, for example, is the study of the history of the earth, especially as recorded in the rocks. Paleontology is the study of fossils. Inherent in the work of the geologist and the paleontologist are questions about the relationships of modern animals and plants to ancestral forms, and about the chronology of the history of the earth. Evolution provides the framework within which these questions can be answered.

What do science and education societies say about the study of evolution?

Instructors often look to scientific societies for answers to many questions regarding their teaching. There is one aspect of teaching on which the scientific societies agree and are emphatic. Evolution is key to scientific study, and should be taught in the science classroom. The National Research Council, part of the National Academy of Science, identified evolution as a major unifying idea in science that transcends disciplinary boundaries. Its publication *National Science Education Standards* lists biological evolution as one of the six content areas in the life sciences that are important for all high school students to study. Likewise, the American Association for the Advancement of Science identified the evolution of life as one of six major areas of study in the life sciences in its publication *Benchmarks for Scientific Literacy*. The National Science Teachers Association, the largest organization in the world committed to promoting excellence and innovation "in science teaching and learning, published a position statement on the teaching of evolution in 1997, which states that "evolution is a major unifying concept of science and should be included as part of K—College science frameworks and curricula." The National Association of Biology Teachers, a leading organization in life science education, also issued a position statement on the teaching of evolution in 1997, which states that evolution has a "central, unifying role . . . in nature, and therefore in biology. Teaching biology in an effective and scientifically honest manner requires classroom discussions and laboratory experiences on evolution." Evolution has been identified as the unifying theme of biology by almost all science organizations that focus on the biological sciences.

So why should students learn evolution? Eliminating evolution from the education of students removes the context and unifying theory that underpins and permeates the biological sciences. Students thus learn disparate facts in the science classroom without the thread that ties them together, and they miss the answers to its underlying *why* questions. Without an understanding of evolution, they cannot understand processes based on this science, such as insect resistance to pesticides and microbial resistance to antibiotics. Students will not come to understand evolutionary connections to other scientific fields, nor will they fully understand the world of which we are a part. Evolution is, in fact, one of the most important concepts in attaining scientific literacy.

UNIT 2

Primates

Unit Selections

Key Points to Consider

- If we share 98% of our DNA with chimpanzees, why are we so different?

- How is it possible to objectively study and assess the emotional and mental states of nonhuman primates?

- What are the implications on human evolution of tool use, social hunting, and food sharing by the Ivory Coast chimpanzees?

- Should chimpanzees' behavioral patterns be classified as "cultural"?

- Are primates naturally aggressive?

- Is a "theory of mind" possible without language?

- Under what circumstances have some primates, such as orangutans, become more innovative and intelligent?

- To what extent is cooperation a part of our primitive heritage?

- How does the human ability to communicate compare and contrast with that of our closest living relatives?

Student Website
www.mhcls.com

Internet References

The Dian Fossey Gorilla Fund International
http://www.gorillafund.org

Great Ape Survival Project: United Nations
http://www.unep.org/grasp/ABOUT_GRASP/index.asp

Jane Goodall Institute for Wildlife Research, Education and Conservation
http://www.janegoodall.org/jane/default.asp

Living Links
http://www.emory.edu/LIVING_LINKS/dewaal.html

National Primate Research Center
http://pin.primate.wisc.edu/factsheets

Orangutan Foundation International
http://www.orangutan.org/

San Francisco State University
http://online.sfsu.edu/~,mgriffin/primates.html

African Primates at Home
http://www.indiana.edu/~primate/primates.html

Electronic Zoo/NetVet-Primate Page
http://netvet.wustl.edu/primates.htm

Laboratory Primate Newsletter
http://www.brown.edu/Research/Primate/other.html

Primates are fun. They are active, intelligent, colorful, emotionally expressive, and unpredictable. Because, in some ways, they are very much like us (see "The 2% Difference") observing them is like holding up an opaque mirror to ourselves. The image may not be crystal-clear or, indeed, what some would consider flattering, but it is certainly familiar enough to be illuminating.

Primates are, of course, one of the many orders of mammals that adaptively radiated into the variety of ecological niches, which were vacated at the end of the Age of Reptiles about 65 million years ago. Whereas some mammals took to the sea (cetaceans), and some took to the air (chiroptera, or bats), primates took to the land, and are characterized by an arboreal or forested adaptation. While some mammals can be identified by their food-getting habits, such as the meat-eating carnivores, primates have a penchant for eating almost anything and are best described as omnivorous. In taking to the trees, primates did not simply develop a full-blown set of distinguishing characteristics that set them off easily from other orders of mammals, the way the rodent order can be readily identified by its gnawing set of front teeth. Rather, each primate seems to represent degrees of anatomical, biological, and behavioral characteristics on a continuum of change, in the direction of the particular traits in which we humans happen to be interested.

None of this is meant to imply, of course, that the living primates are our ancestors. Since the prosimians, monkeys, and apes are contemporaries, they are no more our ancestors than we are theirs, and, as living end-products of evolution, we have all descended from a common stock in the distant past. So, if we are interested primarily in our own evolutionary past, why study primates at all? Because, by the criteria we have set up as significant milestones in the evolution of humanity, an inherent reflection of our own bias, primates have not evolved as far as we have. They and their environments, therefore, may give a glimmer of the evolutionary stages and ecological circumstances through which our own ancestors may have gone. What we stand to gain, for instance, is an educated guess as to how our own ancestors might have appeared and behaved as semierect creatures before becoming bipedal. Aside from being a pleasure to observe, then, living primates can teach us something about our past.

This unit demonstrates that the kind of answers obtained depends upon the kind of questions asked, and that we have to be very careful in making inferences about human beings from any one particular study on primates. We may, if we are not careful, draw conclusions that say more about our own skewed perspectives than about that which we claim to understand. Still another benefit of primate field research is that it provides us with perspectives that the bones and stones of the fossil hunters will never reveal: a sense of the richness and variety of social patterns that must have existed in the primate order for many tens of millions of years. (See Jane Goodall's "The Mind of the Chimpanzee" and Frans B. M. de Waal's "How Animals Do Business.")

Even if we had the physical remains of the earliest hominids in front of us, which we do not, there is no way such evidence could thoroughly answer the questions that physical anthropologists care most deeply about: How did these creatures move about and get their food? Did they cooperate and share? At what levels did they think and communicate? Did they have a sense of family, let alone a sense of self? In one way or another, all of the previously mentioned articles on primates relate to these issues, as do some of the subsequent ones on fossil evidence. But what sets off this unit from others is how some of the authors attempt to deal with these matters head-on, even in the absence of direct fossil evidence. Christophe Boesch and Hedwige Boesch-Achermann, in "Dim Forest, Bright Chimps," indicate that some aspects of "hominization" (the acquisition of humanlike qualities such as cooperative hunting and food sharing) may have actually begun in the African rain forest rather than in the dry savanna, as has been proposed usually. They base their suggestions on some remarkable first-hand observations of forest-dwelling

chimpanzees. As Craig Stanford shows in "Got Culture?" chimpanzee behavior may vary according to local circumstances, just as we know human behavior does. He makes a strong case for such differences to be classified as cultural.

Recent research has shown some striking resemblances between apes and humans, hinting that such qualities might have been characteristic of our common ancestor. Following this line of reasoning, Frans de Waal ("How Animals Do Business") argues that we can make educated guesses as to the mental and physical processes of our hominid predecessors. In "Why Are Some Animals So Smart?" Carel Van Shaik concludes from his study of orangutans that social animals are more innovative and intelligent. Lest we make too much of the similarities, Stephen R. Anderson ("A Telling Difference") and Jerry Adler ("Thinking Like a Monkey") remind us that the contrasts between our primate relatives and ourselves serve to highlight how truly special we humans are.

Taken collectively, the articles in this section show how far anthropologists are willing to go to construct theoretical formulations based upon limited data. Although making so much out of so little may be seen as a fault and may generate irreconcilable differences among theorists, a readiness to entertain new ideas should be welcomed for what it is—a stimulus for more intensive and meticulous research.

The 2% Difference

Now that scientists have decoded the chimpanzee genome, we know that 98 percent of our DNA is the same. So how can we be so different?

Robert Sapolsky

If you find yourself sitting close to a chimpanzee, staring face to face and making sustained eye contact, something interesting happens, something that is alternately moving, bewildering, and kind of creepy. When you gaze at this beast, you suddenly realize that the face gazing back is that of a sentient individual, who is recognizably kin. You can't help but wonder, What's the matter with those intelligent design people?

Chimpanzees are close relatives to humans, but they're not identical to us. We are not chimps. Chimps excel at climbing trees, but we beat them hands down at balance-beam routines; they are covered in hair, while we have only the occasional guy with really hairy shoulders. The core differences, however, arise from how we use our brains. Chimps have complex social lives, play power politics, betray and murder each other, make tools, and teach tool use across generations in a way that qualifies as culture. They can even learn to do logic operations with symbols, and they have a relative sense of numbers. Yet those behaviors don't remotely approach the complexity and nuance of human behaviors, and in my opinion there's not the tiniest bit of scientific evidence that chimps have aesthetics, spirituality, or a capacity for irony or poignancy.

What makes the human species brainy are huge numbers of standard-issue neurons.

What accounts for those differences? A few years ago, the most ambitious project in the history of biology was carried out: the sequencing of the human genome. Then just four months ago, a team of researchers reported that they had likewise sequenced the complete chimpanzee genome. Scientists have long known that chimps and humans share about 98 percent of their DNA. At last, however, one can sit down with two scrolls of computer printout, march through the two genomes, and see exactly where our 2 percent difference lies.

Given the outward differences, it seems reasonable to expect to find fundamental differences in the portions of the genome that determine chimp and human brains—reasonable, at least,

to a brainocentric neurobiologist like me. But as it turns out, the chimp brain and the human brain differ hardly at all in their genetic underpinnings. Indeed, a close look at the chimp genome reveals an important lesson in how genes and evolution work, and it suggests that chimps and humans are a lot more similar than even a neurobiologist might think.

DNA, or deoxyribonucleic acid, is made up of just four molecules, called nucleotides: adenine (A), cytosine (C), guanine (G), and thymine (T). The DNA codebook for every species consists of billions of these letters in a precise order. If, when DNA is being copied in a sperm or an egg, a nucleotide is mistakenly copied wrong, the result is a mutation. If the mutation persists from generation to generation, it becomes a DNA difference—one of the many genetic distinctions that separate one species (chimpanzees) from another (humans). In genomes involving billions of nucleotides, a tiny 2 percent difference translates into tens of millions of ACGT differences. And that 2 percent difference can be very broadly distributed. Humans and chimps each have somewhere between 20,000 and 30,000 genes, so there are likely to be nucleotide differences in every single gene.

To understand what distinguishes the DNA of chimps and humans, one must first ask: What is a gene? A gene is a string of nucleotides that specify how a single distinctive protein should be made. Even if the same gene in chimps and humans differs by an A here and a T there, the result may be of no consequence. Many nucleotide differences are neutral—both the mutation and the normal gene cause the same protein to be made. However, given the right nucleotide difference between the same gene in the two species, the resulting proteins may differ slightly in construction and function.

One might assume that the differences between chimp and human genes boil down to those sorts of typographical errors: one nucleotide being swapped for a different one and altering the gene it sits in. But a close look at the two codebooks reveals very few such instances. And the typos that do occasionally occur follow a compelling pattern. It's important to note that genes don't act alone. Yes, each gene regulates the construction of a specific protein. But what tells that gene *when* and *where* to build that protein? Regulation is everything: It's important not to start up genes related to puberty during, say, infancy, or to activate genes that are related to eye color in the bladder.

In the DNA code list, that critical information is contained in a short stretch of As and Cs and Gs and Ts that lie just before each gene and act as a switch that turns the gene on or off. The switch, in turn, is flicked on by proteins called transcription factors, which activate certain genes in response to certain stimuli. Naturally, every gene is not regulated by its own distinct transcription factor; otherwise, a codebook of as many as 30,000 genes would require 30,000 transcription factors—and 30,000 more genes to code for them. Instead, one transcription factor can flick on an array of functionally related genes. For example, a certain type of injury can activate one transcription factor that turns on a bunch of genes in your white blood cells, triggering inflammation.

Accurate switch flickers are essential. Imagine the consequences if some of those piddly nucleotide changes arose in a protein that happened to be a transcription factor: Suddenly, instead of activating 23 different genes, the protein might charge up 21 or 25 of them—or it might turn on the usual 23 but in different ratios than normal. Suddenly, one minor nucleotide difference would be amplified across a network of gene differences. (And imagine the ramifications if the altered proteins are transcription factors that activate the genes coding for still other transcription factors!) When the chimp and human genomes are compared, some of the clearest cases of nucleotide differences are found in genes coding for transcription factors. Those cases are few, but they have far-ranging implications.

The genomes of chimps and humans reveal a history of other kinds of differences as well. Instead of a simple mutation, in which a single nucleotide is copied incorrectly, consider an insertion mutation, where an extra A, C, G, or T is dropped in, or a deletion mutation, whereby a nucleotide drops out. Insertion or deletion mutations can have major consequences: Imagine the deletion mutation that turns the sentence "I'll have the mousse for dessert" into "I'll have the mouse for dessert," or the insertion mutation implicit in "She turned me down for a date after I asked her to go bowling with me." Sometimes, more than a single nucleotide is involved; whole stretches of a gene may be dropped or added. In extreme cases, entire genes may be deleted or added.

More important than how the genetic changes arise—by insertion, deletion, or straight mutation—is where in the genome they occur. Keep in mind that, for these genetic changes to persist from generation to generation, they must convey some evolutionary advantage. When one examines the 2 percent difference between humans and chimps, the genes in question turn out to be evolutionarily important, if banal. For example, chimps have a great many more genes related to olfaction than we do; they've got a better sense of smell because

we've lost many of those genes. The 2 percent distinction also involves an unusually large fraction of genes related to the immune system, parasite vulnerability, and infectious diseases: Chimps are resistant to malaria, and we aren't; we handle tuberculosis better than they do. Another important fraction of that 2 percent involves genes related to reproduction—the sorts of anatomical differences that split a species in two and keep them from interbreeding.

That all makes sense. Still, chimps and humans have very different brains. So which are the brain-specific genes that have evolved in very different directions in the two species? It turns out that there are hardly any that fit that bill. This, too, makes a great deal of sense. Examine a neuron from a human brain under a microscope, then do the same with a neuron from the brain of a chimp, a rat, a frog, or a sea slug. The neurons all look the same: fibrous dendrites at one end, an axonal cable at the other. They all run on the same basic mechanism: channels and pumps that move sodium, potassium, and calcium around, triggering a wave of excitation called an action potential. They all have a similar complement of neurotransmitters: serotonin, dopamine, glutamate, and so on. They're all the same basic building blocks.

The main difference is in the sheer number of neurons. The human brain has 100 million times the number of neurons a sea slug's brain has. Where do those differences in quantity come from? At some point in their development, all embryos—whether human, chimp, rat, frog, or slug—must have a single first cell committed toward generating neurons. That cell divides and gives rise to 2 cells; those divide into 4, then 8, then 16. After a dozen rounds of cell division, you've got roughly enough neurons to run a slug. Go another 25 rounds or so and you've got a human brain. Stop a couple of rounds short of that and, at about one-third the size of a human brain, you've got one for a chimp. Vastly different outcomes, but relatively few genes regulate the number of rounds of cell division in the nervous system before calling a halt. And it's precisely some of those genes, the ones involved in neural development, that appear on the list of differences between the chimp and human genomes.

That's it; that's the 2 percent solution. What's shocking is the simplicity of it. Humans, to be human, don't need to have evolved unique genes that code for entirely novel types of neurons or neurotransmitters, or a more complex hippocampus (with resulting improvements in memory), or a more complex frontal cortex (from which we gain the ability to postpone gratification). Instead, our braininess as a species arises from having humongous numbers of just a few types of off-the-rack neurons and from the exponentially greater number of interactions between them. The difference is sheer quantity: Qualitative distinctions emerge from large numbers. Genes may have something to do with that quantity, and thus with the complexity of the quality that emerges. Yet no gene or genome can ever tell us what sorts of qualities those will be. Remember that when you and the chimp are eyeball to eyeball, trying to make sense of why the other seems vaguely familiar.

From *Discover*, April 2006, pp. 42–45. Copyright © 2006 by Robert Sapolsky. Reprinted by permission of the author.

The Mind of the Chimpanzee

Jane Goodall

O ften I have gazed into a chimpanzee's eyes and wondered what was going on behind them. I used to look into Flo's, she so old, so wise. What did she remember of her young days? David Greybeard had the most beautiful eyes of them all, large and lustrous, set wide apart. They somehow expressed his whole personality, his serene self-assurance, his inherent dignity—and, from time to time, his utter determination to get his way. For a long time I never liked to look a chimpanzee straight in the eye—I assumed that, as is the case with most primates, this would be interpreted as a threat or at least as a breach of good manners. No so. As long as one looks with gentleness, without arrogance, a chimpanzee will understand, and may even return the look. And then—or such is my fantasy—it is as though the eyes are windows into the mind. Only the glass is opaque so that the mystery can never be fully revealed.

I shall never forget my meeting with Lucy, an eight-year-old home-raised chimpanzee. She came and sat beside me on the sofa and, with her face very close to mine, searched in my eyes—for what? Perhaps she was looking for signs of mistrust, dislike, or fear, since many people must have been somewhat disconcerted when, for the first time, they came face to face with a grown chimpanzee. Whatever Lucy read in my eyes clearly satisfied her for she suddenly put one arm round my neck and gave me a generous and very chimp-like kiss, her mouth wide open and laid over mine. I was accepted.

For a long time after that encounter I was profoundly disturbed. I had been at Gombe for about fifteen years then and I was quite familiar with chimpanzees in the wild. But Lucy, having grown up as a human child, was like a changeling, her essential chimpanzeeness overlaid by the various human behaviours she had acquired over the years. No longer purely chimp yet eons away from humanity, she was man-made, some other kind of being. I watched, amazed, as she opened the refrigerator and various cupboards, found bottles and a glass, then poured herself a gin and tonic. She took the drink to the TV, turned the set on, flipped from one channel to another then, as though in disgust, turned it off again. She selected a glossy magazine from the table and, still carrying her drink, settled in a comfortable chair. Occasionally, as she leafed through the magazine she identified something she saw, using the signs of ASL, the American Sign Language used by the deaf. I, of course, did not understand, but my hostess, Jane Temerlin (who was also Lucy's 'mother'),

translated: 'That dog,' Lucy commented, pausing at a photo of a small white poodle. She turned the page. 'Blue,' she declared, pointing then signing as she gazed at a picture of a lady advertising some kind of soap powder and wearing a brilliant blue dress. And finally, after some vague hand movements—perhaps signed mutterings—'This Lucy's, this mine,' as she closed the magazine and laid it on her lap. She had just been taught, Jane told me, the use of the possessive pronouns during the thrice weekly ASL lessons she was receiving at the time.

The book written by Lucy's human 'father,' Maury Temerlin, was entitled *Lucy, Growing Up Human.* And in fact, the chimpanzee is more like us than is any other living creature. There is close resemblance in the physiology of our two species and genetically, in the structure of the DNA, chimpanzees and humans differ by only just over one per cent. This is why medical research uses chimpanzees as experimental animals when they need substitutes for humans in the testing of some drug or vaccine. Chimpanzees can be infected with just about all known human infectious diseases including those, such as hepatitis B and AIDS, to which other non-human animals (except gorillas, orangutans and gibbons) are immune. There are equally striking similarities between humans and chimpanzees in the anatomy and wiring of the brain and nervous system, and—although many scientists have been reluctant to admit to this—in social behaviour, intellectual ability, and the emotions. The notion of an evolutionary continuity in physical structure from pre-human ape to modern man has long been morally acceptable to most scientists. That the same might hold good for mind was generally considered an absurd hypothesis—particularly by those who used, and often misused, animals in their laboratories. It is, after all, convenient to believe that the creature you are using, while it may react in disturbingly human-like ways, is, in fact, merely a mindless and, above all, unfeeling, 'dumb' animal.

When I began my study at Gombe in 1960 it was not permissible—at least not in ethological circles—to talk about an animal's mind. Only humans had minds. Nor was it quite proper to talk about animal personality. Of course everyone knew that they *did* have their own unique characters—everyone who had ever owned a dog or other pet was aware of that. But ethologists, striving to make theirs a 'hard' science, shied away from the task of trying to explain such things objectively. One respected ethologist, while acknowledging that there was 'variability between individual animals,' wrote that it was best that this fact be 'swept under the carpet.' At that time ethological carpets fairly bulged with all that was hidden beneath them.

How naive I was. As I had not had an undergraduate science education I didn't realize that animals were not supposed to have personalities, or to think, or to feel emotions or pain. I had no idea that it would have been more appropriate to assign each of the chimpanzees a number rather than a name when I got to know him or her. I didn't realize that it was not scientific to discuss behaviour in terms of motivation or purpose. And no one had told me that terms such as *childhood* and *adolescence* were uniquely human phases of the life cycle, culturally determined, not to be used when referring to young chimpanzees. Not knowing, I freely made use of all those forbidden terms and concepts in my initial attempt to describe, to the best of my ability, the amazing things I had observed at Gombe.

I shall never forget the response of a group of ethologists to some remarks I made at an erudite seminar. I described how Figan, as an adolescent, had learned to stay behind in camp after senior males had left, so that we could give him a few bananas for himself. On the first occasion he had, upon seeing the fruits, uttered loud, delighted food calls: whereupon a couple of the older males had charged back, chased after Figan, and taken his bananas. And then, coming to the point of the story, I explained how, on the next occasion, Figan had actually suppressed his calls. We could hear little sounds, in his throat, but so quiet that none of the others could have heard them. Other young chimps, to whom we tried to smuggle fruit without the knowledge of their elders, never learned such self-control. With shrieks of glee they would fall to, only to be robbed of their booty when the big males charged back. I had expected my audience to be as fascinated and impressed as I was. I had hoped for an exchange of views about the chimpanzee's undoubted intelligence. Instead there was a chill silence, after which the chairman hastily changed the subject. Needless to say, after being thus snubbed, I was very reluctant to contribute any comments, at any scientific gatherings, for a very long time. Looking back, I suspect that everyone was interested, but it was, of course, not permissible to present a mere 'anecdote' as evidence for anything.

The editorial comments on the first paper I wrote for publication demanded that every *he* or *she* be replaced with *it*, and every *who* be replaced with *which*. Incensed, I, in my turn, crossed out the *its* and *whichs* and scrawled back the original pronouns. As I had no desire to carve a niche for myself in the world of science, but simply wanted to go on living among and learning about chimpanzees, the possible reaction of the editor of the learned journal did not trouble me. In fact I won that round: the paper when finally published did confer upon the chimpanzees the dignity of their appropriate genders and properly upgraded them from the status of mere 'things' to essential Beingness.

However, despite my somewhat truculent attitude, I did want to learn, and I was sensible of my incredible good fortune in being admitted to Cambridge. I wanted to get my PhD, if only for the sake of Louis Leakey and the other people who had written letters in support of my admission. And how lucky I was to have, as my supervisor, Robert Hinde. Not only because I

thereby benefitted from his brilliant mind and clear thinking, but also because I doubt that I could have found a teacher more suited to my particular needs and personality. Gradually he was able to cloak me with at least some of the trappings of a scientist. Thus although I continued to hold to most of my convictions—that animals had personalities; that they could feel happy or sad or fearful; that they could feel pain; that they could strive towards planned goals and achieve greater success if they were highly motivated—I soon realized that these personal convictions were, indeed, difficult to prove. It was best to be circumspect—at least until I had gained some credentials and credibility. And Robert gave me wonderful advice on how best to tie up some of my more rebellious ideas with scientific ribbon. 'You can't *know* that Fifi was jealous,' had admonished on one occasion. We argued a little. And then: 'Why don't you just say *If Fifi were a human child we would say she was jealous.*' I did.

It is not easy to study emotions even when the subjects are human. I know how I feel if I am sad or happy or angry, and if a friend tells me that he is feeling sad, happy or angry, I assume that his feelings are similar to mine. But of course I cannot know. As we try to come to grips with the emotions of beings progressively more different from ourselves the task, obviously, becomes increasingly difficult. If we ascribe human emotions to non-human animals we are accused of being anthropomorphic—a cardinal sin in ethology. But is it so terrible? If we test the effect of drugs on chimpanzees because they are biologically so similar to ourselves, if we accept that there are dramatic similarities in chimpanzee and human brain and nervous system, is it not logical to assume that there will be similarities also in at least the more basic feelings, emotions, moods of the two species?

In fact, all those who have worked long and closely with chimpanzees have no hesitation in asserting that chimps experience emotions similar to those which in ourselves we label pleasure, joy, sorrow, anger, boredom and so on. Some of the emotional states of the chimpanzee are so obviously similar to ours that even an inexperienced observer can understand what is going on. An infant who hurls himself screaming to the ground, face contorted, hitting out with his arms at any nearby object, banging his head, is clearly having a tantrum. Another youngster, who gambols around his mother, turning somersaults, pirouetting and, every so often, rushing up to her and tumbling into her lap, patting her or pulling her hand towards him in a request for tickling, is obviously filled with *joie de vivre*. There are few observers who would not unhesitatingly ascribe his behaviour to a happy, carefree state of well-being. And one cannot watch chimpanzee infants for long without realizing that they have the same emotional need for affection and reassurance as human children. An adult male, reclining in the shade after a good meal, reaching benignly to play with an infant or idly groom an adult female, is clearly in a good mood. When he sits with bristling hair, glaring at his subordinates and threatening them, with irritated gestures, if they come too close, he is clearly feeling cross and grumpy. We make these judgements because the similarity of so much of a chimpanzee's behaviour to our own permits us to empathize.

It is hard to empathize with emotions we have not experienced. I can image, to some extent, the pleasure of a female chimpanzee during the act of procreation. The feelings of her male partner are beyond my knowledge—as are those of the human male in the same context. I have spent countless hours watching mother chimpanzees interacting with their infants. But not until I had an infant of my own did I begin to understand the basic, powerful instinct of mother-love. If someone accidentally did something to frighten Grub, or threaten his well-being in any way, I felt a surge of quite irrational anger. How much more easily could I then understand the feelings of the chimpanzee mother who furiously waves her arm and barks in threat at an individual who approaches her infant too closely, or at a playmate who inadvertently hurts her child. And it was not until I knew the numbing grief that gripped me after the death of my second husband that I could even begin to appreciate the despair and sense of loss that can cause young chimps to pine away and die when they lose their mothers.

Empathy and intuition can be of tremendous value as we attempt to understand certain complex behavioral interactions, provided that the behaviour, as it occurs, is recorded precisely and objectively. Fortunately I have seldom found it difficult to record facts in an orderly manner even during times of powerful emotional involvement. And "knowing" intuitively how a chimpanzee is feeling—after an attack, for example—may help one to understand what happens next. We should not be afraid at least to try to make use of our close evolutionary relationship with the chimpanzees in our attempts to interpret complex behaviour.

Today, as in Darwin's time, it is once again fashionable to speak of and study the animal mind. This change came about gradually, and was, at least in part, due to the information collected during careful studies of animal societies in the field. As these observations became widely known, it was impossible to brush aside the complexities of social behaviour that were revealed in species after species. The untidy clutter under the ethological carpets was brought out and examined, piece by piece. Gradually it was realized that parsimonious explanations of apparently intelligent behaviours were often misleading. This led to a succession of experiments that, taken together, clearly prove that many intellectual abilities that had been thought unique to humans were actually present, though in a less highly developed form, in other, non-human beings. Particularly, of course, in the non-human primates and especially in chimpanzees.

When first I began to read about human evolution, I learned that one of the hallmarks of our own species was that we, and only we, were capable of making tools. *Man the Toolmaker* was an oft-cited definition—and this despite the careful and exhaustive research of Wolfgang Kohler and Robert Yerkes on the tool-using and tool-making abilities of chimpanzees. Those studies, carried out independently in the early twenties, were received with scepticism. Yet both Kohler and Yerkes were respected scientists, and both had a profound understanding of chimpanzee behaviour. Indeed, Kohler's descriptions of the personalities and behaviour of the various individuals in his colony, published in his book *The Mentality of Apes,* remain some of the most vivid and colourful ever written. And his experiments, showing how chimpanzees could stack boxes, then climb the unstable constructions to reach fruit suspended from the ceiling, or join two short sticks to make a pole long enough to rake in fruit otherwise out of reach, have become classic, appearing in almost all textbooks dealing with intelligent behaviour in non-human animals.

By the time systematic observations of tool-using came from Gombe those pioneering studies had been largely forgotten. Moreover, it was one thing to know that humanized chimpanzees in the lab could use implements: it was quite another to find that this was a naturally occurring skill in the wild. I well remember writing to Louis about my first observations, describing how David Greybeard not only used bits of straw to fish for termites but actually stripped leaves from a stem and thus *made* a tool. And I remember too receiving the now oft-quoted telegram he sent in response to my letter: "Now we must redefine *tool,* redefine *Man,* or accept chimpanzees as humans."

There were initially, a few scientists who attempted to write off the termiting observations, even suggesting that I had taught the chimps! By and large, though, people were fascinated by the information and by the subsequent observations of the other contexts in which the Gombe chimpanzees used objects as tools. And there were only a few anthropologists who objected when I suggested that the chimpanzees probably passed their tool-using traditions from one generation to the next, through observations, imitation and practice, so that each population might be expected to have its own unique tool-using culture. Which, incidentally, turns out to be quite true. And when I described how one chimpanzee, Mike, spontaneously solved a new problem by using a tool (he broke off a stick to knock a banana to the ground when he was too nervous to actually take it from my hand) I don't believe there were any raised eyebrows in the scientific community. Certainly I was not attacked viciously, as were Kohler and Yerkes, for suggesting that humans were not the only beings capable of reasoning and insight.

The mid-sixties saw the start of a project that, along with other similar research, was to teach us a great deal about the chimpanzee mind. This was Project Washoe, conceived by Trixie and Allen Gardner. They purchased an infant chimpanzee and began to teach her the signs of ASL, the American Sign Language used by the deaf. Twenty years earlier another husband and wife team, Richard and Cathy Hayes, had tried, with an almost total lack of success, to teach a young chimp, Vikki, to talk. The Hayes's undertaking taught us a lot about the chimpanzee mind, but Vikki, although she did well in IQ tests, and was clearly an intelligent youngster, could not learn human speech. The Gardners, however, achieved spectacular success with their pupil, Washoe. Not only did she learn signs easily, but she quickly began to string them together in meaningful ways. It was clear that each sign evoked, in her mind, a mental image of the object it represented. If, for example, she was asked, in sign language, to fetch an apple, she would go and locate an apple that was out of sight in another room.

Other chimps entered the project, some starting their lives in deaf signing families before joining Washoe. And finally Washoe adopted an infant, Loulis. He came from a lab where no thought of teaching signs had ever penetrated. When he was with Washoe he was given no lessons in language acquisition—not by humans, anyway. Yet by the time he was eight years old he had made fifty-eight signs in their correct contexts. How did he learn them? Mostly, it seems, by imitating the behaviour of Washoe and the other three signing chimps, Dar, Moja and Tatu. Sometimes, though, he received tuition from Washoe herself. One day, for example, she began to swagger about bipedally, hair bristling, signing *food! food! food!* in great excitement. She had seen a human approaching with a bar of chocolate. Loulis, only eighteen months old, watched passively. Suddenly Washoe stopped her swaggering, went over to him, took his hand, and moulded the sign for *food* (fingers pointing towards mouth). Another time, in a similar context, she made the sign for *chewing gum*—but with *her* hand on *his* body. On a third occasion Washoe, apropos of nothing, picked up a small chair, took it over to Loulis, set it down in front of him, and very distinctly made the *chair* sign three times, watching him closely as she did so. The two food signs became incorporated into Loulis's vocabulary but the sign for chair did not. Obviously the priorities of a young chimp are similar to those of a human child!

When news of Washoe's accomplishments first hit the scientific community it immediately provoked a storm of bitter protest. It implied that chimpanzees were capable of mastering a human language, and this, in turn, indicated mental powers of generalization, abstraction and concept-formation as well as an ability to understand and use abstract symbols. And these intellectual skills were surely the prerogatives of *Homo sapiens*. Although there were many who were fascinated and excited by the Gardners' findings, there were many more who denounced the whole project, holding that the data was suspect, the methodology sloppy, and the conclusions not only misleading, but quite preposterous. The controversy inspired all sorts of other language projects. And, whether the investigators were sceptical to start with and hoped to disprove the Gardners' work, or whether they were attempting to demonstrate the same thing in a new way, their research provided additional information about the chimpanzee's mind.

And so, with new incentive, psychologists began to test the mental abilities of chimpanzees in a variety of different ways; again and again the results confirmed that their minds are uncannily like our own. It had long been held that only humans were capable of what is called 'cross-modal transfer of information'—in other words, if you shut your eyes and someone allows you to feel a strangely shaped potato, you will subsequently be able to pick it out from other differently shaped potatoes simply by looking at them. And vice versa. It turned out that chimpanzees can 'know' with their eyes what they 'feel' with their fingers in just the same way. In fact, we now know that some other non-human primates can do the same thing. I expect all kinds of creatures have the same ability.

Then it was proved, experimentally and beyond doubt, that chimpanzees could recognize themselves in mirrors—that they had, therefore, some kind of self-concept. In fact, Washoe, some years previously, had already demonstrated the ability when she spontaneously identified herself in the mirror, staring at her image and making her name sign. But that observation was merely anecdotal. The proof came when chimpanzees who had been allowed to play with mirrors were, while anaesthetized, dabbed with spots of odourless paint in places, such as the ears or the top of the head, that they could see only in the mirror. When they woke they were not only fascinated by their spotted images, but immediately investigated, with their fingers, the dabs of paint.

The fact that chimpanzees have excellent memories surprised no one. Everyone, after all, has been brought up to believe that 'an elephant never forgets' so why should a chimpanzee be any different? The fact that Washoe spontaneously gave the name-sign of Beatrice Gardner, her surrogate mother, when she saw her after a separation of eleven years was no greater an accomplishment than the amazing memory shown by dogs who recognize their owners after separations of almost as long—and the chimpanzee has a much longer life span than a dog. Chimpanzees can plan ahead, too, at least as regards the immediate future. This, in fact, is well illustrated at Gombe, during the termiting season: often an individual prepares a tool for use on a termite mound that is several hundred yards away and absolutely out of sight.

This is not the place to describe in detail the other cognitive abilities that have been studied in laboratory chimpanzees. Among other accomplishments chimpanzees possess premathematical skills: they can, for example, readily differentiate between *more* and *less*. They can classify things into specific categories according to a given criterion—thus they have no difficulty in separating a pile of food into *fruits* and *vegetables* on one occasion, and, on another, dividing the same pile of food into *large* versus *small* items, even though this requires putting some vegetables with some fruits. Chimpanzees who have been taught a language can combine signs creatively in order to describe objects for which they have no symbol. Washoe, for example, puzzled her caretakers by asking, repeatedly, for a *rock berry*. Eventually it transpired that she was referring to Brazil nuts which she had encountered for the first time a while before. Another language-trained chimp described a cucumber as a *green banana*, and another referred to an Alka-Seltzer as a *listen drink*. They can even invent signs. Lucy, as she got older, had to be put on a leash for her outings. One day, eager to set off but having no sign for *leash*, she signalled her wishes by holding a crooked index finger to the ring on her collar. This sign became part of her vocabulary. Some chimpanzees love to draw, and especially to paint. Those who have learned sign language sometimes spontaneously label their works, 'This [is] apple'—or bird, or sweetcorn, or whatever. The fact that the paintings often look, to our eyes, remarkably unlike the objects depicted by the artists either means that the chimpanzees are poor draughtsmen or that we have much to learn regarding ape-style representational art!

People sometimes ask why chimpanzees have evolved such complex intellectual powers when their lives in the wild are so simple. The answer is, of course, that their lives in the wild are not so simple! They use—and need—all their mental skills during normal day-to-day life in their complex society. They are always having to make choices—where to go, or with whom to travel. They need highly developed social skills—particularly those males who are ambitious to attain high positions in the dominance hierarchy. Low-ranking chimpanzees must learn deception—to conceal their intentions or to do things in secret—if they are to get their way in the presence of their superiors. Indeed, the study of chimpanzees in the wild suggests that their intellectual abilities evolved, over the millennia, to help them cope with daily life. And now, the solid core of data concerning chimpanzee intellect collected so carefully in the lab setting provides a background against which to evaluate the many examples of intelligent, rational behaviour that we see in the wild.

It is easier to study intellectual prowess in the lab where, through carefully devised tests and judicious use of rewards, the chimpanzees can be encouraged to exert themselves, to stretch their minds to the limit. It is more meaningful to study the subject in the wild, but much harder. It is more meaningful because we can better understand the environmental pressures that led

to the evolution of intellectual skills in chimpanzee societies. It is harder because, in the wild, almost all behaviours are confounded by countless variables; years of observing, recording and analysing take the place of contrived testing; sample size can often be counted on the fingers of one hand; the only experiments are nature's own, and only time—eventually—may replicate them.

In the wild a single observation may prove of utmost significance, providing a clue to some hitherto puzzling aspect of behaviour, a key to the understanding of, for example, a changed relationship. Obviously it is crucial to see as many incidents of this sort as possible. During the early years of my study at Gombe it became apparent that one person alone could never learn more than a fraction of what was going on in a chimpanzee community at any given time. And so, from 1964 onwards, I gradually built up a research team to help in the gathering of information about the behaviour of our closest living relatives.

Got Culture?

CRAIG STANFORD

On my first trip to east Africa in the early 1990s, I stood by a dusty, dirt road hitchhiking. I had waited hours in rural Tanzania for an expected lift from a friend who had never shown up, leaving me with few options other than the kindness of strangers. I stood with my thumb out, but the cars and trucks roared by me, leaving me caked in paprika-red dust. I switched to a palm-down gesture I had seen local people using to get lifts. Voilà; on the first try a truck pulled over and I hopped in. A conversation in Kiswahili with the truck driver ensued and I learned my mistake. Hitchhiking with your thumb upturned may work in the United States, but in Africa the gesture can be translated in the way that Americans understand the meaning of an extended, declarative middle finger. Not exactly the best way to persuade a passing vehicle to stop. The universally recognized symbol for needing a lift is not so universal.

Much of culture is the accumulation of thousands of such small differences. Put a suite of traditions together—religion, language, ways of dress, cuisine and a thousand other features— and you have a culture. Of course cultures can be much simpler too. A group of toddlers in a day care center possesses its own culture, as does a multi-national corporation, suburban gardeners, inner-city gang members. Many elements of a culture are functional and hinged to individual survival: thatched roof homes from the tropics would work poorly in Canada, nor would harpoons made for catching seals be very useful in the Sahara. But other features are purely symbolic. Brides in Western culture wear white to symbolize sexual purity. Brides in Hindu weddings wear crimson, to symbolize sexual purity. Whether white or red is more pure is nothing more than a product of the long-term memory and mindset of the two cultures. And the most symbolic of cultural traditions, the one that has always been considered the bailiwick of humanity only, is language. The words "white" and "red" have an entirely arbitrary relationship to the colors themselves. They are simply code names.

Arguing about how to define culture has long been a growth industry among anthropologists. We argue about culture the way the Joint Chiefs of Staff argue about national security: as though our lives depended on it. But given that culture requires symbolism and some linguistic features, can we even talk about culture in other animals?

In 1996 I was attending a conference near Rio de Janeiro when the topic turned to culture.[1] As a biological anthropologist with a decade of field research on African great apes, I offered my perspective on the concept of culture. Chimpanzees, I said with confidence, display a rich cultural diversity. Recent years have shown that each wild chimpanzee population is more than just a gene pool. It is also a distinct culture, comprising a unique assortment of learned traditions in tool use, styles of grooming and hunting, and other features of the sort that can only be seen in the most socially sophisticated primates. Go from one forest to another and you will run into a new culture, just as walking between two human villages may introduce you to tribes who have different ways of building boats or celebrating marriages.

At least that's what I meant to say. But I had barely gotten the word "culture" past my lips when I was made to feel the full weight of my blissful ignorance. The cultural anthropologists practically leaped across the seminar table to berate me for using the words "culture" and "chimpanzee" in the same sentence. I had apparently set off a silent security alarm, and the culture-theory guards came running. How dare you, they said, use a human term like "cultural diversity" to describe what chimpanzees do? Say "behavioral variation," they demanded. "Apes are mere animals, and culture is something that only the human animal can claim. Furthermore, not only can humans alone claim culture, culture alone can explain humanity." It became clear to me that culture, as understood by most anthropologists, is a human concept, and many passionately want it to stay that way. When I asked if this was not just a semantic difference—what are cultural traditions if not learned behavioral variations?—they replied that culture is symbolic, and what animals do lacks symbolism.

When Jane Goodall first watched chimpanzees make simple stick tools to probe into termite mounds, it became clear that tool cultures are not unique to human societies. Of course many animals use tools. Sea otters on the California coast forage for abalones, which they place on their chests and hammer open with stones. Egyptian vultures use stones to break the eggs of ostriches. But these are simple, relatively inflexible lone behaviors. Only among chimpanzees do we see elaborate forms of tools made and used in variable ways, and also see distinct chimp tool cultures across Africa. In Gombe National Park in Tanzania, termite mounds of red earth rise 2 meters high and shelter millions of the almond-colored insects. Chimpanzees pore over the mounds, scratching at plugged tunnels until they find portals into the mound's interior. They will gently insert a twig or blade of grass into a tunnel until the soldier termites latch onto the tools with their powerful mandibles, then they'll withdraw the probe from the mound. With dozens of soldier and worker termites clinging ferociously to the twig, the chimpanzee draws the stick between her lips and reaps a nutritious bounty.

Less than 100 kilometers away from Gombe's termite-fishing apes is another culture. Chimpanzees in Mahale National Park live in a forest that is home to most of the same species of termites, but they practically never use sticks to eat them. If Mahale chimpanzees forage for termites at all, they use their fingers to crumble apart soil and pick out their insect snacks. However, Mahale chimpanzees love to eat ants. They climb up the straight-sided trunks of great trees and poke Gombe-like probes into holes to obtain woodboring species. As adept as Gombe chimpanzees are at fishing for termites, they practically never fish for these ants, even though both the ants and termites occur in both Gombe and Mahale.[2]

Segue 2,000 kilometers westward, to a rainforest in Côte d'Ivoire. In a forest filled with twigs, chimpanzees do not use stick tools. Instead, chimpanzees in Taï National Park and other forests in western Africa use hammers made of rock and wood. Swiss primatologists Christophe and Hedwige Boesch and their colleagues first reported the use of stone tools by chimpanzees twenty years ago.[3] Their subsequent research showed that Taï chimpanzees collect hammers when certain species of nut-bearing trees are in fruit. These hammers are not modified in any way as the stone tools made by early humans were; they are hefted, however, and appraised for weight and smashing value before being carried back to the nut tree. A nut is carefully positioned in a depression in the tree's aboveground root buttresses (the anvil) and struck with precision by the tool-user. The researchers have seen mothers instructing their children on the art of tool use, by assisting them in placing the nut in the anvil in the proper way.

So chimpanzees in East Africa use termite-and ant-fishing tools, and West African counterparts use hammers, but not vice versa. These are subsistence tools; they were almost certainly invented for food-getting. Primatologist William McGrew of Miami University of Ohio has compared the tool technologies of wild chimpanzees with those of traditional human hunter-gatherer societies. He found that in at least some instances, the gap between chimpanzee technology and human technology is not wide. The now-extinct aboriginal Tasmanians, for example, possessed no complex tools or weapons of any kind. Though they are an extreme example, the Tasmanians illustrate that human culture need not be technologically complex.[4]

As McGrew first pointed out, there are three likeliest explanations for the differences we see among the chimpanzee tool industries across Africa.[5] The first is genetic: perhaps there are mutations that arise in one population but not others that govern tool making. This seems extremely unlikely, just as we would never argue that Hindu brides wear red while Western brides wear white due to a genetic difference between Indians and Westerners. The second explanation is ecological: maybe the environment in which the chimpanzee population lives dictates patterns of tool use. Maybe termite-fishing sticks will be invented in places where there are termites and sticks but not

rocks and nuts, and hammers invented in the opposite situation. But a consideration of each habitat raises doubts. Gombe is a rugged, rock-strewn place where it is hard to find a spot to sit that is not within arm's reach of a few stones, but Gombe chimpanzees do not use stone tools. The West African chimpanzees who use stone tools live, by contrast, in lowland rainforests that are nearly devoid of rocks. Yet they purposely forage to find them. The tool-use pattern is exactly the opposite of what we would expect if environment and local availability accounted for differences among chimpanzee communities in tool use.

British psychologist Andrew Whiten and his colleagues recently conducted the first systematic survey of cultural differences in tool use among the seven longest-term field studies, representing more than a century and a half of total observation time. They found thirty-nine behaviors that could not be explained by environmental factors at the various sites.[6] Alone with humans in the richness of their behavior repertoire, chimpanzee cultures show variations that can only be ascribed to learned traditions. These traditions, passed from one generation to the next through observation and imitation, are a simple version of human culture.

But wait. I said earlier that human culture must have a symbolic element. Tools that differ in form and function, from sticks to hammers to sponges made of crushed leaves, are all utterly utilitarian. They tell us much about the environment in which they are useful but little about the learned traditions that led to their creation. Human artifacts, on the other hand, nearly always contain some purely symbolic element, be it the designs carved into a piece of ancient pottery or the "Stanley" logo on my new claw hammer. Is there anything truly symbolic in chimpanzee culture, in the human sense of an object or behavior that is completely detached from its use?

Male chimpanzees have various ways of indicating to a female that they would like to mate. At Gombe, one such courtship behavior involves rapidly shaking a small bush or branch several times, after which a female in proximity will usually approach the male and present her swelling to him. But in Mahale, males have learned to use leaves in their courtship gesture. A male plucks a leafy stem from a nearby plant and noisily uses his teeth and fingers to tear off its leaves. Leaf-clipping is done mainly in the context of wanting to mate with a particular female, and appears to function as a purely symbolic signal of sexual desire (it could also be a gesture of frustration). A second leafy symbol is leaf-grooming. Chimpanzees pick leaves and intently groom them with their fingers, as seriously as though they were grooming another chimpanzee. And this may be the function; leaf-grooming may signal a desire for real grooming from a social partner. Since the signal for grooming involves grooming, albeit of another object, this gesture is not symbolic in the sense that leaf-clipping is. But its distribution across Africa is equally spotty; leaf-grooming is commonly practiced in East African chimpanzee cultures but is largely absent in western Africa.[7]

These two cases of potentially symbolic behavior may not seem very impressive. After all, the briefest consideration of human culture turns up a rich array of symbolism, from language to the arts. But are all human cultures highly symbolic?

If we use language and other forms of symbolic expression as the criterion for culture, then how about a classroom full of two-year-old toddlers in a day care center? They communicate by a very simple combination of gestures and half-formed sentences. Toddlers have little symbolic communication or appreciation for art and are very little different from chimpanzees in their cultural output. We grant them human qualities because we know they will mature into symbol-using, linguistically expert adults, leaving chimpanzees in the dust. But this is no reason to consider them on a different plane from the apes when both are fifteen months old.

Chimpanzee societies are based on learned traditions passed from mother to child and from adult males to eager wannabe males. These traditions vary from place to place. This is culture. Culture is not limited, however, to those few apes that are genetically 99 percent human. Many primates show traditions. These are usually innovations by younger members of a group, which sweep rapidly through the society and leave it just slightly different than before. Japanese primatologists have long observed such traditions among the macaques native to their island nation. Researchers long ago noticed that a new behavior had arisen in one population of Japanese macaque monkeys living on Koshima Island just offshore the mainland. The monkeys were regularly tossed sweet potatoes, rice and other local treats by the locals. One day Imo, a young female in the group, took her potato and carried it to the sea, where she washed it with salty brine before eating it. This behavior rapidly spread throughout the group, a nice example of innovation happening in real time so that researchers could observe the diffusion. Later, other monkeys invented the practice of scooping up rice offered them with the beach sand it was scattered on, throwing both onto the surf and then scraping up the grains that floated while the sand sank.

At a supremely larger scale, such innovations are what human cultural differences are all about. Of course, only in human cultures do objects such as sweet potatoes take on the kind of symbolic meaning that permits them to stand for other objects and thus become a currency. Chimpanzees lack the top-drawer cognitive capacity needed to invent such a currency. Or do they? Wild chimpanzees hunt for a part of their living. All across equatorial Africa, meat-eating is a regular feature of chimpanzee life, but its style and technique vary from one forest to another. In Taï National Park in western Africa, hunters are highly cooperative; Christophe Boesch has reported specific roles such as ambushers and drivers as part of the apes' effort to corral colobus monkeys in the forest canopy.[8] At Gombe in East Africa, meanwhile, hunting is like a baseball game; a group sport performed on an individual basis. This difference may be environmentally influenced; perhaps the high canopy rain forest at Taï requires cooperation more than the broken, low canopy forest at Gombe. There is a culture of hunting in each forest as well, in which young and eager male wannabes copy the predatory skills of their elders. At Gombe, for instance, chimpanzees relish wild pigs and piglets in addition to monkeys and small antelope. At Taï, wild pigs are ignored even when they stroll in front of a hunting party.

There is also a culture of sharing the kill. Sharing of meat is highly nepotistic at Gombe; sons who make the kill share with their mothers and brothers but snub rival males. They also share preferentially with females who have sexual swellings, and with high-ranking females. At Taï, the captor shares with the other members of the hunting party whether or not they are allies or relatives; a system of reciprocity seems to be in place in which the golden rule works. I have argued that since the energy and time that chimpanzees spend hunting is rarely paid back by the calories, protein and fat gotten from a kill, we should consider hunting a social behavior done at least partly for its own sake.[9] When chimpanzees barter a limited commodity such as meat for other services—alliances, sex, grooming—they are engaging in a very simple and primitive form of a currency exchange. Such an exchange relies on the ability of the participants to remember the web of credits and debts owed one another and to act accordingly. It may be that the two chimpanzee cultures 2,000 kilometers apart have developed their distinct uses of meat as a social currency. In one place meat is used as a reward for cooperation, in the other as a manipulative tool of nepotism. Such systems are commonplace in all human societies, and their roots may be seen in chimpanzees' market economy, too.[10]

I have not yet considered one obvious question. If tool use and other cultural innovations can be so valuable to chimpanzees, why have they not arisen more widely among primates and other big-brained animals? Although chimpanzees are adept tool-users, their very close relatives the bonobos are not. Bonobos do a number of very clever things—dragging their hands beside them as they wade through streams to catch fish is one notable example—but they are not accomplished technicians. Gorillas don't use tools at all, and orangutans have only recently been observed to occasionally use sticks as probing tools in their rainforest canopy world.[11]

Other big-brained animals fare even worse. Wild elephants don't use their wonderfully dexterous trunks to manipulate tools in any major way, although when you're strong enough to uproot trees you may not have much use for a pokey little probe. Dolphins and whales, cognitively gifted though they may be, lack the essential anatomical ingredient for tool manufacture—a pair of nimble hands. Wild bottlenose dolphins have been observed to carry natural sponges about on their snouts to ferret food from the sea bottom, the only known form of cetacean tool use.[12] But that may be the limit of how much a creature that lacks any grasping appendages can manipulate its surroundings.

So to be a cultural animal, it is not enough to be big-brained. You must have the anatomical prerequisites for tool cultures to develop. Even if these are in place, there is no guarantee that a species will generate a subsistence culture in the form of tools. Perhaps environmental necessity dictates which ape species use tools and which don't, except it is hard to imagine that bonobos have much less use for tools than chimpanzees do. There is probably a strong element of chance involved. The chance that a cultural tradition—tool use, hunting style or grooming technique—will develop may be very small in any given century or millennium. Once innovated, the chance that the cultural trait will disappear—perhaps due to the death of the main practitioners from whom everyone learned the behavior—may conversely be great. Instead of a close fit between the environment and the cultural traditions that evolve in it—which many scholars believe explains cultural diversity in human societies—the roots of cultural variation may be much more random. A single influential individual who figures out how to make a better mousetrap, so to speak, can through imitation spread his mousetrap through the group and slowly into other groups.

We tend to think of cultural traditions as highly plastic and unstable compared to biological innovation. It takes hundreds of generations for natural selection to bring about biological change, whereas cultural change can happen in one lifetime, even in a few minutes. Because we live in a culture in which we buy the newest cell phone and the niftiest handheld computer—we fail to appreciate how conservative traditions like tool use can be. *Homo erectus,* with a brain nearly the size of our own, invented a teardrop-shaped stone tool called a hand axe 1.5 million years ago. It was presumably used for butchering carcasses, though some archaeologists think it may have also been a weapon. Whatever its purpose, more than a million years later those same stone axes were still being manufactured and used. Fifty thousand generations passed without a significant change in the major piece of material culture in a very big-brained and intelligent human species. *That's* conservatism and it offers us two lessons. First, if it ain't broke don't fix it: when a traditional way of making a tool works and the environment is not throwing any curves your way, there may be no pressure for a change. Second, we see a human species vastly more intelligent than an ape (*Homo erectus'* neocortical brain volume was a third smaller than a modern human's, but two and a half times larger than a chimpanzee's) whose technology didn't change at all. This tells us that innovations, once made, may last a very long time without being either extinguished or improved upon. It suggests that chimpanzee tool cultures may have been in place for all of the 5 million years since their divergence from our shared ancestor.

The very word *culture,* as William McGrew has pointed out, was invented for humans, and this has long blinded cultural theorists to a more expansive appreciation of the concept. Whether apes have culture or not is not really the issue. The heart of the debate is whether scholars who study culture and consider it their intellectual territory will accept a more expansive definition. In purely academic arguments like this one, the power lies with the party who owns the key concepts of the discipline. They define concepts however they choose, and the choice is usually aimed at fencing off their intellectual turf from all others.

Primatologists are latecomers to the table of culture, and they have had to wait their turn before being allowed to sit. We should be most interested in what the continuum of intelligence tells us about the roots of human behavior, not whether what apes do or don't do fits any particular, rigid definition of culture. When it comes to human practices, from building boats to weddings to choosing mates, we should look at the intersections of our biology and our culture for clues about what has made us who we are.

Notes

1. *Changing Views of Primate Societies: The Role of Gender and Nationality,* June 1996, sponsored by the Wenner-Gren Foundation for Anthropological Research.

2. For an enlightening discussion of cross-cultural differences in chimpanzee tool use, see almost anything William McGrew has written, but especially McGrew (1992).

3. See Boesch and Boesch (1989).

4. Again, see McGrew (1992).

5. McGrew (1979).

6. Whiten *et al.* (1999) combined data from seven long-term chimpanzees studies to produce the most systematic examination of cultural variation in these apes.

7. For further discussion of chimpanzee symbolic behavior in the wild, see Goodall (1986), Wrangham *et al.* (1994), and McGrew et al. (1996).

8. See Boesch and Boesch (1989).

9. See Stanford (1999, 2001).

10. See de Waal (1996) and Stanford (2001).

11. For the first report of systematic tool use by wild orangutans, see van Schaik *et al.* (1996).

12. See Smolker *et al.* (1997).

Dim Forest, Bright Chimps

In the rain forest of Ivory Coast, chimpanzees meet the challenge of life by hunting cooperatively and using crude tools.

CHRISTOPHE BOESCH AND HEDWIGE BOESCH-ACHERMANN

Taï National Park, Ivory Coast, December 3, 1985. Drumming, barking, and screaming, chimps rush through the undergrowth, little more than black shadows. Their goal is to join a group of other chimps noisily clustering around Brutus, the dominant male of this seventy-member chimpanzee community. For a few moments, Brutus, proud and self-confident, stands fairly still, holding a shocked, barely moving red colobus monkey in his hand. Then he begins to move through the group, followed closely by his favorite females and most of the adult males. He seems to savor this moment of uncontested superiority, the culmination of a hunt high up in the canopy. But the victory is not his alone. Cooperation is essential to capturing one of these monkeys, and Brutus will break apart and share this highly prized delicacy with most of the main participants of the hunt and with the females. Recipients of large portions will, in turn, share more or less generously with their offspring, relatives, and friends.

In 1979, we began a long-term study of the previously unknown chimpanzees of Taï National Park, 1,600 square miles of tropical rain forest in the Republic of the Ivory Coast (Côte d'Ivoire). Early on, we were most interested in the chimps' use of natural hammers—branches and stones—to crack open the five species of hard-shelled nuts that are abundant here. A sea otter lying on its back, cracking an abalone shell with a rock, is a familiar picture, but no primate had ever before been observed in the wild using stones as hammers. East Africa's savanna chimps, studied for decades by Jane Goodall in Gombe, Tanzania, use twigs to extract ants and termites from their nests or honey from a bees' nest, but they have never been seen using hammerstones.

As our work progressed, we were surprised by the many ways in which the life of the Taï forest chimpanzees differs from that of their savanna counterparts, and as evidence accumulated, differences in how the two populations hunt proved the most intriguing. Jane Goodall had found that chimpanzees hunt monkeys, antelope, and wild pigs, findings confirmed by Japanese biologist Toshida Nishida, who conducted a long-term study 120 miles south of Gombe, in the Mahale Mountains. So we were not surprised to discover that the Taï chimps eat meat. What

intrigued us was the degree to which they hunt cooperatively. In 1953 Raymond Dart proposed that group hunting and cooperation were key ingredients in the evolution of *Homo sapiens*. The argument has been modified considerably since Dart first put it forward, and group hunting has also been observed in some social carnivores (lions and African wild dogs, for instance), and even some birds of prey. Nevertheless, many anthropologists still hold that hunting cooperatively and sharing food played a central role in the drama that enabled early hominids, some 1.8 million years ago, to develop the social systems that are so typically human.

We hoped that what we learned about the behavior of forest chimpanzees would shed new light on prevailing theories of human evolution. Before we could even begin, however, we had to habituate a community of chimps to our presence. Five long years passed before we were able to move with them on their daily trips through the forest, of which "our" group appeared to claim some twelve square miles. Chimpanzees are alert and shy animals, and the limited field of view in the rain forest—about sixty-five feet at best—made finding them more difficult. We had to rely on sound, mostly their vocalizations and drumming on trees. Males often drum regularly while moving through the forest: pant-hooting, they draw near a big buttress tree; then, at full speed they fly over the buttress, hitting it repeatedly with their hands and feet. Such drumming may resound more than half a mile in the forest. In the beginning, our ignorance about how they moved and who was drumming led to failure more often than not, but eventually we learned that the dominant males drummed during the day to let other group members know the direction of travel. On some days, however, intermittent drumming about dawn was the only signal for the whole day. If we were out of earshot at the time, we were often reduced to guessing.

During these difficult early days, one feature of the chimps' routine proved to be our salvation: nut cracking is a noisy business. So noisy, in fact, that in the early days of French colonial rule, one officer apparently even proposed the theory that some unknown tribe was forging iron in the impenetrable and dangerous jungle.

Guided by the sounds made by the chimps as they cracked open nuts, which they often did for hours at a time, we were gradually able to get within sixty feet of the animals. We still seldom saw the chimps themselves (they fled if we came too close), but even so, the evidence left after a session of nut cracking taught us a great deal about what types of nuts they were eating, what sorts of hammer and anvil tools they were using, and—thanks to the very distinctive noise a nut makes when it finally splits open—how many hits were needed to crack a nut and how many nuts could be opened per minute.

After some months, we began catching glimpses of the chimpanzees before they fled, and after a little more time, we were able to draw close enough to watch them at work. The chimps gather nuts from the ground. Some nuts are tougher to crack than others. Nuts of the *Panda oleosa* tree are the most demanding, harder than any of the foods processed by present-day hunter-gatherers and breaking open only when a force of 3,500 pounds is applied. The stone hammers used by the Taï chimps range from stones of ten ounces to granite blocks of four to forty-five pounds. Stones of any size, however, are a rarity in the forest and are seldom conveniently placed near a nut-bearing tree. By observing closely, and in some cases imitating the way the chimps handle hammerstones, we learned that they have an impressive ability to find just the right tool for the job at hand. Taï chimps could remember the positions of many of the stones scattered, often out of sight, around a panda tree. Without having to run around rechecking the stones, they would select one of appropriate size that was closest to the tree. These mental abilities in spatial representation compare with some of those of nine-year-old humans.

To extract the four kernels from inside a panda nut, a chimp must use a hammer with extreme precision. Time and time again, we have been impressed to see a chimpanzee raise a twenty-pound stone above its head, strike a nut with ten or more powerful blows, and then, using the same hammer, switch to delicate little taps from a height of only four inches. To finish the job, the chimps often break off a small piece of twig and use it to extract the last tiny fragments of kernel from the shell. Intriguingly, females crack panda nuts more often than males, a gender difference in tool use that seems to be more pronounced in the forest chimps than in their savanna counterparts.

After five years of fieldwork, we were finally able to follow the chimpanzees at close range, and gradually, we gained insights into their way of hunting. One morning, for example, we followed a group of six male chimps on a three-hour patrol that had taken them into foreign territory to the north. (Our study group is one of five chimpanzee groups more or less evenly distributed in the Taï forest.) As always during these approximately monthly incursions, which seem to be for the purpose of territorial defense, the chimps were totally silent, clearly on edge and on the lookout for trouble. Once the patrol was over, however, and they were back within their own borders, the chimps shifted their attention to hunting. They were after monkeys, the most abundant mammals in the forest. Traveling in large, multi-species groups, some of the forest's ten species of monkeys are more apt than others to wind up as a meal for the chimps.

The relatively sluggish and large (almost thirty pounds) red colobus monkeys are the chimps' usual fare. (Antelope also live in the forest, but in our ten years at Taï, we have never seen a chimp catch, or even pursue, one. In contrast, Gombe chimps at times do come across fawns, and when they do, they seize the opportunity—and the fawn.)

The six males moved on silently, peering up into the vegetation and stopping from time to time to listen for the sound of monkeys. None fed or groomed; all focused on the hunt. We followed one old male, Falstaff, closely, for he tolerates us completely and is one of the keenest and most experienced hunters. Even from the rear, Falstaff set the pace; whenever he stopped, the others paused to wait for him. After thirty minutes, we heard the unmistakable noises of monkeys jumping from branch to branch. Silently, the chimps turned in the direction of the sounds, scanning the canopy. Just then, a diana monkey spotted them and gave an alarm call. Dianas are very alert and fast; they are also about half the weight of colobus monkeys. The chimps quickly gave up and continued their search for easier, meatier prey.

Shortly after, we heard the characteristic cough of a red colobus monkey. Suddenly Rousseau and Macho, two twenty-year-olds, burst into action, running toward the cough. Falstaff seemed surprised by their precipitousness, but after a moment's hesitation, he also ran. Now the hunting barks of the chimps mixed with the sharp alarm calls of the monkeys. Hurrying behind Falstaff, we saw him climb up a conveniently situated tree. His position, combined with those of Schubert and Ulysse, two mature chimps in their prime, effectively blocked off three of the monkeys' possible escape routes. But in another tree, nowhere near any escape route and thus useless, waited the last of the hunters, Kendo, eighteen years old and the least experienced of the group. The monkeys, taking advantage of Falstaff's delay and Kendo's error, escaped.

The six males moved on and within five minutes picked up the sounds of another group of red colobus. This time, the chimps approached cautiously, nobody hurrying. They screened the canopy intently to locate the monkeys, which were still unaware of the approaching danger. Macho and Schubert chose two adjacent trees, both full of monkeys, and started climbing very quietly, taking care not to move any branches. Meanwhile, the other four chimps blocked off anticipated escape routes. When Schubert was halfway up, the monkeys finally detected the two chimps. As we watched the colobus monkeys take off in literal panic, the appropriateness of the chimpanzees' scientific name—*Pan* came to mind: with a certain stretch of the imagination, the fleeing monkeys could be shepherds and shepherdesses frightened at the sudden appearance of Pan, the wild Greek god of the woods, shepherds, and their flocks.

Taking off in the expected direction, the monkeys were trailed by Macho and Schubert. The chimps let go with loud hunting barks. Trying to escape, two colobus monkeys jumped into smaller trees lower in the canopy. With this, Rousseau and Kendo, who had been watching from the ground, sped up into the trees and tried to grab them. Only a third of the weight of the chimps, however, the monkeys managed to make it to the next tree along branches too small for their pursuers. But Falstaff had anticipated this move and was waiting for them. In the following confusion, Falstaff seized a juvenile and killed it with a bite to the neck. As the chimps met in a rush on the ground, Falstaff began to eat, sharing with Schubert and Rousseau. A juvenile colobus does not provide much meat, however, and this time, not all the chimps got a share. Frustrated individuals soon started off on another hunt, and relative calm returned fairly quickly: this sort of hunt, by a small band of chimps acting on their own at the edge of their territory, does not generate the kind of high excitement that prevails when more members of the community are involved.

So far we have observed some 200 monkey hunts and have concluded that success requires a minimum of three motivated hunters acting cooperatively. Alone or in pairs, chimps succeed less than 15 percent of the time, but when three or four act as a group, more than half the hunts result in a kill. The chimps seem well aware of the odds; 92 percent of all the hunts we observed were group affairs.

Gombe chimps also hunt red colobus monkeys, but the percentage of group hunts is much lower: only 36 percent. In addition, we learned from Jane Goodall that even when Gombe chimps do hunt in groups, their strategies are different. When Taï chimps arrive under a group of monkeys, the hunters scatter, often silently, usually out of sight of one another but each aware of the others' positions. As the hunt progresses, they gradually close in, encircling the quarry. Such movements require that each chimp coordinate his movements with those of the other hunters, as well as with those of the prey, at all times.

Coordinated hunts account for 63 percent of all those observed at Taï but only 7 percent of those at Gombe. Jane Goodall says that in a Gombe group hunt, the chimpanzees typically travel together until they arrive at a tree with monkeys. Then, as the chimps begin climbing nearby trees, they scatter as each pursues a different target. Goodall gained the impression that Gombe chimps boost their success by hunting independently but simultaneously, thereby disorganizing their prey; our impression is that the Taï chimps owe their success to being organized themselves.

Just why the Gombe and Taï chimps have developed such different hunting strategies is difficult to explain, and we plan to spend some time at Gombe in the hope of finding out. In the meantime, the mere existence of differences is interesting enough and may perhaps force changes in our understanding of human evolution. Most currently accepted theories propose that some three million years ago, a dramatic climate change in Africa east of the Rift Valley turned dense forest into open, drier habitat. Adapting to the difficulties of life under these new conditions, our ancestors supposedly evolved into cooperative hunters and began sharing food they caught. Supporters of this idea point out that plant and animal remains indicative of dry, open environments have been found at all early hominid excavation sites in Tanzania, Kenya, South Africa, and Ethiopia. That the large majority of apes in Africa today live west of the Rift Valley appears to many anthropologists to lend further support to the idea that a change in environment caused the common ancestor of apes and humans to evolve along a different line from those remaining in the forest.

Our observations, however, suggest quite another line of thought. Life in dense, dim forest may require more sophisticated behavior than is commonly assumed: compared with their savanna relatives, Taï chimps show greater complexity in both hunting and tool use. Taï chimps use tools in nineteen different ways and have six different ways of making them, compared with sixteen uses and three methods of manufacture at Gombe.

Anthropologist colleagues of mine have told me that the discovery that some chimpanzees are accomplished users of hammerstones forces them to look with a fresh eye at stone tools turned up at excavation sites. The important role played by female Taï chimps in tool use also raises the possibility that in the course of human evolution, women may have been decisive in the development of many of the sophisticated manipulative skills characteristic of our species. Taï mothers also appear to pass on their skills by actively teaching their offspring. We have observed mothers providing their young with hammers and then stepping in to help when the inexperienced youngsters encounter difficulty. This help may include carefully showing how to position the nut or hold the hammer properly. Such behavior has never been observed at Gombe.

Similarly, food sharing, for a long time said to be unique to humans, seems more general in forest than in savanna chimpanzees. Taï chimp mothers share with their young up to 60 percent of the nuts they open, at least until the latter become sufficiently adept, generally at about six years old. They also share other foods acquired with tools, including honey, ants, and bone marrow. Gombe mothers share such foods much less often, even with their infants. Taï chimps also share meat more frequently than do their Gombe relatives, sometimes dividing a chunk up and giving portions away, sometimes simply allowing beggars to grab pieces.

Any comparison between chimpanzees and our hominid ancestors can only be suggestive, not definitive. But our studies lead us to believe that the process of hominization may have begun independently of the drying of the environment. Savanna life could even have delayed the process; many anthropologists have been struck by how slowly hominid-associated remains, such as the hand ax, changed after their first appearance in the Olduvai age.

Will we have the time to discover more about the hunting strategies or other, perhaps as yet undiscovered abilities of these forest chimpanzees? Africa's tropical rain forests, and their inhabitants, are threatened with extinction by extensive logging, largely to provide the Western world with tropical timber and such products as coffee, cocoa, and rubber. Ivory Coast has lost 90 percent of its original forest, and less than 5 percent of the remainder can be considered pristine. The climate has changed dramatically. The harmattan, a cold, dry wind from the Sahara previously unknown in the forest, has now swept through the Taï forest every year since 1986. Rainfall has diminished; all the rivulets in our study region are now dry for several months of the year.

In addition, the chimpanzee, biologically very close to humans, is in demand for research on AIDS and hepatitis vaccines. Captive-bred chimps are available, but they cost about twenty times more than wild-caught animals. Chimps taken from the wild for these purposes are generally young, their mothers having been shot during capture. For every chimp arriving at its sad destination, nine others may well have died in the forest or on the way. Such priorities—cheap coffee and cocoa and chimpanzees—do not do the economies of Third World countries any good in the long run, and they bring suffering and death to innocent victims in the forest. Our hope is that Brutus, Falstaff, and their families will survive, and that we and others will have the opportunity to learn about them well into the future. But there is no denying that modern times work against them and us.

From *Natural History,* September 1991, pp. 50, 52–56. Copyright © 1991 by Natural History Magazine. Reprinted by permission.

Thinking Like a Monkey

What do our primate cousins know and when do they know it? Researcher Laurie Santos is trying to read their minds.

JERRY ADLER

On a hot morning in early August, the primate census of Cayo Santiago, a 38-acre island just off the coast of Puerto Rico, numbers approximately 875. Of those, 861 are resident Macaca mulatta, commonly known as rhesus macaques, the descendants of a colony transported here from Calcutta in 1938 to provide a permanent breeding stock for medical researchers. The rest are Homo sapiens who have made the trip in a motorboat, including workers stocking the feeding bins with dun-colored biscuits of monkey chow, and researchers for whom the island provides a rare opportunity to study free-ranging primates without the drudgery of having to locate them deep in some remote forest.

The researchers comprise two distinct disciplines, with widely divergent interests and approaches. Ever since E. O. Wilson visited here in 1956 and came away with the ideas that would eventually become the foundation of a whole new field of research he called sociobiology, the island has been a mecca for ethologists, who study the monkeys' social hierarchies and interactions. It has also been discovered by experimental psychologists, who study the animals' thinking processes. Since the former try to stay as unobtrusive as possible, while the latter employ attention-getting constructions of colored posterboard and bags of fruit, there's a certain unavoidable tension between the disciplines. Trailed by three undergraduates toting armloads of gear up a path sodden with monkey droppings, Laurie Santos, a psychologist at Yale, is in the latter camp. "This is what we do," she says, "hike around looking for monkeys by themselves who are hungry and want to play It's hard to find social creatures by themselves," she adds as she backs out of the field of view of a primatologist's video camera, "and even harder to find ones that aren't being followed by other researchers."

Santos has been coming to Cayo every year since 1993, when she was a freshman at Harvard and volunteered to work here with her psychology professor, Marc Hauser.

She keeps that tradition alive with her own undergraduates. With her bright smile and mass of curly dark hair, Santos, 32, could pass for an undergraduate herself. Her boyfriend, Mark Maxwell, actually is an undergrad-albeit one who dropped out of MIT and supported himself for years by playing poker before returning this year to finish his degree at Yale. Santos teaches a class, "Sex, Evolution and Human Nature" with a course description ("Topics include . . . human mating strategies, the biology of warfare, sex differences in behavior, love and lust . . .") that all but guaranteed it would have to be held in the largest classroom on campus, the law school auditorium. She was embarrassed last year when her mother attended one of her lectures and by happenstance chose the day that she was discussing the female orgasm. "I had to cover it, but my mom was in the auditorium, so I kind of rushed through it," Santos says. "I hope the students didn't notice."

She has built a growing and impressive list of publications in cognitive neuroscience (mostly having to do with how primates understand physical objects and relations) and evolutionary psychology the field that grew out of sociobiology "If you see something in a primate," Santos reasons, "you can use it as a window into the evolutionary past of human beings."

On this summer day, if her undergraduate volunteers expected to be investigating the exuberant and promiscuous sex life of the rhesus macaque, they must be disappointed. Santos' interest here is in what psychologists call "theory of mind," the ability to impute thoughts and intentions to another individual, one of the cornerstones of human cognition. "Sitting here talking with you," Santos explains, "all I can see is your behavior, but I draw inferences about your desires and thoughts. The interesting question is, how far back in evolutionary time does that ability extend? Can it exist without language?" As recently as a decade ago, the conventional wisdom doubted that even chimpanzees, which are more closely related to human beings than are monkeys, possessed theory of mind. This view is changing, in large measure because of the work of Santos and her collaborators. With her students in tow and a small bag of grapes in her pocket, Santos is now out to demonstrate the phenomenon—if a Macaca mulatta can be induced to cooperate.

Trial 1: The experiment relies on one of the most predictable traits of rhesus monkeys: their tendency to steal food at every opportunity. Santos discovered this a few years ago when she and her colleagues were running experiments in cognition and tool use involving lemons, and frequently had to quit early because the animals stole all the fruit. The island's monkeys are supplied with food, of course, and they also forage, but to leave so much as a raisin unguarded is to invite larceny; the researchers eat their own lunches inside a locked cage of cyclone fencing.

The theory-of-mind experiment is designed to test whether the monkeys, who obsessively guard their own food, assume that people do the same. If so, Santos reasons, they should prefer to steal from people who are looking away. So Santos enlists Olivia Scheck and Katharine Jan, Yale student volunteers here for the month. They are dressed alike in blue slacks and white shirts to minimize any confounding effect from their appearance—although there are differences Santos cannot do anything about, because Olivia is several inches shorter than Katharine, and blond, where Katharine is dark-haired. In general, Santos has found, rhesus macaques prefer to steal from the shorter person, although top-ranking dominant males sometimes do the opposite, apparently just to show off.

The goal is to locate a monkey that isn't busy doing something else and isn't distracted by other monkeys. That's not always easy on this crowded island; monkeys who seem to be off by themselves are often low-ranking males skulking around a female in hopes of getting a quick copulation—out of sight of the dominant males. Once Santos has a monkey's attention, she holds up two grapes for it to see and impales each on a stick placed a few feet apart on the ground. Each student stands behind one of the grapes. Then Katharine turns her back on the monkey, while Olivia stares straight ahead. If the monkey doesn't fall asleep, wander off or lose interest, it will scamper, saunter or nervously edge over to one grape or the other and snatch it up. Based on published results, says Santos, nine times out of ten the person whose back is turned is the one who gets robbed.

This time, the monkey, who apparently hadn't read the literature, heads straight for Olivia's grape, grabs it from right under her nose and runs off.

Santos has traveled a long and (to her) unexpected path to this patch of tropical forest. She grew up in New Bedford, Massachusetts, the daughter of a high-school guidance counselor mother and a computer programmer father. She's French-Canadian on her mother's side, and on her father's is descended from Cape Verdean fishermen who settled in New England generations ago. In high school, all she knew about college was that she wanted to attend one in Boston; she chose Harvard because, taking financial aid into account, it was the least expensive. She enrolled in Hauser's psychology class, on which her own is modeled, because she was closed out of a course she'd needed for her intended career as a lawyer, and was won over by the charismatic professor and the intellectual challenge of a rapidly evolving field.

Santos did not originate the idea that has fueled several breakthroughs in the past decade, but she has been one of the most imaginative and successful in applying it. The concept, known as "domain specificity," holds that the cognitive abilities of primates evolved for particular tasks and can be tested only in a context that is meaningful to the animal itself. The early theory-of-mind experiments tried to enlist monkeys or chimps in begging for food, sharing it or cooperating to find it—behaviors, says Santos, that do not come naturally to them. As she and co-author and Yale colleague Derek E. Lyons put it in a recent paper in the journal Philosophy Compass, "though primates are social creatures, they are not exactly sociable ones." Colleagues say Santos has a talent for thinking like a monkey. Her experiments cleverly elicit and exploit primates' natural gifts for competitiveness, stealthiness, hoarding and deceit.

Trial 2: This time Olivia is the one facing away, and the monkey, better versed in theory-of-mind, makes a dash for her grape.

Rhesus Macaques, especially juveniles, are capable of simulating cuteness, but it's not their defining characteristic. Scrappy and long-limbed, with pink hairless faces framed by gray or brown fur, they fight convincingly among themselves. At least two here appear to have lost limbs in their perpetual struggle for rank, and they will stand up to a human being if the stakes are high enough a grape, for example. They have been known to carry a variety of herpes that can be fatal to human beings, and scattered around the island are first-aid stations holding disinfectant kits to be used in case of a bite. (On the other hand, a single human visitor with active tuberculosis could wipe out the entire colony.) Santos recognizes many of the individual monkeys here by sight or by the letter-and-number code tattooed on their chests, but she says she has never been even tempted to name them.

She has somewhat more affection for the 11 capuchin monkeys in her lab at Yale, who are named after characters in James Bond movies (Goldfinger, Jaws, Holly Goodhead). Her work with them involves experiments on "social decision-making." She equips them with tokens they can trade for food and studies the development of their rudimentary economy. Like human beings, they are loss-averse: if the going price is two grapes for a token, they prefer to trade with an experimenter who shows them one grape and then adds one, compared with one who shows three and takes one away. They are also sneaky. After swapping for an apple, she says, they will sometimes take a bite of it, then present the untouched side to the researcher and try to sell it back. And they have an entrepreneurial bent. At times they would offer their feces in exchange for a token, behavior that baffled the researchers until a student pointed out that every morning someone comes into the cage and scoops out the droppings—which may have given them the idea that people value them.

Trial 3: Katharine faces away again, and the monkey sidles up and grabs her grape, just as science would predict. Then it does a quick sideways dash and snatches up Olivia's as well.

T he experiments done so far are tests of first-order knowledge: the monkey sees the human experimenter either facing or facing away from the grape. Now Santos intends to test whether macaques possess the more sophisticated concept of "false belief"—the recognition that another individual may be mistaken. The classic test for this in people is the "Sally-Anne" experiment. The subject watches "Sally" put a ball in a box, then leave the room. While she's gone, "Anne" moves the ball to a different box. The experimenter asks the subject: Where will Sally look for the ball? The expected answer from adults is the first box, where Sally last saw it. Children younger than about 4, and those with autism, more often say the second box, where the ball actually is; they cannot conceive that Sally has a false belief.

To test if monkeys are capable of false belief, Santos has devised an experiment involving two grapes, three open boxes and four researchers, including Santos herself and someone to record the whole thing on video. Again, the premise is that the monkeys are more likely to steal things that, from their point of view, are unguarded. The protocol is as follows: the three boxes are arranged side by side on the ground with their open sides facing the monkey, and a student puts one grape in each of two boxes—B and C, say. Then she stands behind the boxes and turns her back, and a different student moves the grapes—into A and B. The monkey now knows where the grapes are, but the first student does not. When she turns and faces the monkey, which box is the monkey more likely to rob? If the monkey understands "false belief," it will expect the student to be guarding boxes B and C, and so will be more likely to steal from A.

"Make sure you don't both have your backs turned to the monkey at the same time," Santos warns the students. "Some of these monkeys will just rush the boxes."

Trial 1: After finally locating a suitable monkey, setting up the boxes and going through the pantomime with the grapes, Santos drifts back into the trees and watches as the monkey languidly scratches itself. Almost ostentatiously, it seems, the animal turns and looks out over the rocks to the sea.

Trials 2 and 3: No approach.

With her students, Santos tramps up and down the now-familiar hills, across a rocky isthmus, to the sounds of wind and crashing waves, chattering monkeys and the continual bang of metal lids slamming on the chow bins. Santos tries to enlist one young monkey gnawing a biscuit, only to be stared down by a nearby male that was about to mount a different female. "Don't worry," Santos says placatingly as she backs away, "she's gonna mate with you, I promise."

Trial 4: Boxes blow over, trial aborted.

Trial 5: As soon as the grapes are displayed, the monkey gets up and walks away

Trial 6: Finally a monkey that seems interested. Actually, a little too interested. As the second student is approaching the boxes to move the grapes, the monkey gets off his haunches and walks swiftly toward her. "Turn around!" Santos calls. The student pivots, pulls herself up to her full height and stares right at the monkey it snarls menacingly back at her; she shrieks and runs to hide behind a colleague. The monkey grabs both grapes and runs away, chewing.

S tudents must commit to a month in Puerto Rico, but it is the prerogative of the professor to fly home at the end of the first week. Before Santos leaves, she makes some modifications to the false-belief experiment, and by the end of the month she hears that it's working better. In the months after returning to New Haven, she begins to formulate some tentative conclusions about what she has found: monkeys can gauge the knowledge and intentions of others when they correspond to their own perceptions of reality, but they cannot make the leap to the concept of a false belief.

So is the mental gap between monkeys and human beings closing or widening? In a sense, both: if Santos is right, monkeys manage to navigate complex social hierarchies, hiding from and deceiving others as necessary, all without an ability that human beings develop by the age of 4. The more she works with monkeys, the more Santos is convinced that their abilities are limited to specific contexts and tasks, such as competing for food or establishing dominance. It's rather like the honeybee dance, a fantastically ingenious way to communicate geographic information. Still, honeybees can't use it to talk about their feelings. "My guess," says Hauser, "is that we will eventually come to see that the gap between human and animal cognition, even a chimpanzee, is greater than the gap between a chimp and a beetle." Perhaps, Santos says. Monkeys can reason quite competently about human beings' intentions with respect to grapes, but only by imputing to them what they themselves experience: a readiness to grab and hoard whenever possible. She speculates that it is our capacity for language that enables us to understand mental states different from our own. We may not be hungry now, but because we have a word for the concept we can imagine what it feels like. "The more you hang out with monkeys," she says, "the more you realize just how special people really are."

JERRY ADLER is a *NewsWeek* senior editor specializing in science and medicine.

Sylwia Kapuscinski usually photographs human primates, and focuses on immigrants.

Why Are Some Animals So Smart?

The unusual behavior of orangutans in a Sumatran swamp suggests a surprising answer.

CAREL VAN SCHAIK

Even though we humans write the textbooks and may justifiably be suspected of bias, few doubt that we are the smartest creatures on the planet. Many animals have special cognitive abilities that allow them to excel in their particular habitats, but they do not often solve novel problems. Some of course do, and we call them intelligent, but none are as quick-witted as we are.

What favored the evolution of such distinctive brainpower in humans or, more precisely, in our hominid ancestors? One approach to answering this question is to examine the factors that might have shaped other creatures that show high intelligence and to see whether the same forces might have operated in our forebears. Several birds and nonhuman mammals, for instance, are much better problem solvers than others: elephants, dolphins, parrots, crows. But research into our close relatives, the great apes, is surely likely to be illuminating.

Scholars have proposed many explanations for the evolution of intelligence in primates, the lineage to which humans and apes belong (along with monkeys, lemurs, and lorises). Over the past 13 years, though, my group's studies of orangutans have unexpectedly turned up a new explanation that we think goes quite far in answering the question.

Incomplete Theories

One influential attempt at explaining primate intelligence credits the complexity of social life with spurring the development of strong cognitive abilities. This Machiavellian intelligence hypothesis suggests that success in social life relies on cultivating the most profitable relationships and on rapidly reading the social situation—for instance, when deciding whether to come to the aid of an ally attacked by another animal. Hence, the demands of society foster intelligence because the most intelligent beings would be most successful at making self-protective choices and thus would survive to pass their genes to the next generation. Machiavellian traits may not be equally beneficial to other lineages, however, or even to all primates, and so this notion alone is unsatisfying.

One can easily envisage many other forces that would promote the evolution of intelligence, such as the need to work

Overview/The Orangutan Connection

- The author has discovered extensive tool use among orangutans in a Sumatran swamp. No one has observed orangutans systematically using tools in the wild before.
- This unexpected finding suggests to the author a resolution to a long-standing puzzle: Why are some animals so smart?
- He proposes that culture is the key. Primatologists define culture as the ability to learn—by observation—skills invented by others. Culture can unleash ever increasing accomplishments and can bootstrap a species toward greater and greater intelligence.

hard for one's food. In that situation, the ability to figure out how to skillfully extract hidden nourishment or the capacity to remember the perennially shifting locations of critical food items would be advantageous, and so such cleverness would be rewarded by passing more genes to the next generation.

My own explanation, which is not incompatible with these other forces, puts the emphasis on social learning. In humans, intelligence develops over time. A child learns primarily from the guidance of patient adults. Without strong social—that is, cultural—inputs, even a potential wunderkind will end up a bungling bumpkin as an adult. We now have evidence that this process of social learning also applies to great apes, and will argue that, by and large, the animals that are intelligent are the ones that are cultural: they learn from one another innovative solutions to ecological or social problems. In short, I suggest that culture promotes intelligence.

I came to this proposition circuitously, by way of the swamps on the western coast of the Indonesian island of Sumatra, where my colleagues and I were observing orangutans. The orangutan is Asia's only great ape, confined to the islands of Borneo and Sumatra and known to be something of a loner. Compared with its more familiar relative, Africa's chimpanzee, the red ape is serene rather than hyperactive and reserved socially rather than convivial. Yet we discovered in them the conditions that allow culture to flourish.

Technology in the Swamp

We were initially attracted to the swamp because it sheltered disproportionately high numbers of orangutans—unlike the islands' dryland forests, the moist swamp habitat supplies abundant food for the apes year-round and can thus support a large population. We worked in an area near Suaq Balimbing in the Kluet swamp, which may have been paradise for orangutans but, with its sticky mud, profusion of biting insects, and oppressive heat and humidity, was hell for researchers.

One of our first finds in this unlikely setting astonished us: the Suaq orangutans created and wielded a variety of tools. Although captive red apes are avid tool users, the most striking feature of tool use among the wild orangutans observed until then was its absence. The animals at Suaq ply their tools for two major purposes. First, they hunt for ants, termites and, especially, honey (mainly that of stingless bees)—more so than all their fellow orangutans elsewhere. They often cast discerning glances at tree trunks, looking for air traffic in and out of small holes. Once discovered, the holes become the focus of visual and then manual inspection by a poking and picking finger. Usually the finger is not long enough, and the orangutan prepares a stick tool. After carefully inserting the tool, the ape delicately moves it back and forth, and then withdraws it, licks it off and sticks it back in. Most of this "manipulation" is done with the tool clenched between the teeth; only the largest tools, used primarily to hammer chunks off termite nests, are handled.

The second context in which the Suaq apes employ tools involves the fruit of the *Neesia*. This tree produces woody, five-angled capsules up to 10 inches long and four inches wide. The capsules are filled with brown seeds the size of lima beans, which, because they contain nearly 50 percent fat, are highly nutritious—a rare and sought-after treat in a natural habitat without fast food. The tree protects its seeds by growing a very tough husk. When the seeds are ripe, however, the husk begins to split open; the cracks gradually widen, exposing neat rows of seeds, which have grown nice red attachments (arils) that contain some 80 percent fat. To discourage seed predators further, a mass of razor-sharp needles fills the husk. The orangutans at Suaq strip the bark off short, straight twigs, which they then hold in their mouths and insert into the cracks. By moving the tool up and down inside the crack, the animal detaches the seeds from their stalks. After this maneuver, it can drop the seeds straight into its mouth. Late in the season, the orangutans eat only the red arils, deploying the same technique to get at them without injury.

Both these methods of fashioning sticks for foraging are ubiquitous at Suaq. In general, "fishing" in tree holes is occasional and lasts only a few minutes, but when *Neesia* fruits ripen, the apes devote most of their waking hours to ferreting out the seeds or arils, and we see them grow fatter and sleeker day by day.

Why the Tool Use Is Cultural

What explains this curious concentration of tool use when wild orangutans elsewhere show so little propensity? We doubt that the animals at Suaq are intrinsically smarter: the observation that most captive members of this species can learn to use tools suggests that the basic brain capacity to do so is present.

So we reasoned that their environment might hold the answer. The orangutans studied before mostly live in dry forest, and the swamp furnishes a uniquely lush habitat. More insects make their nests in the tree holes there than in forests on dry land, and *Neesia* grows only in wet places, usually near flowing water. Tempting as the environmental explanation sounds, however, it does not explain why orangutans in several populations outside Suaq ignore altogether these same rich food sources. Nor does it explain why some populations that do eat the seeds harvest them without tools (which results, of course, in their eating much less than the orangutans at Suaq do). The same holds for tree-hole tools. Occasionally, when the nearby hills—which have dryland forests—show massive fruiting, the Suaq orangutans go there to indulge, and while they are gathering fruit they use tools to exploit the contents of tree holes. The hill habitat is a dime a dozen throughout the orangutan's geographic range, so if tools can be used on the hillsides above Suaq, why not everywhere?

Another suggestion we considered, captured in the old adage that necessity is the mother of invention, is that the Suaq animals, living at such high density, have much more competition for provisions. Consequently, many would be left without food unless they could get at the hard-to-reach supplies—that is, they *need* tools in order to eat. The strongest argument against this possibility is that the sweet or fat foods that the tools make accessible sit very high on the orangutan preference list and should therefore be sought by these animals everywhere. For instance, red apes in all locations are willing to be stung many times by honeybees to get at their honey. So the necessity idea does not hold much water either.

A different possibility is that these behaviors are innovative techniques a couple of clever orangutans invented, which then spread and persisted in the population because other individuals learned by observing these experts. In other words, the tool use is cultural. A major obstacle to studying culture in nature is that, barring experimental introductions, we can never demonstrate convincingly that an animal we observe invents some new trick rather than simply applying a well remembered but rarely practiced habit. Neither can we prove that one individual learned a new skill from another group member rather than figuring out what to do on its own. Although we can show that orangutans in the lab are capable of observing and learning socially, such studies tell us nothing about culture in nature—neither what it is generally about nor how much of it exists. So field-workers have had to develop a system of criteria to demonstrate that a certain behavior has a cultural basis.

First, the behavior must vary geographically, showing that it was invented somewhere, and it must be common where it is found, showing that it spread and persisted in a population. The tool uses at Suaq easily pass these first two tests. The second step is to eliminate simpler explanations that produce the same spatial pattern but without involving social learning. We have already excluded an ecological explanation, in which individuals exposed to a particular habitat independently converge on the same skill. We can also eliminate genetics because of the fact that most captive orangutans can learn to use tools.

The third and most stringent test is that we must be able to find geographic distributions of behavior that can be explained by culture and are not easily explained any other way. One key pattern would be the presence of a behavior in one place and its absence beyond some natural barrier to dispersal. In the case of the tool users at Suaq, the geographic distribution of *Neesia* gave us decisive clues. *Neesia* trees (and orangutans) occur on both sides of the wide Alas River. In the Singkil swamp, however, just south of Suaq and on the same side of the Alas River tools littered the floor, whereas in Batu-Batu swamp across the river they were conspicuously absent, despite our numerous visits in different years. In Batu-Batu, we did find that many of the fruits were ripped apart, showing that these orangutans ate *Neesia* seeds in the same way as their colleagues did at a site called Gunung Palung in distant Borneo but in a way completely different from their cousins right across the river in Singkil.

Batu-Batu is a small swamp area, and it does not contain much of the best swamp forest; thus, it supports a limited number of orangutans. We do not know whether tool use was never invented there or whether it could not be maintained in the smaller population, but we do know that migrants from across the river never brought it in because the Alas is so wide there that it is absolutely impassable for an orangutan. Where it is passable, farther upriver, *Neesia* occasionally grows, but the orangutans in that area ignore it altogether, apparently unaware of its rich offerings. A cultural interpretation, then, most parsimoniously explains the unexpected juxtaposition of knowledgeable tool users and brute-force foragers living practically next door to one another, as well as the presence of ignoramuses farther upriver.

Tolerant Proximity

Why do we see these fancy forms of tool use at Suaq and not elsewhere? To look into this question, we first made detailed comparisons among all the sites at which orangutans have been studied. We found that even when we excluded tool use, Suaq had the largest number of innovations that had spread throughout the population. This finding is probably not an artifact of our own interest in unusual behaviors, because some other sites have seen far more work by researchers eager to discover socially learned behavioral innovations.

We guessed that populations in which individuals had more chances to observe others in action would show a greater diversity of learned skills than would populations offering fewer learning opportunities. And indeed, we were able to confirm that sites in which individuals spend more time with others have greater repertoires of learned innovations—a relation, by the way, that also holds among chimpanzees. This link was strongest for food-related behavior, which makes sense because acquiring feeding skills from somebody else requires more close-range observation than, say, picking up a conspicuous communication signal. Put another way, those animals exposed to the fewest

educated individuals have the smallest collection of cultural variants, exactly like the proverbial country bumpkin.

When we looked closely at the contrasts among sites, we noticed something else. Infant orangutans everywhere spend over 20,000 daylight hours in close contact with their mothers, acting as enthusiastic apprentices. Only at Suaq, however, did we also see adults spending considerable time together while foraging. Unlike any other orangutan population studied so far, they even regularly fed on the same food item, usually termite-riddled branches, and shared food—the meat of a slow loris, for example. This unorthodox proximity and tolerance allowed less skilled adults to come close enough to observe foraging methods, which they did as eagerly as kids.

Acquisition of the most cognitively demanding inventions, such as the tool uses found only at Suaq, probably requires face time with proficient individuals, as well as several cycles of observation and practice. The surprising implication of this need is that even though infants learn virtually all their skills from their mothers, a population will be able to perpetuate particular innovations only if tolerant role models other than the mother are around; if mom is not particularly skillful, knowledgeable experts will be close at hand, and a youngster will still be able to learn the fancy techniques that apparently do not come automatically. Thus, the more connected a social network, the more likely it is that the group will retain any skill that is invented, so that in the end tolerant populations support a greater number of such behaviors.

Our work in the wild shows us that most learning in nature, aside from simple conditioning, may have a social component, at least in primates. In contrast, most laboratory experiments that investigate how animals learn are aimed at revealing the subject's ability for individual learning. Indeed, if the lab psychologist's puzzle were presented under natural conditions, where myriad stimuli compete for attention, the subject might never realize that a problem was waiting to be solved. In the wild, the actions of knowledgeable members of the community serve to focus the attention of the naive animal.

The Cultural Roots of Intelligence

Our analyses of orangutans suggest that not only does culture—social learning of special skills—promote intelligence, it favors the evolution of greater and greater intelligence in a population over time. Different species vary greatly in the mechanisms that enable them to learn from others, but formal experiments confirm the strong impression one gets from observing great apes in the wild: they are capable of learning by watching what others do. Thus, when a wild orangutan, or an African great ape for that matter, pulls off a cognitively complex behavior, it has acquired the ability through a mix of observational learning and individual practice, much as a human child has garnered his or her skills. And when an orangutan in Suaq has acquired more of these tricks than its less fortunate cousins elsewhere, it has done so because it had greater opportunities for social learning throughout its life. In brief, social learning may bootstrap an animal's intellectual performance onto a higher plane.

To appreciate the importance of social inputs to the evolution of ever higher intelligence, let us do a thought experiment. Imagine an individual that grows up without any social inputs yet is provided with all the shelter and nutrition it needs. This situation is equivalent to that in which no contact exists between the generations or in which young fend for themselves after they emerge from the nest. Now imagine that some female in this species invents a useful skill—for instance, how to open a nut to extract its nutritious meat. She will do well and perhaps have more offspring than others in the population. Unless the skill gets transferred to the next generation, however, it will disappear when she dies.

Now imagine a situation in which the offspring accompany their mother for a while before they strike out on their own. Most youngsters will learn the new technique from their mother and thus transfer it—and its attendant benefits—to the next generation. This process would generally take place in species with slow development and long association between at least one parent and offspring, but it would get a strong boost if several individuals form socially tolerant groups.

We can go one step further. For slowly developing animals that live in socially tolerant societies, natural selection will tend to reward a slight improvement in the ability to learn through observation more strongly than a similar increase in the ability to innovate, because in such a society, an individual can stand on the shoulders of those in both present and past generations. We will then expect a feed-forward process in which animals can become more innovative and develop better techniques of social learning because both abilities rely on similar cognitive mechanisms. Hence, being cultural predisposes species with some innovative capacities to evolve toward higher intelligence. This, then, brings us to the new explanation for cognitive evolution.

This new hypothesis makes sense of an otherwise puzzling phenomenon. Many times during the past century people reared great ape infants as they would human children. These so-called enculturated apes acquired a surprising set of skills, effortlessly imitating complex behavior—understanding pointing, for example, and even some human language, becoming humorous pranksters and creating drawings. More recently, formal experiments such as those performed by E. Sue Savage-Rumbaugh of Georgia State University, involving the bonobo Kanzi, have revealed startling language abilities. Though often dismissed as lacking in scientific rigor, these consistently replicated cases reveal the astonishing cognitive potential that lies dormant in great apes. We may not fully appreciate the complexity of life in the jungle, but guess that these enculturated apes have truly become overqualified. In a process that encapsulates the story of human evolution, an ape growing up like a human can be bootstrapped to cognitive peaks higher than any of its wild counterparts.

The same line of thinking solves the long-standing puzzle of why many primates in captivity readily use—and sometimes even make—tools, when their counterparts in the wild seem to lack any such urges. The often-heard suggestion that they do not need tools is belied by observations of orangutans, chimpanzees and capuchin monkeys showing that some of this tool use makes available the richest food in the animals' natural habitats or tides the creatures over during lean periods. The conundrum is resolved if we realize that two individuals of the same species can differ dramatically in their intellectual performance, depending on the social environment in which they grew up.

Orangutans epitomize this phenomenon. They are known as the escape artists of the zoo world, cleverly unlocking the doors of their cages. But the available observations from the wild, despite decades of painstaking monitoring by dedicated field-workers, have uncovered precious few technological accomplishments outside Suaq. Wild-caught individuals generally never take to being locked up, always retaining their deeply ingrained shyness and suspicion of humans. But zoo-born apes happily consider their keepers valuable role models and pay attention to their activities and to the objects strewn around the enclosures, learning to learn and thus accumulating numerous skills.

The critical prediction of the intelligence-through-culture theory is that the most intelligent animals are also likely to live in populations in which the entire group routinely adopts innovations introduced by members. This prediction is not easily tested. Animals from different lineages vary so much in their senses and in their ways of life that a single yardstick for intellectual performance has traditionally been hard to find. For now, we can merely ask whether lineages that show incontrovertible signs of intelligence also have innovation-based cultures, and vice versa. Recognizing oneself in a mirror, for example, is a poorly understood but unmistakable sign of self-awareness, which is taken as a sign of high intelligence. So far, despite widespread attempts in numerous lineages, the only mammalian groups to pass this test are great apes and dolphins, the same animals that can learn to understand many arbitrary symbols and that show the best evidence for imitation, the basis for innovation-based culture. Flexible, innovation-based tool use, another expression of intelligence, has a broader distribution in mammals: monkeys and apes, cetaceans, and elephants—all lineages in which social learning is common. Although so far only these very crude tests can be done, they support the intelligence-through-culture hypothesis.

Another important prediction is that the propensities for innovation and social learning must have coevolved. Indeed, Simon Reader, now at Utrecht University in the Netherlands, and Kevin N. Laland, currently at the University of St. Andrews in Scotland, found that primate species that show more evidence of innovation are also those that show the most evidence for social learning. Still more indirect tests rely on correlations among species between the relative size of the brain (after statistically correcting for body size) and social and developmental variables. The well-established correlations between gregariousness and relative brain size in various mammalian groups are also consistent with the idea.

Although this new hypothesis is not enough to explain why our ancestors, alone among great apes, evolved such extreme intelligence, the remarkable bootstrapping ability of the great apes in rich cultural settings makes the gap seem less formidable. The explanation for the historical trajectory of change involves many details that must be painstakingly pieced together from a sparse and confusing fossil and archaeological record.

Many researchers suspect that a key change was the invasion of the savanna by tool-wielding, striding early *Homo*. To dig up tubers and deflesh and defend carcasses of large mammals, they had to work collectively and create tools and strategies. These demands fostered ever more innovation and more interdependence, and intelligence snowballed.

Once we were human, cultural history began to interact with innate ability to improve performance. Nearly 150,000 years after the origin of our own species, sophisticated expressions of human symbolism, such as finely worked nonfunctional artifacts (art, musical instruments and burial gifts), were widespread. The explosion of technology in the past 10,000 years shows that cultural inputs can unleash limitless accomplishments, all with Stone Age brains. Culture can indeed build a new mind from an old brain.

CAREL VAN SCHAIK is director of the Anthropological Institute and Museum at the University of Zurich in Switzerland. A native of the Netherlands, he earned his doctorate at Utrecht University in 1985. After a postdoc at Princeton University and another short stint at Utrecht, he went to Duke University, where he was professor of biological anthropology until he returned to the Old World in 2004. His book *Among Orangutans: Red Apes and the Rise of Human Culture* (Harvard University Press, 2004) gives a more detailed treatment of the ideas covered in this article.

How Animals Do Business

Humans and other animals share a heritage of economic tendencies—including cooperation, repayment of favors and resentment at being shortchanged.

Frans B. M. de Waal

Just as my office would not stay empty for long were I to move out, nature's real estate changes hands all the time. Potential homes range from holes drilled by woodpeckers to empty shells on the beach. A typical example of what economists call a "vacancy chain" is the housing market among hermit crabs. To protect its soft abdomen, each crab carries its house around, usually an abandoned gastropod shell. The problem is that the crab grows, whereas its house does not. Hermit crabs are always on the lookout for new accommodations. The moment they upgrade to a roomier shell, other crabs line up for the vacated one.

One can easily see supply and demand at work here, but because it plays itself out on a rather impersonal level, few would view the crab version as related to human economic transactions. The crab interactions would be more interesting if the animals struck deals along the lines of "you can have my house if I can have that dead fish." Hermit crabs are not deal makers, though, and in fact have no qualms about evicting homeowners by force. Other, more social animals do negotiate, however, and their approach to the exchange of resources and services helps us understand how and why human economic behavior may have evolved.

The New Economics

Classical economics views people as profit maximizers driven by pure selfishness. As 17th-century English philosopher Thomas Hobbes put it, "Every man is presumed to seek what is good for himself naturally, and what is just, only for Peaces sake, and accidentally." In this still prevailing view, sociality is but an afterthought, a "social contract" that our ancestors entered into because of its benefits, not because they were attracted to one another. For the biologist, this imaginary history falls as wide off the mark as can be. We descend from a long line of group-living primates, meaning that we are naturally equipped with a strong desire to fit in

Overview/Evolved Economics

- The new field of behavioral economics views the way humans conduct business as an evolved heritage of our species.
- Just as tit for tat and supply and demand influence the trading of goods and services in human economies, they also affect trading activities among animals.
- Emotional reactions—such as outrage at unfair arrangements—underlie the negotiations of both animals and humans.
- This shared psychology may explain such curious behaviors as altruism—they are part of our background as cooperative primates.

and find partners to live and work with. This evolutionary explanation for why we interact as we do is gaining influence with the advent of a new school, known as behavioral economics, that focuses on actual human behavior rather than on the abstract forces of the marketplace as a guide for understanding economic decision making. In 2002 the school was recognized by a shared Nobel Prize for two of its founders: Daniel Kahneman and Vernon L. Smith.

Animal behavioral economics is a fledgling field that lends support to the new theories by showing that basic human economic tendencies and preoccupations—such as reciprocity, the division of rewards, and cooperation—are not limited to our species. They probably evolved in other animals for the same reasons they evolved in us—to help individuals take optimal advantage of one another without undermining the shared interests that support group life.

Take a recent incident during my research at the Yerkes National Primate Research Center in Atlanta. We had taught capuchin monkeys to reach a cup of food on a tray by pulling on a bar attached to the tray. By making the tray too heavy for a single individual, we gave the monkeys a reason to work together.

On one occasion, the pulling was to be done by two females, Bias and Sammy. Sitting in adjoining cages, they successfully brought a tray bearing two cups of food within reach. Sammy, however, was in such a hurry to collect her reward that she released the bar and grabbed her cup before Bias had a chance to get hers. The tray bounced back, out of Bias's reach. While Sammy munched away, Bias threw a tantrum. She screamed her lungs out for half a minute until Sammy approached her pull bar again. She then helped Bias bring in the tray a second time. Sammy did not do so for her own benefit, because by now the cup accessible to her was empty.

Sammy's corrective behavior appeared to be a response to Bias's protest against the loss of an anticipated reward. Such action comes much closer to human economic transactions than that of the hermit crabs, because it shows cooperation, communication and the fulfillment of an expectation, perhaps even a sense of obligation. Sammy seemed sensitive to the quid pro quo of the situation. This sensitivity is not surprising given that the group life of capuchin monkeys revolves around the same mixture of cooperation and competition that marks our own societies.

The Evolution of Reciprocity

Animals and people occasionally help one another without any obvious benefits for the helper. How could such behavior have evolved? If the aid is directed at a family member, the question is relatively easy to answer. "Blood is thicker than water," we say, and biologists recognize genetic advantages to such assistance: if your kin survive, the odds of your genes making their way into the next generation increase. But cooperation among unrelated individuals suggests no immediate genetic advantages. Pëtr Kropotkin, a Russian prince, offered an early explanation in his book *Mutual Aid,* published in 1902. If helping is communal, he reasoned, all parties stand to gain—everyone's chances for survival go up. We had to wait until 1971, however, for Robert L. Trivers, then at Harvard University, to phrase the issue in modern evolutionary terms with his theory of reciprocal altruism.

Trivers contended that making a sacrifice for another pays off if the other later returns the favor. Reciprocity boils down to "I'll scratch your back, if you scratch mine." Do animals show such tit for tat? Monkeys and apes form coalitions; two or more individuals, for example, gang up on a third. And researchers have found a positive correlation between how often A supports B and how often B supports A. But does this mean that animals actually keep track of given and received favors? They may just divide the world into "buddies," whom they prefer, and "nonbuddies," whom they care little about. If such feelings are mutual, relationships will be either mutually helpful or mutually unhelpful.

Such symmetries can account for the reciprocity reported for fish, vampire bats (which regurgitate blood to their buddies), dolphins and many monkeys.

Just because these animals may not keep track of favors does not mean they lack reciprocity. The issue rather is how a favor done for another finds its way back to the original altruist. What exactly is the reciprocity mechanism? Mental record keeping is just one way of getting reciprocity to work, and whether animals do this remains to be tested. Thus far chimpanzees are the only exception. In the wild, they hunt in teams to capture colobus monkeys. One hunter usually captures the prey, after which he tears it apart and shares it. Not everyone gets a piece, though, and even the highest-ranking male, if he did not take part in the hunt, may beg in vain. This by itself suggests reciprocity: hunters seem to enjoy priority during the division of spoils.

To try to find the mechanisms at work here, we exploited the tendency of these apes to share—which they also show in captivity—by handing one of the chimpanzees in our colony a watermelon or some branches with leaves. The owner would be at the center of a sharing cluster, soon to be followed by secondary clusters around individuals who had managed to get a major share, until all the food had trickled down to everyone. Claiming another's food by force is almost unheard of among chimpanzees—a phenomenon known as "respect of possession." Beggars hold out their hand, palm upward, much like human beggars in the street. They whimper and whine, but aggressive confrontations are rare. If these do occur, the possessor almost always initiates them to make someone leave the circle. She whacks the offenders over the head with a sizable branch or barks at them in a shrill voice until they leave her alone. Whatever their rank, possessors control the food flow.

We analyzed nearly 7,000 of these approaches, comparing the possessor's tolerance of specific beggars with previously received services. We had detailed records of grooming on the mornings of days with planned food tests. If the top male, Socko, had groomed May, for example, his chances of obtaining a few branches from her in the afternoon were much improved. This relation between past and present behavior proved general. Symmetrical connections could not explain this outcome, as the pattern varied from day to day. Ours was the first animal study to demonstrate a contingency between favors given and received. Moreover, these food-for-grooming deals were partner-specific—that is, May's tolerance benefited Socko, the one who had groomed her, but no one else.

This reciprocity mechanism requires memory of previous events as well as the coloring of memory such that it induces friendly behavior. In our own species, this coloring process is known as "gratitude," and there is no reason to call it something else in chimpanzees. Whether apes also feel obligations remains unclear, but it is interesting that the tendency to return favors is not the same for all relationships. Between individuals who associate and groom a great deal,

What Makes Reciprocity Tick

Humans and other animals exchange benefits in several ways, known technically as reciprocity mechanisms. No matter what the mechanism, the common thread is that benefits find their way back to the original giver.

RECIPROCITY MECHANISM	KEY FEATURES
Symmetry-based "We're buddies"	Mutual affection between two parties prompts similar behavior in both directions without need to keep track of daily give-and-take, so long as the overall relationship remains satisfactory. Possibly the most common mechanism of reciprocity in nature, this kind is typical of humans and chimpanzees in close relationships. **Example:** Chimpanzee friends associate, groom together and support each other in fights.
Attitudinal "If you're nice, I'll be nice"	Parties mirror one another's attitudes, exchanging favors on the spot. Instant attitudinal reciprocity occurs among monkeys, and people often rely on it with strangers. **Example:** Capuchins share food with those who help them pull a treat-laden tray.
Calculated "What have you done for me lately?"	Individuals keep track of the benefits they exchange with particular partners, which helps them decide to whom to return favors. This mechanism is typical of chimpanzees and common among people in distant and professional relationships. **Example:** Chimpanzees can expect food in the afternoon from those they groomed in the morning.

Roberto Osti

a single grooming session carries little weight. All kinds of daily exchanges occur between them, probably without their keeping track. They seem instead to follow the buddy system discussed before. Only in the more distant relationships does grooming stand out as specifically deserving reward. Because Socko and May are not close friends, Socko's grooming was duly noticed.

A similar difference is apparent in human behavior, where we are more inclined to keep track of give-and-take with strangers and colleagues than with our friends and family. In fact, scorekeeping in close relationships, such as between spouses, is a sure sign of distrust.

Biological Markets

Because reciprocity requires partners, partner choice ranks as a central issue in behavioral economics. The hand-me-down housing of hermit crabs is exceedingly simple compared with the interactions among primates, which involve multiple partners exchanging multiple currencies, such as grooming, sex, support in fights, food, babysitting and so on. This "marketplace of services," as I dubbed it in *Chimpanzee Politics,* means that each individual needs to be on good terms with higher-ups, to foster grooming partnerships

and—if ambitious—to strike deals with like-minded others. Chimpanzee males form coalitions to challenge the reigning ruler, a process fraught with risk. After an overthrow, the new ruler needs to keep his supporters contented: an alpha male who tries to monopolize the privileges of power, such as access to females, is unlikely to keep his position for long. And chimps do this without having read Niccoló Machiavelli.

With each individual shopping for the best partners and selling its own services, the framework for reciprocity becomes one of supply and demand, which is precisely what Ronald Noë and Peter Hammerstein, then at the Max Planck Institute for Behavioral Physiology in Seewiesen, Germany, had in mind with their biological market theory. This theory, which applies whenever trading partners can choose with whom to deal, postulates that the value of commodities and partners varies with their availability. Two studies of market forces elaborate this point: one concerns the baby market among baboons, the other the job performance of small fish called cleaner wrasses.

Like all primate females, female baboons are irresistibly attracted to infants-not only their own but also those of others. They give friendly grunts and try to touch them. Mothers are highly protective, however, and reluctant to let anyone

Roberto Osti

Tray-Pulling Experiment demonstrates that capuchin monkeys are more likely to share food with cooperative partners than with those who are not helpful. The test chamber houses two capuchins, separated by mesh. To reach their treat cups, they must use a bar to pull a counterweighted tray; the tray is too heavy for one monkey to handle alone. The "laborer" (*on left*), whose transparent cup is obviously empty, works for the "winner," who has food in its cup. The winner generally shares food with the laborer through the mesh. Failing to do so will cause the laborer to lose interest in the task.

handle their precious newborns. To get close, interested females groom the mother while peeking over her shoulder or underneath her arm at the baby. After a relaxing grooming session, a mother may give in to the groomer's desire for a closer look. The other thus buys infant time. Market theory predicts that the value of babies should go up if there are fewer around. In a study of wild chacma baboons in South Africa, Louise Barrett of the University of Liverpool and Peter Henzi of the University of Central Lancashire, both in England, found that, indeed, mothers of rare infants were able to extract a higher price (longer grooming) than mothers in a troop full of babies.

Cleaner wrasses (*Labroides dirnidiatus*) are small marine fish that feed on the external parasites of larger fish. Each cleaner owns a "station" on a reef where clientele come to spread their pectoral fins and adopt postures that offer the cleaner a chance to do its job. The exchange exemplifies a perfect mutualism.

The cleaner nibbles the parasites off the client's body surface, gills and even the inside of its mouth. Sometimes the cleaner is so busy that clients have to wait in line. Client fish come in two varieties: residents and roamers. Residents belong to species with small territories; they have no choice but to go to their local cleaner. Roamers, on the other hand, either hold large territories or travel widely, which means that they have several cleaning stations to choose from. They want short waiting times, excellent service and no cheating. Cheating occurs when a cleaner fish takes a bite out of its client, feeding on healthy mucus. This makes clients jolt and swim away.

Research on cleaner wrasses by Redouan Bshary of the Max Planck institute in Seewiesen consists mainly of observations on the reef but also includes ingenious experiments in the laboratory. His papers read much like a manual for good business practice. Roamers are more likely to change stations if a cleaner has ignored them for too long or cheated them. Cleaners seem to know this and treat roamers better than they do residents. If a roamer and a resident arrive at the same time, the cleaner almost always services the roamer first. Residents have nowhere else to go, and so they can be kept waiting. The only category of fish that cleaners never cheat are predators, who possess a radical counterstrategy, which is to swallow the cleaner. With predators, cleaner fish wisely adopt, in Bshary's words, an "unconditionally cooperative strategy."

Biological market theory offers an elegant solution to the problem of freeloaders, which has occupied biologists for a long time because reciprocity systems are obviously vulnerable to those who take rather than give. Theorists often assume that offenders must be punished, although this has yet to be demonstrated for animals. Instead cheaters can be taken care of in a much simpler way. If there is a choice of partners, animals can simply abandon unsatisfactory relationships and replace them with those offering more benefits. Market mechanisms are all that is needed to sideline profiteers. In our own societies, too, we neither like nor trust those who take more than they give, and we tend to stay away from them.

Fair Is Fair

To reap the benefits of cooperation, an individual must monitor its efforts relative to others and compare its rewards with the effort put in. To explore whether animals actually carry out such monitoring, we turned again to our capuchin monkeys, testing them in a miniature labor market inspired by field observations of capuchins attacking giant squirrels. Squirrel hunting is a group effort, but one in which all rewards end up in the hands of a single individual: the captor. If captors were to keep the prey solely for themselves, one can imagine that others would lose interest in joining them in the future. Capuchins share meat for the same reason chimpanzees (and people) do: there can be no joint hunting without joint payoffs.

We mimicked this situation in the laboratory by making certain that only one monkey (whom we called the winner) of a tray-pulling pair received a cup with apple pieces. Its partner (the laborer) had no food in its cup, which was obvious from the outset because the cups were transparent. Hence, the laborer pulled for the winner's benefit. The monkeys sat side by side, separated by mesh. From previous tests we knew that food possessors might bring food to the partition and permit their neighbor to reach for it through the mesh. On rare occasions, they push pieces to the other.

How Humans Do Business

The emotions that Frans de Waal describes in the economic exchanges of social animals have parallels in our own transactions. Such similarities suggest that human economic interactions are controlled at least in part by ancient tendencies and emotions. Indeed, the animal work supports a burgeoning school of research known as behavioral economics. This new discipline is challenging and modifying the "standard model" of economic research, which maintains that humans base economic decisions on rational thought processes. For example, people reject offers that strike them as unfair, whereas classical economics predicts that people take anything they can get. In 2002 the Noble Prize in Economics went to two pioneers of the field: Daniel Kahneman, a psychologist at Princeton University, and Vernon L. Smith, an economist at George Mason University.

Kahneman, with his colleague Amos Tversky, who died in 1996 and thus was not eligible for the prize, analyzed how humans make decisions when confronted by uncertainty and risk. Classical economists had thought of human decisions in terms of expected utility—the sum of the gains people think they will get from some future event multiplied by its probability of occurring. But Kahneman and Tversky demonstrated that people are much more frightened of losses than they are encouraged by potential gains and that people follow that herd. The bursting of the stock-market bubble in 2000 provides a potent example: the desire to stay with the herd may have led people to shell out far more for shares than any purely rational investor would have paid.

Smith's work demonstrated that laboratory experiments would function in economics, which had traditionally been considered a nonexperimental science that relied solely on observation. Among his findings in the lab: emotional decisions are not necessarily unwise.

—The Editors

We contrasted collective pulls with solo pulls. In one condition, both animals had a pull bar and the tray was heavy; in the other, the partner lacked a bar and the winner handled a lighter tray on its own. We counted more acts of food sharing after collective than solo pulls: winners were in effect compensating their partners for the assistance they had received. We also confirmed that sharing affects future cooperation. Because a pair's success rate would drop if the winner failed to share, payment of the laborer was a smart strategy.

Sarah F. Brosnan, one of my colleagues at Yerkes, went further in exploring reactions to the way rewards are divided. She would offer a capuchin monkey a small pebble, then hold up a slice of cucumber as enticement for returning the pebble. The monkeys quickly grasped the principle of exchange. Placed side by side, two monkeys would gladly exchange pebbles for cucumber with the researcher. If one of them got grapes, however, whereas the other stayed on cucumber, things took an unexpected turn. Grapes are much preferred. Monkeys who had been perfectly willing to work for cucumber suddenly went on strike. Not only did they perform reluctantly seeing that the other was getting a better deal, but they became agitated, hurling the pebbles out of the test chamber and sometimes even the cucumber slices. A food normally never refused had become less than desirable.

To reject unequal pay—which people do as well—goes against the assumptions of traditional economics. If maximizing benefits were all that mattered, one should take what one can get and never let resentment or envy interfere. Behavioral economists, on the other hand, assume evolution has led to emotions that preserve the spirit of cooperation and that such emotions powerfully influence behavior. In the short run, caring about what others get may seem irrational, but in the long run it keeps one from being taken advantage of. Discouraging exploitation is critical for continued cooperation.

It is a lot of trouble, though, to always keep a watchful eye on the flow of benefits and favors. This is why humans protect themselves against freeloading and exploitation by forming buddy relationships with partners—such as spouses and good friends—who have withstood the test of time. Once we have determined whom to trust, we relax the rules. Only with more distant partners do we keep mental records and react strongly to imbalances, calling them "unfair."

We found indications for the same effect of social distance in chimpanzees. Straight tit for tat, as we have seen, is rare among friends who routinely do favors for one another. These relationships also seem relatively immune to inequity. Brosnan conducted her exchange task using grapes and cucumbers with chimpanzees as well as capuchins. The strongest reaction among chimpanzees concerned those who had known one another for a relatively short time, whereas the members of a colony that had lived together for more than 30 years hardly reacted at all. Possibly, the greater their familiarity, the longer the time frame over which chimpanzees evaluate their relationships. Only distant relations are sensitive to day-to-day fluctuations.

All economic agents, whether human or animal, need to come to grips with the freeloader problem and the way yields are divided after joint efforts. They do so by sharing most with those who help them most and by displaying strong emotional reactions to violated expectations. A truly evolutionary discipline of economics recognizes this shared psychology and considers the possibility that we embrace the golden rule not accidentally, as Hobbes thought, but as part of our background as cooperative primates.

More To Explore

"The Chimpanzee's Service Economy: Food for Grooming." Frans B. M. de Waal in *Evolution and Human Behavior,* Vol. 18, No. 6, pages 375–386; November 1997.

"Payment for Labour in Monkeys." Frans B. M. de Waal and Michelle L. Berger in *Nature,* Vol. 404, page 563; April 6, 2000.

"Choosy Reef Fish Select Cleaner Fish That Provide High-Quality Service." R. Bshary and D. Schäffer in *Animal Behaviour,* Vol. 63, No. 3, pages 557–564; March 2002.

"Infants as a Commodity in a Baboon Market." S. P. Henzi and L. Barrett in *Animal Behaviour,* Vol. 63, No. 5, pages 915–921; 2002.

"Monkeys Reject Unequal Pay." Sarah F. Brosnan and Frans B. M. de Waal in *Nature,* Vol. 425, pages 297–299; September 18, 2003.

Living Links Center site: www.emory.edu/LIVING-LINKS/

Classic cooperation experiment with chimpanzees: www.emory.edu/LIVING-LINKS/crawfordvideo.html

F RANS B. M. DE WAAL is C. H. Candler Professor of Primate Behavior at Emory University and director of the Living Links Center at the university's Yerkes National Primate Research Center. De Waal specializes in the social behavior and cognition of monkeys, chimpanzees and bonobos, especially cooperation, conflict resolution and culture. His books include *Chimpanzee Politics, Peacemaking among Primates, The Ape and the Sushi Master* and the forthcoming *Our Inner Ape.*

A Telling Difference

Animals can communicate, but evidence that any of them can emulate human language remains elusive.

STEPHEN R. ANDERSON

Doctor Dolittle, the fictional hero of Hugh Lofting's novels, was said to be able to talk with animals. Whether he, or any of his would-be imitators in real life today, could actually speak with an animal is an entirely different question.

Clearly animals can communicate; communication is virtually universal among living things. Cats meow; songbirds sing; whales call: A dog wagging its tail can be providing information about how it feels and what it wants. Surely, though, such communication is not of a piece with the languages people use. Describing any of those behaviors with the word "talk" would be nothing more than a (feeble) attempt to be clever.

Animals communicate—without language—for a variety of purposes. The vocal sac of a male frog, ready to mate, expands; a randy male sage grouse's feathers ruffle. Threats provoke communication: a cobra hisses; a porcupine bristles its quills, and a dog responds by barking and baring its teeth. Some animal communication is inadvertent, such as the scents exuded by and covering scavenging ants.

But people do use words such as "talk" to describe certain kinds of animal communication. In fact, since the 1970s many claims have been made about the potential abilities of apes to talk with people in sign languages or via other means. What is the nonspecialist to make of such claims? Are animals simply handicapped by their vocal anatomy? Could they, like Dr. Dolittle's friends, one day be taught to converse with us, via some vocal or nonvocal channel, and perhaps even to pass along their newly acquired linguistic "culture" to their offspring? Or is the evidence presented so far, purportedly in support of such claims, at best irrelevant to them, and at worst a gross overstatement of what the data really mean?

One evening I returned home to find my wife correcting papers. When I asked her what we were doing for dinner, she said, "I want to go out." Her words left no doubt that she wanted us to go to a restaurant, where we would have dinner.

When I came home the following night, I found my cat Pooh in the kitchen. She looked at me, walked over to an oriental rug in the next room, and began to sharpen her claws on it. Pooh knows I hate that, and as I went to stop her, she ran to the sliding glass door that leads outside. I yelled at her, but my wife said, "Don't get mad; she's just saying, 'I want to go out.'"

Voila! Both my wife and my cat can say, "I want to go out." But do they both have language? Surely that is at best an oversimplification. Each can behave in such a way as to convey information to me. But the means by which they do this are radically different.

One way of approaching the distinction between communication and language is to note that communication is something we—and lots of other animals—do, whereas language is a tool that people can use to do that. People can, of course, communicate without language, though the range of information we can transmit by such means is limited. The same is true of the communication by animals and other organisms: it can transmit some fairly complex information or requests, but it still falls far short of something that is uniquely human: language.

Psychologists and others seeking to establish that such and such an animal either has language or at least has the cognitive ability to acquire language need to be able to say what language is. Their approach is commonly to make a list of characteristics and show that their animal does indeed exhibit all of them, or at least that they can teach it enough to pass a battery of tests.

That strategy poses a number of problems. Any specific set of characteristics is liable to need constant revision, because as linguists learn more about language, its characteristics change. Nevertheless, at least two of them—the use of arbitrary symbols for nouns and verbs, and the use of syntax—are critical to assessing language ability.

Investigators exploring the cognitive capacities of other species, particularly the people who study the putative language abilities of apes, have often complained about what seems to them a double standard. E. Sue Savage-Rumbaugh, a biologist at Georgia State University in Atlanta, objects that linguists "keep raising the bar."

First the linguists said we had to get our animals to use signs in a symbolic way if we wanted to say they learned language, OK, we did that, and then they said "No, that's not language, because you don't have syntax." So we proved our apes could produce some combinations of signs, but the linguists said that wasn't enough syntax, or the right syntax. They'll never agree that we've done enough.

But linguists are not being capricious. What gives human language its power and its centrality in our lives is its capacity to articulate a range of novel expressions, thoughts, and ideas, bounded only by imagination. In our native language, you and I can produce and understand sentences we have never encountered before. Human languages have the property of including such a potentially infinite number of distinct sentences with discrete meanings because they are organized in a hierarchical and recursive fashion. Words are not just strung out one after another. Rather, they are organized into phrases, which themselves can be constituents of larger phrases, and so on—in principle, without any limit.

To see why that property is so important, suppose language did not have any syntax. Suppose that knowing how to speak a language were really just knowing a collection of words—lots of words, perhaps, but still a finite collection. In that case, speakers could talk only about a fixed range of things—namely, what they happen to have words for. Imagine you and I were at a baseball game, and our communication were restricted, somehow; to just such a finite collection of words. If the language did not have a specific word for "the third person in from the aisle in the front row of the upper deck," without syntax I could not refer to that specific individual. I might be able to say something like "catchperson!" and point to the spectator I meant. But with the resources of English, even without special words, I can tell you that "the third person in from the aisle in the front row of the upper deck caught Bonds's home run, but the guy behind him grabbed it away from him." You can understand all that instantly and unambiguously, even if neither one of us, or the individuals referred to, are present. And the reason I can put this expression together, and that you can understand it, is that we share the syntax of English.

What gives us the power to talk about an unlimited range of things, even though we only know a fixed set of words at any-one time, is our capacity for putting those words together into larger structures, the meanings of which are a function of both the meaning of the individual words and the way the words are put together. Thus we can make up new expressions of arbitrary complexity (such as the preceding sentence!) by putting together known pieces in regular ways.

Kanzi, a bonobo that can communicate via a symbol-laden keyboard, is at the center of the debate about whether nonhumans can acquire language.

Furthermore, the system of combination is recursive. What that means is that language users only need to know how to construct a limited number of different kinds of structures, because those structures can be used repeatedly as building blocks. Recursion enables speakers to build linguistic entities of unlimited complexity from a few basic patterns.

Among animals in the wild, there is simply no evidence that their communication incorporates any of these structures. Instead, communication is limited to a rather small, fixed set of "words." Vervet monkeys, for instance, distinguish among a small number of different predators (eagle, leopard, and snake) and warn their fellow monkeys with a few distinct calls of alarm. Some groups have even adapted certain calls to announce something like "unfamiliar human coming"; others have developed a call for warning of dogs accompanying human hunters. Impressive as those behaviors may be, such an augmentation of the call system happened slowly, and the system itself remains limited. What's more, vervets have no way of saying anything about "the leopard that almost sneaked up on us yesterday."

The most persuasive claims about animal language come not from observing animals in the wild, but from attempting to teach various species of great apes to communicate via sign language or electronic consoles of symbols. Perhaps the best-known such project is Francine (Penny) Patterson's effort to teach American Sign Language (ASL) to a gorilla named Koko. Koko is, by Patterson's account, the ape that "really" learned sign language, using it the way humans do—swearing, using metaphors, telling jokes, making puns. Unfortunately, we have nothing but Patterson's word for any of that. She says she has kept systematic records, but no one else has been able to study them. And without a way to assess Koko's behavior independently, the project is the best illustration imaginable of the adage that "the plural of 'anecdote' is not 'data.'"

Koko was a year old when Patterson began working with her in 1972. Patterson initially trained Koko by molding the gorilla's hands into the desired form, as she exposed the animal to whatever the sign symbolized. Koko caught on after a while and began to imitate. By the age of three and a half, Koko reportedly had acquired about a hundred signs, and by age five, almost 250.

Patterson also spoke aloud while signing, and it is reasonably clear that Koko's input was a kind of pidgin signed English rather than genuine ASL. That circumstance turns out to be a problem affecting several of the ape-language projects. Real ASL is a fully structured natural language, as expressively rich as English is. Hardly any of the investigators pursuing this research, however, have been fluent in ASL. As a result, the apes have not really been exposed to ASL, and so it is not surprising that they have come far short of learning it.

Since 1981, information about Koko has come only in forms such as *NOVA* or *National Geographic* television features, stories in the popular press, children's books, Internet chat sessions with Koko (mediated by Patterson, who acts as both interpreter and translator for the gorilla), and the ongoing public relations activities of Patterson's Gorilla Foundation. Such accounts make bold claims about how clever and articulate Koko is, but in the absence of evidence it is impossible to evaluate those claims.

And the information in the popular accounts does not inspire great confidence. Here is dialogue from a *NOVA* program filmed ten years after the start of the project (with translations for Koko's and Patterson's signing in capital letters):

Koko: YOU KOKO LOVE DO KNEE YOU

Patterson: KOKO LOVE WHAT?

Koko: LOVE THERE CHASE KNEE DO

Observer: The tree, she wants to play in it!

Patterson: No, the girl behind the tree!

Patterson's interpretation, that Koko wanted to chase the girl behind the tree, is not self-evident, to say the least.

Sue Savage-Rumbaugh, whom I quoted above, has undertaken—along with her husband Duane Rumbaugh and others—what has proved to be the most substantial attempt so far to teach language to apes. Their subject, a bonobo named Kanzi, presents the most serious and genuine challenge to those who doubt the linguistic capacities of any nonhuman animal. Kanzi displays fascinating cognitive abilities that have not been documented before in any nonhuman primate. Yet he still falls well short of what an animal would have to do to truly acquire the structural essence of a human language.

Monkeys can say nothing about "the leopard that almost sneaked up on us yesterday."

What sets Kanzi's experience apart is that no one tried to teach him ASL or any other naturally occurring language. Instead, Savage-Rumbaugh and her team taught him a completely artificial symbol system, based on associations between meanings and arbitrary graphic designs called lexigrams. The lexigrams were available to the animal on a computer keyboard. Thus instead of issuing a series of signing gestures with his hands, Kanzi was expected to press the keys corresponding to what he (presumably) meant to say.

Actually, the research did not begin with Kanzi, but with his mother, Matata. At first, Matata was to have been trained to use the lexigram keyboard, but she turned out to be a rather poor student. The experimenters spent many long training sessions pressing lexigram keys on a keyboard connected to a computer, and indicating the intended referent. The computer responded by lighting up the key and uttering the spoken English word, but the training seemed to get nowhere.

Then something remarkable happened. Matata's infant son, Kanzi, was too young to be separated from her during the training sessions. When he was about two-and-a-half years old, however, Matata was removed to another facility for breeding. Suddenly Kanzi emerged from her shadow. Even though he had had no explicit training at all, he had learned to use the lexigram keyboard in a systematic way. He would make the natural bonobo hand-clapping gesture to provoke chasing, for instance, and then immediately hit the CHASE lexigram on the keyboard.

From then on, the focus of study became the abilities Kanzi had developed without direct instruction. In his subsequent training, the keyboard was carried around, and the trainers would press lexigrams as they spoke in English about what they and the animals were doing. While tickling Kanzi, the teacher said, "Liz is tickling Kanzi," and pressed the three keyboard keys LIZ TICKLE KANZI. Kanzi himself used the keyboard freely to express objects he wanted, places he wanted to go, and things he wanted to do. The experimenters also tested Kanzi in more structured interactions, and Kanzi could still identify objects with lexigrams and vice versa.

By the time he was about four years old, Kanzi had roughly forty-four lexigrams in his productive vocabulary, and he could recognize the corresponding spoken English words. He performed almost flawlessly on double-blind tests that required him to match pictures, lexigrams, and spoken words. He also used his lexigrams in ways that clearly showed an extension from an initial, highly specific reference to a more generalized one. COKE, for instance, came to be used for all dark liquids, and BREAD for all kinds of bread—including taco shells.

Certainly further questions can be (and have been) raised about just what the lexigrams represent for Kanzi. Nearly all the lexigrams for which his comprehension can be tested are associated with objects, not actions, and so it is hard to assess the richness of his internal representations of meaning. Nevertheless, the lexigrams do appear to function as symbols, independent of specific exemplars or other contextual conditions. And there is no question that he has learned a collection of "words," in the sense that he has associated arbitrary shapes (the abstract lexigram patterns) with an arbitrary sound (the spoken English equivalent), and he has associated each of those with a meaning of some sort.

Assessing Kanzi's use of syntax is another matter. A major difficulty is that one must evaluate two different systems, those of language production and of language recognition. Kanzi's production centers on the keyboard; his recognition, on spoken English. To be sure not to underestimate Kanzi's abilities, one must examine both systems for evidence of syntactic understanding.

Kanzi uses his keyboard, but he does not produce enough multi-lexigram sequences to permit a detailed analysis of their structure. That is not to say he does not produce complex utterances. In addition to his keyed-in lexigrams, he expresses himself with a number of natural, highly iconic gestures, with meanings such as "come," "go," and "chase." He also employs pointing gestures to designate people, and he frequently combines a lexigram with a gesture to make a complex utterance.

Such combinations, taken out of context, might look like evidence for internalized rules of syntax. Kanzi does exhibit some reliable tendencies, such as combining words in certain orders: an action word precedes an agent word, a goal precedes an action, an object precedes an agent. But the full data make a semantic analysis of those orderings beside the point, because virtually all Kanzi's complex utterances follow a single rule: lexigram first, then gesture. The combining principle is intriguing, but it is not evidence of syntax, because it has nothing to do with the role that the "words" involved play in the meaning of a communication. It is as if, in English, we wrote the first word of the sentence, spoke the second, and emailed the third. Comparing the way the words were expressed, however, would tell us nothing about their meaning.

Because of such problems in interpreting his productions, arguments for Kanzi's command of syntax rely instead on his comprehension of spoken English. Investigators compared Kanzi's understanding with that of a child named Alia, the daughter of one of Kanzi's trainers. The two were studied at a similar stage of language development, at least in terms of the size of their vocabularies and the average length of their utterances.

Both Kanzi and Alia were quite skilled at responding appropriately to requests such as "put the ball on the pine needles," "put the ice water in the potty," "give the lighter to Rose," and "take the snake outdoors." Many of the actions requested (squeezing hot dogs, washing the TV, and the like) were entirely novel, so the subjects could not succeed simply by doing what one normally does with the object named.

The range of possibilities to which both Kanzi and Alia correctly responded was broad enough to show that each of them could form a conceptual representation of an action involving one, two, or more roles—that is, words could correspond to participants in action or locations of participants or actions. Both were then able to connect information in the utterance with those roles. Kanzi is the first nonhuman to show evidence for such an ability.

Kanzi can also make connections between word order and what the words express about the world. For example, he can distinguish between the sentences "make the doggie bite the snake" and "make the snake bite the doggie." His success, at a minimum, implies he must be sensitive to regularities in word order. Such an ability is unprecedented in studies of animal cognition. Still, it does not in itself prove that Kanzi represents sentences in terms of the kind of structure that characterize human understanding of language.

Remarkably, Kanzi can distinguish "make the doggie bite the snake" from "make the snake bite the doggie."

In contrast, when the understanding of a sentence depends on "grammatical" words, such as prepositions or conjunctions, Kanzi's performance is quite poor. He does not seem to distinguish between putting something *in, on,* or *next to* something else. Sentences in which the word *and* links two nouns (as in "give the peas and the sweet potatoes to Kelly,") or two sentences (as in "go to the refrigerator and get the banana") frequenly lead to mistakes that suggest Kanzi cannot interpret such words.

It is also not clear that Kanzi can understand subordinating conjunctions, such as *that* or *which.* It is true that he can correcdy respond to sentences such as: "Go get the carrot that's in the microwave." But appropriate behavior alone does not imply that he has understood the sentence as having a hierarchical structure with an embedded clause, specifying a particular carrot (the one in the microwave) rather than any other (such as one on the counter or on the floor). The content words alone ("go," "get," "carrot," "microwave") are enough to convey the command: "carrot" has to be the object of "go get," but "microwave" has no role to play in that action and can only be interpreted as a property of the carrot (its location). Kanzi needn't understand the grammar to get the right carrot.

Concrete verbs and nouns correspond to observable actions and things in the world, and they can constitute the meanings of symbols for Kanzi. Prepositions and conjunctions, however, are important because they govern how words and phrases relate to one another. Kanzi can associate lexigrams and some spoken words with parts of complex concepts in his mind, but words that are solely grammatical in content can only be ignored, because he has no grammar in which they might play a role.

What then does it mean to use a natural language? Here is a classic example: "The chickens are ready to eat." The sentence has two strikingly different interpretations, but the ambiguity has nothing to do with grammatical words, ambiguous words, or the multiple ways of organizing words into phrases. One interpretation is that someone has chickens that are ready for people to eat. The other interpretation is that some chickens are hungry.

The point is that the syntax of a language involves more than merely combining elements into sequences of words. Sentences incorporate that kind of structure, to be sure, but they also have much more structure, involving abstractions that are not readily apparent in the superficial form of the sentence—abstractions that allow the same group of words to communicate very different pieces of information in systematic ways.

As speakers of a natural language, we manage such abstractions without noticing them. But without them, language would not be the flexible instrument of expression and communication that it is. Perhaps that is the most important "take-home lesson" from the studies of animal communication. Nonhuman animals lack the kind of system that linguists are still hard at work trying to understand, and without such a capacity, animals can communicate only in much more restricted ways. The ability to use language is probably grounded in the biological nature that makes us the particular animal we are.

Reprinted from *Natural History,* November 2004, pp. 38–43. Adapted from the book *Doctor Dolittle's Delusion: Animals and the Uniqueness of Human Language* by Stephen R. Anderson. Copyright 2004 by Yale University Press. Reprinted by permission.

UNIT 3

Sex and Gender

Unit Selections

Key Points to Consider

- Why is friendship important to olive baboons? What implications does this have for the origin of pair-bonding?

- Under what circumstances are female primates more likely than males to express territoriality?

- How does the study of bonobo sexual behavior help us understand human evolution?

- How do social bonds help provide protection to female apes against abusive male apes?

Student Website

www.mhcls.com

Internet References

American Anthropologist
   http://www.aaanet.org/aa/index.htm

American Scientist
   http://www.amsci.org/amsci.html

Bonobo Sex and Society
   http://songweaver.com/info/bonobos.html

Any account of hominid evolution would be remiss if it did not attempt to explain that which is most mystifying of all human experiences—our sexuality. No other aspect of humanity—whether it be upright posture, tool-making ability, or intelligence in general—seems to elude our intellectual grasp at least as much as it dominates our subjective consciousness. While we are a long way from reaching a consensus as to why it arose and what it is all about, there is widespread agreement that our very preoccupation with sex is in itself one of the hallmarks of being human. Even as we experience it and analyze it, we exalt it and condemn it. Beyond seemingly irrational fixations, however, there is the further tendency to project our own values onto the observations we make and the data we collect.

There are many who argue quite reasonably that the human bias has been more male-oriented than otherwise and that the recent "feminization" of anthropology has resulted in new kinds of research and refreshingly new, theoretical perspectives. Not only should we consider the source when evaluating the old theories, but we should also welcome the source when considering the new.

One reason for studying the sexual and social lives of primates is that they allow us to test certain notions too often taken for granted. For instance, Barbara Smuts, in "What Are Friends For?" reveals that friendship bonds, as illustrated by the olive baboons of East Africa, have little if anything to do with a sex-based division of labor or with sexual exclusivity between a pair-bonded male and female. Smuts challenges the traditional male-oriented idea that primate societies are dominated solely by males and for males.

To take another example, traditional theory would have predicted that male primates are the natural aggressors when territoriality is an issue for a primate troop, especially since they tend to be less pre-occupied with caring for infants. Instead, Marina Cords has found, as a result of her career-long research of the blue monkeys of Kenya, that it is the females that lead the attack and that they probably do so because there is more at stake for them with respect to available resources than there is for males. This just goes to show that, even among monkeys, nothing can be taken for granted.

Finally, there is the question of the social significance of sexuality in humans. In "Mothers and Others," Sarah Blaffer Hrdy points out that reproductive success often depends upon how much assistance the mother gets from others, including males. In "What's Love Got to Do With It?" Meredith Small shows that

© Brand X Pictures/PunchStock

the chimp-like bonobos of Zaire use sex to reduce tensions and cement social relations and, in so doing, have achieved a high degree of equality between the sexes. Whether we see parallels in the human species, says Small, depends on our willingness to interpret bonobo behavior as a "modern version of our own ancestors' sex play," and this, in turn, may depend on our prior theoretical beliefs.

What Are Friends For?

Among East African baboons, friendship means companions, health, safety . . . and, sometimes, sex.

Barbara Smuts

Virgil, a burly adult male olive baboon, closely followed Zizi, a middle-aged female easily distinguished by her grizzled coat and square muzzle. On her rump Zizi sported a bright pink swelling, indicating that she was sexually receptive and probably fertile. Virgil's extreme attentiveness to Zizi suggested to me—and all rival males in the troop—that he was her current and exclusive mate.

Zizi, however, apparently had something else in mind. She broke away from Virgil, moved rapidly through the troop, and presented her alluring sexual swelling to one male after another. Before Virgil caught up with her, she had managed to announce her receptive condition to several of his rivals. When Virgil tried to grab her, Zizi screamed and dashed into the bushes with Virgil in hot pursuit. I heard sounds of chasing and fighting coming from the thicket. Moments later Zizi emerged from the bushes with an older male named Cyclops. They remained together for several days, copulating often. In Cyclops's presence, Zizi no longer approached or even glanced at other males.

Primatologists describe Zizi and other olive baboons (*Papio cynocephalus anubis*) as promiscuous, meaning that both males and females usually mate with several members of the opposite sex within a short period of time. Promiscuous mating behavior characterizes many of the larger, more familiar primates, including chimpanzees, rhesus macaques, and gray langurs, as well as olive, yellow, and chacma baboons, the three subspecies of savanna baboon. In colloquial usage, promiscuity often connotes wanton and random sex, and several early studies of primates supported this stereotype. However, after years of laboriously recording thousands of copulations under natural conditions, the Peeping Toms of primate fieldwork have shown that, even in promiscuous species, sexual pairings are far from random.

Some adult males, for example, typically copulate much more often than others. Primatologists have explained these differences in terms of competition: the most dominant males monopolize females and prevent lower-ranking rivals from mating. But exceptions are frequent. Among baboons, the exceptions often involve scruffy, older males who mate in full view of younger, more dominant rivals.

A clue to the reason for these puzzling exceptions emerged when primatologists began to question an implicit assumption of the dominance hypothesis—that females were merely passive objects of male competition. But what if females were active arbiters in this system? If females preferred some males over others and were able to express these preferences, then models of mating activity based on male dominance alone would be far too simple.

Once researchers recognized the possibility of female choice, evidence for it turned up in species after species. The story of Zizi, Virgil, and Cyclops is one of hundreds of examples of female primates rejecting the sexual advances of particular males and enthusiastically cooperating with others. But what is the basis for female choice? Why might they prefer some males over others?

This question guided my research on the Eburru Cliffs troop of olive baboons, named after one of their favorite sleeping sites, a sheer rocky outcrop rising several hundred feet above the floor of the Great Rift Valley, about 100 miles northwest of Nairobi, Kenya. The 120 members of Eburru Cliffs spent their days wandering through open grassland studded with occasional acacia thorn trees. Each night they retired to one of a dozen sets of cliffs that provided protection from nocturnal predators such as leopards.

Most previous studies of baboon sexuality had focused on females who, like Zizi, were at the peak of sexual receptivity. A female baboon does not mate when she is pregnant or lactating, a period of abstinence lasting about eighteen months. The female then goes into estrus, and for about two weeks out of every thirty-five-day cycle, she mates. Toward the end of this two-week period she may ovulate, but usually the female undergoes four or five estrous cycles before she conceives. During pregnancy, she once again resumes a chaste existence. As a result, the typical female baboon is sexually active for less than 10 percent of her adult life. I thought that by focusing on the other 90 percent, I might learn something new. In particular, I suspected that routine, day-to-day relationships between males and pregnant or lactating (nonestrous) females might provide clues to female mating preferences.

Nearly every day for sixteen months, I joined the Eburru Cliffs baboons at their sleeping cliffs at dawn and traveled several miles with them while they foraged for roots, seeds, grass, and occasionally, small prey items, such as baby gazelles or hares (see "Predatory Baboons of Kekopey," *Natural History,* March 1976). Like all savanna baboon troops, Eburru Cliffs functioned as a cohesive unit organized around a core of related females, all of whom were born in the troop. Unlike the females, male savanna baboons leave their natal troop to join another where they may remain for many years, so most of the Eburru Cliffs adult males were immigrants. Since membership in the troop remained relatively constant during the period of my study, I learned to identify each individual. I relied on differences in size, posture, gait, and especially, facial features. To the practiced observer, baboons look as different from one another as human beings do.

As soon as I could recognize individuals, I noticed that particular females tended to turn up near particular males again and again. I came to think of these pairs as friends. Friendship among animals is not a well-documented phenomenon, so to convince skeptical colleagues that baboon friendship was real, I needed to develop objective criteria for distinguishing friendly pairs.

I began by investigating grooming, the amiable simian habit of picking through a companion's fur to remove dead skin and ectoparasites (see "Little Things That Tick Off Baboons," *Natural History,* February 1984). Baboons spend much more time grooming than is necessary for hygiene, and previous research had indicated that it is a good measure of social bonds.

Although eighteen adult males lived in the troop, each nonestrous female performed most of her grooming with just one, two, or occasionally, three males. For example, of Zizi's twenty-four grooming bouts with males, Cyclops accounted for thirteen, and a second male, Sherlock, accounted for all the rest. Different females tended to favor different males as grooming partners.

Another measure of social bonds was simply who was observed near whom. When foraging, traveling, or resting, each pregnant or lactating female spent a lot of time near a few males and associated with the others no more often than expected by chance. When I compared the identities of favorite grooming partners and frequent companions, they overlapped almost completely. This enabled me to develop a formal definition of friendship: any male that scored high on both grooming and proximity measures was considered a friend.

Virtually all baboons made friends; only one female and three males who had most recently joined the troop lacked such companions. Out of more than 600 possible adult female-adult male pairs in the troop, however, only about one in ten qualified as friends; these really were special relationships.

Several factors seemed to influence which baboons paired up. In most cases, friends were unrelated to each other, since the male had immigrated from another troop. (Four friendships, however, involved a female and an adolescent son who had not yet emigrated. Unlike other friends, these related pairs never mated.) Older females tended to be friends with older males; younger females with younger males. I witnessed occasional May–December romances, usually involving older females and young adult males. Adolescent males and females were strongly rule-bound, and with the exception of mother-son pairs, they formed friendships only with one another.

Regardless of age or dominance rank, most females had just one or two male friends. But among males, the number of female friends varied greatly from none to eight. Although high-ranking males enjoyed priority of access to food and sometimes mates, dominant males did not have more female friends than low-ranking males. Instead it was the older males who had lived in the troop for many years who had the most friends. When a male had several female friends, the females were often closely related to one another. Since female baboons spend a lot of time near their kin, it is probably easier for a male to maintain bonds with several related females at once.

When collecting data, I focused on one nonestrous female at a time and kept track of her every movement toward or away from any male; similarly, I noted every male who moved toward or away from her. Whenever the female and male moved close enough to exchange intimacies, I wrote down exactly what happened. When foraging together, friends tended to remain a few yards apart. Males more often wandered away from females than the reverse, and females, more often than males, closed the gap. The female behaved as if she wanted to keep the male within calling distance, in case she needed his protection. The male, however, was more likely to make approaches that brought them within actual touching distance. Often, he would plunk himself down right next to his friend and ask her to groom him by holding a pose with exaggerated stillness. The female sometimes responded by grooming, but more often, she exhibited the most reliable sign of true intimacy: she ignored her friend and simply continued whatever she was doing.

In sharp contrast, when a male who was not a friend moved close to a female, she dared not ignore him. She stopped whatever she was doing and held still, often glancing surreptitiously at the intruder. If he did not move away, she sometimes lifted her tail and presented her rump. When a female is not in estrus, this is a gesture of appeasement, not sexual enticement. Immediately after this respectful acknowledgement of his presence, the female would slip away. But such tense interactions with non-friend males were rare, because females usually moved away before the males came too close.

These observations suggest that females were afraid of most of the males in their troop, which is not surprising: male baboons are twice the size of females, and their canines are longer and sharper than those of a lion. All Eburru Cliffs males directed both mild and severe aggression toward females. Mild aggression, which usually involved threats and chases but no body contact, occurred most often during feeding competition or when the male redirected aggression toward a female after losing a fight with another male. Females and juveniles showed aggression toward other females and juveniles in similar circumstances and occasionally inflicted superficial wounds. Severe aggression by males, which involved body contact and sometimes biting, was less common and also more puzzling, since there was no apparent cause.

An explanation for at least some of these attacks emerged one day when I was watching Pegasus, a young adult male, and his friend Cicily, sitting together in the middle of a small clearing. Cicily moved to the edge of the clearing to feed, and a higher-ranking female, Zora, suddenly attacked her. Pegasus stood up and looked as if he were about to intervene when both females disappeared into the bushes. He sat back down, and I remained with him. A full ten minutes later, Zora appeared at the edge of the clearing; this was the first time she had come into view since her attack on Cicily. Pegasus instantly pounced on Zora, repeatedly grabbed her neck in his mouth and lifted her off the ground, shook her whole body, and then dropped her. Zora screamed continuously and tried to escape. Each time, Pegasus caught her and continued his brutal attack. When he finally released her five minutes later she had a deep canine gash on the palm of her hand that made her limp for several days.

This attack was similar in form and intensity to those I had seen before and labeled "unprovoked." Certainly, had I come upon the scene after Zora's aggression toward Cicily, I would not have understood why Pegasus attacked Zora. This suggested that some, perhaps many, severe attacks by males actually represented punishment for actions that had occurred some time before.

Whatever the reasons for male attacks on females, they represent a serious threat. Records of fresh injuries indicated that Eburru Cliffs adult females received canine slash wounds from males at the rate of one for every female each year, and during my study, one female died of her injuries. Males probably pose an even greater threat to infants. Although only one infant was killed during my study, observers in Botswana and Tanzania have seen recent male immigrants kill several young infants.

Protection from male aggression, and from the less injurious but more frequent aggression of other females and juveniles, seems to be one of the main advantages of friendship for a female baboon. Seventy times I observed an adult male defend a female or her offspring against aggression by another troop member, not infrequently a high-ranking male. In all but six of these cases, the defender was a friend. Very few of these confrontations involved actual fighting; no male baboon, subordinate or dominant, is anxious to risk injury by the sharp canines of another.

Males are particularly solicitous guardians of their friends' youngest infants. If another male gets too close to an infant or if a juvenile female plays with it too roughly, the friend may intervene. Other troop members soon learn to be cautious when the mother's friend is nearby, and his presence provides the mother with a welcome respite from the annoying pokes and prods of curious females and juveniles obsessed with the new baby. Male baboons at Gombe Park in Tanzania and Amboseli Park in Kenya have also been seen rescuing infants from chimpanzees and lions. These several forms of male protection help to explain why females in Eburru Cliffs stuck closer to their friends in the first few months after giving birth than at any other time.

The male-infant relationship develops out of the male's friendship with the mother, but as the infant matures, this new bond takes on a life of its own. My co-worker Nancy Nicolson found that by about nine months of age, infants actively sought out their male friends when the mother was a few yards away,

suggesting that the male may function as an alternative care-giver. This seemed to be especially true for infants undergoing unusually early or severe weaning. (Weaning is generally a gradual, prolonged process, but there is tremendous variation among mothers in the timing and intensity of weaning. See "Mother Baboons," *Natural History,* September 1980). After being rejected by the mother, the crying infant often approached the male friend and sat huddled against him until its whimpers subsided. Two of the infants in Eburru Cliffs lost their mothers when they were still quite young. In each case, their bond with the mother's friend subsequently intensified, and—perhaps as a result—both infants survived.

A close bond with a male may also improve the infant's nutrition. Larger than all other troop members, adult males monopolize the best feeding sites. In general, the personal space surrounding a feeding male is inviolate, but he usually tolerates intrusions by the infants of his female friends, giving them access to choice feeding spots.

Although infants follow their male friends around rather than the reverse, the males seem genuinely attached to their tiny companions. During feeding, the male and infant express their pleasure in each other's company by sharing spirited, antiphonal grunting duets. If the infant whimpers in distress, the male friend is likely to cease feeding, look at the infant, and grunt softly, as if in sympathy, until the whimpers cease. When the male rests, the infants of his female friends may huddle behind him, one after the other, forming a "train," or, if feeling energetic, they may use his body as a trampoline.

When I returned to Eburru Cliffs four years after my initial study ended, several of the bonds formed between males and the infants of their female friends were still intact (in other cases, either the male or the infant or both had disappeared). When these bonds involved recently matured females, their long-time male associates showed no sexual interest in them, even though the females mated with other adult males. Mothers and sons, and usually maternal siblings, show similar sexual inhibitions in baboons and many other primate species.

The development of an intimate relationship between a male and the infant of his female friend raises an obvious question: Is the male the infant's father? To answer this question definitely we would need to conduct genetic analysis, which was not possible for these baboons. Instead, I estimated paternity probabilities from observations of the temporary (a few hours or days) exclusive mating relationships, or consortships, that estrous females form with a series of different males. These estimates were apt to be fairly accurate, since changes in the female's sexual swelling allow one to pinpoint the timing of conception to within a few days. Most females consorted with only two or three males during this period, and these males were termed likely fathers.

In about half the friendships, the male was indeed likely to be the father of his friend's most recent infant, but in the other half he was not—in fact, he had never been seen mating with the female. Interestingly, males who were friends with the mother but not likely fathers nearly always developed a relationship with her infant, while males who had mated with the female but were not her friend usually did not. Thus friendship with the mother, rather than paternity, seems to mediate the development of male-infant bonds. Recently, a similar pattern was documented for South American capuchin monkeys in a laboratory study in which paternity was determined genetically.

These results fly in the face of a prominent theory that claims males will invest in infants only when they are closely related. If males are not fostering the survival of their own genes by caring for the infant, then why do they do so? I suspected that the key was female choice. If females preferred to mate with males who had already demonstrated friendly behavior, then friendships with mothers and their infants might pay off in the future when the mothers were ready to mate again.

To find out if this was the case, I examined each male's sexual behavior with females he had befriended before they resumed estrus. In most cases, males consorted considerably more often with their friends than with other females. Baboon females typically mate with several different males, including both friends and nonfriends, but prior friendship increased a male's probability of mating with a female above what it would have been otherwise.

This increased probability seemed to reflect female preferences. Females occasionally overtly advertised their disdain for certain males and their desire for others. Zizi's behavior, described above, is a good example. Virgil was not one of her friends, but Cyclops was. Usually, however, females expressed preferences and aversions more subtly. For example, Delphi, a petite adolescent female, found herself pursued by Hector, a middle-aged adult male. She did not run away or refuse to mate with him, but whenever he wasn't watching, she looked around for her friend Homer, an adolescent male. When she succeeded in catching Homer's eye, she narrowed her eyes and flattened her ears against her skull, the friendliest face one baboon can send another. This told Homer she would rather be with him. Females expressed satisfaction with a current consort partner by staying close to him, initiating copulations, and not making advances toward other males. Baboons are very sensitive to such cues, as indicated by an experimental study in which rival hamadryas baboons rarely challenged a male-female pair if the female strongly preferred her current partner. Similarly, in Eburru Cliffs, males were less apt to challenge consorts involving a pair that shared a long-term friendship.

Even though females usually consorted with their friends, they also mated with other males, so it is not surprising that friendships were most vulnerable during periods of sexual activity. In a few cases, the female consorted with another male more often than with her friend, but the friendship survived nevertheless. One female, however, formed a strong sexual bond with a new male. This bond persisted after conception, replacing her previous friendship. My observations suggest that adolescent and young adult females tend to have shorter, less stable friendships than do older females. Some friendships, however, last a very long time. When I returned to Eburru Cliffs six years after my study began, five couples were still together. It is possible that friendships occasionally last for life (baboons probably live twenty to thirty years in the wild), but it will require longer studies, and some very patient scientists to find out.

By increasing both the male's chances of mating in the future and the likelihood that a female's infant will survive, friendship contributes to the reproductive success of both partners. This clarifies the evolutionary basis of friendship-forming tendencies in baboons, but what does friendship mean to a baboon? To answer this question we need to view baboons as sentient beings with feelings and goals not unlike our own in similar circumstances. Consider, for example, the friendship between Thalia and Alexander.

The affair began one evening as Alex and Thalia sat about fifteen feet apart on the sleeping cliffs. It was like watching two novices in a singles bar. Alex stared at Thalia until she turned and almost caught him looking at her. He glanced away immediately, and then she stared at him until his head began to turn toward her. She suddenly became engrossed in grooming her toes. But as soon as Alex looked away, her gaze returned to him. They went on like this for more than fifteen minutes, always with split-second timing. Finally, Alex managed to catch Thalia looking at him. He made the friendly eyes-narrowed, ears-back face and smacked his lips together rhythmically. Thalia froze, and for a second she looked into his eyes. Alex approached, and Thalia, still nervous, groomed him. Soon she calmed down, and I found them still together on the cliffs the next morning. Looking back on this event months later, I realized that it marked the beginning of their friendship. Six years later, when I returned to Eburru Cliffs, they were still friends.

If flirtation forms an integral part of baboon friendship, so does jealousy. Overt displays of jealousy, such as chasing a friend away from a potential rival, occur occasionally, but like humans, baboons often express their emotions in more subtle ways. One evening a colleague and I climbed the cliffs and settled down near Sherlock, who was friends with Cybelle, a middle-aged female still foraging on the ground below the cliffs. I observed Cybelle while my colleague watched Sherlock, and we kept up a running commentary. As long as Cybelle was feeding or interacting with females, Sherlock was relaxed, but each time she approached another male, his body would stiffen, and he would stare intently at the scene below. When Cybelle presented politely to a male who had recently tried to befriend her, Sherlock even made threatening sounds under his breath. Cybelle was not in estrus at the time, indicating that male baboon jealousy extends beyond the sexual arena to include affiliative interactions between a female friend and other males.

Because baboon friendships are embedded in a network of friendly and antagonistic relationships, they inevitably lead to repercussions extending beyond the pair. For example, Virgil once provoked his weaker rival Cyclops into a fight by first attacking Cyclops's friend Phoebe. On another occasion, Sherlock chased Circe, Hector's best friend, just after Hector had chased Antigone, Sherlock's friend.

In another incident, the prime adult male Triton challenged Cyclops's possession of meat. Cyclops grew increasingly tense and seemed about to abandon the prey to the younger male. Then Cyclops's friend Phoebe appeared with her infant Phyllis. Phyllis wandered over to Cyclops. He immediately grabbed her, held her close, and threatened Triton away from the prey. Because any challenge to Cyclops now involved a threat to

Phyllis as well, Triton risked being mobbed by Phoebe and her relatives and friends. For this reason, he backed down. Males frequently use the infants of their female friends as buffers in this way. Thus, friendship involves costs as well as benefits because it makes the participants vulnerable to social manipulation or redirected aggression by others.

Finally, as with humans, friendship seems to mean something different to each baboon. Several females in Eburru Cliffs had only one friend. They were devoted companions. Louise and Pandora, for example, groomed their friend Virgil and no other male. Then there was Leda, who, with five friends, spread herself more thinly than any other female. These contrasting patterns of friendship were associated with striking personality differences. Louise and Pandora were unobtrusive females who hung around quietly with Virgil and their close relatives. Leda seemed to be everywhere at once, playing with infants, fighting with juveniles, and making friends with males. Similar differences were apparent among the males. Some devoted a great deal of time and energy to cultivating friendships with females, while others focused more on challenging other males. Although we probably will never fully understand the basis of these individual differences, they contribute immeasurably to the richness and complexity of baboon society.

Male-female friendships may be widespread among primates. They have been reported for many other groups of savanna baboons, and they also occur in rhesus and Japanese Macaques, capuchin monkeys, and perhaps in bonobos (pygmy chimpanzees). These relationships should give us pause when considering popular scenarios for the evolution of male-female relationships in humans. Most of these scenarios assume that, except for mating, males and females had little to do with one another until the development of a sexual division of labor, when, the story goes, females began to rely on males to provide meat in exchange for gathered food. This, it has been argued,

set up new selection pressures favoring the development of long-term bonds between individual males and females, female sexual fidelity, and as paternity certainty increased, greater male investment in the offspring of these unions. In other words, once women began to gather and men to hunt, presto—we had the nuclear family.

This scenario may have more to do with cultural biases about women's economic dependence on men and idealized views of the nuclear family than with the actual behavior of our hominid ancestors. The nonhuman primate evidence challenges this story in at least three ways.

First, long-term bonds between the sexes can evolve in the absence of a sexual division of labor of food sharing. In our primate relatives, such relationships rest on exchanges of social, not economic, benefits.

Second, primate research shows that highly differentiated, emotionally intense male-female relationships can occur without sexual exclusivity. Ancestral men and women may have experienced intimate friendships long before they invented marriage and norms of sexual fidelity.

Third, among our closest primate relatives, males clearly provide mothers and infants with social benefits even when they are unlikely to be the fathers of those infants. In return, females provide a variety of benefits to the friendly males, including acceptance into the group and, at least in baboons, increased mating opportunities in the future. This suggests that efforts to reconstruct the evolution of hominid societies may have overemphasized what the female must supposedly do (restrict her mating to just one male) in order to obtain male parental investment.

Maybe it is time to pay more attention to what the male must do (provide benefits to females and young) in order to obtain female cooperation. Perhaps among our ancestors, as in baboons today, sex and friendship went hand in hand. As for marriage—well, that's another story.

From *Natural History*, February 1987, pp. 36, 38–44. Copyright © 1987 by Natural History Magazine. Reprinted by permission.

Face-Offs of the Female Kind

Turf battles between gangs of female blue monkeys reveal a complex social organization.

MARINA CORDS

U rgent, low-pitched growls emanate from dense foliage in the Kakamega Forest in western Kenya. The growls are punctuated by birdlike chirps and, every so often, a deep, resonant boom. The sounds get louder as two groups of blue monkeys, which are gray and black rather than blue, face off across an invisible line in the tangle of branches. Each group is about forty strong. In the front lines are adult females, the size of house cats, literally shoulder to shoulder, glaring and threatening. The opposing phalanxes move in parallel, sometimes pushing forward, sometimes retreating. Individual "soldiers" join and leave the front ranks; behind them, others—adult females, the juveniles, and the group's one resident male—chirp and growl in support, or simply sit and watch. Still others, usually at a distance from the commotion, seem completely unconcerned and uninvolved in the battle. In my fieldwork on blue monkeys (*Cercopithccus mitis*), my colleagues and I have witnessed fierce encounters of that kind every month or so, while less dramatic confrontations, such as a couple of animals growling at their neighbors, occur every day or two. What's in dispute is territory, territory that contains the fruits, insects, flowers, and leaves that make up most of the diet of these monkeys. The battles are remarkable both for the ganglike cohesiveness they bring to what can otherwise seem a scattered, unconnected group, and for the intensity of the aggression that can erupt among females with normally peaceful demeanors. For it is the females that participate in these turf wars, grabbing and biting their opponents when aggressive threats are not enough.

Chimpanzees, our close relatives, are sometimes compared to politicians: they engage in power plays; they use diplomacy; they assign perks to various positions in a complicated social hierarchy. Blue monkeys, which seem calmer and less prone to form coalitions, appear to be more egalitarian. And yet my study of the group dynamics of territorial battles, and how these may figure into the way a group later splits into smaller new groups, has revealed unexpected complexity in blue monkey social structure. As in some human political organizations, those on top may depend more on those at the bottom than first meets the eye.

T he feeding territories over which blue monkeys battle are often so specific that a person could draw lines to demarcate them: this tree belongs to this group, the next tree over doesn't. Groups can coexist peacefully very near one another as long as each stays on its side of these imaginary lines.

Territorial behavior occurs in many animals that defend feeding grounds, breeding areas, and in a few cases, courtship arenas. Among primates, territorial defense is just one way a group cooperates to compete with the neighbors. Not all primates are territorial in the way blue monkeys are, defending a specific piece of land. However, many primate groups react aggressively toward neighboring groups wherever they meet. Biologists would not call such populations territorial, but there is nevertheless cooperative defense of resources.

Quite a few researchers have investigated what certain primate species fight over; less often have they looked at how group members differ in their participation. Of those studies, almost all involve species in which the males do most of the fighting. My study focused on the question of why certain individual females did the fighting.

At first glance, it seems unfair that only some members of a blue monkey group would fight to defend a food supply that benefits all the group members—an effort that economists call "collective action for a public good." Indeed, those monkeys that sit out the battles are getting a free ride. As a matter of fact, any individual monkey would seem well advised to avoid joining an intergroup battle: it's a way to get the benefit (more food) without paying any cost (potential injury or even death).

The most severe wounds I've seen a female sustain in my twenty-nine years of study occurred during a group battle. For more than an hour, members of the front lines had taken each other on, sometimes grappling fiercely in a tangle as a roar of growls, chirps, and loud screams erupted. When the losing group finally retreated, I moved forward to get a closer look. Normally monkeys are wary of people, so I was amazed that I could come within six feet of an adult female. She was breathing heavily as she lay prostrate on some low branches, just level with my eyes. Her body was covered with flecks of blood—she must have been bitten all over, severely and repeatedly. Only after lying perfectly still for a half hour did she pull herself together and slowly move off to a safer distance.

More recently, in another prolonged, loud, and vicious group fight, another female had the skin ripped off the back of her calf, starting from the knee. The skin bunched down at her ankle like a frilly bobby sock, leaving the red calf muscle fully exposed; eventually she limped away, though carefully and in obvious pain. Both of those animals survived their injuries, but that was a matter of chance: open wounds in a tropical environment can become infected and lead to death.

And yet, if every monkey chose to take a free ride to avoid such risks, no cooperative territorial defense would occur, and all would lose out. This dilemma is what economists refer to as a "collective action problem." Evolutionary biologists think in a parallel manner, because natural selection should act on animal decision making in a way that maximizes individual fitness. In other words, natural selection should favor selfish and self-protective decision making, which maximizes an individual's chances to survive and reproduce. If taking a free ride offers the best deal to the individual, collective action should always fall apart.

To understand from an evolutionary perspective why some members of a group of blue monkeys fight even though others ride free, it seems that there must be additional important factors that a simple model of cooperation does not take into account. For one thing, individual group members are not identical: one might expect some difference in participation if the costs and benefits of territorial defense are not the same for all potential participants.

Over a five-year period, my colleagues and I monitored individuals' participation in territorial encounters in five study groups of the blue monkey subspecies *C.m. stuhimanni* in the Kakamega Forest to see if such disparities in individuals' costs and benefits offered a compelling explanation for divergences in participation. As noted before, adult females regularly joined the fray, while adult males engaged infrequently—and when they did, it was mostly to vocalize from the back lines. (Although each blue monkey group usually contains only one resident adult male, an influx of male adults sometimes swells the group during the three- to five-month breeding season.) Juveniles were less likely than adults to get involved in the intergroup aggression; generally, however, the older the juveniles were, the more likely they were to join in. At every age, juvenile females participated more than juvenile males—foreshadowing the adult pattern.

We can in fact begin to explain these results in terms of the relative costs and benefits of participating in intergroup battles. From an evolutionary perspective, the relative reproductive success of female mammals is limited mainly by access to food: enduring a pregnancy, and in particular, lactating to support a growing infant, are energy-intensive life stages limited to adult females. Thus females have especially much to gain from defending a source of food, and it makes sense that they are more involved than males in defending feeding territories.

In contrast to females, the relative reproductive success of male mammals depends mainly on their access to female mates, at least in cases where paternal care is minimal (as is the case in blue monkeys). When male primates participate in intergroup aggression, they are usually defending mates, not food. Some exceptions to this generalization have recently been discovered: Eastern black-and-white colobus monkey males seem to defend feeding areas directly, for example. But researchers believe this may actually be a way to attract potential mates, rather than a defense of feeding grounds for their own sake. In blue monkeys, however, males are obviously less involved in battles between groups than females are, and it seems clear that defending rood sources is not one of their strategies for attracting mates. The age-related difference in participation, by contrast, may reflect the differing risk to individuals. Given the potential for extreme violence, smaller and more vulnerable individuals may be less inclined to take a risk. Not only juvenile monkeys, but also females with infants, are less likely to take part in intergroup aggression. This observation is also consistent with the idea that individuals make decisions based on their personal risks: a female carrying an infant is probably less agile in the branches, and agility is at a premium in the fast-moving action of escalated encounters.

Why, then, do females of higher rank in the dominance hierarchy participate more in territorial battles than do those of lower rank? Rank structure in blue monkeys is linear: if A is dominant to B and B is dominant to C, then A is dominant to C as well. In that respect blue monkey hierarchies resemble those of many other Old World monkeys, such as the rhesus macaque and the baboon. What's different is that blue monkey rank structure is less "in your face": dominance interactions are rare, especially those more aggressive ones in which there is a clear loser. Instead, dominance is revealed over the long term by how a lower-ranking individual will tend to avoid a higher-ranking one or withdraw in her favor. It's a muted dance of approach and retreat in which the dancers perform occasionally. In fact, only after piecing together years of observations to detect repeated patterns did we perceive a hierarchy in blue monkeys at all.

Rank is generally a poor predictor of female blue monkey behavior, so we had not expected dominance rank to play a role during territorial battles. For example, females of lower rank do not travel more or farther to get food, do not spend more time feeding, and do not have a lower-quality diet than those of higher rank. Nor do they occupy spatial positions in trees (at the edges of a tree's crown) or in the group as a whole (on the edge of the group) that would expose them more to predators. Most important, there is no evidence that they breed less successfully: neither the rate at which they produce offspring nor the survival of their infants suffers compared with that of higher-ranking females.

If high-ranking females possessed an advantage in any of those ways, one might understand their greater participation in group battles: they are the animals with the most to gain. But for blue monkeys there must be a more subtle explanation.

I can suggest two possibilities. The first is that participation in cooperative territorial defense is traded for other social services. Here behavioral biologists use another economics analogy: the idea that cooperative exchange can involve multiple "currencies." At the simplest level, one animal takes on the risks of an intergroup battle, while another pays back with a different social good. In some primate species, teaming up in aggressive alliances to sort out squabbles within a group is a significant service provided by friends, but in blue monkeys this seems too rare to be important. Other obvious contenders are social grooming, or perhaps tolerance while feeding: a monkey is allowed to feed undisturbed, rather than be chased away by a higher-ranking group member. And, for reasons that are as yet unclear, high- and low-ranking animals "play" with different currencies. At present we don't know whether such exchanges occur, but our team is monitoring exchange in all three currencies (territorial fighting, grooming, and feeding tolerance) to find out.

When two animals exchange services with each other, reciprocity is direct: I give something to you, and you pay me back in some way. But reciprocity can also be indirect, when an individual provides services to another and is paid back (whether in the same currency or not) by a third party or parties. In theoretical models, indirect reciprocity can persist when individuals have reputations, and when their fate in a marketplace of social partners depends on their reputations. Both theoretical models and experiments with human players suggest that investment in reputation occurs. For example, human subjects will donate to a public good if doing so enhances their reputation, and if others can use information about their reputation to make decisions about cooperating with them in the future. So, contribution to the public good can eventually bring benefits to the contributor, lessening the temptation to ride free. Whether nonhuman primates attend to reputations or practice indirect reciprocity is, however, currently unknown.

The second potential explanation for why high-ranking females fight invokes the theory of "reproductive skew." This theory was originally devised to explain how reproduction is distributed among the members of a society. One might ask, for example, why high-ranking individuals do not always prevent lower-ranking ones from reproducing. A possible answer to this question is that lower-ranking individuals have something the members of higher rank need. For example, perhaps the social unit needs all of its members alive and well for any of them to reproduce successfully. If so, a higher-ranking individual might need to give up some control over reproduction to keep lower-ranking individuals around. Without such an incentive, the latter might go elsewhere.

That general idea may indeed apply to blue monkeys. Specifically, high-ranking females may need to keep low-ranking ones around to cope effectively with the aftermath of group fissions. Blue monkey groups tend to split when they reach fifty to seventy members. The reasons for such divisions are not well known in this species, but the consequences seem clear. The two new daughter groups, which are seldom the same size, engage in a series of intense intergroup battles to divvy up the original territory. In fact, that is when territorial boundaries—normally stable over generations—change the most. Invariably, the smaller daughter group ends up with the smaller parcel of land, which may not be big enough for its needs. That new home range seldom includes the most visited portions of the original group's range, and it often includes areas that were relatively infrequently used. The fact that there are different consequences for large and small daughter groups is one piece of the puzzle. Another is that lower-ranking females appear to have some control over how the group divides. They may choose not to join higher-ranking females in a new group, for example; in addition, they may actively and collectively exclude higher-ranking females. In one fission, we witnessed lower-ranking females harassing a higher-ranking matriarch that tried to join their subgroup. She was highly motivated to join it, as it included almost all of her many offspring. In the face of repeated, targeted threats and chases by lower-ranking females, however, she ended up with the smaller subgroup of females, all higher ranking than she was. She was thus at the bottom of the hierarchy in her new group, and separated from all of her family except her young daughter—and this position seemed to be imposed on her from below.

Presumably it is in the best interest of high-ranking females to join the larger subgroup during a group fission, but they risk being abandoned by lower-ranking individuals looking for a better situation elsewhere. If high-ranking individuals take on a greater share of territorial defense, they may create the staying incentive needed to retain a loyal following, thus ensuring the most advantageous outcome.

Our field research continues to investigate such questions of social structure by focusing on the behavior of individuals and their exchanges with one another, both one-on-one and in the context of group territoriality. This may prove to be a long undertaking, as some of the relevant social events occur rarely. Escalated attacks happen only once a month or so, and group fissions take place on average only once in ten years. With females living as long as thirty years or more, perhaps one should expect social lives that play out over a protracted period, but that presents scientists with a challenge. It's a good thing that human researchers live longer than their subjects!

MARINA CORDS is a professor of ecology, evolution, and environmental biology at Columbia University. Her research focuses on the social behavior, ecology, and reproduction of non-human primates, especially Old World monkeys. She has led a field study of blue monkeys in the Kakamega Forest since 1979, in which she combines behavioral observations with laboratory-based investigations of DNA and hormones.

What's Love Got to Do with It?

Sex among Our Closest Relatives Is a Rather Open Affair

MEREDITH F. SMALL

Maiko and Lana are having sex. Maiko is on top, and Lana's arms and legs are wrapped tightly around his waist. Lina, a friend of Lana's, approaches from the right and taps Maiko on the back, nudging him to finish. As he moves away, Lina enfolds Lana in her arms, and they roll over so that Lana is now on top. The two females rub their genitals together, grinning and screaming in pleasure.

This is no orgy staged for an X-rated movie. It doesn't even involve people—or rather, it involves them only as observers. Lana, Maiko, and Lina are bonobos, a rare species of chimplike ape in which frequent couplings and casual sex play characterize every social relationship—between males and females, members of the same sex, closely related animals, and total strangers. Primatologists are beginning to study the bonobos' unrestrained sexual behavior for tantalizing clues to the origins of our own sexuality.

In reconstructing how early man and woman behaved, researchers have generally looked not to bonobos but to common chimpanzees. Only about 5 million years ago human beings and chimps shared a common ancestor, and we still have much behavior in common: namely, a long period of infant dependency, a reliance on learning what to eat and how to obtain food, social bonds that persist over generations, and the need to deal as a group with many everyday conflicts. The assumption has been that chimp behavior today may be similar to the behavior of human ancestors.

Bonobo behavior, however, offers another window on the past because they, too, shared our 5-million-year-old ancestor, diverging from chimps just 2 million years ago. Bonobos have been less studied than chimps for the simple reason that they are difficult to find. They live only on a small patch of land in Zaire, in central Africa. They were first identified, on the basis of skeletal material, in the 1920s, but it wasn't until the 1970s that their behavior in the wild was studied, and then only sporadically.

Bonobos, also known as pygmy chimpanzees, are not really pygmies but welterweights. The largest males are as big as chimps, and the females of the two species are the same size. But bonobos are more delicate in build, and their arms and legs are long and slender.

On the ground, moving from fruit tree to fruit tree, bonobos often stand and walk on two legs—behavior that makes them seem more like humans than chimps. In some ways their sexual behavior seems more human as well, suggesting that in the sexual arena, at least, bonobos are the more appropriate ancestral model. Males and females frequently copulate face-to-face, which is an uncommon position in animals other than humans. Males usually mount females from behind, but females seem to prefer sex face-to-face. "Sometimes the female will let a male start to mount from behind," says Amy Parish, a graduate student at the University of California at Davis who's been watching female bonobo sexual behavior in several zoo colonies around the world. "And then she'll stop, and of course he's really excited, and then she continues face-to-face." Primatologists assume the female preference is dictated by her anatomy: her enlarged clitoris and sexual swellings are oriented far forward. Females presumably prefer face-to-face contact because it feels better.

Sex is fun. Sex makes them feel good and keeps the group together.

Like humans but unlike chimps and most other animals, bonobos separate sex from reproduction. They seem to treat sex as a pleasurable activity, and they rely on it as a sort of social glue, to make or break all sorts of relationships. "Ancestral humans behaved like this," proposes Frans de Waal, an ethologist at the Yerkes Regional Primate Research Center at Emory University. "Later, when we developed the family system, the use of sex for this sort of purpose became more limited, mainly occurring within families. A lot of the things we see, like pedophilia and homosexuality, may be leftovers that some now consider unacceptable in our particular society."

Depending on your morals, watching bonobo sex play may be like watching humans at their most extreme and perverse. Bonobos seem to have sex more often and in more combinations than the average person in any culture, and most of the time bonobo sex has nothing to do with making babies. Males mount females and females sometimes mount them back; females rub against other females just for fun; males stand rump to rump and press their scrotal areas together. Even juveniles participate by rubbing their genital areas against adults, although ethologists don't think that males actually insert their penises into juvenile females. Very young animals also have sex with each other: little males suck on each other's penises or French-kiss. When two animals initiate sex, others freely join in by poking their fingers and toes into the moving parts.

One thing sex does for bonobos is decrease tensions caused by potential competition, often competition for food. Japanese primatologists observing bonobos in Zaire were the first to notice that when bonobos come across a large fruiting tree or encounter piles of provisioned sugarcane, the sight of food triggers a binge of sex. The atmosphere of this sexual free-for-all is decidedly friendly, and it eventually calms the group down. "What's striking is how rapidly the sex drops off," says Nancy Thompson-Handler of the State University of New York at Stony Brook, who has observed bonobos at a site in Zaire called Lomako. "After ten minutes, sexual behavior decreases by fifty percent." Soon the group turns from sex to feeding.

But it's tension rather than food that causes the sexual excitement. "I'm sure the more food you give them, the more sex you'll get," says De Waal. "But it's not really the food, it's competition that triggers this. You can throw in a cardboard box and you'll get sexual behavior." Sex is just the way bonobos deal with competition over limited resources and with the normal tensions caused by living in a group. Anthropologist Frances White of Duke University, a bonobo observer at Lomako since 1983, puts it simply: "Sex is fun. Sex makes them feel good and therefore keeps the group together."

Females rule the business. It's a good species for feminists, I think.

Sexual behavior also occurs after aggressive encounters, especially among males. After two males fight, one may reconcile with his opponent by presenting his rump and backing up against the other's testicles. He might grab the penis of the other male and stroke it. It's the male bonobo's way of shaking hands and letting everyone know that the conflict has ended amicably.

Researchers also note that female bonobo sexuality, like the sexuality of female humans, isn't locked into a monthly cycle. In most other animals, including chimps, the female's interest in sex is tied to her ovulation cycle. Chimp females sport pink swellings on their hind ends for about two weeks, signaling their fertility, and they're only approachable for sex during that time. That's not the case with humans, who show no outward signs that they are ovulating, and can mate at all phases of the cycle. Female bonobos take the reverse tack, but with similar results. Their large swellings are visible for weeks before and after their fertile periods, and there is never any discernibly wrong time to mate. Like humans, they have sex whether or not they are ovulating.

What's fascinating is that female bonobos use this boundless sexuality in all their relationships. "Females rule the business—sex and food," says De Waal. "It's a good species for feminists, I think." For instance, females regularly use sex to cement relationships with other females. A genital-genital rub, better known as GG-rubbing by observers, is the most frequent behavior used by bonobo females to reinforce social ties or relieve tension. GG-rubbing takes a variety of forms. Often one female rolls on her back and extends her arms and legs. The other female mounts her and they rub their swellings right and left for several seconds, massaging their clitorises against each other. GG-rubbing occurs in the presence of food because food causes tension and excitement, but the intimate contact has the effect of making close friends.

Sometimes females would rather GG-rub with each other than copulate with a male. Parish filmed a 15-minute scene at a bonobo colony at the San Diego Wild Animal Park in which a male, Vernon, repeatedly solicited two females, Lisa and Loretta. Again and again he arched his back and displayed his erect penis—the bonobo request for sex. The females moved away from him, tactfully turning him down until they crept behind a tree and GG-rubbed with each other.

Unlike most primate species, in which males usually take on the dangerous task of leaving home, among bonobos females are the ones who leave the group when they reach sexual maturity, around the age of eight, and work their way into unfamiliar groups. To aid in their assimilation into a new community, the female bonobos make good use of their endless sexual favors. While watching a bonobo group at a feeding tree, White saw a young female systematically have sex with each member before feeding. "An adolescent female, presumably a recent transfer female, came up to the tree, mated with all five males, went into the tree, and solicited GG-rubbing from all the females present," says White.

Once inside the new group, a female bonobo must build a sister-hood from scratch. In groups of humans or chimps, unrelated females construct friendships through the rituals of shopping together or grooming. Bonobos do it sexually. Although pleasure may be the motivation behind a female-female assignation, the function is to form an alliance.

These alliances are serious business, because they determine the pecking order at food sites. Females with powerful friends eat first, and subordinate females may not get any food at all if the resource is small. When times are rough, then, it pays to have close female friends. White describes a scene at Lomako in which an adolescent female, Blanche, benefited from her established friendship with Freda. "I was following Freda and her boyfriend, and they found a tree that they didn't expect to be there. It was a small tree, heavily in fruit with one of their favorites. Freda went straight up the tree and made a food call to Blanche. Blanche came tearing over—she was quite far away—and went tearing up the tree to join Freda, and they GG-rubbed like crazy."

Alliances also give females leverage over larger, stronger males who otherwise would push them around. Females have discovered there is strength in numbers. Unlike other species of primates, such as chimpanzees or baboons (or, all too often,

Hidden Heat

Standing upright is not a position usually—or easily—associated with sex. Among people, at least, anatomy and gravity prove to be forbidding obstacles. Yet our two-legged stance may be the key to a distinctive aspect of human sexuality: the independence of women's sexual desires from a monthly calendar.

Males in the two species most closely related to us, chimpanzees and bonobos, don't spend a lot of time worrying, "Is she interested or not?" The answer is obvious. When ovulatory hormones reach a monthly peak in female chimps and bonobos, and their eggs are primed for fertilization, their genital area swells up, and both sexes appear to have just one thing on their mind. "These animals really turn on when this happens. Everything else is dropped," says primatologist Frederick Szalay of Hunter College in New York.

Women, however, don't go into heat. And this departure from our relatives' sexual behavior has long puzzled researchers. Clear signals of fertility and the willingness to do something about it bring major evolutionary advantages: ripe eggs lead to healthier pregnancies, which leads to more of your genes in succeeding generations, which is what evolution is all about. In addition, male chimps give females that are waving these red flags of fertility first chance at high-protein food such as meat.

So why would our ancestors give this up? Szalay and graduate student Robert Costello have a simple explanation. Women gave heat up, they say, because our ancestors stood up. Fossil footprints indicate that somewhere around 3.5 million years ago hominids—non-ape primates—began walking on two legs. "In hominids, something dictated getting up. We don't know what it was," Szalay says. "But once it did, there was a problem with the signaling system." The problem was that it didn't work. Swollen genital areas that were visible when their owners were down on all fours became hidden between the legs. The mating signal was lost.

"Uprightness meant very tough times for females working with the old ovarian cycle," Szalay says. Males wouldn't notice them, and the swellings themselves, which get quite large, must have made it hard for two-legged creatures to walk around.

Those who found a way out of this quandary, Szalay suggests, were females with small swellings but with a little less hair on their rears and a little extra fat. It would have looked a bit like the time-honored mating signal. They got more attention, and produced more offspring. "You don't start a completely new trend in signaling," Szalay says. "You have a little extra fat, a little nakedness to mimic the ancestors. If there was an ever-so-little advantage because, quite simply, you look good, it would be selected for."

And if a little nakedness and a little fat worked well, Szalay speculates, then a lot of both would work even better. "Once you start a trend in sexual signaling, crazy things happen," he notes. "It's almost like: let's escalate, let's add more. That's what happens in horns with sheep. It's a particular part of the body that brings an advantage." In a few million years human ancestors were more naked than ever, with fleshy rears not found in any other primate. Since these features were permanent, unlike the monthly ups and downs of swellings, sex was free to become a part of daily life.

It's a provocative notion, say Szalay's colleagues, but like any attempt to conjure up the past from the present, there's no real proof of cause and effect. Anthropologist Helen Fisher of the American Museum of Natural History notes that Szalay is merely assuming that fleshy buttocks evolved because they were sex signals. Yet their mass really comes from muscles, which chimps don't have, that are associated with walking. And anthropologist Sarah Blaffer Hrdy of the University of California at Davis points to a more fundamental problem: our ancestors may not have had chimplike swellings that they needed to dispense with. Chimps and bonobos are only two of about 200 primate species, and the vast majority of those species don't have big swellings. Though they are our closest relatives, chimps and bonobos have been evolving during the last 5 million years just as we have, and swollen genitals may be a recent development. The current unswollen human pattern may be the ancestral one.

"Nobody really knows what happened," says Fisher. "Everybody has an idea. You pays your money and you takes your choice."

—Joshua Fischman

humans), where tensions run high between males and females, bonobo females are not afraid of males, and the sexes mingle peacefully. "What is consistently different from chimps," says Thompson-Handler, "is the composition of parties. The vast majority are mixed, so there are males and females of all different ages."

Female bonobos cannot be coerced into anything, including sex. Parish recounts an interaction between Lana and a male called Akili at the San Diego Wild Animal Park. "Lana had just been introduced into the group. For a long time she lay on the grass with a huge swelling. Akili would approach her with a big erection and hover over her. It would have been easy for him to do a mount. But he wouldn't. He just kept trying to catch her eye, hovering around her, and she would scoot around the ground, avoiding him. And then he'd try again. She went around full circle." Akili was big enough to force himself on her. Yet he refrained.

In another encounter, a male bonobo was carrying a large clump of branches. He moved up to a female and presented his erect penis by spreading his legs and arching his back. She rolled onto her back and they copulated. In the midst of their joint ecstasy, she reached out and grabbed a branch from the male. When he pulled back, finished and satisfied, she moved away, clutching the branch to her chest. There was no tension between them, and she essentially traded copulation for food. But the key here is that the male allowed her to move away with the branch—it didn't occur to him to threaten her, because their status was virtually equal.

Although the results of sexual liberation are clear among bonobos, no one is sure why sex has been elevated to such a high position in this species and why it is restricted merely to reproduction among chimpanzees. "The puzzle for me," says De Waal, "is that chimps do all this bonding with kissing and embracing, with body contact. Why do bonobos do it in a sexual manner?" He speculates that the use of sex as a standard way to underscore relationships began between adult males and adult females as an extension of the mating process and later spread to all members of the group. But no one is sure exactly how this happened.

It is also unclear whether bonobo sexually became exaggerated only after their split from the human lineage or whether the behavior they exhibit today is the modern version of our common ancestor's sex play. Anthropologist Adrienne Zihlman of the University of California at Santa Cruz, who has used the evidence of fossil bones to argue that our earliest known non-ape ancestors, the australopithecines, had body proportions similar to those of bonobos, says, "The path of evolution is not a straight line from either species, but what I think is important is that the bonobo information gives us more possibilities for looking at human origins."

Some anthropologists, however, are reluctant to include the details of bonobo life, such as wide-ranging sexuality and a strong sisterhood, into scenarios of human evolution. "The researchers have all these commitments to male dominance [as in chimpanzees], and yet bonobos have egalitarian relationships," says De Waal. "They also want to see humans as unique, yet bonobos fit very nicely into many of the scenarios, making humans appear less unique."

Our divergent, non-ape path has led us away from sex and toward a culture that denies the connection between sex and social cohesion. But bonobos, with their versatile sexuality, are here to remind us that our heritage may very well include a primordial urge to make love, not war.

Mothers and Others

SARAH BLAFFER HRDY

Mother apes—chimpanzees, gorillas, orangutans, humans—dote on their babies. And why not? They give birth to an infant after a long gestation and, in most cases, suckle it for years. With humans, however, the job of providing for a juvenile goes on and on. Unlike all other ape babies, ours mature slowly and reach independence late. A mother in a foraging society may give birth every four years or so, and her first few children remain dependent long after each new baby arrives; among nomadic foragers, grown-ups may provide food to children for eighteen or more years. To come up with the 10–13 million calories that anthropologists such as Hillard Kaplan calculate are needed to rear a young human to independence, a mother needs help.

So how did our prehuman and early human ancestresses living in the Pleistocene Epoch (from 1.6 million until roughly 10,000 years ago) manage to get those calories? And under what conditions would natural selection allow a female ape to produce babies so large and slow to develop that they are beyond her means to rear on her own?

The old answer was that fathers helped out by hunting. And so they do. But hunting is a risky occupation, and fathers may die or defect or take up with other females. And when they do, what then? New evidence from surviving traditional cultures suggests that mothers in the Pleistocene may have had a significant degree of help—from men who thought they just might have been the fathers, from grandmothers and great-aunts, from older children.

These helpers other than the mother, called allomothers by sociobiologists, do not just protect and provision youngsters. In groups such as the Efe and Aka Pygmies of central Africa, allomothers actually hold children and carry them about. In these tight-knit communities of communal foragers—within which men, women, and children still hunt with nets, much as humans are thought to have done tens of thousands of years ago—siblings, aunts, uncles, fathers, and grandmothers hold newborns on the first day of life. When University of New Mexico anthropologist Paula Ivey asked an Efe woman, "Who cares for babies?" the immediate answer was, "We all do!" By three weeks of age, the babies are in contact with allomothers 40 percent of the time. By eighteen weeks, infants actually spend more time with allomothers than with their gestational mothers. On average, Efe babies have fourteen different caretakers, most of whom are close kin. According to Washington State University anthropologist Barry Hewlett, Aka babies

are within arm's reach of their fathers for more than half of every day.

Accustomed to celebrating the antiquity and naturalness of mother-centered models of child care, as well as the nuclear family in which the mother nurtures while the father provides, we Westerners tend to regard the practices of the Efe and the Aka as exotic. But to sociobiologists, whose stock in trade is comparisons across species, all this helping has a familiar ring. It's called cooperative breeding. During the past quarter century, as anthropologists and sociobiologists started to compare notes, one of the spectacular surprises has been how much allomaternal care goes on, not just within various human societies but among animals generally. Evidently, diverse organisms have converged on cooperative breeding for the best of evolutionary reasons.

A broad look at the most recent evidence has convinced me that cooperative breeding was the strategy that permitted our own ancestors to produce costly, slow-maturing infants at shorter intervals, to take advantage of new kinds of resources in habitats other than the mixed savanna-woodland of tropical Africa, and to spread more widely and swiftly than any primate had before. We already know that animal mothers who delegate some of the costs of infant care to others are thereby freed to produce more or larger young or to breed more frequently. Consider the case of silver-backed jackals. Patricia Moehlman, of the World Conservation Union, has shown that for every extra helper bringing back food, jackal parents rear one extra pup per litter. Cooperative breeding also helps various species expand into habitats in which they would normally not be able to rear any young at all. Florida scrub-jays, for example, breed in an exposed landscape where unrelenting predation from hawks and snakes usually precludes the fledging of young; survival in this habitat is possible only because older siblings help guard and feed the young. Such cooperative arrangements permit animals as different as naked mole rats (the social insects of the mammal world) and wolves to move into new habitats and sometimes to spread over vast areas.

When animal mothers delegate some infant-care costs to others, they can produce more or larger young and raise them in less-than-ideal habitats.

What does it take to become a cooperative breeder? Obviously, this lifestyle is an option only for creatures capable of living in groups. It is facilitated when young but fully mature individuals (such as young Florida scrub-jays) do not or cannot immediately leave their natal group to breed on their own and instead remain among kin in their natal location. As with delayed maturation, delayed dispersal of young means that teenagers, "spinster" aunts, real and honorary uncles will be on hand to help their kin rear young. Flexibility is another criterion for cooperative breeders. Helpers must be ready to shift to breeding mode should the opportunity arise. In marmosets and tamarins—the little South American monkeys that are, besides us, the only full-fledged cooperative breeders among primates—a female has to be ready to be a helper this year and a mother the next. She may have one mate or several. In canids such as wolves or wild dogs, usually only the dominant, or alpha, male and female in a pack reproduce, but younger group members hunt with the mother and return to the den to regurgitate predigested meat into the mouths of her pups. In a fascinating instance of physiological flexibility, a subordinate female may actually undergo hormonal transformations similar to those of a real pregnancy: her belly swells, and she begins to manufacture milk and may help nurse the pups of the alpha pair. Vestiges of cooperative breeding crop up as well in domestic dogs, the distant descendants of wolves. After undergoing a pseudopregnancy, my neighbors' Jack Russell terrier chased away the family's cat and adopted and suckled her kittens. To suckle the young of another species is hardly what Darwinians call an adaptive trait (because it does not contribute to the surrogate's own survival). But in the environment in which the dog family evolved, a female's tendency to respond when infants signaled their need—combined with her capacity for pseudopregnancy—would have increased the survival chances for large litters born to the dominant female.

According to the late W.D. Hamilton, evolutionary logic predicts that an animal with poor prospects of reproducing on his or her own should be predisposed to assist kin with better prospects so that at least some of their shared genes will be perpetuated. Among wolves, for example, both male and female helpers in the pack are likely to be genetically related to the alpha litter and to have good reasons for not trying to reproduce on their own: in a number of cooperatively breeding species (wild dogs, wolves, hyenas, dingoes, dwarf mongooses, marmosets), the helpers do try, but the dominant female is likely to bite their babies to death. The threat of coercion makes postponing ovulation the better part of valor, the least-bad option for females who must wait to breed until their circumstances improve, either through the death of a higher-ranking female or by finding a mate with an unoccupied territory.

One primate strategy is to line up extra fathers. Among common marmosets and several species of tamarins, females mate with several males, all of which help rear her young. As primatologist Charles T. Snowdon points out, in three of the four genera of Callitrichidae (*Callithrix, Saguinus,* and *Leontopithecus*), the more adult males the group has available to help, the more young survive. Among many of these species, females ovulate just after giving birth, perhaps encouraging males to stick around until after babies are born. (In cotton-top tamarins, males also undergo hormonal changes that prepare them to care for infants at the time of birth.) Among cooperative breeders of certain other species, such as wolves and jackals, pups born in the same litter can be sired by different fathers.

Human mothers, by contrast, don't ovulate again right after birth, nor do they produce offspring with more than one genetic father at a time. Ever inventive, though, humans solve the problem of enlisting help from several adult males by other means. In some cultures, mothers rely on a peculiar belief that anthropologists call partible paternity—the notion that a fetus is built up by contributions of semen from all the men with whom women have had sex in the ten months or so prior to giving birth. Among the Canela, a matrilineal tribe in Brazil studied for many years by William Crocker of the Smithsonian Institution, publicly sanctioned intercourse between women and men other than their husbands—sometimes many men—takes place during villagewide ceremonies. What might lead to marital disaster elsewhere works among the Canela because the men believe in partible paternity. Across a broad swath of South America—from Paraguay up into Brazil, westward to Peru, and northward to Venezuela—mothers rely on this convenient folk wisdom to line up multiple honorary fathers to help them provision both themselves and their children. Over hundreds of generations, this belief has helped children thrive in a part of the world where food sources are unpredictable and where husbands are as likely as not to return from the hunt empty-handed.

The Bari people of Venezuela are among those who believe in shared paternity, and according to anthropologist Stephen Beckerman, Bari children with more than one father do especially well. In Beckerman's study of 822 children, 80 percent of those who had both a "primary" father (the man married to their mother) and a "secondary" father survived to age fifteen, compared with 64 percent survival for those with a primary father alone. Not surprisingly, as soon as a Bari woman suspects she is pregnant, she accepts sexual advances from the more successful fishermen or hunters in her group. Belief that fatherhood can be shared draws more men into the web of possible paternity, which effectively translates into more food and more protection.

But for human mothers, extra mates aren't the only source of effective help. Older children, too, play a significant role in family survival. University of Nebraska anthropologists Patricia Draper and Raymond Hames have just shown that among !Kung hunters and gatherers living in the Kalahari Desert, there is a significant correlation between how many children a parent successfully raises and how many older siblings were on hand to help during that person's own childhood.

One primate strategy is to line up extra "fathers." In some species of marmosets, females mate with several males, all of which help her raise her young.

Older matrilineal kin may be the most valuable helpers of all. University of Utah anthropologists Kristen Hawkes and James O'Connell and their UCLA colleague Nicholas Blurton Jones, who have demonstrated the important food-gathering role of older women among Hazda hunter-gatherers in Tanzania, delight in explaining that since human life spans may extend for a few decades after menopause, older women become available to care for—and to provide vital food for—children born to younger kin. Hawkes, O'Connell, and Blurton Jones further believe that dating from the earliest days of Homo erectus, the survival of weaned children during food shortages may have depended on tubers dug up by older kin.

At various times in human history, people have also relied on a range of customs, as well as on coercion, to line up allomaternal assistance—for example, by using slaves or hiring poor women as wet nurses. But all the helpers in the world are of no use if they're not motivated to protect, carry, or provision babies. For both humans and nonhumans, this motivation arises in three main ways: through the manipulation of information about kinship; through appealing signals coming from the babies themselves; and, at the heart of it all, from the endocrinological and neural processes that induce individuals to respond to infants' signals. Indeed, all primates and many other mammals eventually respond to infants in a nurturing way if exposed long enough to their signals. Trouble is, "long enough" can mean very different things in males and females, with their very different response thresholds.

For decades, animal behaviorists have been aware of the phenomenon known as priming. A mouse or rat encountering a strange pup is likely to respond by either ignoring the pup or eating it. But presented with pup after pup, rodents of either sex eventually become sensitized to the baby and start caring for it. Even a male may gather pups into a nest and lick or huddle over them. Although nurturing is not a routine part of a male's repertoire, when sufficiently primed he behaves as a mother would. Hormonal change is an obvious candidate for explaining this transformation. Consider the case of the cooperatively breeding Florida scrub-jays studied by Stephan Schoech, of the University of Memphis. Prolactin, a protein hormone that initiates the secretion of milk in female mammals, is also present in male mammals and in birds of both sexes. Schoech showed that levels of prolactin go up in a male and female jay as they build their nest and incubate eggs and that these levels reach a peak when they feed their young. Moreover, prolactin levels rise in the jays' nonbreeding helpers and are also at their highest when they assist in feeding nestlings.

As it happens, male, as well as immature and nonbreeding female, primates can respond to infants' signals, although quite different levels of exposure and stimulation are required to get them going. Twenty years ago, when elevated prolactin levels were first reported in common marmoset males (by Alan Dixson, for *Callithrix jacchus*), many scientists refused to believe it. Later, when the finding was confirmed, scientists assumed this effect would be found only in fathers. But based on work by Scott Nunes, Jeffrey Fite, Jeffrey French, Charles Snowdon, Lucille Roberts, and many others—work that deals with a variety of species of marmosets and tamarins—we now know that all sorts of hormonal changes are associated with increased nurturing in males. For example, in the tufted-eared marmosets studied by French and colleagues, testosterone levels in males

went down as they engaged in caretaking after the birth of an infant. Testosterone levels tended to be lowest in those with the most paternal experience.

Genetic relatedness alone, in fact, is a surprisingly unreliable predictor of love. What matters are cues from infants and how we process these cues emotionally.

The biggest surprise, however, has been that something similar goes on in males of our own species. Anne Storey and colleagues in Canada have reported that prolactin levels in men who were living with pregnant women went up toward the end of the pregnancy. But the most significant finding was a 30 percent drop in testosterone in men right after the birth. (Some endocrinologically literate wags have proposed that this drop in testosterone levels is due to sleep deprivation, but this would probably not explain the parallel testosterone drop in marmoset males housed with parturient females.) Hormonal changes during pregnancy and lactation are, of course, indisputably more pronounced in mothers than in the men consorting with them, and no one is suggesting that male consorts are equivalent to mothers. But both sexes are surprisingly susceptible to infant signals—explaining why fathers, adoptive parents, wet nurses, and day-care workers can become deeply involved with the infants they care for.

Genetic relatedness alone, in fact, is a surprisingly unreliable predictor of love. What matters are cues from infants and how these cues are processed emotionally. The capacity for becoming emotionally hooked—or primed—also explains how a fully engaged father who is in frequent contact with his infant can become more committed to the infant's well-being than a detached mother will.

But we can't forget the real protagonist of this story: the baby. From birth, newborns are powerfully motivated to stay close, to root—even to creep—in quest of nipples, which they instinctively suck on. These are the first innate behaviors that any of us engage in. But maintaining contact is harder for little humans to do than it is for other primates. One problem is that human mothers are not very hairy, so a human mother not only has to position the baby on her breast but also has to keep him there. She must be motivated to pick up her baby even *before* her milk comes in, bringing with it a host of hormonal transformations.

Within minutes of birth, human babies can cry and vocalize just as other primates do, but human newborns can also read facial expressions and make a few of their own. Even with blurry vision, they engage in eye-to-eye contact with the people around them. Newborn babies, when alert, can see about eighteen inches away. When people put their faces within range, babies may reward this attention by looking back or even imitating facial expressions. Orang and chimp babies, too, are strongly attached to and interested in their mothers' faces. But unlike humans, other ape mothers and infants do not get absorbed in gazing deeply into each other's eyes.

To the extent that psychiatrists and pediatricians have thought about this difference between us and the other apes, they tend to attribute it to human mental agility and our ability to use language. Interactions between mother and baby, including vocal play and babbling, have been interpreted as protoconversations: revving up the baby to learn to talk. Yet even babies who lack face-to-face stimulation—babies born blind, say—learn to talk. Furthermore, humans are not the only primates to engage in the continuous rhythmic streams of vocalization known as babbling. Interestingly, marmoset and tamarin babies also babble. It may be that the infants of cooperative breeders are specially equipped to communicate with caretakers. This is not to say that babbling is not an important part of learning to talk, only to question which came first—babbling so as to develop into a talker, or a predisposition to evolve into a talker because among cooperative breeders, babies that babble are better tended and more likely to survive.

If humans evolved as cooperative breeders, the degree of a human mother's commitment to her infant should be linked to how much social support she herself can expect. Mothers in cooperatively breeding primate species can afford to bear and rear such costly offspring as they do only if they have help on hand. Maternal abandonment and abuse are very rarely observed among primates in the wild. In fact, the only primate species in which mothers are anywhere near as likely to abandon infants at birth as mothers in our own species are the other cooperative breeders. A study of cotton-top tamarins at the New England Regional Primate Research Center showed a 12 percent chance of abandonment if mothers had older siblings on hand to help them rear twins, but a 57 percent chance when no help was available. Overburdened mothers abandoned infants within seventy-two hours of birth.

This new way of thinking about our species' history, with its implications for children, has made me concerned about the future. So far, most Western researchers studying infant development have presumed that living in a nuclear family with a fixed division of labor (mom nurturing, dad providing) is the normal human adaptation. Most contemporary research on children's psychosocial development is derived from John Bowlby's theories of attachment and has focused on such variables as how available and responsive the mother is, whether the father is present or absent, and whether the child is in the mother's care or in day care. Sure enough, studies done with this model in mind always show that children with less responsive mothers are at greater risk.

In cooperative breeders, the degree of a mother's commitment to her infant should correlate with how much social support she herself can expect.

It is the baby, first and foremost, who senses how available and how committed its mother is. But I know of no studies that take into account the possibility that humans evolved as cooperative breeders and that a mother's responsiveness also happens to be a good indicator of her social supports. In terms of developmental outcomes, the most relevant factor might not be how securely or insecurely attached to the mother the baby is—the variable that developmental psychologists are trained to measure—but rather how secure the baby is in relation to all the people caring for him or her. Measuring attachment this way might help explain why even children whose relations with their mother suggest they are at extreme risk manage to do fine because of the interventions of a committed father, an older sibling, or a there-when-you-need-her grandmother.

The most comprehensive study ever done on how nonmaternal care affects kids is compatible with both the hypothesis that humans evolved as cooperative breeders and the conventional hypothesis that human babies are adapted to be reared exclusively by mothers. Undertaken by the National Institute of Child Health and Human Development (NICHD) in 1991, the seven-year study included 1,364 children and their families (from diverse ethnic and economic backgrounds) and was conducted in ten different U.S. locations. This extraordinarily ambitious study was launched because statistics showed that 62 percent of U.S. mothers with children under age six were working outside the home and that the majority of them (willingly or unwillingly) were back at work within three to five months of giving birth. Because this was an entirely new social phenomenon, no one really knew what the NICHD's research would reveal.

The study's main finding was that both maternal and hired caretakers' sensitivity to infant needs was a better predictor of a child's subsequent development and behavior (such traits as social "compliance," respect for others, and self-control were measured) than was actual time spent apart from the mother. In other words, the critical variable was not the continuous presence of the mother herself but rather how secure infants felt when cared for by someone else. People who had been convinced that babies need full-time care from mothers to develop normally were stunned by these results, while advocates of day care felt vindicated. But do these and other, similar findings mean that day care is not something we need to worry about anymore?

Not at all. We should keep worrying. The NICHD study showed only that day care was better than mother care if the mother was neglectful or abusive. But excluding such worst-case scenarios, the study showed no detectable ill effects from day care only when infants had a secure relationship with parents to begin with (which I take to mean that babies felt wanted) and only when the day care was of high quality. And in this study's context, "high quality" meant that the facility had a high ratio of caretakers to babies, that it had the same caretakers all the time, and that the caretakers were sensitive to infants' needs—in other words, that the day care staff acted like committed kin.

Bluntly put, this kind of day care is almost impossible to find. Where it exists at all, it's expensive. Waiting lists are long, even for cheap or inadequate care. The average rate of staff turnover in day care centers is 30 percent per year, primarily because these workers are paid barely the minimum wage (usually less, in fact, than parking-lot attendants). Furthermore, day care tends to be age-graded, so even at centers where staff members stay put, kids move annually to new teachers. This kind of day care is unlikely to foster trusting relationships.

What conclusion can we draw from all this? Instead of arguing over "mother care" versus "other care," we need to make day care better. And this is where I think today's evolution-minded researchers have something to say. Impressed by just how variable child-rearing conditions can be in human societies, several anthropologists and psychologists (including Michael Lamb, Patricia Draper, Henry Harpending, and James Chisholm) have suggested that babies are up to more than just maintaining the relationship with their mothers. These researchers propose that babies actually monitor mothers to gain information about the world they have been born into. Babies ask, in effect, Is this world filled with people who are going to provide for me and help me survive? Can I count on them to care about me? If the answer to those questions is yes, they begin to sense that developing a conscience and a capacity for compassion would be a great idea. If the answer is no, they may then be asking, Can I not afford to count on others? Would I be better off just grabbing what I need, however I can? In this case, empathy, or thinking about others' needs, would be more of a hindrance than a help.

For a developing baby and child, the most practical way to behave might vary drastically, depending on whether the mother has kin who help, whether the father is around, whether foster parents are well-meaning or exploitative. These factors, however unconsciously perceived by the child, affect important developmental decisions. Being extremely self-centered or selfish, being oblivious to others or lacking in conscience—traits that psychologists and child-development theorists may view as pathological—are probably quite adaptive traits for an individual who is short on support from other group members.

If I am right that humans evolved as cooperative breeders, Pleistocene babies whose mothers lacked social support and were less than fully committed to infant care would have been unlikely to survive. But once people started to settle down—10,000 or 20,000 or perhaps 30,000 years ago—the picture changed. Ironically, survival chances for neglected children increased. As people lingered longer in one place, eliminated predators, built walled houses, stored food—not to mention inventing things such as rubber nipples and pasteurized milk—infant survival became decoupled from continuous contact with a caregiver.

Since the end of the Pleistocene, whether in preindustrial or industrialized environments, some children have been surviving levels of social neglect that previously would have meant certain death. Some children get very little attention, even in the most benign of contemporary homes. In the industrialized world, children routinely survive caretaking practices that an Efe or a !Kung mother would find appallingly negligent. In traditional societies, no decent mother leaves her baby alone at any time, and traditional mothers are shocked to learn that Western mothers leave infants unattended in a crib all night.

In effect, babies ask: Is this world filled with people who are going to provide for me and help me survive? Can I count on them to care about me?

Without passing judgment, one may point out that only in the recent history of humankind could infants deprived of supportive human contact survive to reproduce themselves. Certainly there are a lot of humanitarian reasons to worry about this situation: one wants each baby, each child, to be lovingly cared for. From my evolutionary perspective, though, even more is at stake.

Even if we manage to survive what most people are worrying about—global warming, emergent diseases, rogue viruses, meteorites crashing into earth—will we still be human thousands of years down the line? By that I mean human in the way we currently define ourselves. The reason our species has managed to survive and proliferate to the extent that 6 billion people currently occupy the planet has to do with how readily we can learn to cooperate when we want to. And our capacity for empathy is one of the things that made us good at doing that.

At a rudimentary level, of course, all sorts of creatures are good at reading intentions and movements and anticipating what other animals are going to do. Predators from gopher snakes to lions have to be able to anticipate where their quarry will dart. Chimps and gorillas can figure out what another individual is likely to know or not know. But compared with that of humans, this capacity to entertain the psychological perspective of other individuals is crude.

During early childhood, through relationships with mothers and other caretakers, individuals learn to look at the world from someone else's perspective.

The capacity for empathy is uniquely well developed in our species, so much so that many people (including me) believe that along with language and symbolic thought, it is what makes us human. We are capable of compassion, of understanding other people's "fears and motives, their longings and griefs and vanities," as novelist Edmund White puts it. We spend time and energy worrying about people we have never even met, about babies left in dumpsters, about the existence of more than 12 million AIDS orphans in Africa.

Psychologists know that there is a heritable component to emotional capacity and that this affects the development of compassion among individuals. By fourteen months of age, identical twins (who share all genes) are more alike in how they react to an experimenter who pretends to painfully pinch her finger on a clipboard than are fraternal twins (who share only half their genes). But empathy also has a learned component, which has more to do with analytical skills. During the first years of life, within the context of early relationships with mothers and other committed caretakers, each individual learns to look at the world from someone else's perspective.

And this is why I get so worried. Just because humans have evolved to be smart enough to chronicle our species' histories, to speculate about its origins, and to figure out that we have about 30,000 genes in our genome is no reason to assume that evolution has come to a standstill. As gene frequencies change, natural selection acts on the outcome, the expression of those genes. No one doubts, for instance, that fish benefit from being able to see. Yet species reared in total darkness—as are the small, cave-dwelling characin of Mexico—fail to develop their visual capacity. Through evolutionary time, traits that are unexpressed are eventually lost. If populations of these fish are isolated in caves long enough, youngsters descended from those original populations will no longer be able to develop eyesight at all, even if reared in sunlight.

If human compassion develops only under particular rearing conditions, and if an increasing proportion of the species survives to breeding age without developing compassion, it won't make any difference how useful this trait was among our ancestors. It will become like sight in cave-dwelling fish.

No doubt our descendants thousands of years from now (should our species survive) will still be bipedal, symbol-generating apes. Most likely they will be adept at using sophisticated technologies. But will they still be human in the way we, shaped by a long heritage of cooperative breeding, currently define ourselves?

This article was adapted from *"Cooperation, Empathy, and the Needs of Human Infants,"* a Tanner Lecture delivered at the University of Utah. It is used with the permission of the Tanner Lectures on Human Values, a Corporation, University of Utah, Salt Lake City.

This article was reprinted from *Natural History,* May 2001, pp. 50–62, adapted from *Cooperation, Empathy, and the Needs of Human Infants,* a Tanner Lecture. Copyright (c) 2001 Tanner Lectures on Human Values, Inc., University of Utah, Salt Lake City.

UNIT 4

The Fossil Evidence

Unit Selections

Key Points to Consider

- Is the naming of species as if they were discontinuously separate categories a "convenient fiction"?

- Where would you place "Lucy" in our family tree?

- What did the last common ancestor of hominids and chimpanzees look like?

- Under what circumstances did bipedalism evolve? What are its advantages?

- What is the "man the hunter" hypothesis, and how might the "scavenging theory" better suit the early hominid data?

- How would you draw the early hominid family tree?

- Was "Peking Man" a cannibal, a hunter, or the hunted?

Student Website

www.mhcls.com

Internet References

Institute of Human Origins
   http://iho.asu.edu/node/27
The African Emergence and Early Asian Dispersals of the Genus *Homo*
   http://www.uiowa.edu/~bioanth/homo.html
Long Foreground: Human Prehistory
   http://www.wsu.edu/gened/learn-modules/top_longfor/lfopen-index.html

A primary focal point of this book, as well as of the whole of biological anthropology, is the search for and the interpretation of fossil evidence for hominid (meaning human or humanlike) evolution. Paleoanthropologists are those who carry out this task by conducting painstaking excavations and detailed analyses that serve as a basis for understanding our past. Every fragment found is cherished like a ray of light that may help to illuminate the path taken by our ancestors in the process of becoming "us." At least, that is what we would like to believe. In reality, each discovery leads to further mystery, and for every fossil-hunting paleoanthropologist who thinks his or her find supports a particular theory, there are many others anxious to express their disagreement. (See "The Woman Who Shook up Man's Family Tree," "Hunting the First Hominid" and "Made in Savannahstan.") How wonderful it would be, we sometimes think, in moments of frustration over inconclusive data, if the fossils would just speak for themselves, and every primordial piece of humanity were to carry with it a self-evident explanation for its place in the evolutionary story. Paleoanthropology would then be more of a quantitative problem of amassing enough material to reconstruct our ancestral development than a qualitative problem of interpreting what it all means. It would certainly be a simpler process, but would it be as interesting?

Most scientists tolerate, welcome, or even (dare it be said?) thrive on controversy, recognizing that diversity of opinion refreshes the mind, rouses students, and captures the imagination of the general public. After all, where would paleoanthropology be without the gadflies, the near-mythic heroes, and, lest we forget, the research funds they generate? Consider, for example, the issue of the differing roles played by males and females in the transition to humanity and all that it implies with regard to bipedalism, toolmaking, and the origin of the family. Did bipedalism really evolve in the grasslands? Did bipedalism develop as a means of pursuing prey? Should the primary theme of human evolution be summed up as "man the hunter" and "woman the gatherer?" Indeed, for early hominid evolution, how about "man the hunted?"

Not all the research and theoretical speculations taking place in the field of paleoanthropology are so controversial. Most scientists, in fact, go about their work quietly and methodically, generating hypotheses that are much less explosive and yet have the cumulative effect of enriching our understanding of the details of human evolution. In "The Salamander's Tale," Richard Dawkins reminds us that we should not take the names we

give to "species" too seriously. In "The Scavenging of 'Peking Man'," we learn how new methods of analysis are enhancing our understanding of the fossil evidence. In "Scavenger Hunt," Pat Shipman tells how modern technology, in the form of the scanning electron microscope, combined with meticulous detailed analysis of cut marks on fossil animal bones, can help us better understand the locomotor and food-getting adaptations of our early hominid ancestors. In one stroke, Shipman is able to challenge the traditional "man the hunter" theme that has pervaded most early hominid research and writing, and simultaneously set forth an alternative hypothesis that will, in turn, inspire further research.

As we mull over the controversies outlined in this unit, we should not take them as reflecting an inherent weakness of the field of paleoanthropology, but rather as symbolic of its strength: the ability and willingness to scrutinize, question, and reflect (endlessly) on every bit of evidence.

Contrary to the way that the proponents of creationism or "intelligent design theory" would have it, an admission of doubt is not an expression of ignorance but simply a frank recognition of the imperfect state of our knowledge. If we are to increase our understanding of ourselves, we must maintain an atmosphere of free inquiry without preconceived notions and unquestioning commitment to a particular point of view.

To paraphrase anthropologist Ashley Montagu, *whereas creationism seeks certainty without proof, science seeks proof without certainty.*

The Salamander's Tale

RICHARD DAWKINS

Names are a menace in evolutionary history. It is no secret that palaeontology is a controversial subject in which there are even some personal enmities. At least eight books called *Bones of Contention* are in print. And if you look at what two palaeontologists are quarrelling about, as often as not it turns out to be a name. Is this fossil *Homo erectus,* or is it an archaic *Homo sapiens?* Is this one an early *Homo habilis* or a late *Australopithecus?* People evidently feel strongly about such questions they often turn out to be splitting hairs. Indeed, they resemble theological questions, which I suppose gives a clue to why they arouse such passionate disagreements. The Obsession with discrete names is an example of what I call the tyranny of the discontinuous mind. The Salamander's Tale strikes a blow against the discontinuous mind.

The Central Valley runs much of the length of California, bound the Coastal Range to the west and by the Sierra Nevada to the east. These long mountain ranges link up at the north and the south ends of the valley, which is therefore surrounded by high ground. Throughout this high ground lives a genus of salamanders called *Ensatina*. The Central Valley itself, about 40 miles wide, is not friendly to salamanders, and they are not found there. They can move all round the valley but normally not across it, in an elongated ring of more or less continuous population. In practice any one salamander's short legs in its short lifetime don't carry it far from its birthplace. But genes, persisting through a longer timescale are another matter. Individual salamanders can interbreed with neighbours whose parents may have interbred with neighbours further round the ring, and so on. There is therefore potentially gene flow all around the ring. Potentially. What happens in practice has been elegantly worked out by the research of my old colleagues at the University of California at Berkeley, initiated by Robert Stebbins and continued by David Wake.

In a study area called Camp Wolahi, in the mountains to the south of the valley, there are two clearly distinct species of *Ensatina* which do not interbreed. One is conspicuously marked with yellow and black blotches. The other is a uniform light brown with no blotches. Camp Wolahi is in a zone of overlap, but wider sampling shows that the blotched species is typical of the eastern side of the Central Valley which, here in Southern California, is known as the San Joaquin Valley. The light brown species, on the contrary, is typically found on the western side of the San Joaquin.

Non-interbreeding is the recognised criterion for whether two populations deserve distinct species names. It therefore should be straightforward to use the name *Ensatina eschscholtzii* for the plain western species and *Ensatina klauberi* for the blotched eastern species—straightforward but for one remarkable circumstance, which is the nub of the tale.

If you go up to the mountains that bound the north end of the Central Valley, which up there is called the Sacramento Valley, you'll find only one species of *Ensatina.* Its appearance is intermediate between the blotched and the plain species: mostly brown, with rather indistinct blotches. It is not a hybrid between the two: that is the wrong way to look at it. To discover the right way, make two expeditions south, sampling the salamander populations as they fork to west and east on either side of Central Valley. On the east side, they become progressively more pitched until they reach the extreme of *klauberi* in the far south. On the west side, the salamanders become progressively more like the plain *escholtzii* that we met in the zone of overlap at Camp Wolahi.

This is why it is hard to treat *Ensatina eschscholtzii* and *Ensatina klauberi* with confidence as separate species. They constitute a 'ring species'. You'll recognise them as separate species if you only sample in the south. Move north, however, and they gradually turn into each other. Zoogists normally follow Stebbins's lead and place them all in the same species, *Ensatina eschscholtzii,* but give them a range of subspecies names. Starting in the far south with *Ensatina eschscholtzii eschscholtzii,* the plain brown form, we move up the west side of the valley through *Ensatina eschscholtzii xanthoptica* and *Ensatina eschscholtzii oregonensis* which as its name suggests, is also found further north in Oregon and Washington. At the north end of California's Central Valley is *Ensatina eschscholtzii picta,* the semi-blotched form mentioned before. Moving on round the ring and down the east side of the valley, we pass through *Ensatina eschscholtzii platensis* which is a bit more blotched than *picta,* then *Ensatina eschscholtzii croceater* until we reach *Ensatina eschsd klauberi* (which is the very blotched one that we previously called *Ensatina klauberi* when we were considering it to be a separate species).

Stebbins believes that the ancestors of *Ensatina* arrived at the north end of the Central Valley and evolved gradually down the two sides the valley, diverging as they went. An alternative possibility is that started in the south as, say, *Ensatina eschscholtzii eschscholtzii,* then evolved their way up the west side of the valley, round the top and down the other side, ending up as *Ensatina eschscholtzii klauberi* at the other end of the ring. Whatever the history, what happens today is that there is hybridization all round the ring, except where the two ends of the line meet, in the far south of California.

As a complication, it seems that the Central Valley is not a total barrier to gene flow. Occasionally, salamanders seem to have made it across for there are populations of, for example, *xanthoptica,* one of the western subspecies, on the eastern side of the valley, where they hybridise with the eastern subspecies, *platensis.* Yet another complication is that there is a small break near the south end of the ring, where there seem to be no salamanders at all. Presumably they used to be there, but have died out. Or maybe they are still there but have not been found: I am told that the mountains in this area are rugged and hard to search. The ring is complicated, but a ring of continuous gene flow is, nevertheless, the predominant pattern in this genus, as it is with the better-known case of herring gulls and lesser black-backed gulls around the Arctic Circle.

In Britain the herring gull and the lesser black-backed gull are clearly distinct species. Anybody can tell the difference, most easily by the colour of the wing backs. Herring gulls have silver-grey wing backs, lesser black-backs, dark grey, almost black. More to the point, the birds themselves can tell the difference too, for they don't hybridise although they often meet and sometimes even breed alongside one another in mixed colonies. Zoologists therefore feel fully justified in giving them different names, *Larus argentatus* and *Larus fuscus.*

But now here's the interesting observation, and the point of resemblance to the salamanders. If you follow the population of herring gulls westward to North America, then on around the world across Siberia and back to Europe again, you notice a curious fact. The 'herring gulls', as you move round the pole, gradually become less and less like herring gulls and more and more like lesser black-backed gulls until it turns out that our Western European lesser black-backed gulls actually are the other end of a ring-shaped continuum which started with herring gulls At every stage around the ring, the birds are sufficiently similar to their immediate neighbours in the ring to interbreed with them. Until, that is the ends of the continuum are reached, and the ring bites itself in the tail. The herring gull and the lesser black-backed gull in Europe never interbreed, although they are linked by a continuous series of interbreeding colleagues all the way round the other side of the world.

Ring species like the salamanders and the gulls are only showing us in the spatial dimension something that must always happen in the time dimension. Suppose we humans, and the chimpanzees, were a ring species. It could have happened: a ring perhaps moving up one side of the Rift Valley, and down the other side, with two completely separate species coexisting at the southern end of the ring, but an unbroken continuum of interbreeding all the way up and back round the other side. If this were true, what would it do to our attitudes to other species? To apparent discontinuities generally?

Many of our legal and ethical principles depend on the separation between *Homo sapiens* and all other species. Of the

people who regard abortion as a sin, including the minority who go to the lengths of assassinating doctors and blowing up abortion clinics, many are unthinking meat-eaters, and have no worries about chimpanzees being imprisoned in zoos and sacrificed in laboratories. Would they think again, if we could lay out a living continuum of intermediates between ourselves and chimpanzees, linked in an unbroken chain of interbreeders like the Californian salamanders? Surely they would. Yet it is the merest accident that the intermediates all happen to be dead. It is only because of this accident that we can comfortably and easily imagine a huge gulf between our species—or between any two species, for that matter.

I have previously recounted the case of the puzzled lawyer who questioned me after a public lecture. He brought the full weight of his legal acumen to bear on the following nice point. If species A evolves into species B, he reasoned closely, there must come a point when a child belongs to the new species B but his parents still belong to the old species A. Members of different species cannot, by definition, interbreed with one another, yet surely a child would not be so different from its parents as to be incapable of interbreeding with their kind. Doesn't this, he wound up, wagging his metaphorical finger in the special way that lawyers, at least in courtroom dramas, have perfected as their own, undermine the whole idea of evolution?

That is like saying, 'When you heat a kettle of cold water, there is no particular moment when the water ceases to be cold and becomes hot, therefore it is impossible to make a cup of tea.' Since I always try to turn questions in a constructive direction, I told my lawyer about the herring gulls, and I think he was interested. He had insisted on placing individuals firmly in this species or that. He didn't allow for the possibility that an individual might lie half way between two species, or a tenth of the way from species A to species B. Exactly the same limitation of thought hamstrings the endless debates about exactly when in the development of an embryo it becomes human (and when, by implication, abortion should be regarded as tantamount to murder). It is no use saying to these people that, depending upon the human characteristic that interests you, a focus can be 'half human' or 'a hundredth human'. 'Human', to the qualitative, absolutist mind, is like 'diamond'. There are no halfway houses. Absolutist minds can be a menace. They cause real misery, human misery. This is what I call the tyranny of the discontinuous mind, and it leads me to develop the moral of the Salamander's Tale.

For certain purposes names, and discontinuous categories, are exactly what we need. Indeed, lawyers need them all the time. Children are not allowed to drive; adults are. The law needs to impose a threshold, for example the seventeenth birthday. Revealingly, insurance companies take a very different view of the proper threshold age.

Some discontinuities are real, by any standards. You are a person and I am another person and our names are discontinuous labels that correctly signal our separateness. Carbon monoxide really is distinct from carbon dioxide. There is no overlap. A molecule consists of a carbon and one oxygen, or a carbon and two oxygens. None has a carbon and 1.5 oxygens. One gas is deadly poisonous, the other is needed by plants to make the organic substances that we all depend upon. Gold really is distinct from silver. Diamond crystals really are different from graphite crystals. Both are made of carbon, but the carbon atoms naturally arrange themselves in two quite distinct ways. There are no intermediates.

But discontinuities are often far from so clear. My newspaper carried the following item during a recent flu epidemic. Or was it an epidemic! That question was the burden of the article.

Official statistics show there are 144 people in every 100,000 suffering from flu, said a spokeswoman for the Department of Health. As the usual gauge of an epidemic is 400 in every 100,000, it is not being officially treated by the Government. But the spokeswoman added: 'Professor Donaldson is happy to stick by his version that this is an epidemic. He believes it is many more than 144 per 100,000. It is very confusing and it depends on which definition you choose. Professor Donaldson has looked at his graph and said it is a serious epidemic.'

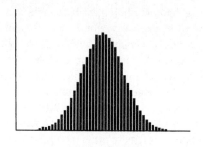

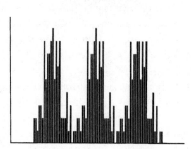

What we know is that some particular number of people are suffering from flu. Doesn't that, in itself, tell us what we want to know? Yet for the spokeswomen, the important question is whether this counts as an 'epidemic'. Has the proportion of sufferers crossed the rubicon of 400 per 100,000? This is the great decision which Professor Donaldson had to make, as he pored over his graph. You'd think he might have been better employed trying to do something about it, whether or not it counted officially as an epidemic.

As it happens, in the case of epidemics, for once there really is a natural rubicon: a critical mass of infections above which the virus, or bacterium, suddenly 'takes off' and dramatically increases its rate of spreading. This is why public health officials try so hard to vaccinate more than a threshold proportion of the population against, say whooping cough. The purpose is not just to protect the individuals vaccinated. It is also to deprive the pathogens of the opportunity to reach their own critical mass for 'take off'. In the case of our flu epidemic, what should really worry the spokeswomen for the Ministry of Health is whether the flu virus has yet crossed it rubicon for take-off, and leapt abrupt into high gear in its spread through the population. This should be decided by some means other than reference to magic numbers like 400 per 100,000. Concern with magic numbers is a mark of the discontinuous mine, or qualitative mind. The funny thing is that, in the case, the discontinous mind overlooks a genuine discontinuity, the take-off point for an epidemic. Usually there isn't a genuine discontinuity to overlook.

Many Western countries at present are suffering what is described as an epidemic of obesity. I seem to see evidence of this all around me, but I am not impressed by the preferred way of turning it into numbers. A percentage of population is described as 'clinically obese'. Once again, the discontinuous mind insists on separating people out into the obese on one side of a line, the non-obese on the other. That is not the way real life works. Obesity is continuously distributed. You can measure how obese each individual is, and you can compute group statistics from such measurements. Counts of numbers of people who lie above some arbitrarily defined threshold of obesity are

not illuminating, if only because they immediately prompt a demand for the threshold to be specified and maybe redefined.

The same discontinuous mind also lurks behind all those official figures detailing the numbers of people 'below the poverty line'. You can meaningfully express a family's poverty by telling us their income, preferably expressed in real terms of what they can buy. Or you can say 'X is as poor as a church mouse' or 'y is as rich as Croesus' and everybody will know what you mean. But spuriously precise counts or percentages of people said to fall above or below some arbitrarily defined poverty line are pernicious. They are pernicious because the precision implied by the percentage is instantly belied by the meaningless artificiality of the 'line'. Lines are impositions of the discontinuous mind. Even more politically sensitive is the label 'black', as opposed to 'white', in the context of modern society—especially American society. This is the central issue in the Grasshopper's Tale, and I'll leave it for now, except to say that I believe race is yet another of the many cases where we don't need discontinuous categories, and where we should do without them unless an extremely strong case in their favour is made.

Here's another example. Universities in Britain award degrees that are classified into three distinct classes, First, Second and Third Class. Universities in other countries do something equivalent, if under different names, like A, B, C, etc. Now, my point is this. Students do not really separate neatly into good, middling and poor. There are not discrete and distinct classes of ability or diligence. Examiners go to some trouble to assess students on a finely continuous numerical scale, awarding marks or points that are designed to be added to other such marks, or otherwise manipulated in mathematically continuous ways. The score on such a continuous numerical scale conveys far more information than classification into one of three categories. Nevertheless, only the discontinuous categories are published.

In a very large sample of students, the distribution of ability and prowess would normally be a bell curve with few doing very well, few doing very badly and many in between. It might not actually be a symmetrical bell like the picture, but it would certainly be smoothly continuous and it would become smoother as more and more students are added in.

A few examiners (especially, I hope I'll be forgiven for adding, in non-scientific subjects) seem actually to believe that there really is a discrete entity called the First-Class Mind, or the 'alpha' mind, and a student either definitely has it or definitely hasn't. The task of the examiner is to sort out the Firsts from the Seconds and Seconds from the Thirds, just as one might sort sheep from goats. The likelihood that in reality there is a smooth continuum, sliding from pure sheepiness through all intermediates to pure goatiness, is a difficult one for some kinds of mind to grasp.

If, against all my expectations, it should turn out that the more students you add in, the more the distribution of exam marks approximates to a discontinuous distribution with three peaks, it would be a fascinating result. The awarding of First, Second and Third Class degrees might then actually be justifiable.

But there is certainly no evidence for this, and it would be very surprising given everything we know about human variation. As things are, it is clearly unfair: there is far more difference between the top of one class and the bottom of the same class, than there is between the bottom of one class and the top of the next class. It would be fairer to publish the actual marks obtained, or a rank order based upon those marks. But the discontinuous or qualitative mind insists on forcing people into one or other discrete category.

Returning to our topic of evolution, what about sheep and goats themselves? Are there sharp discontinuities between species, or do they merge into each other like first-class and second-class exam performances? If we look only at surviving animals, the answer is normally yes, are sharp discontinuities. Exceptions like the gulls and the Californian salamanders are rare, but revealing because they translate into the spatial domain the continuity which is normally found only in the temporal domain. People and chimpanzees are certainly linked via a continuous chain of intermediates and a shared ancestor, but the intermediates are extinct: what remains is a discontinuous distribution. The same is true of people and monkeys, and of people and kangaroos, except that the extinct intermediates lived longer ago. Because the intermediates are nearly always extinct, we can usually get away with assuming that there is a sharp discontinuity between every species and every other. But in this book we are concerned with evolutionary history, with the dead as well as the living. When we are talking about all the animals that have ever lived, not just those that are living now, evolution tells us there are lines of gradual continuity linking literally every species to every other. When we are talking history, even apparently discontinuous modern species like sheep and dogs are linked, via their common ancestor, in unbroken lines of smooth continuity.

Ernst Mayr, distinguished elder statesman of twentieth-century evolution, has blamed the delusion of discontinuity—under its philosophical name of Essentialism—as the main reason why evolutionary understanding came so late in human history. Plato, whose philosophy can be seen as the inspiration for Essentialism, believed that actual things are imperfect versions of an ideal archetype of their kind. Hanging somewhere in ideal space is an essential, perfect rabbit, which bears the same relation to a real rabbit as a mathematician's perfect circle bears to a circle drawn in the dust. To this day many people are deeply imbued with the idea that sheep are sheep and goats are goats, and no species can ever give rise to another because to do so they'd have to change their 'essence'.

There is no such thing as essence.

No evolutionist thinks that modern species change into other modern species. Cats don't turn into dogs or vice versa. Rather, cats and dogs have evolved from a common ancestor, who lived tens of millions of years ago. If only all the intermediates were still alive, attempting to separate cats from dogs would be a doomed enterprise, as it is with the salamanders and the gulls. Far from being a question of ideal essences, separating cats from dogs turns out to be possible only because of the lucky (from the point of view of the essentialist) fact that the intermediates happen to be dead. Plato might find it ironic to learn that it is actually an imperfection—the sporadic ill-fortune of death—that makes the ration of anyone species from another possible. This of course applies to the separation of human beings from our nearest relatives—and, indeed, from our more distant relatives too. In a world of perfect and complete information, fossil information as well as recent, discrete names for animals would become impossible. Instead of discrete names we would need sliding scales, just as the words hot, warm, cool and cold are better replaced by a sliding scale such as Celsius or Fahrenheit.

Evolution is now universally accepted as a fact by thinking people, so one might have hoped that essentialist intuitions in biology would have been finally overcome. Alas, this hasn't happened. Essentialism refuses to lie down. In practice, it is usually not a problem. Everyone agrees that *Homo sapiens* is a different species (and most would say a different genus) from *Pan troglodytes,* the chimpanzee. But everyone also agrees that if you follow human ancestry backward to the shared ancestor and then forward to chimpanzees, the intermediates all along the way will form a gradual continuum in which every generation would have been capable mating with its parent or child of the opposite sex.

By the interbreeding criterion every individual is a member of the same species as its parents. This is an unsurprising, not to say platitudinously obvious conclusion, until you realise that it raises an intolerable paradox in the essentialist mind. Most of our ancestors throughout evolutionary history have belonged to different species from us by any criterion and we certainly couldn't have interbred with them. In the Devonian Period our direct ancestors were fish. Yet, although we couldn't interbreed with them, we are linked by an unbroken chain of ancestral generations, every one of which could have interbred with their immediate predecessors and immediate successors in the chain.

In the light of this, see how empty are most of those passionate arguments about the naming of particular hominid fossils. *Homo ergaster* is widely recognised as the predecessor species that gave rise to *Homo sapiens,* so I'll play along with that for what follows. To call *Homo ergaster* a separate species from *Homo sapiens* could have a precise meaning in principle, even if it is impossible to test in practice. It means that if we could go back in our time machine and meet our *Homo ergaster* ancestors, we could not interbreed with them.* But suppose that, instead of zooming directly to the time of *Homo ergaster,* or indeed any other extinct species in our ancestral lineage, we stopped our time machine every thousand years along the way and picked up a young and fertile passenger. We transport this passenger back to the next thousand-year stop and release her (or him: let's take a female and a male at alternate stops). Provided our one-stop time traveller could accommodate to local social and linguistic customs (quite a tall order) there would be no biological barrier to her interbreeding with a member of the opposite sex from 1,000 years earlier. Now we pick up a new passenger, say a male this time, and transport him back another 1,000 years. Once again, he too would be biologically capable of fertilising a female from 1,000 years before his native time. The daisy chain would continue on back to when our ancestors were swimming in the sea. It could go back without a break, to the fishes, and it would still be true that each and every passenger transported, 1,000 years before its own time would be able to interbreed with its predecessors. Yet at some point, which might be a million years back but might be longer or shorter, there would come a time when we moderns could not interbreed with an ancestor, even though our latest one-stop passenger could. At this point we could say that we have travelled back to a different species.

The barrier would not come suddenly. There would never be a generation in which it made sense to say of an individual that he is *Homo sapiens* but his parents are *Homo ergaster.* You can

---

* I am not asserting that as a fact. I don't know if it is a fact, although I suspect that it is. It is an implication of our plausibly agreeing to give *Homo ergaster* a different species name.

think of it as a paradox if you like, but there is no reason to think that any child was ever a member of a different species from its parents, even though the daisy chain of parents and children stretches back from humans to fish and beyond. Actually it isn't paradoxical to anybody but a dyed-in-the-wool essentialist. It is no more paradoxical than the statement that there is never a moment when a growing child ceases to be short and becomes tall. Or a kettle ceases to be cold and becomes hot. The legal mind may find it necessary to impose a barrier between childhood and majority—the stroke of midnight on the eighteenth birthday, or whenever it is. But anyone can see that it is a (necessary for some purposes) fiction. If only more people could see that the same applies to when, say, a developing embryo becomes 'human'.

Creationists love 'gaps' in the fossil record. Little do they know, biologists have good reason to love them too. Without gaps in the fossil record, our whole system for naming species would break down. Fossil could not be given names, they'd have to be given numbers, or positions on a graph. Or instead of arguing heatedly over whether a fossil is 'really', say, an early *Homo ergaster* or a late *Homo habilis,* we might call it *habigaster.* There's a lot to be said for this. Nevertheless, perhaps because our brains evolved in a world where most things do fall into discrete categories, and in particular where most of the intermediates between living species are dead, we often feel more comfortable if we can use separate names for things when we talk about them. I am no exception and neither are you, so I shall not bend over backwards to avoid using discontinuous names for species in this book. But the Salamander's Tale explains why this is a human imposition rather than something deeply built into the natural world. Let us use names as if they really reflected a discontinuous reality, but by all means let's privately remember that, at least in the world of evolution, it is no more than a convenient fiction, a pandering to our own limitations.

The Woman Who Shook up Man's Family Tree

Donald C. Johanson and Kate Wong

Never in my wildest fantasies did I imagine that I would discover a fossil as earthshaking as Lucy. When I was a teenager, I dreamed of traveling to Africa and finding a "missing link." Lucy is that and more: a 3.2-million-year-old skeleton who has become the spokeswoman for human evolution. She is perhaps the best known and most studied fossil hominid of the twentieth century, the bench-mark by which other discoveries of human ancestors are judged.

Whenever I tell the story, I am instantly transported back to the thrilling moment when I first saw her thirty-four years ago on the sandy slopes of Hadar in Ethiopia's Afar region. I can feel the searing, noonday sun beating down on my shoulders, the beads of sweat on my forehead, the dryness of my mouth—and then the shock of seeing a small fragment of bone lying inconspicuously on the ground. Most dedicated fossil hunters spend the majority of their lives in the field without finding anything remarkable, and there I was, a thirty-one-year-old newly minted Ph.D., staring at my childhood dream at my feet.

Sunday, November 24, 1974, began, as it usually does for me in the field. I had slept well in my tent, with the glittering stars visible through the small screen that kept out the mosquitoes, and as sunrise announced a brilliant new day, I got up and went to the dining tent for a cup of thick, black Ethiopian coffee. Listening to the morning sounds of camp life, I planned with some disinclination the day's activities: catching up on correspondence, fossil cataloging, and a million other tasks that had been set aside to accommodate a visit from anthropologists Richard and Mary Leakey. I looked up as Tom Gray, my grad student, appeared.

"I'm plotting the fossil localities on the Hadar map," he said. "Can you show me Afar Locality 162, where the pig skull was found last year?"

"I have a ton of paperwork and am not sure I want to leave camp today."

"Can you do the paperwork later?"

"Even if I start it now I'll be doing it later," I grumbled. But something inside—a gut sense that I had learned to heed—said I should put the paperwork aside and head to the outcrops with Tom.

A couple of geologists joined us in one of our old, dilapidated Land Rovers, and in a cloud of dust we headed out to the field.

I sat in the passenger seat enjoying the passing landscape peppered with animal fossils. Flocks of quacking guinea fowl ran for cover, and a giant warthog, annoyed by our intrusion, hurried off, its tail straight up in the air. Unlike many mammals that had been hunted to extinction in the area, the Hadar warthogs were left alone by the Afar locals, whose Islamic faith forbade eating pork. Tom put the Land Rover through its paces, and as we picked up speed in the sandy washes, my mind switched gears into fossil-finding mode. After we dropped off the geologists, who needed to inspect a troublesome geological fault that had disturbed the sedimentary layers near Locality 162, Tom and I threaded our way along smaller and smaller gullies.

"Somewhere around here," I said. "Pull over." Then I laughed as it occurred to me that in the remote desert you don't have to pull over, you just stop driving. We got out and spent a few minutes locating the cairn that had been left to mark the pig skull's locality, a little plateau of clay and silt sediments bordered by harder layers of sand-stone. A year earlier, a geologist had been out on a mapping mission and the plateau was obvious on the aerial photographs we had toted along: otherwise we might have overlooked it. After carefully piercing a pinhole into the aerial photo to mark the spot and labeling it "162" on the reverse side, we lingered. I was reluctant to return to camp and my paperwork. Even though the area was known to be fossil poor, we decided to look around while we were there. But after two hours of hunting all we had to show were some unremarkable fossil antelope and horse teeth, a bit of a pig skull, and a fragment of monkey jaw.

"I've had it. When do we head back?" Tom said.

"Right now." With my gaze still glued to the ground, I cut across the midportion of the plateau toward the Land Rover. Then a glint caught my eye, and when I turned my head I saw a two-inch-long, light brownish gray fossil fragment shaped like a wrench, which my knowledge of osteology told me instantly was part of an elbow. I knelt and picked it up for closer inspection. As I examined it, an image clicked into my brain and a subconscious template announced hominid. (The term *hominid* is used throughout this book to refer to the group of creatures in the human lineage since they diverged from a common ancestor to the African apes. Some other scholars employ the word *hominin* in its place.) The only other thing it could have been was monkey, but it lacked the telltale flare on the back that characterizes monkey elbows. Without a doubt, this was the elbow end of a hominid ulna, the larger of the two bones in the forearm. Raising my eyes, I scanned the immediate surroundings and spotted other bone fragments of similar color—a piece of thighbone, rib fragments, segments of the backbone, and, most important, a shard of skull vault.

"Tom, look!" I showed him the ulna, then pointed at the fragments. Like me, he dropped to a crouch. With his jaw hanging open, he picked up a chunk of mandible that he wordlessly held out for me to see. "Hominid!" I gushed. "All hominid!" Our excitement mounted as we examined every splinter of bone. "I don't believe this! Do you believe this?" we shouted over and over. Drenched in sweat, we hugged each other and whooped like madmen.

"I'm going to bring the ulna to camp," I said. "We'll come back for the others." I wanted to mark the exact location of each bone fragment scattered on the landscape, but there were too many pieces and time was short.

"Good idea. Don't lose it," Tom joked, as I carefully wrapped the ulna in my bandanna. I decided to take a fragment of lower jaw, too, for good measure. I marked the exact spots where the bones had lain, scribbled a few words in my field notebook, and then got back into the Land Rover.

The two geologists relaxing in the shade of a small acacia tree looked relieved when we drove up to rescue them from the stultifying heat. As they stood and greeted us, they could tell from our giddy grins that we'd found something.

"Feast your eyes!" I said, and opened the bandanna. I held the ulna next to my elbow. Being geologists, they didn't know a lot about bones, but they understood the importance of the find. Back into the bandanna the bones went, and then into my khaki hat for the trip to camp in the safety of my lap. Thirty minutes later Tom announced our arrival by honking the horn, and as we pulled to a stop our inquisitive teammates surrounded the car.

I jumped out of the Land Rover and everyone followed me to the work area, where a large tent fly protected our plywood worktables. Still in a state of semidisbelief, I sat and unpacked the precious remains. Reassured that they were in fact real, I sighed with relief. Everyone leaned over to see the tiny fragments of arm and jaw. The questions came fast and furious. Is there more? Where'd you find it? How did you find it? And then there was a stunned silence as the import of what we'd found sunk in. It hit me that if I had walked just a few more paces and looked to my left rather than my right, the bones would still be there on the slope. And in the ever-changing landscape of the Afar, a single desert thunderstorm could have washed them off the plateau, over a cliff and into oblivion, forever.

Suddenly someone slapped me on the back and exhilaration replaced awe. We all started talking at once, and we had to keep raising our voices to be heard so that eventually no one could hear what anyone else was saying. A hurried lunch followed and then everyone wanted to see the spot where I had found the ulna. At the locality my colleagues stood back as I carefully pointed to the bone fragments on the slope. Immediately my team understood that what they were looking at was a partial hominid skeleton. It was a special moment for all of us, though I don't think any of us truly realized how special at the time.

We celebrated the discovery with a delicious dinner of roasted goat and panfried potatoes washed down with a case of Bati beer my students had somehow managed to smuggle into camp. Conversation became less animated and more technical, focusing on morphology and size. I felt from the beginning that the fossils belonged to a single individual because there was no duplication of parts in the remains we collected; the pieces all had the same proportions and exhibited the same fossilization color. I further argued that the skeleton was a female specimen of *Australopithecus*—a primitive human forebear—because of the small size of the bones relative to those of other australopithecines. All australopithecines were sexually dimorphic, which is to say males and females exhibited physical differences beyond those pertaining to the sex organs. So if the lightly built ulna we discovered were from a male, then a female would have to be unbelievably tiny.

While we were all talking, *Sgt. Pepper's Lonely Hearts Club Band* was playing on a small Sony tape deck. When "Lucy in the Sky with Diamonds" came on, my girlfriend Pamela Alderman, who had come to spend some time in the field with me, said, "Why don't you call her Lucy?" I smiled politely at the suggestion, but I didn't like it because I thought it was frivolous to refer to such an important find simply as Lucy. Nicknaming hominid fossils was not unheard of, however. Mary and Louis Leakey, giants in the field of paleoanthropology, dubbed a flattened hominid skull found in Tanzania's Olduvai Gorge "Twiggy," and a specimen their son Jonathan found received the moniker "Jonny's Child." But most of the scientists I knew wouldn't give their fossils a cute name based on a song by the Beatles. The next morning, however, everyone wanted to know if we were going to the Lucy site. Someone asked how tall Lucy was. Another inquired how old I thought Lucy was when she died. As I sat there eating my breakfast of peanut butter and jelly on toast, I conceded that the name Lucy had a better ring to it than A.L. 288, the locality number that had been assigned to the site.

At my request, the government representative from the Antiquities Administration who had escorted our expedition sent word to the director general of the Ministry of Culture, Bekele Negussie. He arrived a few days later with some of his colleagues. While I answered their questions, I resisted referring to our australopithecine as Lucy because I was uncomfortable about an Ethiopian fossil bearing an English name. When the team returned that afternoon from the site bursting with news of more Lucy fragments, additional information about Lucy, endless speculations about Lucy, my discomfort grew. After dinner Bekele and I sat outside the dining tent looking up at a brilliant starlit sky. I talked about the implications of the discovery, how it might impact prevailing theories about hominid evolution. And we discussed arrangements for a press announcement in Addis Ababa in December.

He listened in silence, then regarded me very seriously and said, "You know, she is an Ethiopian. She needs an Ethiopian name."

"Yes!" I agreed, relieved. "What do you suggest?"

"Dinkinesh is the perfect name for her."

I mentally inventoried my Amharic vocabulary, which was just enough to shop for basics, greet people, ask directions, and, most important, order a cup of the best coffee in the world. The word *Dinkinesh* wasn't there. "What does it mean?"

With a broad smile, as if he were naming his own child, he answered, "Dinkinesh means 'you are marvelous.'"

He was right, it was the perfect name. Of course, today most of the world, including nearly every Ethiopian I have spoken to, calls her Lucy. And Lucy is the name that has appeared in crossword puzzles, on *Jeopardy!,* in cartoons, and on African Red Bush Tazo tea bags. In Ethiopia she has lent her name to numerous coffee shops, a rock band, a typing school, a fruit juice bar, and a political magazine. There is even an annual Lucy Cup soccer competition in Addis Ababa. Once, while driving through the town of Kombolcha on the way back to Addis after a field season, years after the discovery, I spotted a small sign that said LUSSY BAR. I brought the car to a screeching halt and my colleagues and I went in to have a beer. When we asked the proprietress how the place got its name, she explained in a solemn voice that many years ago a young American found a skeleton named Lucy in the Afar region, and that she took great pride in naming her bar after the fossil that proved Ethiopia's status as the original homeland to all people. With a grin, I told her I was the American who had found Lucy. She shrieked in delight and insisted that we have our picture taken together to mount on the wall. I sent the photo to her, and for all I know, it hangs there still. But sometimes I still think of Lucy as Dinkinesh, because she truly is marvelous.

At the end of the 1974 field season, Lucy, painstakingly wrapped and packed in a cardboard box, made the day-and-a-half journey from Hadar to the National Museum of Ethiopia in Addis Ababa. Lucy was expected, and when my colleagues and I pulled up to the museum in my Land Rover, the director, Mamo Tessema, and his curatorial staff greeted us warmly. The cardboard box, a temporary home for Lucy, was whisked off and locked in a carefully guarded room.

Over the next few days I worked with Woldesenbet, the non-nonsense collections manager, to officially tally every fragment and formally catalog Lucy as part of the National Museum of Ethiopia's collections. The entire Ministry of Culture was abuzz with the news that she was now in Addis Ababa, and Bekele and the minister made preparations for her official coming-out party, a public announcement at the ministry. A throng of scientists, antiquities people, ministry officials, university faculty, and journalists jammed the room that had been specially prepared by the ministry. Resplendent on a black cloth, Lucy was an instant hit. Everyone in the room jostled to catch a glimpse of her bones.

The press conference was intense, and Bekele had to finally call a stop to the questions. Three million two hundred thousand years after her death her image would grace the front page of newspapers all over the world. Not exactly an overnight success, I thought. In a way, we had both arrived, Lucy and I. Her path to that press conference was quite different from mine, to be sure. But the reason we were there together was because we had met in the right place at the right time.

My own path could be characterized as a combination of hard work, perseverance, and more than a few lucky breaks. My first opportunity to travel to Africa had come four years earlier, in 1970, when one of my professors at the University of Chicago, F. Clark Howell, invited me to work as an assistant on his expedition to the Omo area in extreme southwestern Ethiopia, where he was looking for hominids. This was the chance I had been dreaming of ever since I had read as a kid the *National Geographic* articles describing the Leakeys' finds at Olduvai Gorge. I was utterly mesmerized by their fascinating field work and the photos of Africa. But when I stepped out of the light plane at the Omo airstrip I was astounded by the brutal heat as I staggered to the waiting Land Rover. Soon I suffered an attack of malaria that could have quickly terminated my career as a field scientist, but eventually I became acclimated to the rigors of working in Africa. During my first expedition, the week passed swiftly as I grew more and more comfortable in the field and learned many of the skills necessary to conduct fieldwork. After three months I was hooked, and I knew that Africa would forever be a part of my life.

In the summer of 1971 I returned to the Omo and was given greater responsibility in running the camp alongside Gerry Eck, our camp manager extraordinaire. More than anything in the world I wanted an expedition of my own someday, and I knew that all the work I was doing on the Omo Research Expedition was the best preparation I could ever have.

In the fall of 1971 I spent several weeks in Europe gathering data for my doctoral dissertation. I was studying variation in chimpanzee teeth, which could inform assessments of similar variation in early hominids. My time working in Paris proved to be the most memorable and rewarding of my young career, for many reasons. From my experience in the Omo I knew several members of the French contingent, who looked after me in Paris. One evening I attended a dinner party where I met a young Tunisian-born French geologist named Maurice Taieb, a gregarious, handsome, and heavily tanned man with a highly animated personality. As he sipped a glass of red wine and took deep drags off one Gauloise after another, he regaled me with stories of his fieldwork in the Afar Triangle. The Afar, Africa's most northern reach of the Great Rift Valley, is a geologist's dream because it is where three rifting systems intersect and buckle the landscape. It is the ideal place to study the process of continental drift. Maurice wanted to survey the area in hopes of piecing together its geological history. He called it "a geological and paleoanthropological paradise" and explained that it contained great expanses of sediments eroded by wind and water that were literally oozing fossils. Full of enthusiasm, he invited me to visit his lab the next day to see his photographs and maps of the place.

I stood in Maurice's lab electrified by his pictures of entire elephant skulls, pig jaws, antelope bones, crocodile skulls—complete specimens, not fragments like the Omo fossils. What impressed me even more was that the Afar pig and elephant fossils closely resembled the Omo samples that were in excess of 3 million years old. Maurice paced back and forth as he recounted stories of the Afar region, with its exotic people, its treasures, and its dangers. The Afar didn't like strangers, he explained. But once one got to know them they were wonderful. "You should go out there with me!" he said, exhaling thick, blue smoke and adjusting his heavy-rimmed glasses. I was floored; usually scientists weren't inclined to share information about a fossil-rich area, particularly if it was as promising as the Afar.

It didn't appear to matter to him that I wasn't French: He just wanted to launch a full-fledged expedition to the region and, wonder of wonders, he wanted me to come along! A once-in-a-lifetime opportunity, for sure. I felt torn. I had to finish my dissertation, I had committed to another season in the Omo, and I had no money and no job lined up. But there was no way I could say no to Maurice; this was my chance to get in on the ground floor in a fossil paradise and perhaps find the hominid fossils of my dreams. "Okay," I said, "when do we leave?"

In March 1972 Maurice picked me up at Bole Airport in Addis Ababa. After quickly assembling food and equipment, we set off for a monthlong reconnaissance of the Afar. It was an endless expanse of badlands littered with tons of animal fossils exposed by erosion. "Terra incognita" Maurice called it, as each day we penetrated deeper and deeper into the uncharted territory. Escorting us was a spindly, gentle Afar man named Ali Axinum, who knew the region like the back of his hand and had served as Maurice's guide for several years. Without Ali we would have been lost, literally. The geology of the Afar was overwhelming. Texan geologist Jon Kalb provided additional expertise. The Afar region held such an allure for Jon that he moved his family to Ethiopia, where he had initiated worked for the Ministry of Mines. And rounding out our small expeditionary force was Yves Coppens, an ambitious French paleontologist I had met when he was directing the French team in the Oro. Yves, like me, was especially motivated to find fossil hominids, and his background in mammalian paleontology would be invaluable for this first foray into the Afar region.

We arrived at Hadar in the afternoon. Maurice, who had acquired his driving skills on treacherous French roads and packed Paris streets, managed to brake just before he pitched our Land Rover over a cliff. Hot, dusty, but mostly relieved when he stopped, I climbed out and beheld a veritable El Dorado of paleoanthropology. I stood on the edge of the vast expanse of eroded sediments confident that it was ideal: no vegetation, clear stratigraphy, and, most important, fossils everywhere.

After our six-week reconnaissance we limped back to Addis Ababa exhausted and suntanned but immensely satisfied with the potential we had seen in the Afar for finding fossils. We formalized our collaboration as the International Afar Research Expedition (IARE) and decided that of all the places we had visited, Hadar was the most promising. So in the fall of 1973, with a modest grant from the National Science Foundation (NSF) and funds from the Centre National de la Recherche Scientifique (CNRS), we set up Camp Hadar. Day after day, bent over with my hands behind my back and my eyes to the ground, I scoured the hillsides in search of that illusive first hominid fossil. For weeks there was nothing. The heat, effort, and constant backache began to sap my enthusiasm. But I knew in my gut that it was just a matter of time and persistence. The fossil hominids were there; they had to be.

Late in the afternoon of October 30, I saw what looked like hippo rib protruding from the ground. I gently tapped it with my shoe, and the proximal end of a tibia (the top end of the shinbone) emerged from the loose soil. Crouching, I also spotted parts of a distal femur (the bottom end of the thighbone). When I placed them together, they formed a knee joint, missing only the kneecap. From the angle at which the shaft of the femur ascended I knew it was from an upright walking animal—the first hominid fossil ever discovered in the Afar region. I also knew that I now had important leverage to justify expanded funding for Hadar research.

While yielding valuable information about locomotion, the knee joint by itself held few clues about the species of its owner. When anatomist Raymond Dart discovered the Taung baby in 1924, he named his hominid *Australopithecus africanus,* the "southern ape of Africa." I surmised that the knee was *Australopithecus* but could not be certain whether it was the same species as Dart's or perhaps a new species. Despite the claims of some critics during my subsequent presentations that its small size indicated that it was nothing more than a monkey knee, I never veered from my original assertion that the knee belonged to a biped. The way the femur and tibia articulated with each other, making maximum contact, was a distinctly hominid trait.

With the fossil securely bundled in a small cardboard box labeled Afar Locality (A.L.) 128/129, I returned victorious to Case Western Reserve University in Cleveland where I had begun teaching, a big-game hunter bringing home his trophy from an African safari. I spent many humid summer nights completing my thesis, and late in August 1974 I successfully defended my daunting 444-page doctoral dissertation on chimp teeth. I had a little NSF money remaining and with some additional private funds I was able to enlist a few more students and colleagues who would accompany us back into the field. In early September we set off for Ethiopia and the next great adventure.

The IARE departed in a convoy of heavily laden Land Rovers, trailers, and a lorry from Addis Ababa. Even before camp had been fully set up, a few team members began eagerly searching the geological deposits within walking distance of Camp Hadar in hope of finding a hominid. One of the most motivated and keen-eyed was a young Ethiopian colleague from the Ministry of Culture, Alemayehu Aslaw, who was possessed by what I call "hominid fever." The outline of his figure could be seen roaming the hills until sunset, when it was too dark to survey. His perseverance eventually paid off when he found two jaws containing beautifully preserved teeth in the very deposits that others had searched near camp. Were they the same species as the owner of the knee joint? And was that species *A, africanus,* like Dart's Taung baby, or something new?

Friendly rivalry is at times a good thing because it motivates us all to work a little harder, a little longer, and take chances we otherwise might not take. Chief among my rivals was Richard Leakey, son of Louis and Mary, who had made some spectacular finds at Lake Turkana in Kenya, including a specimen known as 1470, then considered the earliest evidence of *Homo.* Tall and lanky with sun-bleached hair and boyish good looks, Richard exuded authority and confidence. We'd met several times, and the previous year I'd brought the fossil knee to Nairobi so that his team at the National Museums of Kenya could make a cast of it. He graciously allowed me to see their hominid fossil collection, including specimens that hadn't been published yet or even announced. Honored to be a member of the "inner circle" of scholars who were granted such access, I felt it was now my turn to return that favor, so I invited Richard; his wife, Meave; and his mother, Mary, to Hadar. A licensed pilot, he flew to Ethiopia in his own plane and landed at our hastily cleared airstrip, dubbed Hadar International Airport. In addition to Meave and Mary, Richard brought his brother-in-law, a paleontologist named John Harris. As they walked Hadar's astonishingly fossil-rich hillsides, I enjoyed watching their dumbstruck expressions, thinking that was how I must have looked to Maurice when I first came here.

Over dinner we debated the fossil identification of the new hominid jaws that Alemayehu had found. Richard favored classifying the larger one as part of a member of our own genus, *Homo,* whereas I thought it belonged to a male australopithecine. We weren't just arguing about the jaws, though. Richard believed that the 1470 skull was 3 million years old. But like many other experts in the field, I suspected that the geological dating was wrong because the animal fossils found along with it, particularly the pigs, were identical to those from the Omo that were dated at about 2 million years. Although we disagreed, I was thrilled to be exchanging ideas with some of the giants in the field. The stimulating conversation, which included students and other Hadar team members, left everyone excited but exhausted.

On Saturday we drove Richard and his group out to the airstrip, helped them load up, and waved good-bye as they took off for the flight back to Kenya. The following day I found Lucy.

During the 1974 field season at Hadar, Ethiopia's emperor, Haile Selassie, was overthrown by the Derg, a violent military junta who capitalized on Selassie's decreasing popularity following a poorly managed famine in the very region where we were working. I was deeply concerned about how this turn of events would impact our future plans to work at Hadar. Sure enough, when we returned in 1975, the political atmosphere had changed from calm to violence and fear. With increased funding from both the United States and France, the IARE team had grown to include more students and more specialists in paleontology and geology. I had always been concerned about medical issues in the field—dysentery, malaria, snake bites, appendicitis—so I was pleased when Mike Bush, a young, soft-spoken medical doctor with a passion for archaeology, expressed interest in joining my expedition. Not only was Mike a great guy to have in camp, as well as a competent physician, he also turned out to be a keen-eyed and avid surveyor. Late in the morning on November 2, Mike's dedication paid off. I was in the middle of a conversation with David Brill, a *National Geographic* photographer, when Mike interrupted us to say that he had found what he thought might be some huminid teeth. David, a tall, skinny guy from Wisconsin, was excited because after hounding me for days, this might just be the photo op he had been pushing for—a hominid find. We followed Mike back to the spot.

"Right there," Mike said, pointing. I crouched, squinted, and was amazed to see two gray teeth embedded almost invisibly in gray stone. How had he managed to spot them? "Upper premolars," he added.

I grinned, looking up at David. "Here's the hominid I promised you."

David looked at the teeth, then at the sky. "You couldn't have discovered them when the lighting was better?"

I thought he was kidding, but he just shook his head and refused to take any photographs until the next day, when the sun would be lower on the horizon. We headed out to Mike's find first thing next morning, when the light was warmer and shadows gave the landscape a more three-dimensional feel. David began snapping away. I could tell he wasn't very impressed with the amorphous block of stone containing two little blobs of gray, but he was doing his best.

Hoping for a noteworthy discovery, Maurice had persuaded a French film crew to spend most of the field season with us. One of them had positioned herself upslope from us near a little bush, and suddenly she called down to me, "*Quels sont ceux-ci?*" She was holding up a couple of fossils, and as I approached her, much to my astonishment, I could see that one was a heel bone and the other a femur, both unmistakably hominid.

"Could this be another skeleton?" I yelled, and everyone scrambled up the steep hillside. It turned out to be a mother lode of hominid fossils: During the rest of that season and the next, location A.L. 333 furnished more than two hundred fossils, including a partial baby skull, portions of an articulated foot, some articulated hand bones, most of an adult male brain case, parts of faces, and numerous mandible fragments. Together these represented, in our best estimate, at least thirteen individuals—nine adults and four children or infants. From the title of my 1976 *National Geographic* article, the 333 collection was dubbed "the First Family."

Maurice speculated after careful inspection of the geological strata that the fossil-bearing layer was the result of a single geological event such as a flash flood; a snapshot of a group of hominids who lived, died, and were buried together. Unlike the usual discoveries of single specimens, the 333 assemblage offered unprecedented insight into the anatomy not only of a single species but of individuals who had actually known one another millions of years ago. Again, I marveled at the circumstances that had led to the discovery. Had I turned down Mike's request to join our expedition, the well-concealed teeth might not have been found, and A.L. 333 could have gone unnoticed.

By 1977 Ethiopia was under the ruthless leadership of Mengistu Haile Mariam, and it was too dangerous to conduct fieldwork. I was now the curator of physical anthropology at the Cleveland Museum of Natural History, and the major part of my job was to oversee the study of the unmatched hominid harvest from Hadar. The process involved cleaning the stone matrix from each piece of bone in order to obtain a clear picture of its surface anatomy, taking color and black-and-white record photos, molding and casting each specimen, as well as describing each fragment in meticulous detail for publication. All of this had to be accomplished by 1980, when the fossils would be returned to the National Museum of Ethiopia for safe-keeping.

I assembled a team—consulting experts, researchers, students, and colleagues—to systematically undertake a comprehensive study of the Hadar collection. Mike Bush used his expertise in anatomy and his interest in hands to catalog the hand bones; Owen Lovejoy, a leading expert on hominid bipedalism and postcranial anatomy at Kent State University, was assigned to the limbs and the pelvis; William Kimbel, Lovejoy's graduate student, worked on the cranial remains. I recruited Tim White of Berkeley to document the mandibles. Tim, a promising young paleoanthropologist with a curmudgeonly streak, had worked with Mary Leakey at Laetoli, in Tanzania, where similar fossils had been found. We had met in 1975 when I brought the First Family to the National Museums of Kenya, where he was working for the Leakeys, and we struck up a friendship. Having parted ways with Richard's expedition and then Mary's, he joined mine. Meanwhile, ever the dental expert, I worked on the teeth. The final analysis was eventually published in a 352-page single issue of the *American Journal of Physical Anthropology.*

While we were working on detailed descriptions of the bones in early June 1977, I was unexpectedly invited to present an evaluation of the Hadar hominids at a Nobel Symposium in Sweden. Convened by the Royal Swedish Academy of Sciences to address the "Current Argument on Early Man," the symposium commemorated the two hundredth anniversary of the death of the Swedish botanist Carolus Linnaeus, whose taxonomy (the practice of describing, classifying, and assigning Latinized binomial names to all biological organisms, living or extinct, for placement in a hierarchical system) is still the basis of modern classification. I could think of no occasion more fitting than a Nobel Symposium to present our results. My parents had emigrated from Sweden in the early 1900s, and I felt honored to deliver a paper in the country of my ancestors. I knew that some of paleoanthropology's most accomplished scholars would be in the audience listening carefully for speculative claims or factual errors. My presentation had to be meticulously researched, and I was grateful for colleagues like Tim and Owen and others who agreed to review draft after draft, sometimes offering brutal criticism.

On May 21, 1978, a clear, cool Sunday evening in Stockholm, I attended a gala reception and dinner hosted by the Royal Swedish Academy of Sciences. Early the next morning we set off by bus for the town of Karlskoga, some 240 kilometers west of Stockholm, home of Bofors, the major sponsor of the symposium. Alfred Nobel had owned the company in the late nineteenth century when it became important in the chemical industry and the manufacture of cannons. Unfortunately, I was too preoccupied with my upcoming presentation to appreciate the passing countryside.

Richard Leakey opened the conference with a relatively short talk on his work at Lake Turkana in Kenya, describing the many hominid discoveries found there. Then it was my turn to walk to the podium. With my stomach in knots, I presented my paper, "Early African Hominid Phylogenesis: A Re-evaluation," describing the Hadar hominid collection and delivering evidence that they represented the same species as fossils found at Laetoli, in Tanzania, by Richard's mother, Mary. I made my case that all of the fossils bore more primitive anatomical features than any other known hominid species. And then I announced that these hominids belonged to a new species: *Australopithecus afarensis.* As I listened to my words reverberating through the small auditorium, I thought about the sixteen-year-old who dreamed of finding the missing link: He was now standing, dressed in a three-piece suit, before the most distinguished audience on the planet, publicly pronouncing Lucy's scientific name for the first time. It was a provocative thing to do. Many researchers thought that the fossils were simply east African versions of *A. africanus.*

From the sound of people shuffling in their seats and a few audible aspirations I could sense the immediate skepticism. My mouth went dry and I took a sip of water. In my next slide I showed a redrawing of the human family tree and elaborated on the major implications of the new species for understanding the shape of that tree. I was fully aware that most of the assembled favored placing Dart's Taung baby, *A. africanus,* at the base of the tree, the common ancestor to all later hominids, including modern humans. But I boldly maintained that it was now time to relegate *A. africanus* to an extinct side branch of human evolution, and to position *A. afarensis* as the trunk of the tree, the last common ancestor to all post-3-million-year-old hominids. Dead silence. I took another sip of water, the lights came on, and Carl Gustaf Bernhard, the moderator, called for questions. Not a single hand went up. The silence was broken when the moderator suggested that we break for high tea.

During the remaining days of the symposium I continued to argue the main points of my paper, but most of the guests were unconvinced. How could I be sure that all the Hadar hominids were of a single species, they wondered. Based upon what evidence did I put Hadar and Laetoli fossils in the same species? I knew that my colleagues and I faced months of work, possibly years, before our conclusions were accepted and Lucy could assume her proper position on the human family tree.

Hunting the First Hominid

Pat Shipman

Self-centeredly, human beings have always taken an exceptional interest in their origins. Each discovery of a new species of hominid—both our human ancestors and the near-relatives arising after the split from the gorilla-chimp lineage—is reported with great fanfare, even though the First Hominid remains elusive. We hope that, when our earliest ancestor is finally captured, it will reveal the fundamental adaptations that make us *us.*

There is no shortage of ideas about the essential nature of the human species and the basic adaptations of our kind. Some say hominids are fundamentally thinkers; others favor tool-makers or talkers; still others argue that hunting, scavenging or bipedal walking made hominids special. Knowing what the First Hominid looked like would add some meat to a soup flavored with speculation and prejudice.

Genetic and molecular studies provide one sort of insight, showing what sort of *stuff* we are made of, and that it is only slightly different stuff from that which makes up the apes (gorillas, chimps, orangutans and gibbons). From the molecular differences among the genes of humans and apes, geneticists estimate the time when each of the various ape and hominid lineages diverged from the common stem. The result is a sort of hairy Y diagram, with multiple branches instead of simply two as is usual on a Y. Each terminus represents a living species; each branching point or node represents the appearance of some new evolutionary trait, such as new molecules, new genes, new shapes or new proportions of limb, skull and tooth. Unfortunately, this way of diagramming the results tends to lull us into thinking (falsely) that all the evolutionary changes occurred at those nodes, and none along the branches.

Such studies omit a crucial part of our history: the extinct species. Only the fossil record contains evidence, in context, of the precise pathway that evolution took. In this technological age, when sophisticated instrumentation and gee-whiz algorithms seem downright necessary, the most basic information about the evolution of our lineage still comes from branches of science that operate in rather old-fashioned ways. The primary discoveries in paleontology (the study of old things), paleoanthropology (the study of old humans) and archaeology (the study of the old stuff that old humans leave around) still rely on the efforts of handful of investigators who slog around on foot or excavate in desolate landscapes. Fancy equipment can't replace eyes and brains, although instrumentation plays a crucial role in the dating an analysis of fossil remains.

Finding the evolutionary origin of hominids is little like stalking big game. Paleoanthropologist struggle to establish when and where their quarry was last seen and what it was like—hoping to follow its tracks backward in time. (*Why* hominids or any other group arose is such a metaphysical question that most paleoanthropologists run away screaming when it is asked.)

When the first hominid slinked through the underbush has been estimated from molecular clock and confirmed by radiometric dates. These line of evidence converge on a period between 5 million and 7 million years ago as the time when primitive, perhaps vaguely apelike species evolved some definitive new adaptation that transformed it into the First Hominid. But like the point of inflection on a line graph, the first species in any new lineage is only readily apparent after the fact. The emergence of the first hominid was probably not obvious in prospect but only now, in retrospect—in the context of the entire evolutionary record of the hominids—when the long-term evolutionary trends can be seen.

Where this dangerous creature once lived has to be Africa, since both our closest living relatives (chimpanzees and gorillas) and all early hominids (older than about 2 million years ago) are African.

What to Look For?

What happened, exactly, and to *whom,* remain to be discovered. Two newly discovered fossil species have each been proposed to be the First Hominid. This circumstance raises a significant issue: How would we know the First Hominid if we saw it?

Making a list of key features that differentiate apes from people is not difficult, but misleading. It is absurd to expect that all of these differences arose simultaneously during a single evolutionary event represented by the final fork on the hairy Y diagram. The first ape on the gorilla-chimp lineage was neither a gorilla nor a chimpanzee, for modem gorillas and chimps have had at least 5 million years to evolve in isolation before arriving at their modem form. In the same way the First Hominid on our lineage was not a human and did not possess all of the characteristics of modem humans.

Using a hairy Y diagram, we can limit the number of contenders for the essential or basal hominid adaptation:

- Hominids might be essentially bipeds. All known hominids are bipedal; no apes are.

- Wishful thinking aside, hominids are not simply brainy apes. Alas, until about 2 million years ago no hominid had a brain larger than an ape's relative to its body size.

- Hominids might be apelike creatures that have lost their sexual dimorphism. Sexual dimorphism is exhibited as male-female differences that are not related to reproduction. For example, male orangs are typically much larger than females and have longer canine teeth that hone sharper with wear. The fossil record shows that hominids lost their dental sexual dimorphism first, since all known hominids have small and flat-wearing canines. In contrast, sexual dimorphism in body size persisted in hominids until about 2 million years ago, when the genus *Homo* first appeared.

- Thick dental enamel may be a key hominid trait. All hominids have thick enamel, whereas all fossil and living apes (except those in the orangutan lineage) have thin enamel. Because the fossil record of apes is so poor, we do not know whether the primitive condition for apes and hominids was thick or thin enamel. Indeed, how enamel thickness is to be measured and evaluated has generated many pages of debate.

- Hominids are hand-graspers or manipulators (from the Latin for hand, *manus*), whereas apes are foot-graspers. These differences are reflected in the sharp contrasts in the hand and foot anatomy of apes and humans. Apes have divergent big toes and long, curved toe bones for holding onto branches; their thumbs are short and cannot be opposed to the other fingers for skillful manipulation. Human beings are the opposite, with long, opposable thumbs and big toes that are closely aligned with the remaining short, straight toes. Human feet are nearly useless for grasping but are well adapted to bipedalism. An intermediate condition occurs in early hominids such as Lucy (the best-known individual of *Australopithecus afarensis*), who had opposable thumbs and numerous adaptations to bipedalism, and yet retained rather long and curved toes. Lucy and probably other types of *Australopithecus* were walkers, hand-graspers *and* somewhat compromised foot-graspers.

A description of our desired prey, then, might read like this:

An ape-brained and small-canined creature, with dental enamel of unknown thickness. Large if male but smaller if female. May be spotted climbing adeptly in trees or walking bipedally on the ground. Last seen in Africa between 5 million and 7 million years ago.

From this description, can we identify the First Hominid? Well, no—not yet.

A Tale of Two Trophies

Yohannes Haile-Selassie of the University of California, Berkeley, described a likely contender from Ethiopia in July of 2001. His material comes from Ethiopian sediments between 5.2 million and 5.8 million years old and is called *Ardipithecus ramidus kadabba,* a new subspecies. *Ardipithecus* means "root ape" in the Mar language, and the species has been explicitly proposed to be a "root species" ancestral to all later hominids.

Haile-Selassie's specimens include more than 20 teeth, some associated with a mandible or lower jaw; substantial pieces of two left humeri, or upper arm bones; a partial ulna from the same forearm as one humerus; a partial clavicle or collarbone; a half of one finger bone; and a complete toe bone.

No ironclad evidence of bipedality in any *Ardipithecus* specimen has yet been published. In this collection, the only evidence about habitual patterns of locomotion comes from the single toe bone. Its weight-bearing surface faces downward as in bipeds, not inward as in apes. Any jury might be suspicious that *Ardipithecus* was bipedal, but none of the really telltale body parts—pelvis, complete femur, tibia, or ankle bones—has yet been recovered. The preserved bones of the arm, finger and shoulder closely resemble those of Lucy and may have been used in grasping and tree-climbing. *Ardipithecus* is as yet too poorly known for its relative brain size or sexual dimorphism in body size to be assessed.

The other candidate that has already been bagged is a 6 million-year-old find from the Tugen Hills of Kenya called *Orrorin tugenensis.* Its generic name is derived from the Tugen language and means "original man"—a claim as bold as "root ape." Found by a joint French-Kenyan team headed by Brigitte Senut of the Centre nationale de la recherche scientifique, the *Orrorin* fossils include a few teeth, some embedded in a jaw fragment; a partial humerus; a finger bone; and substantial parts of three femurs, or thigh bones.

The femurs, which might provide definitive evidence of bipedality, are incomplete. The sole evidence for bipedality lies in the head of the femur in *Orrorin,* which is proportionately larger than Lucy's. One reason to evolve a large-headed femur is to dissipate the forces produced by bipedalism. The team concludes that *Orrorin* evolved bipedalism separately from Lucy (and from other species of *Australopithecus*), making *Orrorin* the only known ancestor of *Homo. Australopithecus* is displaced to an extinct side-branch of the hominid lineage.

Their surprising conclusion is not universally accepted. Skeptics reply that the femoral differences between *Orrorin* and *Australopithecus* might disappear if *Orrorin*'s femur were compared with that of a large male individual rather than with the diminutive Lucy.

As in *Ardipithecus,* the bones from the upper limb of *Orrorin* show tree-climbing adaptations. Neither relative brain size nor body size dimorphism can be evaluated in *Orrorin.*

Where *Orrorin* and *Ardipithecus* differ are in their teeth. *Orrorin* appears to have thick enamel, like a hominid or an orangutan, and *Ardipithecus* seems to have thin enamel, like other apes. This dental comparison might resolve the question "Who is the First Hominid?" in favor of *Orrorin,* except that

Orrorin's canine teeth imply the opposite conclusion. *Orrorin*'s single known canine is sizable and pointed and wears like an ape's canine. In contrast, the several known canines of *Ardipithecus* are all small-crowned and flat-wearing, like a hominid's canines.

Puzzlingly, *Ardipithecus* and *Orrorin* show different mosaics of hominid and ape features. Both may be bipeds, although *Ardipithecus* is a biped in the manner of *Australopithecus* and *Orrorin* is not. If one of these two newly announced species is the First Hominid, then the other must be banished to the ape lineage. The situation is deliciously complex and confusing.

It is also humbling. We thought we knew an ape from a person; we thought we could even identify a man in an ape suit or an ape in a tuxedo for what they were. Humans have long prided themselves on being very different from apes—but pride goeth before a fall. In this case, embarrassingly, we can't tell the ape from the hominid even though we have teeth, jaws, and arm and leg bones.

Paleoanthropologists must seriously reconsider the defining attributes of apes and hominids while we wait for new fossils. In the meantime, we should ponder our complicity, too, for we have been guilty of expecting evolution to be much simpler than it ever is.

PAT SHIPMAN is an adjunct professor of anthropology at the Pennsylvania State University. Address: Department of Anthropology, 315 Carpenter Building, Pennsylvania State University, University Park, PA 16801. Internet: pls10@psu.edu

Made in Savannahstan

MAREK KOHN

The archaeological excavations at Dmanisi, in the Republic of Georgia, are a glorious exception to the rule that if you are in a hole, you should stop digging. What began as the excavation of a medieval town has turned into a pivotal site for our understanding of human evolution. So far, palaeoarchaeologists working there have unearthed five ancestral human skulls and other remains: the individuals they represent are now the central characters in a story whose plot is poised to undergo a major twist.

The story is known as Out of Africa. It tells of Africa as the centre of evolutionary innovation in our ancestors, and the springboard from which some of these hominins struck out into other continents. There are two main parts to the tale. The most familiar one charts the evolution of our own species in Africa around 200,000 years ago, and the subsequent migration of these modern humans throughout the world. The less well known part of the story concerns the first migration of our ancestors out of Africa, more than 1 million years earlier. It is this part of the story that is now being challenged for the first time. Last December, *Nature* ran a provocative critique by Robin Dennell of the University of Sheffield, UK, and Wil Roebroeks of Leiden University, the Netherlands, that concluded: "Most probably, we are on the threshold of a profound transformation of our understanding of early hominin evolution."

The "Out of Africa 1" story begins more than 2 million years ago when small upright African apes, known as australopithecines, start evolving into large and recognisably human creatures—the first members of our own genus, *Homo.* Eventually one of these, *Homo erectus,* strikes out to conquer Eurasia. At the heart of the tale of this first transcontinental migration lies the assumption that what made us human also propelled us out across the rest of the planet. This idea has a powerful romantic appeal, suggesting that exploration and settlement are primordial and defining human instincts. *H. erectus* had "a typically insatiable human wanderlust", according to palaeoanthropologist Ian Tattersall of the American Museum of Natural History in New York. What enabled these beings to satisfy the urge to boldly go was their package of characteristically human traits that distinguished them from the australopithecines: longer limbs, increased body and brain size, an omnivorous diet and the use of stone tools.

Until quite recently, all the evidence seemed to support this view and version of events. The earliest remains of *H. erectus* in Africa are about 1.8 million years old. At first these beings seem to have produced only simple flaked stone tools, but around 1.5 million years ago these are joined in the archaeological record by teardrop-shaped hand axes, suggesting that their creators had reached a new level of sophistication. In addition, the various hominin fossils found in east Asia over the past century had been dated at a million years old at most. The timing of all this seemed to attest to the emergence of *H. erectus* in Africa, its growing ingenuity there and then gradual spread eastward.

In the past decade, however, this sequence has begun to unravel. Fossils of *H. erectus* found at the Indonesian sites of Sangiran and Mojokerto are now believed to be over 1.5 million years old—possibly as much as 1.8 million years old. Those at Dmanisi have been dated at 1.7 million years or more. With these startlingly early dates from both ends of Asia it looks as though *H. erectus* materialised almost simultaneously in Africa, east Asia and a point in between. What's more, hand axes have proved to be red herrings. The stone tools associated with the migrant populations are no technological advance on the first ones to appear in the archaeological record, half a million years previously. As for brain size: with an adult average of about 700 cubic centimetres these colonisers had the edge on australopithecines, whose brains were under half a litre, but they were at the bottom end of the *H. erectus* range, and had only about half the volume of a modern human brain. It looks as though increased intelligence was not a prerequisite for migration.

A still more radical challenge to the supposed role of superior cognitive abilities in the dispersal of hominins comes from a mid-1990s fossil discovery that Dennell considers one of the most important of the past two decades. Australopithecine fossils had hitherto been found in the Great Rift Valley of eastern Africa and in the south of the continent. Then one turned up in Chad, in the middle of the continent, 2500 kilometres away from the Rift Valley. If australopithecines were able to colonise that region between 3 and 3.5 million years ago, argues Dennell, there is no reason why they should have stopped at the Red Sea. Ancient hominins would not have distinguished between Africa and Asia, and neither should we, he and Roebroeks argue. Those australopithecines in Chad date from an era when grasslands stretched from northern Africa to eastern Asia. Other animals moved freely across this landscape, so why not hominins? "If you were a herbivore that took grass seriously," Dennell remarks, "you could munch your way all across south-west Asia to northern China." He and Roebroeks suggest that we should re-imagine this vast transcontinental band of grass as a zone throughout which our ancestors also roamed. Dennell has dubbed it "Savannahstan."

The savannahs were the product of global cooling, which dried out moist woodlands, shifting the balance to grass. Over millions of years, the global climate gradually cooled, but there were also times when conditions altered quite abruptly. These shifts rearranged the fauna—species vanished, new species emerged. One of these climatic pulses occurred around 2.5 million years ago. In the Arctic, ice sheets spread. In eastern Africa, forest-adapted antelopes were replaced by those suited to savannah. New, robust australopithecines appeared, as did somewhat larger-brained hominins, *Homo habilis,* the first members of the *Homo* genus, and we also find the earliest known stone tools.

In a bold challenge to the conventional story, Dennell argues that hominins migrated out of Africa before *H. erectus* even evolved, and long before the dates of the oldest known hominin fossils in Asia. These first migrants were either australopithecines or *H. habilis*—he, like some prominent palaeoanthropologists, regards these two as much the same kind of creatures. For evidence that small stature was no obstacle to dispersal he points to the Dmanisi hominins. Not only do their brain sizes fit within the *H. habilis* range, evidence from a femur and a tibia, as yet unpublished, indicates that one of them may have weighed only about 54 kilograms and stood just 1.4 metres tall. Although the stature of the individuals at Sangiran and Mojokerto is unknown, hominins clearly did not need long legs to stride out of Africa.

What's more, Dennell has the makings of a story set in Savannahstan that could explain a key mystery of human evolution—what spurred the evolution of *H. erectus* itself. While *H. habilis* seems to have evolved in response to the cold snap around 2.5 million years ago, there is no such climate change in Africa coinciding with the emergence of the earliest known examples of *H. erectus,* around 1.8 million years ago. Nor does *H. erectus* have any clearly identifiable immediate predecessors. "Not for nothing has it been described as a hominin 'without an ancestor, without a clear past'," observe Dennell and Roebroeks.

Dennell's solution to the problem is beguilingly simple: perhaps we have been looking in the wrong place. "Maybe the Rift Valley was a cul-de-sac," Dennell suggests. Tongue in cheek perhaps, but the remark conveys his strong conviction that the importance of Asia has been unfairly neglected. At around the time *H. erectus* emerged some 1.8 million years ago, selective pressures to evolve would have been greater in Asia than in Africa, he argues. Traces of the global cooling pulse starting around 2.5 million years ago have been detected in the soils of China's Loess Plateau.

Beneath the silty loess are layers of red clay, which appear to have been blown there by westerly winds before the cooling began. Above these, the particles of loess decrease in size from north to south, indicating that they were deposited by northerly winds, the heavier particles falling to the ground first. So it appears that the winds changed when the climate cooled. This would have brought monsoons and polarised the years into seasons, with summers becoming increasingly arid over subsequent millennia, causing the grasslands to expand. Asia was the core of this process and Africa was peripheral, according to Dennell.

In this perspective the Dmanisi hominins may represent a missing link in the evolution of *H. erectus,* responding to climatic pressures but still retaining much in common with *H. habilis.* Australopithecines were adapted to open spaces in woodlands, ranging around relatively small areas, living off plants, seeds, small mammals and perhaps carcasses. As these open spaces expanded into savannah, the Dmanisi hominins would have faced pressures to evolve more human-like traits, increasing the distances over which they ranged, and turning more to animals as a source of food.

Dennell even goes so far as to suggest that the Dmanisi hominins might be ancestors of the later *H. erectus* in Africa. The most celebrated representative there is the 1.6-million-year-old "Turkana Boy." His tall stature, long limbs and body proportions epitomise adaptation to a hot, dry climate. In other words, African *H. erectus* might have Asian roots. If this is the case, Out of Africa 1 is a crucial part of the story of our own evolution, since *H. erectus* is generally thought to be a direct ancestor of modern humans.

Since Dennell and Roebroeks wrote their *Nature* review, American and Georgian researchers studying the Dmanisi finds have published a paper that points in a similar direction (*Journal of Human Evolution,* vol 50(2), p 115). Suggesting the finds be classed as *Homo erectus georgicus,* Philip Rightmire of Binghamton University, New York, and his colleagues conclude that Dmanisi may be "close to the stem from which *H. erectus* evolved." They also point to the possibility that the Dmanisi population's ancestors were *H. habilis* emigrants from Africa, and that the dates do not rule out the possibility that *H. erectus* evolved in Asia. "For me, the evidence from Dmanisi is critical," says Rightmire. "It seems to me that such a population could well be ancestral to *H. erectus* in Africa and also to *H. erectus* in the Far East." But he anticipates that rewriting the origin and dispersal of *H. erectus* will be a slow process. "We're not likely to see a major breakthrough immediately."

Further research that broadly chimes with Dennell and Roebroeks's arguments comes from Alan Templeton of Washington University, St Louis (*Yearbook of Physical Anthropology,* vol 48, p 33). By comparing clusters of DNA that vary between individuals and tend to be inherited together, geneticists can identify when particular mutations arose, and use these to map relationships within or between species. Until a few years ago, they had to rely on DNA from mitochondria or sex chromosomes, but it is now becoming possible to increase the resolution of such maps by using data from the rest of the genome. Comparing 25 DNA regions in the genomes of people from across the world, Templeton found evidence for an expansion out of Africa around 1.9 million years ago, and that gene flow between African and Eurasian populations—in both directions—was established by 1.5 million years ago. Not only do these findings suggest that migration began earlier than previously thought, it also looks as though hominins were moving back and forth between Eurasia and Africa.

"The hypotheses Dennell and Roebroeks present are testable with molecular genetic data," Templeton says, "so I think that the prospects for testing some of their alternatives to 'Out of Africa 1' will be excellent in the near future." Only four years ago, when he first conducted an analysis of this kind, there were insufficient results for him to detect any expansion out of Africa between 1 and 3 million years ago. Increasingly, however, researchers looking for genetic variation among individuals are also recording their geographical origins—just the information Templeton needs to do his analysis. "I anticipate greater and greater statistical resolution of these older events in human evolutionary history," he says. "Genetics will play an increasing and important role in testing their ideas in conjunction with new fossil and archaeological discoveries."

For Dennell, however, the objects in the ground are what matters. He is keen to look for hominin remains in Asia to balance the generous legacies of the Rift Valley and southern Africa. Unfortunately, the countries he most wants to search—Saudi Arabia, Iran, Afghanistan—read like a list of places not to visit these days. A site in Pakistan where he found stone tools in the 1980s dating from 1.9 million years ago is also now off limits because of the political turbulence that has spread across the region. It seems that Asia will not give up its secrets easily, but Dennell is convinced that in this case, absence of evidence is not evidence of absence. The search may prove difficult but the rewards are potentially enormous, amounting to nothing less than the rewriting of human prehistory.

MAREK KOHN is based in Brighton, UK. His book *As We Know It: Coming to Terms with on Evolved Mind* is published by Granta Books.

Scavenger Hunt

As paleoanthropologists close in on their quarry, it may turn out to be a different beast from what they imaged.

PAT SHIPMAN

In both textbooks and films, ancestral humans (hominids) have been portrayed as hunters. Small-brained, big-browed, upright, and usually mildly furry, early hominid males gaze with keen eyes across the gold savanna, searching for prey. Skillfully wielding a few crude stone tools, they kill and dismember everything from small gazelles to elephants, while females care for young and gather roots, tubers, and berries. The food is shared by group members at temporary camps. This familiar image of Man the Hunter has been bolstered by the finding of stone tools in association with fossil animal bones. But the role of hunting in early hominid life cannot be determined in the absence of more direct evidence.

I discovered one means of testing the hunting hypothesis almost by accident. In 1978, I began documenting the microscopic damage produced on bones by different events. I hoped to develop a diagnostic key for identifying the post-mortem history of specific fossil bones, useful for understanding how fossil assemblages were formed. Using a scanning electron microscope (SEM) because of its excellent resolution and superb depth of field, I inspected high-fidelity replicas of modern bones that had been subjected to known events or conditions. (I had to use replicas, rather than real bones, because specimens must fit into the SEM's small vacuum chamber.) I soon established that such common events as weathering, root etching, sedimentary abrasion, and carnivore chewing produced microscopically distinctive features.

In 1980, my SEM study took an unexpected turn. Richard Potts (now of Yale University), Henry Bunn (now of the University of Wisconsin at Madison), and I almost simultaneously found what appeared to be stone-tool cut marks on fossils from Olduvai Gorge, Tanzania, and Koobi Fora, Kenya. We were working almost side by side at the National Museums of Kenya, in Nairobi, where the fossils are stored. The possibility of cut marks was exciting, since both sites preserve some of the oldest known archaeological materials. Potts and I returned to the United States, manufactured some stone tools, and started "butchering" bones and joints begged from our local butchers. Under the SEM, replicas of these cut marks looked very different from replicas of carnivore tooth scratches, regardless of the species of carnivore or the type of tool involved. By comparing the marks on the fossils with our hundreds of modern bones of known history, we were able

to demonstrate convincingly that hominids using stone tools had processed carcasses of many different animals nearly two million years ago. For the first time, there was a firm link between stone tools and at least some of the early fossil animal bones.

This initial discovery persuaded some paleoanthropologists that the hominid hunter scenario was correct. Potts and I were not so sure. Our study had shown that many of the cut-marked fossils also bore carnivore tooth marks and that some of the cut marks were in places we hadn't expected—on bones that bore little meat in life. More work was needed.

In addition to more data about the Olduvai cut marks and tooth marks, I needed specific information about the patterns of cut marks left by known hunters performing typical activities associated with hunting. If similar patterns occurred on the fossils, then the early hominids probably behaved similarly to more modern hunters; if the patterns were different, then the behavior was probably also different. Three activities related to hunting occur often enough in peoples around the world and leave consistent enough traces to be used for such a test.

First, human hunters systematically disarticulate their kills, unless the animals are small enough to be eaten on the spot. Disarticulation leaves cut marks in a predictable pattern on the skeleton. Such marks cluster near the major joints of the limbs: shoulder, elbow, carpal joint (wrist), hip, knee, and hock (ankle). Taking a carcass apart at the joints is much easier than breaking or cutting through bones. Disarticulation enables hunters to carry food back to a central place or camp, so that they can share it with others or cook it or even store it by placing portions in trees, away from the reach of carnivores. If early hominids were hunters who transported and shared their kills, disarticulation marks would occur near joints in frequencies comparable to those produced by modern human hunters.

Second, human hunters often butcher carcasses, in the sense of removing meat from the bones. Butchery marks are usually found on the shafts of bones from the upper part of the front or hind limb, since this is where the big muscle masses lie. Butchery may be carried out at the kill site—especially if the animal is very large and its bones very heavy—or it may take place at the base camp, during the process of sharing food with others. Compared with disarticulation, butchery leaves relatively few marks. It is hard for a hunter to locate an animal's joints without leaving cut marks on the bone. In contrast, it is easier to cut the meat away from the midshaft of the bone without making such marks. If early hominids shared their food, however, there ought to be a number of cut marks located on the midshaft of some fossil bones.

Finally, human hunters often remove skin or tendons from carcasses, to be used for clothing, bags, thongs, and so on. Hide or tendon must be separated from the bones in many areas where there is little flesh, such as the lower limb bones of pigs, giraffes, antelopes, and zebras. In such cases, it is difficult to cut the skin without leaving a cut mark on the bone. Therefore, one expects to find many more cut marks on such bones than on the flesh-covered bones of the upper part of the limbs.

Unfortunately, although accounts of butchery and disarticulation by modern human hunters are remarkably consistent, quantitative studies are rare. Further, virtually all modern hunter-gatherers use metal tools, which leave more cut marks than stone tools. For these reasons I hesitated to compare the fossil evidence with data on modern hunters. Fortunately, Diane Gifford of the University of California, Santa Cruz, and her colleagues had recently completed a quantitative study of marks and damage on thousands of antelope bones processed by Neolithic (Stone Age) hunters in Kenya some 2,300 years ago. The data from Prolonged Drift, as the site is called, were perfect for comparison with the Olduvai material.

Assisted by my technician, Jennie Rose, I carefully inspected more than 2,500 antelope bones from Bed I at Olduvai Gorge, which is dated to between 1.9 and 1.7 million years ago. We made high-fidelity replicas of every mark that we thought might be either a cut mark or a carnivore tooth mark. Back in the United States, we used the SEM to make positive identifications of the marks. (The replication and SEM inspection was time consuming, but necessary: only about half of the marks were correctly identified by eye or by light microscope.) I then compared the patterns of cut mark and tooth mark distributions on Olduvai fossils with those made by Stone Age hunters at Prolonged Drift.

By their location, I identified marks caused either by disarticulation or meat removal and then compared their frequencies with those from Prolonged Drift. More than 90 percent of the Neolithic marks in these two categories were from disarticulation, but to my surprise, only about 45 percent of the corresponding Olduvai cut marks were from disarticulation. This difference is too great to have occurred by chance; the Olduvai bones did not show the predicted pattern. In fact, the Olduvai cut marks attributable to meat removal and disarticulation showed essentially the same pattern of distribution as the carnivore tooth marks. Apparently, the early hominids were not regularly disarticulating carcasses. This finding casts serious doubt on the idea that early hominids carried their kills back to camp to share with others, since both transport and sharing are difficult unless carcasses are cut up.

When I looked for cut marks attributable to skinning or tendon removal, a more modern pattern emerged. On both the Neolithic and Olduvai bones, nearly 75 percent of all cut marks occurred on bones that bore little meat; these cut marks probably came from skinning. Carnivore tooth marks were much less common on such bones. Hominids were using carcasses as a source of skin and tendon. This made it seem more surprising that they disarticulated carcasses so rarely.

A third line of evidence provided the most tantalizing clue. Occasionally, sets of overlapping marks occur on the Olduvai fossils. Sometimes, these sets include both cut marks and carnivore tooth marks. Still more rarely, I could see under the SEM which mark had been made first, because its features were over-laid by those of the later mark, in much the same way as old tire tracks on a dirt road are obscured by fresh ones. Although only thirteen such sets of marks were found, in eight cases the hominids made the cut marks after the carnivores made their tooth marks. This finding suggested a new hypothesis. Instead of hunting for prey and leaving the remains behind for carnivores to scavenge, perhaps hominids were scavenging from the carnivores. This might explain the hominids' apparently unsystematic use of carcasses: they took what they could get, be it skin, tendon, or meat.

Man the Scavenger is not nearly as attractive an image as Man the Hunter, but it is worth examining. Actually, although hunting and scavenging are different ecological strategies, many mammals do both. The only pure scavengers alive in Africa today are vultures; not one of the modern African mammalian carnivores is a pure scavenger. Even spotted hyenas, which have massive, bone-crushing teeth well adapted for eating the bones left behind by others, only scavenge about 33 percent of their food. Other carnivores that scavenge when there are enough carcasses around include lions, leopards, striped hyenas, and jackals. Long-term behavioral studies suggest that these carnivores scavenge when they can and kill when they must. There are only two nearly pure predators, or hunters—the cheetah and the wild dog—that rarely, if ever, scavenge.

What are the costs and benefits of scavenging compared with those of predation? First of all, the scavenger avoids the task of making sure its meal is dead: a predator has already endured the energetically costly business of chasing or stalking animal after animal until one is killed. But while scavenging may be cheap, it's risky. Predators rarely give up their prey to scavengers without defending it. In such disputes, the larger animal, whether a scavenger or a predator, usually wins, although smaller animals in a pack may defeat a lone, larger animal. Both predators and scavengers suffer the dangers inherent in fighting for possession of a carcass. Smaller scavengers such as jackals or striped hyenas avoid disputes to some extent by specializing in darting in and removing a piece of a carcass without trying to take possession of the whole thing. These two strategies can be characterized as that of the bully or that of the sneak: bullies need to be large to be successful, sneaks need to be small and quick.

Because carcasses are almost always much rarer than live prey, the major cost peculiar to scavenging is that scavengers must survey much larger areas than predators to find food. They can travel slowly, since their "prey" is already dead, but endurance is important. Many predators specialize in speed at the expense of endurance, while scavengers do the opposite.

The more committed predators among the East African carnivores (wild dogs and cheetahs) can achieve great top speeds when running, although not for long. Perhaps as a consequence, these "pure" hunters enjoy a much higher success rate in hunting (about three-fourths of their chases end in kills) than any of the scavenger-hunters do (less than half of their chases are successful). Wild dogs and cheetahs are efficient hunters, but they are neither big enough nor efficient enough in their locomotion to make good scavengers. In fact, the cheetah's teeth are so specialized for meat slicing that they probably cannot withstand the stresses of bone crunching and carcass dismembering carried out by scavengers. Other carnivores are less successful at hunting, but have specializations of size, endurance, or (in the case of the hyenas) dentition that make successful scavenging possible. The small carnivores seem to have a somewhat higher hunting success rate than the large ones, which balances out their difficulties in asserting possession of carcasses.

In addition to endurance, scavengers need an efficient means of locating carcasses, which, unlike live animals, don't move or make noises. Vultures, for example, solve both problems by flying. The soaring, gliding flight of vultures expends much less energy than walking or cantering as performed by the part-time mammalian scavengers. Flight enables vultures to maintain a foraging radius two to three times larger than that of spotted hyenas, while providing a better vantage point. This explains why vultures can scavenge all of their food in the same habitat in which it is impossible for any mammal to be a pure scavenger. (In fact, many mammals learn where carcasses are located from the presence of vultures.)

Since mammals can't succeed as full-time scavengers, they must have another source of food to provide the bulk of their diet. The large carnivores rely on hunting large animals to obtain food when scavenging doesn't work. Their size enables them to defend a carcass against others. Since the small carnivores—jackals and striped hyenas—often can't defend carcasses successfully, most of their diet is composed of fruit and insects. When they do hunt, they usually prey on very small animals, such as rats or hares, that can be consumed in their entirety before the larger competitors arrive.

The ancient habitat associated with the fossils of Olduvai and Koobi Fora would have supported many herbivores and carnivores. Among the latter were two species of large saber-toothed cats, whose teeth show extreme adaptations for meat slicing. These were predators with primary access to carcasses. Since their teeth were unsuitable for bone crushing, the saber-toothed cats must have left behind many bones covered with scraps of meat, skin, and tendon. Were early hominids among the scavengers that exploited such carcasses?

All three hominid species that were present in Bed I times (*Homo habilis, Australopithecus africanus, A. robustus*) were adapted for habitual, upright bipedalism. Many anatomists see evidence that these hominids were agile tree climbers as well. Although upright bipedalism is a notoriously peculiar mode of locomotion, the adaptive value of which has been argued for years (See Matt Cartmill's article, "Four Legs Good, Two Legs Bad," *Natural History,* November 1983), there are three general points of agreement.

First, bipedal running is neither fast nor efficient compared to quadrupedal gaits. However, at moderate speeds of 2.5 to 3.5 miles per hour, bipedal *walking* is more energetically efficient than quadrupedal walking. Thus, bipedal walking is an excellent means of covering large areas slowly, making it an unlikely adaptation for a hunter but an appropriate and useful adaptation for a scavenger. Second, bipedalism elevates the head, thus improving the hominid's ability to spot items on the ground—an advantage both to scavengers and to those trying to avoid becoming a carcass. Combining bipedalism with agile tree climbing improves the vantage point still further. Third, bipedalism frees the hands from locomotive duties, making it possible to carry items. What would early hominids have carried? Meat makes a nutritious, easy-to-carry package; the problem is that carrying meat attracts scavengers. Richard Potts suggests that carrying stone tools or unworked stones for toolmaking to caches would be a more efficient and less dangerous activity under many circumstances.

In short, bipedalism is compatible with a scavenging strategy. I am tempted to argue that bipedalism evolved because it provided a substantial advantage to scavenging hominids. But I doubt hominids could scavenge effectively without tools, and bipedalism predates the oldest known stone tools by more than a million years.

Is there evidence that, like modern mammalian scavengers, early hominids had an alternative food source, such as either hunting or eating fruits and insects? My husband, Alan Walker, has shown that the microscopic wear on an animal's teeth reflects its diet. Early hominid teeth wear more like that of chimpanzees and other modern fruit eaters than that of carnivores. Apparently, early hominids ate mostly fruit, as the smaller, modern scavengers do. This accords with the estimated body weight of early hominids, which was only about forty to eighty pounds—less than that of any of the modern carnivores that combine scavenging and hunting but comparable to the striped hyena, which eats fruits and insects as well as meat.

Would early hominids have been able to compete for carcasses with other carnivores? They were too small to use a bully strategy, but if they scavenged in groups, a combined bully-sneak strategy might have been possible. Perhaps they were able to drive off a primary predator long enough to grab some meat, skin, or marrow-filled bone before relinquishing the carcass. The effectiveness of this strategy would have been vastly improved by using tools to remove meat or parts of limbs, a task at which hominid teeth are poor. As agile climbers, early hominids may have retreated into the trees to eat their scavenged trophies, thus avoiding competition from large terrestrial carnivores.

In sum, the evidence on cut marks, tooth wear, and bipedalism, together with our knowledge of scavenger adaptation in general, is consistent with the hypothesis that two million years ago hominids were scavengers rather than accomplished hunters. Animal carcasses, which contributed relatively little to the hominid diet, were not systematically cut up and transported for sharing at base camps. Man the Hunter may not have appeared until 1.5 to 0.7 million years ago, when we do see a shift toward omnivory, with a greater proportion of meat in the diet. This more heroic ancestor may have been *Homo erectus,* equipped with Acheulean-style stone tools and, increasingly, fire. If we wish to look further back, we may have to become accustomed to a less flattering image of our heritage.

PAT SHIPMAN is an assistant professor in the Department of Cell Biology and Anatomy at The Johns Hopkins University School of Medicine.

From *Natural History,* April 1984, pp. 21–22, 24–27. Copyright © 1984 by Natural History Magazine. Reprinted by permission.

The Scavenging of "Peking Man"

New evidence shows that a venerable cave was neither hearth nor home.

Noel T. Boaz and Russell L. Ciochon

China is filled with archaeological wonders, but few can rival the Peking Man Site at Zhoukoudian, which has been inscribed on UNESCO's World Heritage List. Located about thirty miles southwest of Beijing, the town of Zhoukoudian boasts several attractions, including ruins of Buddhist monasteries dating from the Ming Dynasty (1368–1644). But the town's main claim to fame is Longgushan, or Dragon Bone Hill, the site of the cave that yielded the first (and still the largest) cache of fossils of *Homo erectus pekinensis,* historically known as Peking man—a human relative who walked upright and whose thick skull bones and beetling brow housed a brain three-quarters the size of *H. sapiens's.*

The remains of about forty-five individuals—more than half of them women and children—along with thousands of stone stools, debris from tool manufacturing, and thousands of animal bones, were contained within the hundred-foot-thick deposits that once completely filled the original cave. The task of excavation, initiated in 1921, was not completed until 1982. Some evidence unearthed at the site suggested that these creatures, who lived from about 600,000 to 300,000 years ago, had mastered the use of fire and practiced cannibalism. But despite years of excavation and analysis, little is certain about what occurred here long ago. In the past two years we have visited the cave site, reexamined the fossils, and carried out new tests in an effort to sort out the facts.

To most of the early excavators, such as anatomist Davidson Black, paleontologist Pierre Teilhard de Chardin, and archaeologist Henri Breuil, the likely scenario was that these particular early humans lived in the cave where their bones and stone tools were found and that the animal bones were the remains of meals, proof of their hunting expertise. Excavation exposed ash in horizontal patches within the deposits or in vertical patches along the cave's walls; these looked very much like the residue of hearths built up over time.

A more sensational view, first advanced by Breuil in 1929, was that the cave contained evidence of cannibalism. If the animal bones at the site were leftovers from the cave dwellers' hunting forays, he argued, why not the human bones as well? And skulls were conspicuous among the remains, suggesting to him that these might be the trophies of headhunters. Perhaps, Breuil even proposed, the dull-witted *H. erectus* had been prey to a contemporary, advanced cousin, some ancestral form of *H. sapiens.* Most paleoanthropologists rejected this final twist, but the cannibalism hypothesis received considerable support.

In the late 1930s Franz Weidenreich, an eminent German paleoanthropologist working at Peking Union Medical College, described the *H. erectus* remains in scientific detail. A trained anatomist and medical doctor, he concluded that some of the skulls showed signs of trauma, including scars and fresh injuries from attacks with both blunt and sharp instruments, such as clubs and stone tools. Most convincing to him and others was the systematic destruction of the skulls, apparently at the hands of humans who had decapitated the victims and then broken open the skull bases to retrieve the brains. Weidenreich also believed that the large longitudinal splits seen, for example, in some of the thighbones could only have been caused by humans and were probably made in an effort to extract the marrow.

Others held dissenting views. Chinese paleoanthropologist Pei Wenzhong, who codirected the early Zhoukoudian excavations, disagreed with Breuil and suggested in 1929 that the skulls had been chewed by hyenas. Some Western scientists also had doubts. In 1939 German paleontologist Helmuth Zapfe published his findings on the way hyenas at the Vienna zoo fed on cow bones. Echoing Pei's earlier observations, of which he was aware, Zapfe convincingly argued that many of the bones found at sites like Longgushan closely resembled modern bones broken up by hyenas. In fact, a new term, taphonomy, was coined shortly

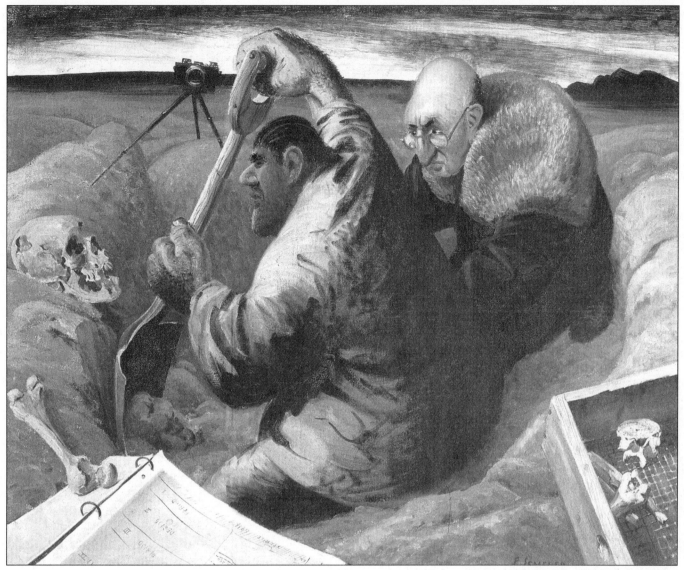

Franz Weidenreich, who in the 1930s studied the fossils of *Homo erectus* unearthed in China, is caricatured along with Ralph Von Koenigswald (wielding the shovel), who found fossils of *H. erectus* in Java. The fanciful setting is, according to the artist, "any place where the dead are disturbed."

thereafter for the field Zapfe pioneered: the study of how, after death, animal and plant remains become modified, moved, buried, and fossilized. Franz Weidenreich soon revised his prior interpretation of several *H. erectus* bones whose condition he had attributed to human cannibalistic activity, but he continued to argue that the long-bone splinters and broken skull bases must have resulted from human action.

Following disruptions in fieldwork during World War II (including the loss of all the *H. erectus* fossils collected at Longgushan up to that time, leaving only the casts that had been made of them), Chinese paleoanthropologists resumed investigation of the site. While rejecting the idea of cannibalism, they continued to look upon the cave as a shelter used by early humans equipped with stone tools and fire, as reflected in the title of paleoanthropologist Jia Lampo's book *The Cave Home of Peking Man,* published in 1975.

About this time, Western scientists began to appreciate and develop the field of taphonomy. A few scholars, notably U.S. archaeologist Lewis R. Binford, then reexamined the Longgushan evidence, but only from a distance, concluding that the burning of accumulated bat or bird guano may have accounted for the ash in the cave. With the founding in 1993 of the Zhoukoudian International Paleoanthropological Research Center at Beijing's

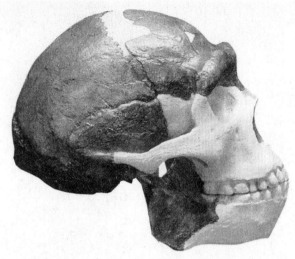

Reconstruction by G.J. Sawyer and Ian Tattersall. Photograph by Rod Mickens; AMNH

Above: A model of an *H. erectus* skull, based on fossils of several individuals from the Peking Man Site at Zhoukoudian. Most of the missing bones, represented in white, mirror existing parts on the opposite side of the skull.

AMNH

The early investigations at Zhoukoudian were coordinated by the Cenozoic Research Laboratory in Beijing. Staff members there included (left to right in foreground) Teilhard de Chardin, Franz Weidenreich, Yang Zhongjian, Pei Wenzhong, and Bian Meinian.

Institute of Vertebrate Paleontology and Paleoanthropology, a new era of multidisciplinary and international research at Longgushan began. At the institute, we have been able to collaborate with paleontologists Xu Qinqi and Liu Jinyi and with other scholars in a reassessment of the excavations.

It looked as if *H. erectus* had smashed open the skulls to cannibalize the brains.

One of taphonomy's maxims is that the most common animals at a fossil site and/or the animals whose remains there are the most complete are most likely the ones to have inhabited the area in life. Standing in the Beijing institute amid row after row of museum cases filled with mammal fossils from the cave, we were immediately struck by how few belonged to *H. erectus*—perhaps only 0.5 percent. This suggests that most of the time, this species did not live in the cave. Furthermore, none of the *H. erectus* skeletons is complete. There is a dearth of limb bones, especially of forearms, hands, lower leg bones, and feet—indicating to us that these individuals died somewhere else and that their partial remains were subsequently brought to the cave. But how?

The answer was suggested by the remains of the most common and complete animal skeletons in the cave deposit: those of the giant hyena, *Pachycrocuta brevirostris.* Had *H. erectus,* instead of being the mighty hunters

of anthropological lore, simply met the same ignominious fate as the deer and other prey species in the cave? This possibility, which had been raised much earlier by Pei and Zapfe, drew backing from subsequent studies by others. In 1970, for example, British paleontologist Anthony J. Sutcliffe reported finding a modern hyena den in Kenya that contained a number of human bones, including skulls, which the animals had apparently obtained from a nearby hospital cemetery. In the same year, South African zoologist C. K. Brain published the findings of his extensive feeding experiments with captive carnivores, akin to those of Zapfe three decades earlier. One of Brain's conclusions was that carnivores tend to chew up and destroy the ends of the extremities, leaving, in the case of primates, very little of the hands and feet.

To test the giant hyena hypothesis, we examined all the fossil casts and the few actual fossils of *H. erectus* from Longgushan. We looked for both carnivore bite marks and the shallow, V-shaped straight cuts that would be left by stone tools (although we realized that cut marks would probably not be detectable on the casts). We also analyzed each sample's fracture patterns. Breaks at right angles indicate damage long after death, when the bone is fossilized or fossilizing; fractures in fresh bone tend to

During the 1930s, excavators dug down through the hundred-foot-thick deposits that contained the remains of "Peking man." The deposits, which also yielded animal bones, stone tools, and layers of ash, had completely filled an ancient cave.

Franz Weidenreich at his laboratory at the American Museum of Natural History in the 1940s, with ape and human skulls

We were surprised by our findings. Two-thirds of Longgushan's *H. erectus* fossils display what we are convinced are one or more of the following kinds of damage: puncture marks from a carnivore's large, pointed front teeth, most likely the canines of a hyena; long, scraping bite marks, typified by U-shaped grooves along the bone; and fracture patterns comparable to those created by modern hyenas when they chew bone. Moreover, we feel that the longitudinal splitting of large bones—a feature that Weidenreich considered evidence of human activity—can also be attributed to a hyena, especially one the size of the extinct *Pachycrocuta,* the largest hyena known, whose preferred prey was giant elk and woolly rhinoceros. One of the *H. erectus* bones, part of a femur, even reveals telltale surface etchings from stomach acid, indicating it was swallowed and then disgorged.

The pattern of damage on some of the skulls sheds light on how hyenas may have handled them. Bite marks on the brow ridge above the eyes indicate that this protrusion had been grasped and bitten by an animal in the course of chewing off the face. Most animals' facial bones are quite thin, and modern hyenas frequently attack or bite the face first; similarly, their ancient predecessors would likely have discovered this vulnerable region in *H. erectus.* Practically no such facial bones, whose structure is known to us from discoveries at other sites, have been found in the Longgushan cave.

The rest of the skull is a pretty tough nut to crack, however, even for *Pachycrocuta,* since it consists of bones half again as thick as those of a modern human, with massive mounds called tori above the eyes and ears and around the back of the skull. Puncture marks and elongated bite

be irregular, following natural structural lines. Breakage due to crushing by cave rocks is usually massive, and the fracture marks characteristically match rock fragments pushed into the bone.

Will Thomson

An artist's depiction of the cave shows hyenas consuming the remains of an *H. erectus*.

marks around the skulls reveal that the hyenas gnawed at and grappled with them, probably in an effort to crack open the cranium and consume the tasty, lipid-rich brain. We concluded that the hyenas probably succeeded best by chewing through the face, gaining a purchase on the bone surrounding the foramen magnum (the opening in the cranium where the spinal cord enters), and then gnawing away until the skull vault cracked apart or the opening was large enough to expose the brain. This is how we believe the skull bases were destroyed—not by the actions of cannibalistic *H. erectus*.

Two-thirds of the fossils show bite marks or fractures inflicted by carnivores.

We know from geological studies of the cave that the animal bones found there could not have been washed in by rains or carried in by streams: the sediments in which the bones are found are either very fine-grained—indicating gradual deposition by wind or slow-moving water—or they contain angular, sharp-edged shards that would not have survived in a stream or flood. Some of the bones may have belonged to animals that died inside the cave during the course of living in it or frequenting it. Other bones were probably brought in and chewed on by hyenas and other carnivores.

Cut marks we observed on several mammal bones from the cave suggest that early humans did sometimes make use of Longgushan, even if they were not responsible for accumulating most of the bones. Stone tools left near the cave entrance also attest to their presence. Given its long history, the cave may have served a variety of occupants or at times have been configured as several separate, smaller shelters. Another possibility is that, in a form of time-sharing, early humans ventured partway into the cave during the day to scavenge on what the hyenas had not eaten and to find temporary shelter. They may not have realized that the animals, which roamed at twilight

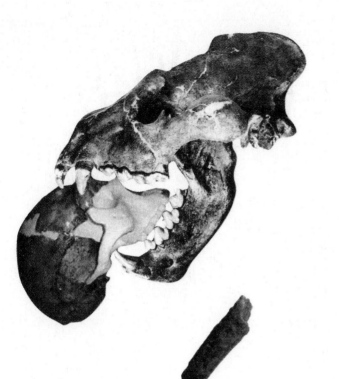

Russell L. Ciochon

A composite image of the skulls of Pachycrocuta and *H. erectus*, shows how the giant hyena may have attacked the face. Beneath is a disgorged piece of an *H. erectus thighbone*.

and at night, were sleeping in the dark recesses a couple of hundred feet away.

What about the ash in the cave, which has been taken as evidence that *H. erectus* used fire? Recently published work by geochemist Steve Weiner and his team at the Weizmann Institute of Science in Israel suggests that the fires were not from hearths. In detailed studies of the ash levels, they discovered no silica-rich layers, which would be left by the burning of wood. Wood (as well as grass and leaves) contains silica particles known as phytoliths—heat-resistant residues that are ubiquitous in archaeological hearth sites. The results indicate that fire was present in the cave but that its controlled use in hearths was not part of the story.

Still, a human hand may somehow be implicated in these fires. One possibility we are exploring in the next phase of our research is that Longgushan was a place where *Pachycrocuta* and *H. erectus* confronted each other as the early humans sought to snatch some of the meat brought back to the cave by the large hyenas. *Pachycrocuta* would have had the home court advantage, but *H. erectus,* perhaps using fire to hold the carnivore at bay, could have quickly sliced off slivers of meat. Although today we might turn up our noses at such carrion, it may have been a dependable and highly prized source of food during the Ice Age.

From *Natural History,* vol. 110, no. 2, March 2001, pp. 46, 48–51. Copyright © 2001 by Natural History Magazine. Reprinted by permission.

UNIT 5
Late Hominid Evolution

Unit Selections

Key Points to Consider

- What evidence is there to convey the hard times faced by the Neanderthals?

- Are Neanderthals a part of our ancestry? Explain.

- What happened to the Neanderthals?

- When did language ability arise in our ancestry and why?

- Which is more appropriate for understanding the linguistic function of our brains, the modular or the integrative model?

- When, where, and how did modern humans evolve?

- Where does *Homo floresiensis* fit in the hominid family tree and why?

- Why do humans have such an extended period of childhood?

- Why is facial expression an important form of human communication?

Student Website
www.mhcls.com

Internet References

Human Prehistory
http://users.hol.gr/~dilos/prehis.htm
Max Planck Institute for Evolutionary Anthropology
http://www.eva.mpg.de/english/index.htm

The most important aspect of human evolution is also the most difficult to decipher from the fossil evidence: our development as sentient, social beings, capable of communicating by means of language.

We detect hints of incipient humanity in the form of crudely chipped tools, the telltale signs of a home base, or the artistic achievements of ornaments and cave art. Yet none of these indicators of a distinctly hominid way of life can provide us with the nuances of the everyday lives of these creatures, their social relations, or their supernatural beliefs, if any. Most of what remains is the rubble of bones and stones from which we interpret what we can of their lifestyle, thought processes, and ability to communicate. Our ability to glean from the fossil record is not completely without hope, however. In fact, informed speculation is what makes possible essays such as "Hard Times among the Neanderthals" by Erik Trinkaus, "Rethinking Neanderthals" by Joe Alper, "Last of the Neanderthals" by Stephen Hall and "The Gift of Gab" by Matt Cartmill. Each is a fine example of careful, systematic, and thought- provoking work that is based upon an increased understanding of hominid fossil sites, as well as the more general environmental circumstances in which our predecessors lived.

Beyond the technological and anatomical adaptations, questions have arisen as to how our hominid forebears organized themselves socially and whether modern-day human behavior is inherited as a legacy of our evolutionary past or is a learned product of contemporary circumstances. Attempts to address these questions have given rise to the technique referred to as the "ethnographic analogy." This is a method whereby anthropologists use "ethnographies" or field studies of modern-day hunters and gatherers whose lives we take to be the best approximations we have to what life might have been like for our ancestors. (See "The Birth of Childhood.") Granted, these contemporary foragers have been living under conditions of environmental and social change just as industrial peoples have.

© Digital Vision

Nevertheless, it seems that, at least in some aspects of their lives, they have not changed as much as we have. So, if we are to make any enlightened assessments of prehistoric behavior patterns, we are better off looking at them than at ourselves.

As if to show that controversial interpretations of the evidence are not limited to the earlier hominid period, in this unit we also see how long-held beliefs about hominid migrations are being revised by new evidence coming from fossils, archeology, and even DNA. (See "The Great Human Migration" by Guy Gugliotta.) There may have even been a species of hominid living contemporaneously alongside our own ancestors 13,000 years ago (as described in "The Littlest Human"). Finally, high tech recordings of brain activity are shedding new light on the question of how language ability evolved. (See "Language: A Social History of Words.") For some scientists, these revelations fit in quite comfortably with previously held positions; for others it seems that reputations, as well as theories, are at stake.

Hard Times among the Neanderthals

Although life was difficult, these prehistoric people may not have been as exclusively brutish as usually supposed.

ERIK TRINKAUS

Throughout the century that followed the discovery in 1856 of the first recognized human fossil remains in the Neander Valley (*Neanderthal* in German) near Düsseldorf, Germany, the field of human paleontology has been beset with controversies. This has been especially true of interpretations of the Neanderthals, those frequently maligned people who occupied Europe and the Near East from about 100,000 years ago until the appearance of anatomically modern humans about 35,000 years ago.

During the last two decades, however, a number of fossil discoveries, new analyses of previously known remains, and more sophisticated models for interpreting subtle anatomical differences have led to a reevaluation of the Neanderthals and their place in human evolution.

This recent work has shown that the often quoted reconstruction of the Neanderthals as semierect, lumbering caricatures of humanity is inaccurate. It was based on faulty anatomical interpretations that were reinforced by the intellectual biases of the turn of the century. Detailed comparisons of Neanderthal skeletal remains with those of modern humans have shown that there is nothing in Neanderthal anatomy that conclusively indicates locomotor, manipulative, intellectual, or linguistic abilities inferior to those of modern humans. Neanderthals have therefore been added to the same species as ourselves—*Homo sapiens*—although they are usually placed in their own subspecies, *Homo sapiens neanderthalensis.*

Despite these revisions, it is apparent that there are significant anatomical differences between the Neanderthals and present-day humans. If we are to understand the Neanderthals, we must formulate hypotheses as to why they evolved from earlier humans about 100,000 years ago in Europe and the Near East, and why they were suddenly replaced about 35,000 years ago by peoples largely indistinguishable from ourselves. We must determine, therefore, the behavioral significance of the anatomical differences between the Neanderthals and other human groups, since it is patterns of successful behavior that dictate the direction of natural selection for a species.

In the past, behavioral reconstructions of the Neanderthals and other prehistoric humans have been based largely on archeological data. Research has now reached the stage at which behavioral interpretations from the archeological record can be significantly supplemented by analyses of the fossils themselves. These analyses promise to tell us a considerable amount about the ways of the Neanderthals and may eventually help us to determine their evolutionary fate.

One of the most characteristic features of the Neanderthals is the exaggerated massiveness of their trunk and limb bones. All of the preserved bones suggest a strength seldom attained by modern humans. Furthermore, not only is this robustness present among the adult males, as one might expect, but it is also evident in the adult females, adolescents, and even children. The bones themselves reflect this hardiness in several ways.

First, the muscle and ligament attachment areas are consistently enlarged and strongly marked. This implies large, highly developed muscles and ligaments capable of generating and sustaining great mechanical stress. Secondly, since the skeleton must be capable of supporting these levels of stress, which are frequently several times as great as body weight, the enlarged attachments for muscles and ligaments are associated with arm and leg bone shafts that have been reinforced. The shafts of all of the arm and leg bones are modified tubular structures that have to absorb stress from bending and twisting without fracturing. When the habitual load on a bone increases, the bone responds by laying down more bone in those areas under the greatest stress.

In addition, musculature and body momentum generate large forces across the joints. The cartilage, which covers joint surfaces, can be relatively easily overworked to the point where it degenerates, as is indicated by the prevalence of arthritis in joints subjected to significant wear and tear over the years. When the surface area of a joint is increased, the force per unit area of cartilage is reduced, decreasing the pressure on the cartilage.

Most of the robustness of Neanderthal arm bones is seen in muscle and ligament attachments. All of the muscles that go

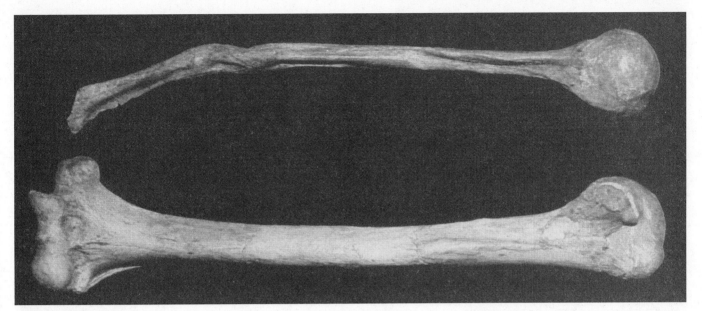

Photograph by Erik Trinkaus

Diagonal lines on these two arm bones from Shanidar 1 are healed fractures. The bottom bone is normal. That on the top is atrophied and has a pathological tip, caused by either amputation or an improperly healed elbow fracture.

from the trunk or the shoulder blade to the upper end of the arm show massive development. This applies in particular to the muscles responsible for powerful downward movements of the arm and, to a lesser extent, to muscles that stabilize the shoulder during vigorous movements.

Virtually every major muscle or ligament attachment on the hand bones is clearly marked by a large roughened area or a crest, especially the muscles used in grasping objects. In fact, Neanderthal hand bones frequently have clear bony crests, where on modern human ones it is barely possible to discern the attachment of the muscle on the dried bone.

In addition, the flattened areas on the ends of the fingers, which provide support for the nail and the pulp of the finger tip, are enormous among the Neanderthals. These areas on the thumb and the index and middle fingers are usually two to three times as large as those of similarly sized modern human hands. The overall impression is one of arms to rival those of the mightiest blacksmith.

Neanderthal legs are equally massive; their strength is best illustrated in the development of the shafts of the leg bones. Modern human thigh and shin bones possess characteristic shaft shapes adapted to the habitual levels and directions of the stresses acting upon them. The shaft shapes of the Neanderthals are similar to those in modern humans, but the cross-sectional areas of the shafts are much greater. This implies significantly higher levels of stress.

Further evidence of the massiveness of Neanderthal lower limbs is provided by the dimensions of their knee and ankle joints. All of these are larger than in modern humans, especially with respect to the overall lengths of the bones.

The development of their limb bones suggests that the Neanderthals frequently generated high levels of mechanical stress in their limbs. Since most mechanical stress in the

body is produced by body momentum and muscular contraction, it appears that the Neanderthals led extremely active lives. It is hard to conceive of what could have required such exertion, especially since the maintenance of vigorous muscular activity would have required considerable expenditure of energy. That level of energy expenditure would undoubtedly have been maladaptive had it not been necessary for survival.

The available evidence from the archeological material associated with the Neanderthals is equivocal on this matter. Most of the archeological evidence at Middle Paleolithic sites concerns stone tool technology and hunting activities. After relatively little change in technology during the Middle Paleolithic (from about 100,000 years to 35,000 years before the present), the advent of the Upper Paleolithic appears to have brought significant technological advances. This transition about 35,000 years ago is approximately coincident with the replacement of the Neanderthals by the earliest anatomically modern humans. However, the evidence for a significant change in hunting patterns is not evident in the animal remains left behind. Yet even if a correlation between the robustness of body build and the level of hunting efficiency could be demonstrated, it would only explain the ruggedness of the Neanderthal males. Since hunting is exclusively or at least predominantly a male activity among humans, and since Neanderthal females were in all respects as strongly built as the males, an alternative explanation is required for the females.

Some insight into why the Neanderthals consistently possessed such massiveness is provided by a series of partial skeletons of Neanderthals from the Shanidar Cave in northern Iraq. These fossils were excavated between 1953 and 1960 by anthropologist Ralph Solecki of Columbia University and have been studied principally by T. Dale Stewart, an anthropologist at

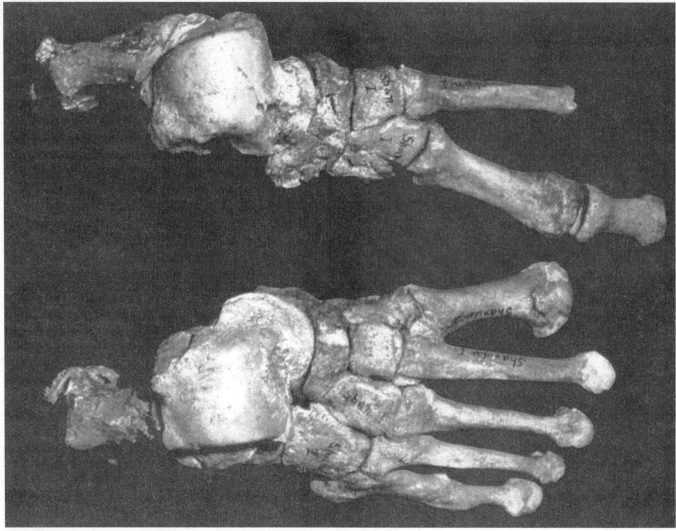

Photograph by Erik Trinkaus

The ankle and big toe of Shanidar 1's bottom foot show evidence of arthritis, which suggests an injury to those parts. The top foot is normal though incomplete.

the Smithsonian Institution, and myself. The most remarkable aspect of these skeletons is the number of healed injuries they contain. Four of the six reasonably complete adult skeletons show evidence of trauma during life.

The identification of traumatic injury in human fossil remains has plagued paleontologists for years. There has been a tendency to consider any form of damage to a fossil as conclusive evidence of prehistoric violence between humans if it resembles the breakage patterns caused by a direct blow with a heavy object. Hence a jaw with the teeth pushed in or a skull with a depressed fracture of the vault would be construed to indicate blows to the head.

The central problem with these interpretations is that they ignore the possibility of damage after death. Bone is relatively fragile, especially as compared with the rock and other sediment in which it is buried during fossilization. Therefore when several feet of sediment caused compression around fossil remains, the fossils will almost always break. In fact,

among the innumerable cases of suggested violence between humans cited over the years, there are only a few exceptional examples that cannot be readily explained as the result of natural geologic forces acting after the death and burial of the individual.

One of these examples is the trauma of the left ninth rib of the skeleton of Shanidar 3, a partially healed wound inflicted by a sharp object. The implement cut obliquely across the top of the ninth rib and probably pierced the underlying lung. Shanidar 3 almost certainly suffered a collapsed left lung and died several days or weeks later, probably as a result of secondary complications. This is deduced from the presence of bony spurs and increased density of the bone around the cut.

The position of the wound on the rib, the angle of the incision, and the cleanness of the cut make it highly unlikely that the injury was accidentally inflicted. In fact, the incision is almost exactly what would have resulted if Shanidar 3 had been stabbed in the side by a right-handed adversary in face-to-face

Photograph by Erik Trinkaus

The scar on the left ninth rib of Shanidar 3 is a partially healed wound inflicted by a sharp object. This wound is one of the few examples of trauma caused by violence.

conflict. This would therefore provide conclusive evidence of violence between humans, the *only* evidence so far found of such violence among the Neanderthals.

In most cases, however, it is impossible to determine from fossilized remains the cause of an individual's death. The instances that can be positively identified as prehistoric traumatic injury are those in which the injury was inflicted prior to death and some healing took place. Shortly after an injury to bone, whether a cut or a fracture, the damaged bone tissue is resorbed by the body and new bone tissue is laid down around the injured area. As long as irritation persists, new bone is deposited, creating a bulge or spurs of irregular bone extending into the soft tissue. If the irritation ceases, the bone will slowly re-form so as to approximate its previous, normal condition. However, except for superficial injuries or those sustained during early childhood, some trace of damage persists for the life of the individual.

In terms of trauma, the most impressive of the Shanidar Neanderthals is the first adult discovered, known as Shanidar 1. This individual suffered a number of injuries, some of which may be related. On the right forehead there are scars from minor surface injuries, probably superficial scalp cuts. The outside of the left eye socket sustained a major blow that partially collapsed that part of the bony cavity, giving it a flat rather than a rounded contour. This injury possibly caused loss of sight in the left eye and pathological alterations of the right side of the body.

Shanidar 1's left arm is largely preserved and fully normal. The right arm, however, consists of a highly atrophied but otherwise normal collarbone and shoulder blade and a highly abnormal upper arm bone shaft. That shaft is atrophied to a fraction of the diameter of the left one but retains most of its original length. Furthermore, the lower end of the right arm bone has a healed fracture of the atrophied shaft and an irregular, pathological tip. The arm was apparently either intentionally amputated just above the elbow or fractured at the elbow and never healed.

This abnormal condition of the right arm does not appear to be a congenital malformation, since the length of the bone is close to the estimated length of the normal left upper arm bone. If, however, the injury to the left eye socket also affected the left side of the brain, directly or indirectly, by disrupting the blood supply to part of the brain, the result could have been partial paralysis of the right side. Motor and sensory control areas for the right side are located on the left side of the brain, slightly behind the left eye socket. This would explain the atrophy of the whole right arm since loss of nervous stimulation will rapidly lead to atrophy of the affected muscles and bone.

The abnormality of the right arm of Shanidar 1 is paralleled to a lesser extent in the right foot. The right ankle joint shows extensive arthritic degeneration, and one of the major joints of the inner arch of the right foot has been completely reworked by arthritis. The left foot, however, is totally free of pathology. Arthritis from normal stress usually affects both lower limbs equally; this degeneration therefore suggests that the arthritis in the right foot is a secondary result of an injury, perhaps a sprain, that would not otherwise be evident on skeletal remains. This conclusion is supported by a healed fracture of the right fifth instep bone, which makes up a major portion of the outer arch of the foot. These foot pathologies may be tied into the damage to the left side of the skull; partial paralysis of the right side would certainly weaken the leg and make it more susceptible to injury.

The trauma evident on the other Shanidar Neanderthals is relatively minor by comparison. Shanidar 3, the individual who died of the rib wound, suffered debilitating arthritis of the right ankle and neighboring foot joints, but lacks any evidence of pathology on the left foot; this suggests a superficial injury similar to the one sustained by Shanidar 1. Shanidar 4 had a healed broken rib. Shanidar 5 received a transverse blow across the left forehead that left a large scar on the bone but does not appear to have affected the brain.

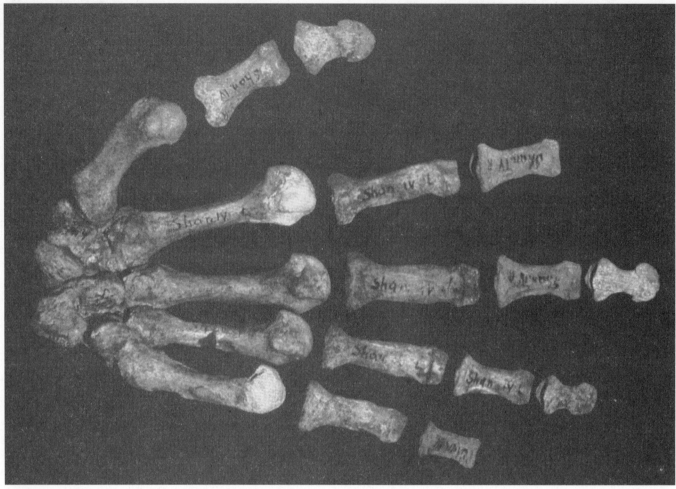

Photograph by Erik Trinkaus

The right hand of Shanidar 4 demonstrates the enlarged finger tips and strong muscle markings characteristic of Neanderthal hands.

None of these injuries necessarily provides evidence of deliberate violence among the Neanderthals; all of them could have been accidentally self-inflicted or accidentally caused by another individual. In either case, the impression gained of the Shanidar Neanderthals is of a group of invalids. The crucial variable, however, appears to be age. All four of these individuals died at relatively advanced ages, probably between 40 and 60 years (estimating the age at death for Neanderthals beyond the age of 25 is extremely difficult); they therefore had considerable time to accumulate the scars of past injuries. Shanidar 2 and 6, the other reasonably complete Shanidar adults, lack evidence of trauma, but they both died young, probably before reaching 30.

Other Neanderthal remains, all from Europe, exhibit the same pattern. Every fairly complete skeleton of an elderly adult shows evidence of traumatic injuries. The original male skeleton from the Neander Valley had a fracture just below the elbow of the left arm, which probably limited movement of that arm for life. The "old man" from La Chapelle-aux-Saints, France, on whom most traditional reconstructions of the Neanderthals have been based, suffered a broken rib. La Ferrassi 1,

the old adult male from La Ferrassie, France, sustained a severe injury to the right hip, which may have impaired his mobility.

In addition, several younger specimens and ones of uncertain age show traces of trauma. La Quina 5, the young adult female from La Quina, France, was wounded on her right upper arm. A young adult from Sala, Czechoslovakia, was superficially wounded on the right forehead just above the brow. And an individual of unknown age and sex from the site of Krapina, Yugoslavia, suffered a broken forearm, in which the bones never reunited after the fracture.

The evidence suggests several things. First, life for the Neanderthals was rigorous. If they lived through childhood and early adulthood, they did so bearing the scars of a harsh and dangerous life. Furthermore, this incident of trauma correlates with the massiveness of the Neanderthals; a life style that so consistently involved injury would have required considerable strength and fortitude for survival.

There is, however, another, more optimistic side to this. The presence of so many injuries in a prehistoric human group, many of which were debilitating and sustained years before death, shows that individuals were taken care of long after their economic usefulness to the social group had ceased. It is perhaps no accident that among the Neanderthals, for the first time in human history, people lived to a comparatively old age. We also find among the Neanderthals the first intentional burials of the dead, some of which involved offerings. Despite the hardships of their life style, the Neanderthals apparently had a deep-seated respect and concern for each other.

Taken together, these different pieces of information paint a picture of life among the Neanderthals that, while harsh and dangerous, was not without personal security. Certainly the hardships the Neanderthals endured were beyond those commonly experienced in the prehistoric record of human caring and respect as well as of violence between individuals. Perhaps for these reasons, despite their physical appearance, the Neanderthals should be considered the first modern humans.

From *Natural History,* December 1978. Copyright © 1978 by Natural History Magazine. Reprinted by permission.

Rethinking Neanderthals

Research suggests the so-called brutes fashioned tools, buried their dead, maybe cared for the sick and even conversed. But why, if they were so smart, did they disappear?

JOE ALPER

Bruno Maureille unlocks the gate in a chain-link fence, and we walk into the fossil bed past a pile of limestone rubble, the detritus of an earlier dig. We're 280 miles southwest of Paris, in rolling farm country dotted with long-haired cattle and etched by meandering streams. Maureille, an anthropologist at the University of Bordeaux, oversees the excavation of this storied site called Los Pradelles, where for three decades researchers have been uncovering, fleck by fleck, the remains of humanity's most notorious relatives, the Neanderthals.

We clamber 15 feet down a steep embankment into a swimming pool-size pit. Two hollows in the surrounding limestone indicate where shelters once stood. I'm just marveling at the idea that Neanderthals lived here about 50,000 years ago when Maureille, inspecting a long ledge that a student has been painstakingly chipping away, interrupts my reverie and calls me over. He points to a whitish object resembling a snapped pencil that's embedded in the ledge. "Butchered reindeer bone," he says. "And here's a tool, probably used to cut meat from one of these bones." The tool, or lithic, is shaped like a hand-size D.

All around the pit, I now see, are other lithics and fossilized bones. The place, Maureille says, was probably a butchery where Neanderthals in small numbers processed the results of what appear to have been very successful hunts. That finding alone is significant, because for a long time paleoanthropologists have viewed Neanderthals as too dull and too clumsy to use efficient tools, never mind organize a hunt and divvy, up the game. Fact is, this site, along with others across Europe and in Asia, is helping overturn the familiar conception of Neanderthals as dumb brutes. Recent studies suggest they were imaginative enough to carve artful objects and perhaps clever enough to invent a language.

Neanderthals, traditionally designated *Homo sapiens neanderthalensis,* were not only "human" but also, it turns out, more "modern" than scientists previously allowed. "In the minds of the European anthropologists who first studied them, Neanderthals were the embodiment of primitive humans, subhumans

if you will," says Fred H. Smith, a physical anthropologist at Loyola University in Chicago who has been studying Neanderthal DNA. "They were believed to be scavengers who made primitive tools and were incapable of language or symbolic thought." Now, he says, researchers believe that Neanderthals "were highly intelligent, able to adapt to a wide variety of ecological zones, and capable of developing highly functional tools to help them do so. They were quite accomplished."

Contrary to the view that Neanderthals were evolutionary failures—they died out about 28,000 years ago—they actually had quite a run. "If you take success to mean the ability to survive in hostile, changing environments, then Neanderthals were a great success," says archaeologist John Shea of the State University of New York at Stony Brook. "They lived 250,000 years or more in the harshest climates experienced by primates, not just humans." In contrast, we modern humans have only been around for 100,000 years or so and moved into colder, temperate regions only in the past 40,000 years.

Though the fossil evidence is not definitive, Neanderthals appear to have descended from an earlier human species, *Homo erectus,* between 500,000 to 300,000 years ago. Neanderthals shared many features with their ancestors—a prominent brow, weak chin, sloping skull and large nose—but were as big-brained as the anatomically modern humans that later colonized Europe, *Homo sapiens.* At the same time, Neanderthals were stocky, a build that would have conserved heat efficiently. From musculature marks on Neanderthal fossils and the heft of arm and leg bones, researchers conclude they were also incredibly strong. Yet their hands were remarkably like those of modern humans; a study published this past March in *Nature* shows that Neanderthals, contrary to previous thinking, could touch index finger and thumb, which would have given them considerable dexterity.

Neanderthal fossils suggest that they must have endured a lot of pain. "When you look at adult Neanderthal fossils, particularly the bones of the arms and skull, you see [evidence of] fractures," says Erik Trinkaus, an anthropologist at Washington University in St. Louis. "I've yet to see an adult Neanderthal skeleton that doesn't have at least one fracture, and in adults in their 30s, it's common to see multiple healed fractures." (That they suffered so many broken bones suggests they hunted large animals up close, probably stabbing prey with heavy spears—a risky tactic.) In addition, fossil evidence indicates that Neanderthals suffered from a wide range of ailments, including pneumonia and malnourishment. Still, they persevered, in some cases living to the ripe old age of 45 or so.

Perhaps surprisingly, Neanderthals must also have been caring: to survive disabling injury or illness requires the help of fellow clan members, paleoanthropologists say. A telling example came from an Iraqi cave known as Shanidar, 250 miles north of Baghdad, near the border with Turkey and Iran. There, archaeologist Ralph Solecki discovered nine nearly complete Neanderthal skeletons in the late 1950s. One belonged to a 40-to 45-year-old male with several major fractures. A blow to the left side of his head had crushed an eye socket and almost certainly blinded him. The bones of his right shoulder and upper arm appeared shriveled, most likely the result of a trauma that led to the amputation of his right forearm. His right foot and lower right leg had also been broken while he was alive. Abnormal wear in his right knee, ankle and foot shows that he suffered from injury-induced arthritis that would have made walking painful, if not impossible. Researchers don't know how he was injured but believe that he could not have survived long without a hand from his fellow man.

"This was really the first demonstration that Neanderthals behaved in what we think of as a fundamentally human way," says Trinkaus, who in the 1970s helped reconstruct and catalog the Shanidar fossil collection in Baghdad. (One of the skeletons is held by the Smithsonian Institution's National Museum of Natural History.) "The result was that those of us studying Neanderthals started thinking about these people in terms of their behavior and not just their anatomy."

Neanderthals inhabited a vast area roughly from present-day England east to Uzbekistan and south nearly to the Red Sea. Their time spanned periods in which glaciers advanced and retreated again and again, But the Neanderthals adjusted. When the glaciers moved in and edible plants became scarcer, they relied more heavily on large, hoofed animals for food, hunting the reindeer and wild horses that grazed the steppes and tundra.

Paleoanthropologists have no idea how many Neanderthals existed (crude estimates are in the many thousands), but archaeologists have found more fossils from Neanderthals than from any extinct human species. The first Neanderthal fossil was uncovered in Belgium in 1830, though nobody accurately identified it for more than a century. In 1848, the Forbes Quarry in Gibraltar yielded one of the most complete Neanderthal skulls ever found, but it, too, went unidentified, for 15 years. The name Neanderthal arose after quarrymen in Germany's Neander Valley found a cranium and several long bones in 1856; they gave the specimens to a local naturalist, Johann Karl Fuhlrott, who soon recognized them as the legacy of a previously unknown type of human. Over the years, France, the Iberian Peninsula, southern Italy and the Levant have yielded abundances of Neanderthal remains, and those finds are being supplemented by newly opened excavations in Ukraine and Georgia. "It seems that everywhere we look, we're finding Neanderthal remains," says Loyola's Smith. "It's an exciting time to be studying Neanderthals."

Clues to some Neanderthal ways of life come from chemical analyses of fossilized bones, which confirm that Neanderthals were meat eaters. Microscopic studies hint at cannibalism; fossilized deer and Neanderthal bones found at the same site bear identical scrape marks, as though the same tool removed the muscle from both animals.

There are hints of cannibalism: deer and Neanderthal bones at the same site bear identical scrape marks.

The arrangement of fossilized Neanderthal skeletons in the ground demonstrates to many archaeologists that Neanderthals buried their dead. "They might not have done so with elaborate ritual, since there has never been solid evidence that they included symbolic objects in graves, but it is clear that they did not just dump their dead with the rest of the trash to be picked over by hyenas and other scavengers," says archaeologist Francesco d'Errico of the University of Bordeaux.

Paleoanthropologists generally agree that Neanderthals lived in groups of 10 to 15, counting children. That assessment is based on a few lines of evidence, including the limited remains at burial sites and the modest size of rock shelters. Also, Neanderthals were top predators, and some top predators, such as lions and wolves, live in small groups.

Steven Kuhn, an archaeologist at the University of Arizona, says experts "can infer quite a bit about who Neanderthal was by studying tools in conjunction with the other artifacts they left behind." For instance, recovered stone tools are typically fashioned from nearby sources of flint or quartz, indicating to some researchers that a Neanderthal group did not necessarily range far.

The typical Neanderthal tool kit contained a variety of implements, including large spear points and knives that would have been hafted, or set in wooden handles. Other tools were suitable for cutting meat, cracking open bones (to get at fat-rich marrow) or scraping hides (useful for clothing, blankets or shelter). Yet other stone tools were used for woodworking; among the very few wooden artifacts associated with Neanderthal sites are objects that resemble spears, plates and pegs.

I get a feel for Neanderthal handiwork in Maureille's office, where plastic milk crates are stacked three high in front of his desk. They're stuffed with plastic bags full of olive and tan flints from Les Pradelles. With his encouragement, I take a palm-size, D-shaped flint out of a bag. Its surface is scarred as though by chipping, and the flat side has a thin edge. I readily imagine I could scrape a hide with it or whittle a stick. The piece, Maureille says, is about 60,000 years old. "As you can see from the number of lithics we've found," he adds, referring to the crates piling up in his office, "Neanderthals were prolific and accomplished toolmakers."

Among the new approaches to Neanderthal study is what might be called paleo-mimicry, in which researchers themselves fashion tools to test their ideas. "What we do is make our own tools out of flint, use them as a Neanderthal might have, and then look at the fine detail of the cutting edges with a high-powered microscope," explains Michael Bisson, chairman of anthropology at McGill University in Montreal. "A tool used to work wood will have one kind of wear pattern that differs from that seen when a tool is used to cut meat from a bone, and we can see those different patterns on the implements recovered from Neanderthal sites." Similarly, tools used to scrape hide show few microscopic scars, their edges having been smoothed by repeated rubbing against skin, just as stropping a straight razor will hone its edge. As Kuhn, who has also tried to duplicate Neanderthal handicraft, says: "There is no evidence of really fine, precise work, but they were skilled in what they did."

Based on the consistent form and quality of the tools found at sites across Europe and western Asia, it appears likely that Neanderthal was able to pass along his toolmaking techniques to others. "Each Neanderthal or Neanderthal group did not have to reinvent the wheel when it came to their technologies," says Bisson.

The kinds of tools that Neanderthals began making about 200,000 years ago are known as Mousterian, after the site in France where thousands of artifacts were first found. Neanderthals struck off pieces from a rock "core" to make an implement, but the "flaking" process was not random; they evidently examined a core much as a diamond cutter analyzes a rough gemstone today, trying to strike just the spot that would yield "flakes," for knives or spear points, requiring little sharpening or shaping.

Around 40,000 years ago, Neanderthals innovated again. In what passes for the blink of an eye in paleoanthropology, some Neanderthals were suddenly making long, thin stone blades and hafting more tools. Excavations in southwest France and northern Spain have uncovered Neanderthal tools betraying a more refined technique involving, Kuhn speculates, the use of soft hammers made of antler or bone.

What happened? According to the conventional wisdom, there was a culture clash. In the early 20th century, when researchers first discovered those "improved" lithics—called Châtelperronian and Uluzzian, depending on where they were found—they saw the relics as evidence that modern humans, Homo sapiens or Cro-Magnon, had arrived in Neanderthal territory. That's because the tools resembled those unequivocally associated with anatomically modern humans, who began colonizing western Europe 38,000 years ago. And early efforts to assign a date to those Neanderthal lithics yielded time frames consistent with the arrival of modern humans.

But more recent discoveries and studies, including tests that showed the lithics to be older than previously believed,

have prompted d'Errico and others to argue that Neanderthals advanced on their own. "They could respond to some change in their environment that required them to improve their technology," he says. "They could behave like modern humans."

Meanwhile, these "late" Neanderthals also discovered ornamentation, says d'Errico and his archaeologist colleague João Zilhão of the University of Lisbon. Their evidence includes items made of bone, ivory and animal teeth marked with grooves and perforations. The researchers and others have also found dozens of pieces of sharpened manganese dioxide—black crayons, essentially—that Neanderthals probably used to color animal skins or even their own. In his office at the University of Bordeaux, d'Errico hands me a chunk of manganese dioxide. It feels silky, like soapstone. "Toward the end of their time on earth," he says, "Neanderthals were using technology as advanced as that of contemporary anatomically modern humans and were using symbolism in much the same way."

Generally, anthropologists and archaeologists today proffer two scenarios for how Neanderthals became increasingly resourceful in the days before they vanished. On the one hand, it may be that Neanderthals picked up a few new technologies from invading humans in an effort to copy their cousins. On the other, Neanderthals learned to innovate in parallel with anatomically modern human beings, our ancestors.

Most researchers agree that Neanderthals were skilled hunters and craftsmen who made tools, used fire, buried their dead (at least on occasion), cared for their sick and injured and even had a few symbolic notions. Likewise, most researchers believe that Neanderthals probably had some facility, for language, at least as we usually think of it. It's not far-fetched to think that language skills developed when Neanderthal groups mingled and exchanged mates; such interactions may have been necessary for survival, some researchers speculate, because Neanderthal groups were too small to sustain the species. "You need to have a breeding population of at least 250 adults, so some kind of exchange had to take place," says archaeologist Ofer Bar-Yosef of Harvard University. "We see this type of behavior in all hunter-gatherer cultures, which is essentially what Neanderthals had."

But if Neanderthals were so smart, why did they go extinct? "That's a question we'll never really have an answer to," says Clive Finlayson, who runs the Gibraltar Museum, "though it doesn't stop any of us from putting forth some pretty elaborate scenarios." Many researchers are loath even to speculate on the cause of Neanderthals' demise, but Finlayson suggests that a combination of climate change and the cumulative effect of repeated population busts eventually did them in. "I think it's the culmination of 100,000 years of climate hitting Neanderthals hard, their population diving during the cold years, rebounding some during warm years, then diving further when it got cold again," Finlayson says.

As Neanderthals retreated into present-day southern Spain and parts of Croatia toward the end of their time, modern human beings were right on their heels. Some researchers, like Smith, believe that Neanderthals and Cro-Magnon humans probably mated, if only in limited numbers. The question of whether Neanderthals and modern humans bred might be resolved within a decade by scientists studying DNA samples from Neanderthal and Cro-Magnon fossils.

As Neanderthals retreated, modern humans were right on their heels. The two may have mated—or tried to.

But others argue that any encounter was likely to be hostile. "Brotherly love is not the way I'd describe any interaction between different groups of humans," Shea says. In fact, he speculates that modern humans were superior warriors and wiped out the Neanderthals. "Modern humans are very competitive and really good at using projectile weapons to kill from a distance," he says, adding they also probably worked together better in large groups, providing a battlefield edge.

In the end, Neanderthals, though handy, big-brained, brawny and persistent, went the way of every human species but one. "There have been a great many experiments at being human preceding us and none of them made it, so we should not think poorly of Neanderthal just because they went extinct," says Rick Potts, head of the Smithsonian's Human Origins Program. "Given that Neanderthal possessed the very traits that we think guarantee our success should make us pause about our place here on earth."

JOE ALPER, a freelance writer in Louisville, Colorado, is a frequent contributor to *Science* magazine. This is his first article for *Smithsonian*. Paris-based ERIC SANDER photographed "Master Class" in the October 2002 issue. STAN FELLOWS' illustrations appeared in "Hamilton Takes Command," in the January issue.

Last of the Neanderthals

A Hunter Retreats

Eurasia was theirs alone for 200,000 years. Then the newcomers arrived.

With their large brains and enormous strength, Neanderthals seemed equipped to face any obstacle. But as the climate changed and a new kind of human appeared on the landscape, their dwindling numbers sought refuge in the highlands.

STEPHEN S. HALL

In March of 1994 some spelunkers exploring an extensive cave system in northern Spain poked their lights into a small side gallery and noticed two human mandibles jutting out of the sandy soil. The cave, called El Sidrón, lay in the midst of a remote upland forest of chestnut and oak trees in the province of Asturias, just south of the Bay of Biscay. Suspecting that the jawbones might date back as far as the Spanish Civil War, when Republican partisans used El Sidrón to hide from Franco's soldiers, the cavers immediately notified the local Guardia Civil. But when police investigators inspected the gallery, they discovered the remains of a much larger—and, it would turn out, much older—tragedy.

Within days, law enforcement officials had shoveled out some 140 bones, and a local judge ordered the remains sent to the national forensic pathology institute in Madrid. By the time scientists finished their analysis (it took the better part of six years), Spain had its earliest cold case. The bones from El Sidrón were not Republican soldiers, but the fossilized remains of a group of Neanderthals who lived, and perhaps died violently, approximately 43,000 years ago. The locale places them at one of the most important geographical intersections of prehistory, and the date puts them squarely at the center of one of the most enduring mysteries in all of human evolution.

The Neanderthals, our closest prehistoric relatives, dominated Eurasia for the better part of 200,000 years. During that time, they poked their famously large and protruding noses into every corner of Europe, and beyond—south along the Mediterranean from the Strait of Gibraltar to Greece and Iraq, north to Russia, as far west as Britain, and almost to Mongolia in the east. Scientists estimate that even at the height of the Neanderthal occupation of western Europe, their total number probably never exceeded 15,000. Yet they managed to endure, even when a cooling climate turned much of their territory into something

like northern Scandinavia today—a frigid, barren tundra, its bleak horizon broken by a few scraggly trees and just enough lichen to keep the reindeer happy.

By the time of the tragedy at El Sidrón, however, the Neanderthals were on the run, seemingly pinned down in Iberia, pockets of central Europe, and along the southern Mediterranean by a deteriorating climate, and further squeezed by the westward spread of anatomically modern humans as they emerged from Africa into the Middle East and beyond. Within another 15,000 years or so, the Neanderthals were gone forever, leaving behind a few bones and a lot of questions. Were they a clever and perseverant breed of survivors, much like us, or a cognitively challenged dead end? What happened during that period, roughly 45,000 to 30,000 years ago, when the Neanderthals shared some parts of the Eurasian landscape with those modern human migrants from Africa? Why did one kind of human being survive, and the other disappear?

Were they a clever and perseverant breed of survivors, much like us, or a cognitively challenged dead end?

On a damp, fog-shrouded morning in September 2007, I stood before the entrance to El Sidrón with Antonio Rosas of the National Museum of Natural Sciences in Madrid, who heads the paleoanthropological investigation. One of his colleagues handed me a flashlight, and I gingerly lowered myself into the black hole. As my eyes adjusted to the interior, 1 began to make out the fantastic contours of a karstic cave. An underground river had hollowed out a deep vein of sandstone, leaving behind a limestone cavern extending hundreds of yards, with side galleries spidering out to at least 12 entrances. Ten minutes into the cave, I arrived at the Galeria del Osario—the "tunnel of bones." Since 2000, some 1,500 bone fragments have been unearthed from this side gallery, representing the remains of at least nine Neanderthals—five young adults, two adolescents, a child of about eight, and a three-year-old toddler. All showed signs of nutritional stress in their teeth—not unusual in young Neanderthalslate in their time on Earth. But a deeper desperation is etched in their bones. Rosas picked up a recently unearthed fragment of a skull and another of a long bone of an arm, both with jagged edges.

"These fractures were—*clop*—made by humans," Rosas said, imitating the blow of a stone tool. "It means these fellows went after the brains and into long bones for the marrow."

In addition to the fractures, cut marks left on the bones by stone tools clearly indicate that the individuals were cannibalized. Whoever ate their flesh, and for whatever reason—starvation? ritual?—the subsequent fate of their remains bestowed upon them a distinct and marvelous kind of immortality. Shortly after the nine individuals died—possibly within days—the ground below them suddenly collapsed, leaving little time for hyenas and other scavengers to scatter the remains. A slurry of bones, sediment, and rocks tumbled 60 feet into a hollow limestone chamber below, much as mud fills the inside walls of a house during a flood.

There, buffered by sand and clay, preserved by the caves constant temperature, and sequestered in their jewel cases of mineralized bone, a few precious molecules of the Neanderthals' genetic code survived, awaiting a time in the distant future when they could be plucked out, pieced together, and examined for clues to how these people lived, and why they vanished.

T he first clue that our kind of human was not the first to inhabit Europe turned up a century and a half ago, about eight miles east of Düsseldorf, Germany. In August 1856 laborers quarrying limestone from a cave in the Neander Valley dug out a beetle-browed skullcap and some thick limb bones. Right from the start, the Neanderthals were saddled with an enduring cultural stereotype as dim-witted, brutish cavemen. The size and shape of the fossils does suggest a short, stout fireplug of a physique (males averaged about five feet, five inches tall and about 185 pounds), with massive muscles and a flaring rib cage presumably encasing capacious lungs. Steven E. Churchill, a paleoanthropologist at Duke University, has calculated that to support his body mass in a cold climate, a typical Neanderthal male would have needed up to 5,000 calories daily, or approaching what a bicyclist burns each day in the Tour de France. Yet behind its bulging browridges, a Neanderthal's low-domed skull housed a brain with a volume slightly larger on average than our own today. And while their tools and weapons were more primitive than those of the modern humans who supplanted them in Europe, they were no less sophisticated than the implements made by their modern human contemporaries living in Africa and the Middle East.

Behind its bulging browridges, a Neanderthal's skull housed a brain slightly larger on average than our own today.

One of the longest and most heated controversies in human evolution rages around the genetic relationship between Neanderthals and their European successors. Did the modern humans sweeping out of Africa beginning some 60,000 years ago completely replace the Neanderthals, or did they interbreed with them? In 1997 the latter hypothesis was dealt a powerful blow by geneticist Svante Pääbo—then at the University of Munich—who used an arm bone from the original Neanderthal man to deliver it. Pääbo and his colleagues were able to extract a tiny 378-letter snippet of mitochondrial DNA (a kind of short genetic appendix to the main text in each cell) from the 40,000-year-old specimen. When they read out the letters of the code, they found that the specimen's DNA differed from living humans to a degree suggesting that the Neanderthal and modern human lineages bad begun to diverge long before the modern human migration out of Africa. Thus the two represent separate geographic and evolutionary branches splitting from a common ancestor. "North of the Mediterranean, this lineage became Neanderthals," said Chris Stringer, research leader on human origins at the Natural History Museum in London, "and south of the Mediterranean, it became us." If there was any interbreeding when they encountered each other later, it was too rare to leave a trace of Neanderthal mitochondrial DNA in the cells of living people.

Pääbo's genetic bombshell seemed to confirm that Neanderthals were a separate species—but it does nothing to solve the mystery of why they vanished, and our species survived.

One obvious possibility is that modern humans were simply more clever, more sophisticated, more "human." Until recently, archaeologists pointed to a "great leap forward" around 40,000 years ago in Europe, when the Neanderthals' relatively humdrum stone tool industry—called Mousterian, after the site of Le Moustier in southwestern France—gave way to the more varied stone and bone tool kits, body ornaments, and other signs of symbolic expression associated with the appearance of modern humans. Some scientists, such as Stanford University anthropologist Richard Klein, still argue for some dramatic genetic change in the brain—possibly associated with a development in language—that propelled early modern humans to cultural dominance at the expense of their beetle-browed forebears.

But the evidence in the ground is not so cut and dried. In 1979 archaeologists discovered a late Neanderthal skeleton at Saint-Césaire in southwestern France surrounded not with typical Mousterian implements, but with a surprisingly modern repertoire of tools. In 1996 Jean-Jacques Hublin of the Max Planck Institute in Leipzig and Fred Spoor of University College London identified a Neanderthal bone in another French cave, near Arcy-sur-Cure, in a layer of sediment also containing ornamental objects previously associated only with modern humans, such as pierced animal teeth and ivory rings. Some scientists, such as British paleoanthropologist Paul Mellars, dismiss such modern "accessorizing" of a fundamentally archaic lifestyle as an "improbable coincidence"—a last gasp of imitative behavior by Neanderthals before the inventive newcomers out of Africa replaced them. But more recently, Francesco d'Errico of the University of Bordeaux and Marie Soressi, also at the Max Planck Institute in Leipzig, analyzed hundreds of crayon-like blocks of manganese dioxide from a French cave

131

called Pech de l'Azé, where Neanderthals lived well before modern humans arrived in Europe. D'Errico and Soressi argue that the Neanderthals used the black pigment for body decoration, demonstrating that they were fully capable of achieving "behavioral modernity" all on their own.

"At the time of the biological transition," says Erik Trinkaus, a paleoanthropologist at Washington University in St. Louis, "the basic behavior [of the two groups] is pretty much the same, and any differences are likely to have been subtle." Trinkaus believes they indeed may have mated occasionally. He sees evidence of admixture between Neanderthals and modern humans in certain fossils, such as a 24,500-year-old skeleton of a young child discovered at the Portuguese site of Lagar Velho, and a 32,000-year-old skull from a cave called Muierii in Romania. "There were very few people on the landscape, and you need to find a mate and reproduce," says Trinkaus. "Why not? Humans are not known to be choosy. Sex happens."

It may have happened, other researchers say, but not often, and not in a way that left behind any evidence. Katerina Harvati, another researcher at the Max Planck Institute in Leipzig, has used detailed 3-D measurements of Neanderthal and early modern human fossils to predict exactly what hybrids between the two would have looked like. None of the fossils examined so far matches her predictions.

The disagreement between Trinkaus and Harvati is hardly the first time that two respected paleoanthropologists have looked at the same set of bones and come up with mutually contradictory interpretations. Pondering—and debating—the meaning of fossil anatomy will always play a role in understanding Neanderthals. But now there are other ways to bring them back to life.

Two days after my first descent into El Sidrón cave, Araceli Soto Flórez, a graduate student at the University of Oviedo, came across a fresh Neanderthal bone, probably a fragment of a femur. All digging immediately ceased, and most of the crew evacuated the chamber. Soto Flórez then squeezed herself into a sterile jumpsuit, gloves, booties, and plastic face mask. Under the watchful eyes of Antonio Rosas and molecular biologist Carles Lalueza-Fox, she delicately extracted the bone from the soil, placed it in a sterile plastic bag, and deposited the bag in a chest of ice. After a brief stop in a hotel freezer in nearby Villamayo, the leg bone eventually arrived at Lalueza-Fox's laboratory at the Institute of Evolutionary Biology in Barcelona. His interest was not in the anatomy of the leg or anything it might reveal about Neanderthal loco motion. All he wanted from it was its DNA.

Prehistoric cannibalism has been very good for modern-day molecular biology. Scraping flesh from a bone also removes the DNA of microorganisms that might otherwise contaminate the sample. The bones of El Sidrón have not yielded the most DNA of any Neanderthal fossil—that honor belongs to a specimen from Croatia, also cannibalized—but so far they have revealed the most compelling insights into Neanderthal appearance and behavior. In October 2007 Lalueza-Fox, Holger Römpler of the University of Leipzig, and their colleagues announced that they had isolated a pigmentation gene from the DNA of an individual

at El Sidrón (as well as another Neanderthal fossil from Italy). The particular form of the gene, called *MC1R*, indicated that at least some Neanderthals would have had red hair, pale skin, and, possibly, freckles. The gene is unlike that of red-haired people today, however—suggesting that Neanderthals and modern humans developed the trait independently, perhaps under similar pressures in northern latitudes to evolve fair skin to let in more sunlight for the manufacture of vitamin D. Just a few weeks earlier, Svante Pääbo, who now heads the genetics laboratory at the Max Planck Institute in Leipzig, Lalueza-Fox, and their colleagues had announced an even more astonishing find: Two El Sidrón individuals appeared to share, with modern humans, a version of a gene called *FOXP2* that contributes to speech and language ability, acting not only in the brain but also on the nerves that control facial muscles. Whether Neanderthals were capable of sophisticated language abilities or a more primitive form of vocal communication (singing, for example) still remains unclear, but the new genetic findings suggest they possessed some of the same vocalizing hardware as modern humans.

All this from a group of ill-fated Neanderthals buried in a cave collapse, soon after they were consumed by their own kind.

"So maybe it's a good thing to eat your con-specifics," says Pääbo.

A tall, cheerful Swede, Pääbo is the main engine behind a breathtaking scientific tour de force: the attempt, expected to be completed next month, to read out not just single Neanderthal genes, but the entire three-billion-letter sequence of the Neanderthal genome. Traces of DNA in fossils are vanishingly faint, and because Neanderthal DNA is ever so close to that of living people, one of the biggest hurdles in sequencing it is the ever present threat of contamination by modern human DNA—especially by the scientists handling the specimens. The precautions taken in excavating at El Sidrón are now becoming standard practice at other Neanderthal sites. Most of the DNA for Pääbo's genome project, however, has come from the Croatian specimen, a 38,000-year-old fragment of leg bone found almost 30 years ago in the Vindija cave. Originally deemed unimportant, it sat in a drawer in Zagreb, largely untouched and thus uncontaminated, for most of its museum life.

Now it is the equivalent of a gold mine for prehistoric human DNA, albeit an extremely difficult mine to work. After the DNA is extracted in a sterile laboratory in the basement of the Max Planck Institute, it is shipped overnight to Branford, Connecticut, where collaborators at 454 Life Sciences have invented machines that can rapidly decipher the sequence of DNA's chemical letters. The vast majority of those letters spell out bacterial contaminants or other non-Neanderthal genetic information. But in the fall of 2006, Pääbo and his colleagues announced they had deciphered approximately one million letters of Neanderthal DNA. (At the same time, a second group, headed by Edward Rubin at the Department of Energy Joint Genome Institute in Walnut Creek, California, used DNA provided by Pääbo to read out snippets of genetic code using a different approach.) By last year, dogged by claims that their work had serious contamination problems, the Leipzig group claimed to have improved accuracy and identified about 70 million letters of DNA—roughly 2 percent of the total.

"We know that the human and chimpanzee sequences are 98.7 percent the same, and Neanderthals are much closer to us than chimps," said Ed Green, head of biomathematics in Pääbo's group in Leipzig, "so the reality is that for most of the sequence, there's no difference between Neanderthals and [modern] humans." But the differences—less than a half percent of the sequence—are enough to confirm that the two lineages had begun to diverge around 700,000 years ago. The Leipzig group also managed to extract mitochondrial DNA from two fossils of uncertain origin that had been excavated in Uzbekistan and southern Siberia; both had a uniquely Neanderthal genetic signature. While the Uzbekistan specimen, a young boy, had long been considered a Neanderthal, the Siberian specimen was a huge surprise, extending the known Neanderthal range some 1,200 miles east of their European stronghold.

So, while the new genetic evidence appears to confirm that Neanderthals were a separate species from us, it also suggests that they may have possessed human language and were successful over a far larger sweep of Eurasia than previously thought. Which brings us back to the same hauntingly persistent question that has shadowed them from the beginning: Why did they disappear?

To coax a Neanderthal fossil to reveal its secrets, you can measure it with calipers, probe it with a CT scan, or try to capture the ghost of its genetic code. Or if you happen to have at your disposal a type of particle accelerator called a synchrotron, you can put it in a lead-lined room and blast it with a 50,000-volt x-ray beam, without disturbing so much as a single molecule.

Over a sleep-deprived week in October 2007, a team of scientists gathered at the European Synchrotron Radiation Facility (ESRF) in Grenoble, France, for an unprecedented "convention of jawbones." The goal was to explore a crucial question in the life history of the Neanderthals: Did they reach maturity at an earlier age than their modern human counterparts? If so, it might have implications for their brain development, which in turn might help explain why they disappeared. The place to look for answers was deep inside the structure of Neanderthal teeth.

"When I was young, I thought that teeth were not so useful in assessing recent human evolution, but now I think they are the most important thing," said Jean-Jacques Hublin, who had accompanied his Max Planck Institute colleague Tanya Smith to Grenoble.

Along with Paul Tafforeau of the ESRF, Hublin and Smith were squeezed into a computer-filled hutch at the facility—one of the three largest synchrotrons in the world, with a storage ring for energized electrons half a mile in circumference—watching on a video monitor as the x-ray beam zipped through the right upper canine of an adolescent Neanderthal from the site of Le Moustier in southwestern France, creating arguably the most detailed dental x-ray in human history. Meanwhile, a dream team of other fossils sat on a shelf nearby, awaiting their turn in the synchrotrons spotlight: two jawbones of Neanderthal juveniles recovered in Krapina, Croatia, dating back 130,000 to 120,000 years; the so-called La Quina skull from a Neanderthal youth, discovered in France and dating from between 75,000

to 40,000 years ago; and two striking 90,000-year-old modern human specimens, teeth intact, found in a rock shelter called Qafzeh in Israel.

When teeth are imaged at high resolution, they reveal a complex, three-dimensional hatch of daily and longer periodic growth lines, like tree rings, along with stress lines that encode key moments in an individual's life history. The trauma of birth etches a sharp neonatal stress line on the enamel; the time of weaning and episodes of nutritional deprivation or other environmental stresses similarly leave distinct marks on developing teeth. "Teeth preserve a continuous, permanent record of growth, from before birth until they finish growing at the end of adolescence," Smith explained. Human beings take longer to reach puberty than chimpanzees, our nearest living relatives—which means more time spent learning and developing within the context of the social group. Early hominin species that lived on the savanna in Africa millions of years ago matured fast, more like chimps. So when in evolution did the longer modern pattern begin?

To address this question, Smith, Tafforeau, and colleagues had previously used the synchrotron to demonstrate that an early modern human child from a site called Jebel Irhoud in Morocco (dated to around 160,000 years ago) showed the modern human life history pattern. In contrast, the "growth rings" in the 100,000-year-old tooth of a young Neanderthal discovered in the Scladina cave in Belgium indicated that the child was eight years old when it died and appeared to be on track to reach puberty several years sooner than the average for modern humans. Another research team, using a single Neanderthal tooth, had found no such difference between its growth pattern and that of living humans. But while a full analysis from the "jawbone convention" would take time, preliminary results, Smith said, were "consistent with what we see in Scladina."

"This would certainly affect Neanderthal social organization, mating strategy, and parenting behavior," says Hublin. "Imagine a society where individuals start to reproduce four years earlier than in modern humans. It's a very different society. It could also mean the Neanderthals' cognitive abilities may have been different from modern humans'."

Neanderthal society may have differed in another way crucial to group survival: what archaeologists call cultural buffering. A buffer is something in a group's behavior—a technology, a form of social organization, a cultural tradition—that hedges its bets in the high-stakes game of natural selection. It's like having a small cache of extra chips at your elbow in a poker game, so you don't have to fold your hand quite as soon. For example, Mary Stiner and Steven Kuhn of the University of Arizona argue that early modern humans emerged from Africa with the buffer of an economically efficient approach to hunting and gathering that resulted in a more diverse diet. While men chased after large animals, women and children foraged for small game and plant foods. Stiner and Kuhn maintain that Neanderthals did not enjoy the benefits of such a marked division of labor. From southern Israel to northern Germany, the archaeological record shows that Neanderthals instead relied almost entirely on hunting big and medium-size mammals like horses, deer, bison, and wild cattle. No doubt they were eating some vegetable material and even shellfish near the Mediterranean, but the lack of milling stones or other evidence far processing plant foods suggests to Stiner and Kuhn that to a Neanderthal vegetables were supplementary foods, "more like salads, snacks, and desserts than energy-rich staple foods."

Their bodies' relentless demand for calories probably forced Neanderthal women and children to join in the hunt.

Their bodies' relentless demand for calories, especially in higher latitudes and during colder interludes, probably forced Neanderthal women and children to join in the hunt—a "rough and dangerous business," write Stiner and Kuhn, judging by the many healed fractures evident on Neanderthal upper limbs and skulls. The modern human bands that arrived on the landscape toward the end of the Neanderthals' time had other options.

"By diversifying diet and having personnel who [did different tasks], you have a formula for spreading risk, and that is ultimately good news for pregnant women and for kids," Stiner told me. "So if one thing falls through, there's something else." A Neanderthal woman would have been powerful and resilient. But without such cultural buffering, she and her young would have been at a disadvantage.

Of all possible cultural buffers, perhaps the most important was the cushion of society itself. According to Erik Trinkaus, a Neanderthal social unit would have been about the size of an extended family. But in early modern human sites in Europe, Trinkaus said, "we start getting sites that represent larger populations." Simply living in a larger group has biological as well as social repercussions. Larger groups inevitably demand more social interactions, which goads the brain into greater activity during childhood and adolescence, creates pressure to increase the sophistication of language, and indirectly increases the average life span of group members. Longevity, in turn, increases intergenerational transmission of knowledge and creates what Chris Stringer calls a "culture of innovation"—the passage of practical survival skills and toolmaking technology from one generation to the next, and later between one group and another.

Whatever the suite of cultural buffers, they may well have provided an extra, albeit thin, layer of insulation against the harsh climatic stresses that Stringer argues peaked right around the time the Neanderthals vanished. Ice core data suggest that from about 30,000 years ago until the last glacial maximum about 18,000 years ago, the Earth's climate fluctuated wildly, sometimes within the space of decades. A few more people in the social unit, with a few more skills, might have given modern humans an edge when conditions turned harsh. "Not a vast edge," Stringer said. "Neanderthals were obviously well adapted to a colder climate. But with the superimposition of these extreme changes in climate on the competition with modern humans, I think that made the difference."

Which leaves the final, delicate—and, as Jean-Jacques Hublin likes to say, politically incorrect—question that has bedeviled Neanderthal studies since the Out of Africa theory became generally accepted: Was the replacement by modern humans attenuated and peaceful, the Pleistocene version of kissing cousins, or was it relatively swift and hostile?

"Most Neanderthals and modern humans probably lived most of their lives without seeing each other," he said, carefully choosing his words. "The way I imagine it is that occasionally in these border areas, some of these guys would see each other at a distance. . . but I think the most likely thing is that they excluded each other from the landscape. Not just avoided, but excluded. We know from recent research on hunter-gatherers that they are much less peaceful than generally believed."

"Sometimes I just turn out the lights in here and think what it must have been like for them."

Evolutionary biologist Clive Finlayson, of the Gibraltar Museum, was standing in the vestibule of Gorham's Cave, a magnificent tabernacle of limestone opening to the sea on the Rock of Gibraltar. Inside, fantastic excretions of flowstone drooled from the ceiling of the massive nave. The stratigraphy in the cave is pocked with evidence of Neanderthal occupation going back 125,000 years, including stone spearpoints and scrapers, charred pine nuts, and the remains of ancient hearths. Two years ago, Finlayson and his colleagues used radiocarbon dating to determine that the embers in some of those fireplaces died out only 28,000 years ago—the last known trace of Neanderthals on Earth. (Other hearths in the cave may be as young as 24,000 years old, but their dating is controversial.)

From pollen and animal remains, Finlayson has reconstructed what the environment was like from 50,000 to 30,000 years ago. Back then, a narrow coastal shelf surrounded Gibraltar, the Mediterranean two or three miles distant. The landscape was scrub savanna scented with rosemary and thyme, its rolling sand dunes interrupted by the occasional cork oak and stone pine, with wild asparagus growing in the coastal flats. Prehistoric vultures, some with nine-foot wingspans, nested high up in the cliff face, scanning the dunes for meals. Finlayson imagines the Neanderthals watching the birds circle and descend, then racing them for food. Their diet was certainly more varied than the typical Neanderthal dependence on terrestrial game. His research team has found rabbit bones, tortoise shells, and mussels in the cave, along with dolphin bones and a seal skeleton with cut marks. "Except for rice, you've almost got a Mousterian paella!" Finlayson joked.

But then things changed. When the coldest fingers of the Ice Age finally reached southern Iberia in a series of abrupt fluctuations between 30,000 and 23,000 years ago, the landscape was transformed into a semiarid steppe. On this more open playing field, perhaps the tall, gracile modern humans moving into the region with projectile spears gained the advantage over the stumpy, muscle-bound Neanderthals. But Finlayson argues that it was not so much the arrival of modern humans as the dramatic shifts in climate that pushed the Iberian Neanderthals to the brink. "A three-year period of intense cold, or a landslide, when you're down to ten people, could be enough," he said. "Once you reach a certain level, you're the living dead."

The larger point may be that the demise of the Neanderthals is not a sprawling yet coherent paleoanthropological novel; rather, it is a collection of related, but unique, short stories of extinction. "Why did the Neanderthals disappear in Mongolia?" Stringer asked. "Why did they disappear in Israel? Why did they disappear in Italy, in Gibraltar, in Britain? Well, the answer could be different in different places, because it probably happened at different times. So we're talking about a large range, and a disappearance and retreat at different times, with pockets of Neanderthals no doubt surviving in different places at different times. Gibraltar is certainly one of their last outposts. It could be the last, but we don't know for sure."

Whatever happened, the denouement of all these stories had a signatory in Gorham's Cave. In a deep recess of the cavern, not far from that last Neanderthal hearth, Finlayson's team recently discovered several red handprints on the wall, a sign that modern humans had arrived in Gibraltar. Preliminary analysis of the pigments dates the handprints between 20,300 and 19,500 years ago. "Its like they were saying, Hey, it's a new world now," said Finlayson.

STEPHEN S. HALL's next book is about the natural history of wisdom.

The Great Human Migration

Why humans left their African homeland 80,000 years ago to colonize the world.

Guy Gugliotta

Seventy-seven thousand years ago, a craftsman sat in a cave in a limestone cliff overlooking the rocky coast of what is now the Indian Ocean. It was a beautiful spot, a workshop with a glorious natural picture window, cooled by a sea breeze in summer, warmed by a small fire in winter. The sandy cliff top above was covered with a white-flowering shrub that one distant day would be known as blombos and give this place the name Blombos Cave.

The man picked up a piece of reddish brown stone about three inches long that he—or she, no one knows—had polished. With a stone point, he etched a geometric design in the flat surface—simple crosshatchings framed by two parallel lines with a third line down the middle.

Today the stone offers no clue to its original purpose. It could have been a religious object, an ornament or just an ancient doodle. But to see it is to immediately recognize it as something only a person could have made. Carving the stone was a very human thing to do.

The scratchings on this piece of red ocher mudstone are the oldest known example of an intricate design made by a human being. The ability to create and communicate using such symbols, says Christopher Henshilwood, leader of the team that discovered the stone, is "an unambiguous marker" of modern humans, one of the characteristics that separate us from any other species, living or extinct.

Henshilwood, an archaeologist at Norway's University of Bergen and the University of the Witwatersrand, in South Africa, found the carving on land owned by his grandfather, near the southern tip of the African continent. Over the years, he had identified and excavated nine sites on the property, none more than 6,500 years old, and was not at first interested in this cliffside cave a few miles from the South African town of Still Bay. What he would find there, however, would change the way scientists think about the evolution of modern humans and the factors that triggered perhaps the most important event in human prehistory, when *Homo sapiens* left their African homeland to colonize the world.

This great migration brought our species to a position of world dominance that it has never relinquished and signaled the extinction of whatever competitors remained—Neanderthals in Europe and Asia, some scattered pockets of *Homo erectus* in the Far East and, if scholars ultimately decide they are in fact a separate species, some diminutive people from the Indonesian island of Flores (see "Were 'Hobbits' Human?"). When the migration was complete, *Homo sapiens* was the last—and only—man standing.

Even today researchers argue about what separates modern humans from other, extinct hominids. Generally speaking, moderns tend to be a slimmer, taller breed: "gracile," in scientific parlance, rather than "robust," like the heavy-boned Neanderthals, their contemporaries for perhaps 15,000 years in ice age Eurasia. The modern and Neanderthal brains were about the same size, but their skulls were shaped differently: the newcomers' skulls were flatter in back than the Neanderthals', and they had prominent jaws and a straight forehead without heavy brow ridges. Lighter bodies may have meant that modern humans needed less food, giving them a competitive advantage during hard times.

The moderns' behaviors were also different. Neanderthals made tools, but they worked with chunky flakes struck from large stones. Modern humans' stone tools and weapons usually featured elongated, standardized, finely crafted blades. Both species hunted and killed the same large mammals, including deer, horses, bison and wild cattle. But moderns' sophisticated weaponry, such as throwing spears with a variety of carefully wrought stone, bone and antler tips, made them more successful. And the tools may have kept them relatively safe; fossil evidence shows Neanderthals suffered grievous injuries, such as gorings and bone breaks, probably from hunting at close quarters with short, stone-tipped pikes and stabbing spears. Both species had rituals—Neanderthals buried their dead—and both made ornaments and jewelry. But the moderns produced their artifacts with a frequency and expertise that Neanderthals never matched. And Neanderthals, as far as we know, had nothing like the etching at Blombos Cave, let alone the bone carvings, ivory flutes and, ultimately, the mesmerizing cave paintings and rock art that modern humans left as snapshots of their world.

Both species had rituals and made ornaments, but the Neanderthals had nothing like the etching at Blombos Cave.

When the study of human origins intensified in the 20th century, two main theories emerged to explain the archaeological and fossil record: one, known as the multi-regional hypothesis, suggested that a species of human ancestor dispersed throughout the globe, and modern humans evolved from this predecessor in several different locations. The other, out-of-Africa theory, held that modern humans evolved in Africa for many thousands of years before they spread throughout the rest of the world.

In the 1980s, new tools completely changed the kinds of questions that scientists could answer about the past. By analyzing DNA in living human populations, geneticists could trace lineages backward in time. These analyses have provided key support for the out-of-Africa theory. *Homo sapiens,* this new evidence has repeatedly shown, evolved in Africa, probably around 200,000 years ago.

The first DNA studies of human evolution didn't use the DNA in a cell's nucleus—chromosomes inherited from both father and mother—but a shorter strand of DNA contained in the mitochondria, which are energy-producing structures inside most cells. Mitochondrial DNA is inherited only from the mother. Conveniently for scientists, mitochondrial DNA has a relatively high mutation rate, and mutations are carried along in subsequent generations. By comparing mutations in mitochondrial DNA among today's populations, and making assumptions about how frequently they occurred, scientists can walk the genetic code backward through generations, combining lineages in ever larger, earlier branches until they reach the evolutionary trunk.

At that point in human history, which scientists have calculated to be about 200,000 years ago, a woman existed whose mitochondrial DNA was the source of the mitochondrial DNA in every person alive today. That is, all of us are her descendants. Scientists call her "Eve." This is something of a misnomer, for Eve was neither the first modern human nor the only woman alive 200,000 years ago. But she did live at a time when the modern human population was small—about 10,000 people, according to one estimate. She is the only woman from that time to have an unbroken lineage of daughters, though she is neither our only ancestor nor our oldest ancestor. She is, instead, simply our "most recent common ancestor," at least when it comes to mitochondria. And Eve, mitochondrial DNA backtracking showed, lived in Africa.

Subsequent, more sophisticated analyses using DNA from the nucleus of cells have confirmed these findings, most recently in a study this year comparing nuclear DNA from 938 people from 51 parts of the world. This research, the most comprehensive to date, traced our common ancestor to Africa and clarified the ancestries of several populations in Europe and the Middle East.

While DNA studies have revolutionized the field of paleoanthropology, the story "is not as straightforward as people think,"

Hominid Family History

Modern humans are a relatively recent offshoot of the family tree.

- Oldest *Homo sapiens* fossils.
- Modern humans' first foray out of Africa.
- Etchings and shell beads in Blombos Cave.
- Modern humans in New Guinea and Australia
- Modern humans reach Europe.
- Modern humans reach the New world.

says University of Pennsylvania geneticist Sarah A. Tishkoff. If the rates of mutation, which are largely inferred, are not accurate, the migration timetable could be off by thousands of years.

To piece together humankind's great migration, scientists blend DNA analysis with archaeological and fossil evidence to try to create a coherent whole—no easy task. A disproportionate number of artifacts and fossils are from Europe—where researchers have been finding sites for well over 100 years—but there are huge gaps elsewhere. "Outside the Near East there is almost nothing from Asia, maybe ten dots you could put on a map," says Texas A&M University anthropologist Ted Goebel.

Scientists blend DNA analysis with archaeological and fossil evidence to create a coherent whole—no easy task.

As the gaps are filled, the story is likely to change, but in broad outline, today's scientists believe that from their beginnings in Africa, the modern humans went first to Asia between 80,000 and 60,000 years ago. By 45,000 years ago, or possibly earlier, they had settled Indonesia, Papua New Guinea and Australia. The moderns entered Europe around 40,000 years ago, probably via two routes: from Turkey along the Danube corridor into eastern Europe, and along the Mediterranean coast. By 35,000 years ago, they were firmly established in most of the Old World. The Neanderthals, forced into mountain strongholds in Croatia, the Iberian Peninsula, the Crimea and elsewhere, would become extinct 25,000 years ago. Finally, around 15,000 years ago, humans crossed from Asia to North America and from there to South America.

Africa is relatively rich in the fossils of human ancestors who lived millions of years ago (see timeline). Lush, tropical lake country at the dawn of human evolution provided one congenial living habitat for such hominids as *Australopithecus afarensis.* Many such places are dry today, which makes for a congenial exploration habitat for paleontologists. Wind erosion exposes old bones that were covered in muck millions of years ago. Remains of early *Homo sapiens,* by

Were "Hobbits" Human?

Debate Rages over an Indonesian Fossil Find

In 2003, Researchers Excavating a limestone cave on the remote Indonesian island of Flores made an extraordinary discovery: the 18,000-year-old bones of a woman whose skull was less than one-third the size of our own.

Modern humans were already living throughout the Old World during her time—yet she was physically very different from them. The researchers, led by paleoanthropologist Peter Brown and archaeologist Michael Morwood, both of Australia's University of New England, concluded that the woman represented a previously undiscovered species of archaic human that had survived for thousands of years after the Neanderthals had died out.

They named her *Homo floresiensis* and nicknamed her the "Hobbit," after the diminutive villagers from J.R.R. Tolkien's *Lord of the Rings* trilogy. The team has since recovered bones from as many as nine such people, all about a yard tall, the most recent of whom lived about 12,000 years ago.

The Hobbits of Flores created an uproar among anthropologists, causing them to question assumptions about evolution and human origins that had held sway for more than half a century. Some agree that the "Hobbits" are a distinct species. But others, such as anthropologist Robert Martin of Chicago's Field Museum, say the bones belong to small *Homo sapiens*—perhaps people who suffered from microcephaly, a condition in which the brain fails to grow to normal size. Five years after the initial discovery, says Martin, "nobody's budging an inch."

Some critics say that it would have been impossible for a hominid with a brain the size of an orange to make the sophisticated tools found at Ling Bua Cave—let alone hunt with them—and that they must have been crafted by modern humans. But supporters of the separate species hypothesis modeled the shape and structure of the Hobbit brain and say it could have made the tools.

When Smithsonian anthropologist Matthew Tocheri and other researchers analyzed the Hobbitt wrist, they found a primitive, wedge-shaped trapezoid bone common to great apes and early hominids but not to Neanderthals and modern humans. That fits a theory that Hobbits are less closely related to *Homo sapiens* than to *Homo erectus*—the human ancestor that is thought to have died out 100,000 years ago. Morwood has found crude *Homo erectus*-type stone tools on Flores that may be 840,000 years old.

The skeptics retort that disease is a more likely explanation for the wrist bones. A study this year speculated that the Flores people could have suffered from hypothyroidism, a form of cretinism found relatively frequently in modern Indonesia that, the researchers say, could also produce deformed, primitive-appearing wrists.

Rick Potts, director of the Smithsonian's Human Origins Program, who once doubted that the Hobbits were a separate species, says he's changed his mind: "Flores was this wing in the building of human evolution that we didn't know about. There is no reason that 800,000 years of experimentation could not evolve a small but advanced brain."

—G.G.

---

contrast, are rare, not only in Africa, but also in Europe. One suspicion is that the early moderns on both continents did not—in contrast to Neanderthals—bury their dead, but either cremated them or left them to decompose in the open.

In 2003, a team of anthropologists reported the discovery of three unusual skulls—two adults and a child—at Herto, near the site of an ancient freshwater lake in northeast Ethiopia. The skulls were between 154,000 and 160,000 years old and had modern characteristics, but with some archaic features. "Even now I'm a little hesitant to call them anatomically modern," says team leader Tim White, from the University of California at Berkeley. "These are big, robust people, who haven't quite evolved into modern humans. Yet they are so close you wouldn't want to give them a different species name."

The Herto skulls fit with the DNA analysis suggesting that modern humans evolved some 200,000 years ago. But they also raised questions. There were no other skeletal remains at the site (although there was evidence of butchered hippopotamuses), and all three skulls, which were nearly complete except for jawbones, showed cut marks—signs of scraping with stone tools. It appeared that the skulls had been deliberately detached from their skeletons and defleshed. In fact, part of the child's skull was highly polished. "It is hard to argue that this is not some kind of mortuary ritual," White says.

Even more provocative were discoveries reported last year. In a cave at Pinnacle Point in South Africa, a team led by Arizona State University paleoanthropologist Curtis Marean found evidence that humans 164,000 years ago were eating shellfish, making complex tools and using red ocher pigment—all modern human behaviors. The shellfish remains—of mussels, periwinkles, barnacles and other mollusks—indicated that humans were exploiting the sea as a food source at least 40,000 years earlier than previously thought.

The first archaeological evidence of a human migration out of Africa was found in the caves of Qafzeh and Skhul, in present-day Israel. These sites, initially discovered in the 1930s, contained the remains of at least 11 modern humans. Most appeared to have been ritually buried. Artifacts at the site, however, were simple: hand axes and other Neanderthal-style tools.

At first, the skeletons were thought to be 50,000 years old—modern humans who had settled in the Levant on their way to Europe. But in 1989, new dating techniques showed them to be 90,000 to 100,000 years old, the oldest modern human remains ever found outside Africa. But this excursion appears to be a dead end: there is no evidence that these moderns survived for long, much less went on to colonize any other parts of the globe. They are therefore not considered to be a part of the migration that followed 10,000 or 20,000 years later.

Intriguingly, 70,000-year-old Neanderthal remains have been found in the same region. The moderns, it would appear, arrived first, only to move on, die off because of disease or natural catastrophe or—possibly—get wiped out. If they shared territory with Neanderthals, the more "robust" species may have outcompeted them here. "You may be anatomically modern and display modern behaviors," says paleoanthropologist Nicholas J. Conard of Germany's University of Tübingen, "but apparently it wasn't enough. At that point the two species are on pretty equal footing." It was also at this point in history, scientists concluded, that the Africans ceded Asia to the Neanderthals.

Then, about 80,000 years ago, says Blombos archaeologist Henshilwood, modern humans entered a "dynamic period" of innovation. The evidence comes from such South African cave sites as Blombos, Klasies River, Diepkloof and Sibudu. In addition to the ocher carving, the Blombos Cave yielded perforated ornamental shell beads—among the world's first known jewelry. Pieces of inscribed ostrich eggshell turned up at Diepkloof. Hafted points at Sibudu and elsewhere hint that the moderns of southern Africa used throwing spears and arrows. Fine-grained stone needed for careful workmanship had been transported from up to 18 miles away, which suggests they had some sort of trade. Bones at several South African sites showed that humans were killing eland, springbok and even seals. At Klasies River, traces of burned vegetation suggest that the ancient hunter-gatherers may have figured out that by clearing land, they could encourage quicker growth of edible roots and tubers. The sophisticated bone tool and stoneworking technologies at these sites were all from roughly the same time period—between 75,000 and 55,000 years ago.

Virtually all of these sites had piles of seashells. Together with the much older evidence from the cave at Pinnacle Point, the shells suggest that seafood may have served as a nutritional trigger at a crucial point in human history, providing the fatty acids that modern humans needed to fuel their outsize brains: "This is the evolutionary driving force," says University of Cape Town archaeologist John Parkington. "It is sucking people into being more cognitively aware, faster-wired, faster-brained, smarter." Stanford University paleoanthropologist Richard Klein has long argued that a genetic mutation at roughly this point in human history provoked a sudden increase in brainpower, perhaps linked to the onset of speech.

Did new technology, improved nutrition or some genetic mutation allow modern humans to explore the world? Possibly, but other scholars point to more mundane factors that may have contributed to the exodus from Africa. A recent DNA study suggests that massive droughts before the great migration split Africa's modern human population into small, isolated groups and may have even threatened their extinction. Only after the weather improved were the survivors able to reunite, multiply and, in the end, emigrate. Improvements in technology may have helped some of them set out for new territory. Or cold snaps may have lowered sea level and opened new land bridges. Whatever the reason, the ancient Africans reached a watershed. They were ready to leave, and they did.

DNA evidence suggests the original exodus involved anywhere from 1,000 to 50,000 people. Scientists do not agree on the time of the departure—sometime more recently than 80,000 years ago—or the departure point, but most now appear to be leaning away from the Sinai, once the favored location, and toward a land bridge crossing what today is the Bab el Mandeb Strait separating Djibouti from the Arabian Peninsula at the southern end of the Red Sea. From there, the thinking goes, migrants could have followed a southern route eastward along the coast of the Indian Ocean. "It could have been almost accidental," Henshilwood says, a path of least resistance that did not require adaptations to different climates, topographies or diet. The migrants' path never veered far from the sea, departed from warm weather or failed to provide familiar food, such as shellfish and tropical fruit.

Tools found at Jwalapuram, a 74,000-year-old site in southern India, match those used in Africa from the same period. Anthropologist Michael Petraglia of the University of Cambridge, who led the dig, says that although no human fossils have been found to confirm the presence of modern humans at Jwalapuram, the tools suggest it is the earliest known settlement of modern humans outside of Africa except for the dead enders at Israel's Qafzeh and Skhul sites.

And that's about all the physical evidence there is for tracking the migrants' early progress across Asia. To the south, the fossil and archaeological record is clearer and shows that modern humans reached Australia and Papua New Guinea—then part of the same landmass—at least 45,000 years ago, and maybe much earlier.

But curiously, the early down under colonists apparently did not make sophisticated tools, relying instead on simple Neanderthal-style flaked stones and scrapers. They had few ornaments and little long-distance trade, and left scant evidence that they hunted large marsupial mammals in their new homeland. Of course, they may have used sophisticated wood or bamboo tools that have decayed. But University of Utah anthropologist James F. O'Connell offers another explanation: the early settlers did not bother with sophisticated technologies because they did not need them. That these people were "modern" and innovative is clear: getting to New Guinea-Australia from the mainland required at least one sea voyage of more than 45 miles, an astounding achievement. But once in place, the colonists faced few pressures to innovate or adapt new technologies. In particular, O'Connell notes, there were few people, no shortage of food and no need to compete with an indigenous population like Europe's Neanderthals.

Modern humans eventually made their first forays into Europe only about 40,000 years ago, presumably delayed by relatively cold and inhospitable weather and a less than welcoming Neanderthal population. The conquest of the continent—if that is what it was—is thought to have lasted about 15,000 years, as the last pockets of Neanderthals dwindled to extinction. The European penetration is widely regarded as the decisive event of the great migration, eliminating as it did our last rivals and enabling the moderns to survive there uncontested.

Did modern humans wipe out the competition, absorb them through interbreeding, outthink them or simply stand by while climate, dwindling resources, an epidemic or some other natural phenomenon did the job? Perhaps all of the above. Archaeologists have found little direct evidence of confrontation between the two peoples. Skeletal evidence of possible interbreeding is sparse, contentious and inconclusive. And while interbreeding may well have taken place, recent DNA studies have failed to show any consistent genetic relationship between modern humans and Neanderthals.

"You are always looking for a neat answer, but my feeling is that you should use your imagination," says Harvard University archaeologist Ofer Bar-Yosef. "There may have been positive interaction with the diffusion of technology from one group to the other. Or the modern humans could have killed off the Neanderthals. Or the Neanderthals could have just died out. Instead of subscribing to one hypothesis or two, I see a composite."

Modern humans' next conquest was the New World, which they reached by the Bering Land Bridge—or possibly by boat—at least 15,000 years ago. Some of the oldest unambiguous evidence of humans in the New World is human DNA extracted from coprolites—fossilized feces—found in Oregon and recently carbon dated to 14,300 years ago.

For many years paleontologists still had one gap in their story of how humans conquered the world. They had no human fossils from sub-Saharan Africa from between 15,000 and 70,000 years ago. Because the epoch of the great migration was a blank slate, they could not say for sure that the modern humans who invaded Europe were functionally identical to those who stayed behind in Africa. But one day in 1999, anthropologist Alan Morris of South Africa's University of Cape Town showed Frederick Grine, a visiting colleague from Stony Brook University, an unusual-looking skull on his bookcase. Morris told Grine that the skull had been discovered in the 1950s at Hofmeyr, in South Africa. No other bones had been found near it, and its original resting place had been befouled by river sediment. Any archaeological evidence from the site had been destroyed—the skull was a seemingly useless artifact.

But Grine noticed that the braincase was filled with a carbonate sand matrix. Using a technique unavailable in the 1950s, Grine, Morris and an Oxford University-led team of analysts measured radioactive particles in the matrix. The skull, they learned, was 36,000 years old. Comparing it with skulls from Neanderthals, early modern Europeans and contemporary humans, they discovered it had nothing in common with Neanderthal skulls and only peripheral similarities with any of today's populations. But it matched the early Europeans elegantly. The evidence was clear. Thirty-six thousand years ago, says Morris, before the world's human population differentiated into the mishmash of races and ethnicities that exist today, "We were all Africans."

GUY GUGLIOTTA has written about cheetahs, Fidel Castro and London's Old Bailey courthouse for *Smithsonian*.

The Littlest Human

A spectacular find in Indonesia reveals that a strikingly different hominid shared the earth with our kind in the not so distant past.

KATE WONG

On the island of Flores in Indonesia, villagers have long told tales of a diminutive, upright-walking creature with a lopsided gait, a voracious appetite, and soft, murmuring speech.

They call it *ebu gogo,* "the grandmother who eats anything." Scientists' best guess was that macaque monkeys inspired the *ebu gogo* lore. But last October, an alluring alternative came to light. A team of Australian and Indonesian researchers excavating a cave on Flores unveiled the remains of a lilliputian human—one that stood barely a meter tall—whose kind lived as recently as 13,000 years ago.

The announcement electrified the paleoanthropology community. *Homo sapiens* was supposed to have had the planet to itself for the past 25 millennia, free from the company of other humans following the apparent demise of the Neandertals in Europe and *Homo erectus* in Asia. Furthermore, hominids this tiny were known only from fossils of australopithecines (Lucy and the like) that lived nearly three million years ago—long before the emergence of *H. sapiens.* No one would have predicted that our own species had a contemporary as small and primitive-looking as the little Floresian. Neither would anyone have guessed that a creature with a skull the size of a grapefruit might have possessed cognitive capabilities comparable to those of anatomically modern humans.

Isle of Intrigue

This is not the first time Flores has yielded surprises. In 1998 archaeologists led by Michael J. Morwood of the University of New England in Armidale, Australia, reported having discovered crude stone artifacts some 840,000 years old in the Soa Basin of central Flores. Although no human remains turned up with the tools, the implication was that *H. erectus,* the only hominid known to have lived in Southeast Asia during that time, had crossed the deep waters

Overview/Mini Humans

- Conventional wisdom holds that *Homo sapiens* has been the sole human species on the earth for the past 25,000 years. Remains discovered on the Indonesian island of Flares have upended that view.
- The bones are said to belong to a dwarf species of *Homo* that lived as recently as 13,000 years ago.
- Although the hominid is as small in body and brain as the earliest humans, it appears to have made sophisticated stone tools, raising questions about the relation between brain size and intelligence.
- The find is controversial, however—some experts wonder whether the discoverers have correctly diagnosed the bones and whether anatomically modern humans might have made those advanced artifacts.

separating Flores from Java. To the team, the find showed *H. erectus* to be a seafarer, which was startling because elsewhere *H. erectus* had left behind little material culture to suggest that it was anywhere near capable of making watercraft. Indeed, the earliest accepted date for boat-building was 40,000 to 60,000 years ago, when modern humans colonized Australia. (The other early fauna on Flores probably got there by swimming or accidentally drifting over on flotsam. Humans are not strong enough swimmers to have managed that voyage, but skeptics say they may have drifted across on natural rafts).

Hoping to document subsequent chapters of human occupation of the island, Morwood and Radien P. Soejono of the Indonesian Center for Archaeology in Jakarta turned their attention to a large limestone cave called Liang Bua located

Dwarfs and giants tend to evolve on islands, with animals larger than rabbits shrinking and animals smaller than rabbits growing. The shifts appear to be adaptive responses to the limited food supplies available in such environments. *Stegodon,* an extinct proboscidean, colonized Flores several times, dwindling from elephant to water buffalo proportions. Some rats, in contrast, became rabbit-sized over time. *H. floresiensis* appears to have followed the island rule as well. It is thought to be a dwarfed descendant of *H. erectus,* which itself was nearly the size of a modern human.

Shared features between LB1 and members of our own genus led to the classification of the Flores hominid as *Homo,* despite its tiny brain size. Noting that the specimen most closely resembles *H. erectus,* the researchers posit that it is a new species, *H. floresiensis,* that dwarfed from a *H. erectus* ancestor. *H. floresiensis* differs from *H. sapiens* in having, among other characteristics, no chin, a relatively projecting face, a prominent brow and a low braincase.

in western Flores. Indonesian archaeologists had been excavating the cave intermittently since the 1970s, depending on funding availability, but workers had penetrated only the uppermost deposits. Morwood and Soejono set their sights on reaching bedrock and began digging in July 2001. Before long, their team's efforts turned up abundant stone tools and bones of a pygmy version of an extinct elephant relative known as *Stegodon.* But it was not until nearly the end of the third season of fieldwork that diagnostic hominid material in the form of an isolated tooth surfaced. Morwood brought a cast of the tooth back to Armidale to show to his department colleague Peter Brown. "It was clear that while the premolar was broadly humanlike, it wasn't from a modern human," Brown recollects. Seven days later Morwood received word that the Indonesians had recovered a skeleton. The Australians boarded the next plane to Jakarta.

Peculiar though the premolar was, nothing could have prepared them for the skeleton, which apart from the missing arms was largely complete. The pelvis anatomy revealed that the individual was bipedal and probably a female, and the tooth eruption and wear indicated that it was an adult. Yet it was only as tall as a modern three-year-old, and its brain was as small as the smallest australopithecine brain known. There were other primitive traits as well, including the broad pelvis and the long neck of the femur. In other respects, however, the specimen looked familiar. Its small teeth and narrow nose, the overall shape of the braincase and the thickness of the cranial bones all evoked *Homo.*

Brown spent the next three months analyzing the enigmatic skeleton, catalogued as LB1 and affectionately nicknamed the Hobbit by some of the team members, after the tiny beings in J.R.R. Tolkien's *The Lord of the Rings* books. The decision about how to classify it did not come easily. Impressed with the characteristics LB1 shared with early hominids such as the australopithecines, he initially proposed that it represented a new genus of human. On further consideration, however, the similarities to *Homo* proved more persuasive. Based on the 18,000-year age of LB1, one might have reasonably expected the bones to belong

to *H. sapiens,* albeit a very petite representative. But when Brown and his colleagues considered the morphological characteristics of small-bodied modern humans— including normal ones, such as pygmies, and abnormal ones, such as pituitary dwarfs—LB1 did not seem to fit any of those descriptions. Pygmies have small bodies and large brains—the result of delayed growth during puberty, when the brain has already attained its full size. And individuals with genetic disorders that produce short stature and small brains have a range of distinctive features not seen in LB1 and rarely reach adulthood, Brown says. Conversely, he notes, the Flores skeleton exhibits archaic traits that have never been documented for abnormal small-bodied *H. sapiens.*

What LB1 looks like most, the researchers concluded, is a miniature *H. erectus.* Describing the find in the journal *Nature,* they assigned LB1 as well as the isolated tooth and an arm bone from older deposits to a new species of human, *Homo floresiensis.* They further argued that it was a descendant of *H. erectus* that had become marooned on Flores and evolved in isolation into a dwarf species, much as the elephant-like *Stegodon* did.

Biologists have long recognized that mammals larger than rabbits tend to shrink on small islands, presumably as an adaptive response to the limited food supply. They have little to lose by doing so, because these environments harbor few predators. On Flores, the only sizable predators were the Komodo dragon and another, even larger monitor lizard. Animals smaller than rabbits, on the other hand, tend to attain brobdingnagian proportions—perhaps because bigger bodies are more energetically efficient than small ones. Liang Bua has yielded evidence of that as well, in the form of a rat as robust as a rabbit.

But attributing a hominid's bantam size to the so-called island rule was a first. Received paleoanthropological wisdom holds that culture has buffered us humans from many of the selective pressures that mold other creatures—we cope with cold, for example, by building fires and making clothes, rather than evolving a proper pelage. The discovery of a dwarf hominid species indicates that, under the right conditions, humans can in fact respond in the same, predictable way that other large mammals do when the going gets tough. Hints that *Homo* could deal with resource fluxes in this manner came earlier in 2004 from the discovery of a relatively petite *H. erectus* skull from Olorgesailie in Kenya, remarks Richard Potts of the Smithsonian Institution, whose team recovered the bones. "Getting small is one of the things *H. erectus* had in its biological tool kit," he says, and the Flores hominid seems to be an extreme instance of that.

Curiouser and Curiouser

H. floresiensis 's teeny brain was perplexing. What the hominid reportedly managed to accomplish with such a modest organ was nothing less than astonishing. Big brains are a hallmark of human evolution. In the space of six million to seven million years, our ancestors more than tripled their cranial capacity, from some 360 cubic centimeters in *Sahelanthropus,* the earliest putative hominid, to a whopping 1,350 cubic centimeters on average in modern folks. Archaeological evidence indicates that behavioral complexity increased correspondingly. Experts were thus fairly certain that large brains are a prerequisite for advanced cultural practices. Yet whereas the pea-brained australopithecines left behind only crude stone tools at best (and most seem not to have done any stone working at all), the comparably gray-matter-impoverished *H. floresiensis* is said to have manufactured implements that exhibit a level of sophistication elsewhere associated exclusively with *H. sapiens.*

The bulk of the artifacts from Liang Bua are simple flake tools struck from volcanic rock and chert, no more advanced than the implements made by late australopithecines and early *Homo.* But mixed in among the pygmy *Stegodon* remains excavators found a fancier set of tools, one that included finely worked points, large blades, awls and small blades that may have been hafted for use as spears. To the team, this association suggests that *H. floresiensis* regularly hunted *Stegodon.* Many of the *Stegodon* bones are those of young individuals that one *H. floresiensis* might have been able to bring down alone. But some belonged to adults that weighed up to half a ton, the hunting and transport of which must have been a coordinated group activity—one that probably required language, surmises team member Richard G. ("Bert") Roberts of the University of Wollongong in Australia.

The discovery of charred animal remains in the cave suggests that cooking, too, was part of the cultural repertoire of *H. floresiensis.* That a hominid as cerebrally limited as this one might have had control of fire gives pause. Humans are not thought to have tamed flame until relatively late in our collective cognitive development: the earliest unequivocal evidence of fire use comes from 200,000-year-old hearths in Europe that were the handiwork of the large-brained Neandertals.

H. *floresiensis.* Earlier hominids with brains similar in size to that of H. floresiensis made only simple flake tools at most. But in the same stratigraphic levels as the hominid remains at Liang Bua, researchers found a suite of sophisticated artifacts—including awls, blades and points—exhibiting a level of complexity previously thought to be the sole purview of H. sapiens.

If the *H. floresiensis* discoverers are correct in their interpretation, theirs is one of the most important paleoanthropological finds in decades. Not only does it mean that another species of human coexisted with our ancestors just yesterday in geological terms, and that our genus is far more variable than expected, it raises all sorts of questions about brain size and intelligence. Perhaps it should come as no surprise, then, that controversy has accompanied their claims.

Classification Clash

It did not take long for alternative theories to surface. In a letter that ran in the October 31 edition of Australia's *Sunday Mail,* just three days after the publication of the *Nature* issue containing the initial reports, paleoanthropologist Maciej Henneberg of the University of Adelaide countered that a pathological condition known as microcephaly (from the Greek for "small brain") could explain LB1's unusual features. Individuals afflicted with the most severe congenital form of microcephaly, primordial microcephalic dwarfism, die in childhood. But those with milder forms, though mentally retarded, can survive into adulthood. Statistically comparing the head and face dimensions of LB1 with those of a 4,000-year-old skull from Crete that is known to have belonged to a microcephalic, Henneberg found no significant differences between the two. Furthermore, he argued, the isolated forearm bone found deeper in the deposit corresponds to a height of 151 to 162 centimeters—the stature of many modern women and some men, not that of a dwarf—suggesting that larger-bodied people, too, lived at Liang Bua. In Henneberg's view, these findings indicate that LB1 is more likely a microcephalic *H. sapiens* than a new branch of *Homo*.

Susan C. Antón of New York University disagrees with that assessment. "The facial morphology is completely different in microcephalic [modern] humans," and their body size is normal, not small, she says. Antón questions whether LB1 warrants a new species, however. "There's little in the shape that differentiates it from *Homo erectus,* " she notes. One can argue that it's a new species, Antón allows, but the difference in shape between LB1 and *Homo erectus* is less striking than that between a Great Dane and a Chihuahua. The possibility exists that the LB1 specimen is a *H. erectus* individual with a pathological growth condition stemming from microcephaly or nutritional deprivation, she observes.

But some specialists say the Flores hominid's anatomy exhibits a more primitive pattern. According to Colin P. Groves of the Australian National University and David W. Cameron of the University of Sydney, the small brain, the long neck of the femur and other characteristics suggest an ancestor along the lines of *Homo habilis,* the earliest member of our genus, rather than the more advanced *H. erectus.* Milford H. Wolpoff of the University of Michigan at Ann Arbor wonders whether the Flores find might even represent an offshoot of *Australopithecus.* If LB1 is a descendant of *H. sapiens* or *H. erectus,* it is hard to imagine how natural selection left her with a brain that's even smaller than expected for her height, Wolpoff says. Granted, if she descended from *Australopithecus,* which had massive jaws and teeth, one has to account for her relatively delicate jaws and dainty dentition. That, however, is a lesser evolutionary conundrum than the one posed by her tiny brain, he asserts. After all, a shift in diet could explain the reduced chewing apparatus, but why would selection downsize intelligence?

Finding an australopithecine that lived outside of Africa—not to mention all the way over in Southeast Asia—18,000 years ago would be a first. Members of this group were thought to have died out in Africa one and a half million years ago, never having left their mother continent. Perhaps, researchers reasoned, hominids needed long, striding limbs, large brains and better technology before they could venture out into the rest of the Old World. But the recent discovery of 1.8 million-year-old *Homo* fossils at a site called Dmanisi in the Republic of Georgia refuted that explanation—the Georgian hominids were primitive and small and utilized tools like those australopithecines had made a million years before. Taking that into consideration, there is no a priori reason why australopithecines (or habilines, for that matter) could not have colonized other continents.

Troubling Tools

Yet if *Australopithecus* made it out of Africa and survived on Flores until quite recently, that would raise the question of why no other remains supporting that scenario have turned up in the region. According to Wolpoff, they may have: a handful of poorly studied Indonesian fossils discovered in the 1940s have been variously classified as *Australopithecus, Meganthropus* and, most recently, *H. erectus.* In light of the Flores find, he says, those remains deserve reexamination.

Many experts not involved in the discovery back Brown and Morwood's taxonomic decision, however. "Most of the differences [between the Flores hominid and known members of *Homo*], including apparent similarities to australopithecines, are almost certainly related to very small body mass," declares David R. Begun of the University of Toronto. That is, as the Flores people dwarfed from *H. erectus,* some of their anatomy simply converged on that of the likewise little australopithecines. Because LB1 shares some key derived features with *H. erectus* and some with other members of *Homo,* "the most straightforward option is to call it a new species of *Homo,* " he remarks. "It's a fair and reasonable interpretation," *H. erectus* expert G. Philip Rightmire of Binghamton University agrees. "That was quite a little experiment in Indonesia."

Even more controversial than the position of the half-pint human on the family tree is the notion that it made those advanced-looking tools. Stanford University paleoanthropologist Richard Klein notes that the artifacts found near LB1 appear to include few, if any, of the sophisticated types found elsewhere in the cave. This brings up the possibility that the modern-looking tools were produced by modern humans, who could have occupied the cave at a different time. Further excavations are necessary to determine the stratigraphic relation between the implements and the hominid remains, Klein opines. Such efforts may turn up modern humans like us. The question then, he says, will be whether there were two species at the site or whether modern humans alone occupied Liang Bua—in which case LB1 was simply a modern who experienced a growth anomaly.

Stratigraphic concerns aside, the tools are too advanced and too large to make manufacture by a primitive, diminutive hominid likely, Groves contends. Although the Liang Bua implements allegedly date back as far as 94,000 years ago, which the team argues makes them too early to be the handiwork of *H. sapiens,* Groves points out that 67,000-year-old tools have turned up in Liujiang, China, and older indications of a modern human presence in the Far East might yet emerge. " *H. sapiens,* once it was out of Africa, didn't take long to spread into eastern Asia," he comments.

"At the moment there isn't enough evidence" to establish that *H. floresiensis* created the advanced tools, concurs

Bernard Wood of George Washington University. But as a thought experiment, he says, "let's pretend that they did." In that case, "I don't have a clue about brain size and ability," he confesses. If a hominid with no more gray matter than a chimp has can create a material culture like this one, Wood contemplates, "why did it take people such a bloody long time to make tools" in the first place?

"If *Homo floresiensis* was capable of producing sophisticated tools, we have to say that brain size doesn't add up to much," Rightmire concludes. Of course, humans today exhibit considerable variation in gray matter volume, and great thinkers exist at both ends of the spectrum. French writer Jacques Anatole Francois Thibault (also known as Anatole France), who won the 1921 Nobel Prize for Literature, had a cranial capacity of only about 1,000 cubic centimeters; England's General Oliver Cromwell had more than twice that. "What that means is that once you get the brain to a certain size, size no longer matters, it's the organization of the brain," Potts states. At some point, he adds, "the internal wiring of the brain may allow competence even if the brain seems small."

LB1's brain is long gone, so how it was wired will remain a mystery. Clues to its organization may reside on the interior of the braincase, however. Paleontologists can sometimes obtain latex molds of the insides of fossil skulls and then create plaster endocasts that reveal the morphology of the organ. Because LBI's bones are too fragile to withstand standard casting procedures, Brown is working on creating a virtual endocast based on CT scans of the skull that he can then use to generate a physical endocast via stereolithography, a rapid prototyping technology.

"If it's a little miniature version of an adult human brain, I'll be really blown away," says paleoneurologist Dean Falk of the University of Florida. Then again, she muses, what happens if the convolutions look chimplike? Specialists have long wondered whether bigger brains fold differently simply because they are bigger or whether the reorganization reflects selection for increased cognition. "This specimen could conceivably answer that," Falk observes.

Return to the Lost World

Since submitting their technical papers to *Nature,* the Liang Bua excavators have reportedly recovered the remains of another five or so individuals, all of which fit the *H. floresiensis* profile. None are nearly so complete as LB1, whose long arms turned up during the most recent field season. But they did unearth a second lower jaw that they say is identical in size and shape to LB1's. Such duplicate bones will be critical to their case that they have a population of these tiny humans (as opposed to a bunch of scattered bones from one person). That should in turn dispel concerns that LB1 was a diseased individual.

Additional evidence may come from DNA: hair samples possibly from *H. floresiensis* are undergoing analysis at the University of Oxford, and the hominid teeth and bones may contain viable DNA as well. "Tropical environments are not the best for long-term preservation of DNA, so we're not holding our breath," Roberts remarks, "but there's certainly no harm in looking."

The future of the bones (and any DNA they contain) is uncertain, however. In late November, Teuku Jacob of the Gadjah Mada University in Yogyakarta, Java, who was not involved in the discovery or the analyses, had the delicate specimens transported from their repository at the Indonesian Center for Archaeology to his own laboratory with Soejono's assistance. Jacob, the dean of Indonesian paleoanthropology, thinks LB1 was a microcephalic and allegedly ordered the transfer of it and the new, as yet undescribed finds for examination and safekeeping, despite strong objections from other staff members at the center. At the time this article was going to press, the team was waiting for Jacob to make good on his promise to return the remains to Jakarta by January 1 of this year, but his reputation for restricting scientific access to fossils has prompted pundits to predict that the bones will never be studied again.

Efforts to piece together the *H. floresiensis* puzzle will proceed, however. For his part, Brown is eager to find the tiny hominid's large-bodied forebears. The possibilities are threefold, he notes. Either the ancestor dwarfed on Flores (and was possibly the maker of the 840,000-year-old Soa Basin tools), or it dwindled on another island and later reached Flores, or the ancestor was small before it even arrived in Southeast Asia. In fact, in many ways, LB1 more closely resembles African *H. erectus* and the Georgian hominids than the geographically closer Javan *H. erectus,* he observes. But whether these similarities indicate that *H. floresiensis* arose from an earlier *H. erectus* foray into Southeast Asia than the one that produced Javan *H. erectus* or are merely coincidental results of the dwarfing process remains to be determined. Future excavations may connect the dots. The team plans to continue digging on Flores and Java and will next year begin work on other Indonesian islands, including Sulawesi to the north.

The hominid bones from Liang Bua now span the period from 95,000 to 13,000 years ago, suggesting to the team that the little Floresians perished along with the pygmy *Stegodon* because of a massive volcanic eruption in the area around 12,000 years ago, although they may have survived later farther east. If *H. erectus* persisted on nearby Java until 25,000 years ago, as some evidence suggests, and *H. sapiens* had arrived in the region by 40,000 years ago, three human species lived cheek by jowl in Southeast Asia for at least 15,000 years. And the discoverers of *H. floresiensis* predict that more will be found. The islands of Lombok and Sumbawa would have been natural stepping-stones for hominids traveling from Java or mainland Asia to Flores. Those that put down roots on these islands may well have set off on their own evolutionary trajectories.

Perhaps, it has been proposed, some of these offshoots of the *Homo* lineage survived until historic times. Maybe they still live in remote pockets of Southeast Asia's dense rain forests, awaiting (or avoiding) discovery. On Flores, oral histories hold that the *ebu gogo* was still in existence when Dutch colonists settled there in the 19th century. And Malay folklore describes another small, humanlike being known as the *orang pendek* that supposedly dwells on Sumatra to this day.

"Every country seems to have myths about these things," Brown reflects. "We've excavated a lot of sites around the world, and we've never found them. But then [in September 2003] we found LB1." Scientists may never know whether tales of the *ebu gogo* and *orang pendek* do in fact recount actual sightings of other hominid species, but the newfound possibility will no doubt spur efforts to find such creatures for generations to come.

KATE WONG is editorial director of ScientificAmerican.com.

The Gift *of* Gab

Grooves and holes in fossil skulls may reveal when our ancestors began to speak. The big question, though, is what drove them to it?

MATT CARTMILL

People can talk. Other animals can't. They can all communicate in one way or another—to lure mates, at the very least—but their whinnies and wiggles don't do the jobs that language does. The birds and beasts can use their signals to attract, threaten, or alert each other, but they can't ask questions, strike bargains, tell stories, or lay out a plan of action.

Those skills make *Homo sapiens* a uniquely successful, powerful, and dangerous mammal. Other creatures' signals carry only a few limited kinds of information about what's happening at the moment, but language lets us tell each other in limitless detail about what used to be or will be or might be. Language lets us get vast numbers of big, smart fellow primates all working together on a single task—building the Great Wall of China or fighting World War II or flying to the moon. It lets us construct and communicate the gorgeous fantasies of literature and the profound fables of myth. It lets us cheat death by pouring out our knowledge, dreams, and memories into younger people's minds. And it does powerful things for us inside our own minds because we do a lot of our thinking by talking silently to ourselves. Without language, we would be only a sort of upright chimpanzee with funny feet and clever hands. With it, we are the self-possessed masters of the planet.

How did such a marvelous adaptation get started? And if it's so marvelous, why hasn't any other species come up with anything similar? These may be the most important questions we face in studying human evolution. They are also the least understood. But in the past few years, linguists and anthropologists have been making some breakthroughs, and we are now beginning to have a glimmering of some answers.

Could Neanderthals talk? They seem to have had nimble tongues, but some scientists think the geometry of their throats prevented them from making many clear vowel sounds.

We can reasonably assume that by at least 30,000 years ago people were talking—at any rate, they were producing carvings, rock paintings, and jewelry, as well as ceremonial graves containing various goods. These tokens of art and religion are high-level forms of symbolic behavior, and they imply that the everyday symbol-handling machinery of human language must have been in place then as well.

Language surely goes back further than that, but archeologists don't agree on just how far. Some think that earlier, more basic human behaviors—hunting in groups, tending fires, making tools—also demanded language. Others think these activities are possible without speech. Chimpanzees, after all, hunt communally, and with human guidance they can learn to tend fires and chip flint.

Paleontologists have pored over the fossil bones of our ancient relatives in search of evidence for speech abilities. Because the most crucial organ for language is the brain, they have looked for signs in the impressions left by the brain on the inner surfaces of fossil skulls, particularly impressions made by parts of the brain called speech areas because damage to them can impair a person's ability to talk or understand language. Unfortunately, it turns out that you can't tell whether a fossil hominid was able to talk simply by looking at brain impressions on the inside of its skull. For one thing, the fit between the brain and the

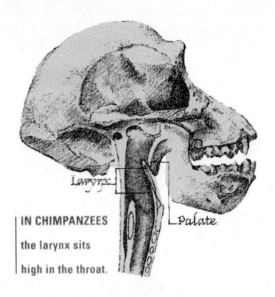

IN CHIMPANZEES the larynx sits high in the throat.

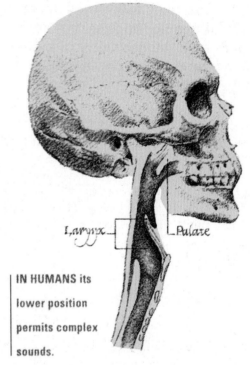

IN HUMANS its lower position permits complex sounds.

Illustrations by Dugald Stermer

bony braincase is loose in people and other large mammals, and so the impressions we derive from fossil skulls are disappointingly fuzzy. Moreover, we now know that language functions are not tightly localized but spread across many parts of the brain.

Faced with these obstacles, researchers have turned from the brain to other organs used in speech, such as the throat and tongue. Some have measured the fossil skulls and jaws of early hominids, tried to reconstruct the shape of their vocal tracts, and then applied the laws of acoustics to them to see whether they might have been capable of producing human speech.

All mammals produce their vocal noises by contracting muscles that compress the rib cage. The air in the lungs is driven out through the windpipe to the larynx, where it flows between the vocal cords. More like flaps than cords, these structures vibrate in the breeze, producing a buzzing sound that becomes the voice. The human difference lies in what happens to the air after it gets past the vocal cords.

In people, the larynx lies well below the back of the tongue, and most of the air goes out through the mouth when we talk. We make only a few sounds by exhaling through the nose—for instance, nasal consonants like *m* or *n,* or the so-called nasal vowels in words like the French *bon* and *vin.* But in most mammals, including apes, the larynx sticks farther up behind the tongue, into the back of the nose, and most of the exhaled air passes out through the nostrils. Nonhuman mammals make mostly nasal sounds as a result.

At some point in human evolution the larynx must have descended from its previous heights, and this change had some serious drawbacks. It put the opening of the windpipe squarely in the path of descending food, making it dangerously easy for us to choke to death if a chunk of meat goes down the wrong way—something that rarely happens to a dog or a cat. Why has evolution exposed us to this danger?

Some scientists think that the benefits outweighed the risks, because lowering the larynx improved the quality of our vowels and made speech easier to understand. The differences between vowels are produced mainly by changing the size and shape of the airway between the tongue and the roof of the mouth. When the front of the tongue almost touches the palate, you get the *ee* sound in *beet;* when the tongue is humped up high in the back (and the lips are rounded), you get the *oo* sound in *boot,* and so on. We are actually born with a somewhat apelike throat, including a flat tongue and a larynx lying high up in the neck, and this arrangement makes a child's vowels sound less clearly separated from each other than an adult's.

Philip Lieberman of Brown University thinks that an ape-like throat persisted for some time in our hominid ancestors. His studies of fossil jaws and skulls persuade him that a more modern throat didn't evolve until some 500,000 years ago, and that some evolutionary lines in the genus *Homo* never did acquire modern vocal organs. Lieberman concludes that the Neanderthals, who lived in Europe until perhaps 25,000 years ago, belonged to a dead-end lineage that never developed our range of vowels, and that their speech—if they had any at all—would have been harder to understand than ours. Apparently, being easily understood wasn't terribly important to them—not important enough, at any rate, to outweigh the risk of inhaling a chunk of steak into a lowered larynx. This suggests that vocal communication wasn't as central to their lives as it is to ours.

Many paleoanthropologists, especially those who like to see Neanderthals as a separate species, accept this story. Others have their doubts. But the study of other parts of the skeleton in fossil hominids supports some of Lieberman's conclusions. During the 1980s a nearly complete skeleton of a young *Homo* male was recovered from 1.5-million-year-old deposits in northern Kenya. Examining the vertebrae attached to the boy's rib cage, the English anatomist Ann MacLarnon discovered that his spinal cord was proportionately thinner in this region than it is in people today. Since that part of the cord controls most of the muscles that drive air in and out of the lungs, MacLarnon concluded that the youth may not have had the kind of precise neural control over breathing movements that is needed for speech.

This year my colleague Richard Kay, his student Michelle Balow, and I were able to offer some insights from yet another part of the hominid body. The tongue's movements are controlled almost solely by a nerve called the hypoglossal. In its course from the brain to the tongue, this nerve passes through a hole in the skull, and Kay, Balow, and I found that this bony canal is relatively big in modern humans—about twice as big in cross section as that of a like-size chimpanzee. Our larger canal presumably reflects a bigger hypoglossal nerve, giving us the precise control over tongue movements that we need for speech.

We also measured this hole in the skulls of a number of fossil hominids. Australopithecines have small canals like those of apes, suggesting that they couldn't talk. But later *Homo* skulls, beginning with a 400,000-year-old skull from Zambia, all have big, humanlike hypoglossal canals. These are also the skulls that were the first to house brains as big as our own. On these counts our work supports Lieberman's ideas. We disagree only on the matter of Neanderthals. While he claims their throats couldn't have produced human speech, we find that their skulls also had human-size canals for the hypoglossal nerve, suggesting that they could indeed talk.

The verdict is still out on the language abilities of Neanderthals. I tend to think they must have had fully human language. After all, they had brains larger than those of most humans.

In short, several lines of evidence suggest that neither the australopithecines nor the early, small-brained species of *Homo* could talk. Only around half a million years ago did the first big-brained *Homo* evolve language. The verdict is still out on the language abilities of Neanderthals.

I tend to think that they must have had fully human language. After all, they had brains larger than those of most modern humans, made elegant stone tools, and knew how to use fire. But if Lieberman and his friends are right about those vowels, Neanderthals may have sounded something like the Swedish chef on *The Muppet Show.*

We are beginning to get some idea of when human language originated, but the fossils can't tell us how it got started, or what the intermediate stages between animal calls and human language might have been like. When trying to understand the origin of a trait that doesn't fossilize, it's sometimes useful to look for similar but simpler versions of it in other creatures living today. With luck, you can find a series of forms that suggest how simple primitive makeshifts could have evolved into more complex and elegant versions. This is how Darwin attacked the problem of the evolution of the eye. Earlier biologists had pointed to the human eye as an example of a marvelously perfect organ that must have been specially created all at once in its final form by God. But Darwin pointed out that animal eyes exist in all stages of complexity, from simple skin cells that can detect only the difference between light and darkness, to pits lined with such cells, and so on all the way to the eyes of people and other vertebrates. This series, he argued, shows how the human eye could have evolved from simpler precursors by gradual stages.

Can we look to other animals to find simpler precursors of language? It seems unlikely. Scientists have sought experimental evidence of language in dolphins and chimpanzees, thus far without success. But even if we had no experimental studies, common sense would tell us that the other animals can't have languages like ours. If they had, we would be in big trouble because they would organize against us. They don't. Outside of Gary Larson's *Far Side* cartoons and George Orwell's *Animal Farm,* farmers don't have to watch their backs when they visit the cowshed. There are no conspiracies among cows, or even among dolphins and chimpanzees. Unlike human slaves or prisoners, they never plot rebellions against their oppressors.

Even if language as a whole has no parallels in animal communication, might some of its peculiar properties be foreshadowed among the beasts around us? If so, that might tell us something about how and in what order these properties were acquired. One such property is reference. Most of the units of human languages refer to things—to individuals (like *Fido*), or to types of objects (*dog*), actions (*sit*), or properties (*furry*). Animal signals don't have this kind of referential meaning. Instead, they have what is called instrumental meaning: this is, they act as stimuli that trigger desired responses from others. A frog's mating croak doesn't *refer* to sex. Its purpose is to get some, not to talk about it. People, too, have signals of

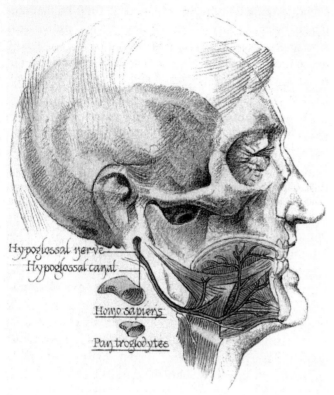

The Tongue-Controlling hypoglossal nerve is larger in humans than in chimps.

this purely animal sort—for example, weeping, laughing, and screaming—but these stand outside language. They have powerful meanings for us but not the kind of meaning that words have.

Some animal signals have a focused meaning that looks a bit like reference. For example, vervet monkeys give different warning calls for different predators. When they hear the "leopard" call, vervets climb trees and anxiously look down; when they hear the "eagle" call, they hide in low bushes or look up. But although the vervets' leopard call is in some sense about leopards, it isn't a word for leopard. Like a frog's croak or human weeping, its meaning is strictly instrumental; it's a stimulus that elicits an automatic response. All a vervet can "say" with it is " *Eeek!* A leopard!"—not "I really hate leopard!" or "No leopards here, thank goodness" or "A leopard ate Alice yesterday."

Australopithecus Africanus and other early hominids couldn't speak.

In these English sentences, such referential words as *leopard* work their magic through an accompanying framework of nonreferential, grammatical words, which set up an empty web of meaning that the referential symbols fill in. When Lewis Carroll tells us in "Jabberwocky" that "the slithy toves did gyre and gimble in the wabe," we have no idea what he is talking about, but we do know certain things—for instance, that all this happened in the past and that there was more than one tove but only one wabe. We know these things because of the grammatical structure of the sentence, a structure that linguists call syntax. Again, there's nothing much like it in any animal signals.

But if there aren't any intermediate stages between animal calls and human speech, then how could language evolve? What was there for it to evolve from? Until recently, linguists have shrugged off these questions—or else concluded that language didn't evolve at all, but just sprang into existence by accident, through some glorious random mutation. This theory drives Darwinians crazy, but the linguists have been content with it because it fits neatly into some key ideas in modern linguistics.

Forty years ago most linguists thought that people learn to talk through the same sort of behavior reinforcement used in training an animal to do tricks: when children use a word correctly or produce a grammatical sentence, they are rewarded. This picture was swept away in the late 1950s by the revolutionary ideas of Noam Chomsky. Chomsky argued that the structures of syntax lie in unconscious linguistic patterns—so-called deep structures—that are very different from the surface strings of words that come out of our mouths. Two sentences that look different on the surface (for instance, "A leopard ate Alice" and "Alice was eaten by a leopard") can mean the same thing because they derive from a single deep structure. Conversely, two sentences with different deep structures and different meanings can look exactly the same on the surface (for example, "Fleeing leopards can be dangerous"). Any models of language learning based strictly on the observable behaviors of language, Chomsky insisted, can't account for these deep-lying patterns of meaning.

Chomsky concluded that the deepest structures of language are innate, not learned. We are all born with the same fundamental grammar hard-wired into our brains, and we are preprogrammed to pick up the additional rules of the local language, just as baby ducks are hard-wired to follow the first big animal they see when they hatch. Chomsky could see no evidence of other animals' possessing this innate syntax machinery. He concluded that we can't learn anything about the origins of language by studying other animals and they can't learn language from us. If language learning were just a matter of proper training, Chomsky reasoned, we ought to be able to teach English to lab rats, or at least to apes.

As we have seen, apes aren't built to talk. But they can be trained to use sign language or to point to word-symbols on a keyboard. Starting in the 1960s, several experimenters trained chimpanzees and other great apes to use such signs to ask for things and answer questions to get rewards. Linguists, however, were unimpressed. They said that the apes' signs had a purely instrumental meaning: the animals were just doing tricks to get a treat. And there was no trace of syntax in the random-looking jumble of signs the apes produced; an ape that signed "You give me cookie please" one minute might sign "Me cookie please you cookie eat give" the next.

Duane Rumbaugh and Sue Savage-Rumbaugh set to work with chimpanzees at the Yerkes Regional Primate Research Center in Atlanta to try to answer the linguists' criticisms. After many years of mixed results, Sue made a surprising break-through with a young bonobo (or pygmy chimp) named Kanzi. Kanzi had watched his mother, Matata, try to learn signs with little success. When Sue gave up on her and started with Kanzi, she was astonished to discover that he already knew the meaning of 12 of the keyboard symbols. Apparently, he had learned them without any training or rewards. In the years that followed, he learned new symbols quickly and used them referentially, both to answer questions and to "talk" about things that he intended to do or had already done. Still more amazingly, he had a considerable understanding of spoken English—including its syntax. He grasped such grammatical niceties as case structures ("Can you throw a potato to the turtle?") and if-then implication ("You can have some cereal if you give Austin your monster mash to play with"). Upon hearing such sentences, Kanzi behaved appropriately 72 percent of the time—more than a 30-month-old human child given the same tests.

Kanzi is a primatologist's dream and a linguist's nightmare. His language-learning abilities seem inexplicable. He didn't need any rewards to learn language, as the old behaviorists would have predicted; but he also defies the Chomskyan model, which can't explain why a speechless ape would have an innate tendency to learn English. It looks as though some animals can develop linguistic abilities for reasons unrelated to language itself.

Brain enlargement in hominids may have been the result of evolutionary pressures that favored intelligence. As a side effect, human evolution crossed a threshold at which language became possible.

Neuroscientist William Calvin of the University of Washington and linguist Derek Bickerton of the University of Hawaii have a suggestion as to what those reasons might be. In their forthcoming book, *Lingua ex Machina*, they argue that the ability to create symbols—signs that refer to things—is potentially present in any animal that can learn to interpret natural signs, such as a trail of footprints. Syntax, meanwhile, emerges from the abstract thought required for a social life. In apes and some other mammals with complex and subtle social relationships, individuals make alliances and act altruistically towards others, with the implicit understanding that their favors will be returned. To succeed in such societies, animals need to choose trustworthy allies and to detect and punish cheaters who take but never give anything in return. This demands fitting a shifting constellation of individuals into an abstract mental model of social roles (debtors, creditors, allies, and so on) connected by social expectations ("If you scratch my back, I'll scratch yours"). Calvin and Bickerton believe that such abstract models of social obligation furnished the basic pattern for the deep structures of syntax.

These foreshadowings of symbols and syntax, they propose, laid the groundwork for language in a lot of social animals but didn't create language itself. That had to wait until our ancestors evolved brains big enough to handle the large-scale operations needed to generate and process complex strings of signs. Calvin and Bickerton suggest that brain enlargement in our ancestry was the result of evolutionary pressures that favored intelligence and motor coordination for making tools and throwing weapons. As a side effect of these selection pressures, which had nothing to do with communication, human evolution crossed a threshold at which language became possible. Big-brained, nonhuman animals like Kanzi remain just on the verge of language.

Fossils hint that language dawned 500,000 years ago.

This story reconciles natural selection with the linguists' insistence that you can't evolve language out of an animal communication system. It is also consistent with what we know about language from the fossil record. The earliest hominids with modern-size brains also seem to be the first ones with modern-size hypoglossal canals. Lieberman thinks that these are also the first hominids with modern vocal tracts. It may be no coincidence that all three of these changes seem to show up together around half a million years ago. If Calvin and Bickerton are right, the enlargement of the brain may have abruptly brought language into being at this time, which would have placed new selection pressures on the evolving throat and tongue.

This account may be wrong in some of its details, but the story in its broad outlines solves so many puzzles and ties up so many loose ends that something like it must surely be correct. It also promises to resolve our conflicting views of the boundary between people and animals. To some people, it seems obvious that human beings are utterly different from any beasts. To others, it's just as obvious that many other animals are essentially like us, only with fewer smarts and more fur. Each party finds the other's view of humanity alien and threatening. The story of language origins sketched above suggests that both parties are right: the human difference is real and profound, but it is rooted in aspects of psychology and biology that we share with our close animal relatives. If the growing consensus on the origins of language can join these disparate truths together, it will be a big step forward in the study of human evolution.

MATT CARTMILL is a professor at Duke, where he teaches anatomy and anthropology and studies animal locomotion. Cartmill is also the author of numerous articles and books on the evolution of people and other animals, including an award-winning book on hunting, *A View to a Death in the Morning*. He is the president of the American Association of Physical Anthropologists.

The Birth of Childhood

Unlike other apes, humans depend on their parents for a long period after weaning. But when—and why—did our long childhood evolve?

Ann Gibbons

Mel was just 3.5 years old when his mother died of pneumonia in 1987 in Tanzania. He had still been nursing and had no siblings, so his prospects were grim. He begged weakly for meat, and although adults gave him scraps, only a 12-year-old named Spindle shared his food regularly, protected him, and let him sleep with him at night. When Spindle took off for a month, another adolescent, Pax, came to Mel's rescue, giving him fruit and a place to sleep until Spindle returned. Mel survived to age 10.

Fortunately for Mel, he was an orphan chimpanzee living in the Gombe Stream National Park rather than a small child living in the slums of a big city. With only sporadic care from older children, a 3-year-old human orphan would not have survived.

Mel's story illustrates the uniqueness of one facet of human life: Unlike our close cousins the chimpanzees, we have a prolonged period of development after weaning, when children depend on their parents to feed them, until at least age 6 or 7. Street children from Kathmandu to Rio de Janeiro do not survive on their own unless they are at least 6. "There's no society where children can feed themselves after weaning," says anthropologist Kristen Hawkes of the University of Utah in Salt Lake City. By contrast, "chimpanzees don't have childhoods. They are independent soon after weaning," says anthropologist Barry Bogin of Loughborough University in Leicestershire, U.K.

Humans are also the only animals that stretch out the teenage years, having a final growth spurt and delaying reproduction until about 6 years after puberty. On average, women's first babies arrive at age 19, with a worldwide peak of first babies at age 22.5. This lengthy period of development—comprised of infancy, juvenile years, and adolescence—is a hallmark of the human condition; researchers have known since the 1930s that we take twice as long as chimpanzees to reach adulthood. Even though we are only a bit bigger than chimpanzees, we mature and reproduce a decade later and live 2 to 3 decades longer, says Bogin.

Given that we are unique among mammals, researchers have been probing how this pattern of growth evolved. They have long scrutinized the few, fragile skulls and skeletons of ancient children and have now developed an arsenal of tools to better gauge how childhood has changed over the past 3 million years. Researchers are scanning skulls and teeth of every known juvenile with electron microscopes, micro-computed tomography scans, or powerful synchrotron x-rays and applying state-of-the-art methods to create three-dimensional virtual reconstructions of the skulls of infants and the pelvises of mothers. They're analyzing life histories in traditional cultures to help understand the advantages of the human condition. In addition, some new fossils are appearing. . . . Researchers report the first nearly complete pelvis of a female *Homo erectus*, which offers clues to the prenatal growth of this key human species.

All of this is creating some surprises. One direct human ancestor, whose skeleton looks much like our own, turns out to have grown up much faster than we do. The life histories of our closest evolutionary cousins, the Neandertals, remain controversial, but some researchers suspect that they may have had the longest childhoods of all. The new lines of evidence are helping researchers close in on the time when childhood began to lengthen. "Evidence suggests that much of what makes our life history unique took shape during the evolution of the genus *Homo* and not before," says anthropologist Holly Smith of the University of Michigan, Ann Arbor.

Live Fast, Die Young

Back in 1925, Australian anatomist Raymond Dart announced the discovery of that rarest of rare specimens, the skull of an early hominin child. Dart estimated that the australopithecine he called the Taung baby had been about 6 years old when it died about 2 million years ago, because its first permanent molar had erupted. As modern parents know, the first of the baby teeth fall out and the first permanent molars appear at about age 6. Dart assumed that early hominins—the group made up of humans and our ancestors but not other apes—matured on much the same schedule as we do, an assumption held for 60 years. Growing up slowly was seen as a defining character of the human lineage.

Childhood Stages

	Age at Weaning (Years)	Age at Eruption of First Molar (Years)	Female Age at First Breeding (Years) (Estimated by 3rd Molar Eruption in Fossils)	Average Maximum Life Span (Years)
Chimpanzees, *Pan troglodytes*	4.0	4.0	11.5	45
Lucy, *Australopithecus afarensis*	4.0?	4.0?	11.5	45
Homo erectus	?	4.5	14.5 (est.)	60? (est.)
Modern humans, *Homo sapiens*	2.5	6.0	19.3	70

Milestones. Key events show that modern humans live slower and die later than our ancestors did.

Then in 1984, anatomists Christopher Dean and Timothy Bromage tested a new method to calculate the chronological ages of fossil children in a lab at University College London (UCL). Just as botanists add up tree rings to calculate the age of a tree, they counted microscopic lines on the surface of teeth that are laid down weekly as humans grow. The pair counted the lines on teeth of australopithecine children about as mature as the Taung child and were confounded: These hominin children were only about 3.5 years old rather than 6. They seemed to be closer to the chimpanzee pattern, in which the first permanent molar erupts at about age 3.5. "We concluded that [the australopithecines] were more like living great apes in their pace of development than modern humans," says Dean.

Their report in *Nature* in 1985 shook the field and focused researchers on the key questions of when and why our ancestors adopted the risky strategy of delaying reproduction. Many other slow-growing, large-bodied animals, such as rhinos, elephants, and chimpanzees, are now threatened with extinction, in part because they delay reproduction so long that their offspring risk dying before they replace themselves. Humans are the latest to begin reproducing, yet we seem immune from those risks, given that there are 6.6 billion of us on the planet. "When did we escape those constraints? When did we extend our childhood?" asks biological anthropologist Steven Leigh of the University of Illinois, Urbana-Champaign.

The Taung baby and the other australopithecine children, including the relatively recent discovery of a stunning fossil of a 3-year-old *Australopithecus afarensis* girl from Dikika, Ethiopia, show that it happened after the australopithecines. So researchers have zeroed in on early *Homo,* which appeared in Africa about 2 million years ago.

Unfortunately, there are only a few jaw bits of early *Homo* infants and young children to nail down their ages. Most of what we know comes from a single skeleton, a *H. erectus* boy who died about 1.6 million years ago near Lake Turkana, Kenya. *H. erectus* was among the first human ancestors to share many key elements of the modern human body plan, with a brain considerably larger than that of earlier hominins. And unlike the petite australopithecines, this Turkana youth was big: He weighed 50 kilograms, stood 163 centimeters tall, and looked like he was 13 years old, based on modern human standards. Yet two independent tooth studies suggested ages from 8 or 9 to 10.5 years old.

Now a fresh look at the skeleton concludes that, despite the boy's size, he was closer to 8 years old when he died. Dean and Smith make this case in a paper in press in an edited volume, *The First Humans: Origin of the Genus* Homo. The skeleton and tooth microstructure of the boy and new data on other members of his species suggest that he attained more of his adult height and mass earlier than modern human children do. Today, "you won't find an 8-year-old boy with body weight, height, and skeletal age that are so much older," says Dean.

He and Smith concluded that the boy did not experience a "long, slow period of growth" after he was weaned but grew up earlier, more like a chimpanzee. They estimate the species' age at first reproduction at about 14.5, based on the eruption of its third molar, which in both humans and chimpanzees erupts at about the age they first reproduce. This 8-year-old Turkana Boy was probably more independent than a 13-year-old modern human, the researchers say, suggesting that *H. erectus* families were quite different from ours and did not stay together as long.

The new, remarkably complete female pelvis, however, suggests that life history changes had begun in *H. erectus.* Researchers led by Sileshi Semaw of the Stone Age Institute at Indiana University, Bloomington, found the pelvis in the badlands of Gona, Ethiopia. They present a chain of inference that leads from pelvis, to brain size, to life history strategy.

They assume that the nearly complete pelvis belongs to *H. erectus,* because other *H. erectus* fossils were found nearby and because it resembles fragmentary pelvises for the species. Lead author Scott Simpson of Case Western Reserve University in Cleveland, Ohio, paints a vivid picture of a short female with wide hips and an "obstetrically capacious" pelvic opening that could have birthed babies with brain sizes of up to 315 milliliters. That's 30% to 50% of the adult brain size for this species and larger than previously predicted based on a reconstruction of the Turkana Boy's incomplete pelvis. However, the new estimate does match with newborn brain size predicted by the size of adult brains in *H. erectus,* says Jeremy DeSilva of Worcester State College in Massachusetts, who made such calculations online in September in the *Journal of Human Evolution.*

The wide pelvis suggests *H. erectus* got a head start on its brain development, putting on extra gray matter in utero rather than later in childhood. That's similar to living people, whose brains

154

grow rapidly before birth, says Simpson. But if *H. erectus*'s fetal growth approached that of modern humans, it built proportionately more of its brain before birth, because its brain never became as massive as our own.

Thus, *H. erectus* grew its brain before birth like a modern human, while during childhood it grew up faster like an ape. With a brain developing early, *H. erectus* toddlers may have spent less time as helpless children than modern humans do, says paleoanthropologist Alan Walker of Pennsylvania State University in State College. This suggests *H. erectus* children were neither chimplike nor humanlike but perhaps somewhere in between: "Early *H. erectus* possessed a life history unlike any species living today," write Dean and Smith. "If you look at its morphology, it fits in our genus, *Homo*," says Smith. "But in terms of life history, they fit with australopithecines."

Live Slow, Die Old?

If *H. erectus* was just beginning to slow down its life history, when did humans take the last steps, to our current late-maturing life plan? Three juvenile fossil members of *H. antecessor,* who died 800,000 years ago in Atapuerca, Spain, offer tantalizing clues. An initial study in 1999, based on rough estimates of tooth eruption, found that this species matured like a modern human, says José María Bermúdez de Castro of the Museo Nacional de Ciencias Naturales in Madrid. Detailed studies of tooth microstructure are eagerly awaited to confirm this.

In the meantime, another recent study has shown that childhood was fully extended by the time the first members of our species, *H. sapiens,* appeared in northern Africa about 200,000 years ago. In 2007, researchers examined the daily, internal tooth lines of a *H. sapiens* child who lived 160,000 years ago in Jebel Irhoud, Morocco. They used x-rays from a powerful particle accelerator in Grenoble, France (*Science,* 7 December 2007, p. 1546), to study the teeth without destroying them and found that the 8-year-old Jebel Irhoud child had grown as slowly as a modern 8-year-old, according to Harvard University paleoanthropologist Tanya Smith, who coled the study.

That analysis narrowed the window of time when humans evolved the last extension of our childhood to between 800,000 years ago and 200,000 years ago. To constrain it still further, Tanya Smith and her colleagues recently trained their x-ray vision on our closest relatives: the extinct Neandertals, who shared their last ancestor with us about 500,000 years ago. First, the researchers sliced a molar of a Belgian Neandertal that was at the same stage of dental development as the 8-year-old Jebel Irhoud child and counted its internal growth lines. They found that it had reached the same dental milestones more rapidly and proposed that Neandertals grew up faster than we do. That suggests that a fully extended childhood evolved only in our species, in the past 200,000 years.

But Tanya Smith's results conflict with earlier studies by Dean and colleagues who also sliced Neandertal teeth and found that they had formed slowly, like those of modern humans. The case is not closed: Smith and paleontologist Paul Tafforeau of the European Synchrotron Radiation Facility in Grenoble, France, spent weeks last year imaging juvenile Neandertals and early members of *H. sapiens,* and they expect to publish within a year.

Meanwhile, new data with implications for Neandertal growth rates are coming in from other sources. The brain sizes of a Neandertal newborn and two infants show that they were at the upper end of the size range for modern humans, suggesting that their brains grew faster than ours after birth, according to virtual reconstructions by Christoph Zollikofer and anthropologist Marcia Ponce de León of the University of Zurich (*Science,* 12 September, p. 1429).

Those rapidly growing brains don't necessarily imply a rapid life history, warn Zollikofer and Ponce de León. They argue that because Neandertals' brains were more massive, they did not complete brain growth earlier than modern humans even though they grew at a faster rate. "They have to get those bigger brains somehow," says Holly Smith. For now, Neandertals' life history remains controversial.

Why Wait?

If childhood began to change in *H. erectus* and continued to get longer in our own species and possibly Neandertals, then the next question is why. What advantage did our ancestors gain from delaying reproduction so long? Many researchers agree that childhood allows us to learn from others, in order to improve our survival skills and prepare us to be better parents. Historically, researchers have also argued that humans need a long childhood to allow enough time for our larger brain to mature.

But in fact, a big brain doesn't directly cause the extension of childhood, because the brain is built relatively early. "Everyone speaks about slow human development, but the human brain develops very fast," says Zollikofer. It doubles in size in the first year of life and achieves 95% of its adult size by the age of 5 (although white matter grows at least to age 18). "We get our brains done; then, we sit around for much longer than other species before we reproduce," says Leigh. "It's almost like humans are building the outside, getting the scaffolding of the house up early, and then filling in after that."

However, there's a less direct connection between brains and life history: Big brains are so metabolically expensive that primates must postpone the age of reproduction in order to build them, according to a paper last year in the *Journal of Human Evolution* (*Science,* 15 June 2007, p. 1560). "The high metabolic costs of rapid brain growth require delayed maturation so that mothers can bear the metabolic burdens associated with high brain growth," says Leigh. "Fast brain growth tells us that maturation is late."

That's why Ponce de León and Zollikofer think that the Neandertals' rapid brain growth implies late, rather than early, maturation: Neandertal mothers must have been large and strong—and by implication, relatively old—to support infants with such big, fast-growing brains. Indeed, say the Zurich pair, Neandertals may have had even longer childhoods than we do now. Childhood, like brain size, may have reached its zenith in Neandertals and early *H. sapiens.* As our brains got smaller over the past 50,000 years, we might have begun reproducing slightly earlier than Neandertals.

To explore such questions, recent interdisciplinary studies are teasing out the reproductive advantages of waiting to become parents. Many analyses cite an influential life history model by evolutionary biologist Eric Charnov of the University of New Mexico, Albuquerque. The model shows that it pays to have babies early if parents face a high risk of death. Conversely, mammals that face a lower risk of dying benefit if they wait to reproduce, because older mothers can grow bigger, stronger bodies that grow bigger babies, who are more likely to survive. "The driving force of a prolonged life history schedule is almost certainly a reduction in mortality rates that allows growth and life span to extend and allows for reproduction to extend further into adulthood in a more spread-out manner," says Dean.

Researchers such as Loughborough's Bogin have applied Charnov's model to modern humans, proposing that delaying reproduction creates higher quality human mothers. Indeed, humans start having babies 8 years later than chimpanzees, and both species stop by about age 45 to 50. But once human mothers begin, they more than make up for their delayed start, pushing out babies on average 3.4 years apart in traditional forager societies without birth control, compared with 5.9 years for wild chimpanzees, says Bogin. This rapid-fire reproduction produces more babies for human hunter-gatherers, who have peak fertility rates of 0.31 babies per given year compared with 0.22 for chimpanzees. And human mothers who start even later than age 19 have more surviving babies. For example, in the 1950s, the Anabaptist Hutterites of North America, who eschewed birth control, had their first babies on average at age 22 and then bore children every 2 years. They produced an amazing nine children per mother, says Bogin, who has studied the group.

Such fecundity, however, requires a village or at least an extended family with fathers and grandmothers around to help provision and care for the young. That's something that other primates cannot provide consistently, if at all, says Hawkes (*Science,* 25 April 1997, p. 535). She proposed that grandmothers' provisioning allows mothers to wean early and have babies more closely together, a vivid example of the way humans use social connections to overcome biological constraints—and allow mothers to have more babies than they could raise on their own. "Late maturation works well for humans because culture lets us escape the constraints other primates have," says Leigh.

The key is to find out when our ancestors were weaned, says Holly Smith. Younger weaning implies that mothers had enough social support to feed weaned children and space babies more closely. "Weaning tells us when *Homo* species start stacking their young," says Smith. Indeed, Dean and Louise Humphrey of the Natural History Museum in London are testing a method that detects the chemical signature of weaning in human teeth. Humans may be slow starters, but our social safety net has allowed us to stack our babies closely together—and so win the reproductive sweepstakes, leaving chimpanzees, and the extinct Neandertals, far behind.

The Brain

CARL ZIMMER

There's more to a happy face than meets the eye. A smirk, a sneer, a wince are the work of evolution Darwin would have loved Botox.

I don't mean that he would have been first in line at the doctor's office to get a needle jabbed into his famously furrowed brow. I mean that Darwin would have loved to use Botox as a scientific tool—to eavesdrop on the intimate conversation between the face and brain.

For much of his life, Darwin was obsessed with faces. On a visit to the London Zoo, he gave mirrors to a pair of orangutans and watched them grimace and pucker their lips as they stared at their reflections. He passed many an afternoon gazing intently at photographs of crying babies and laughing women. He showed his friends pictures of a man whose facial muscles were distorted in various ways by electric shocks and quizzed them about what emotion the man seemed to be feeling. To find out if all humans expressed emotions in the same way, he wrote up a list of 16 questions, which he sent to dozens of acquaintances around the world. His list of questions began:

1. Is astonishment expressed by the eyes and mouth being opened wide, and by the eyebrows being raised?
2. Does shame excite a blush when the colour of the skin allows it to be visible? and especially how low down the body does the blush extend?
3. When a man is indignant or defiant does he frown, hold his body and head erect, square his shoulders and clench his fists?

Darwin took the answers he got from his correspondents—from such places as Borneo, Calcutta, and New Zealand—and combined them with the rest of his notes on faces to publish a book in 1872 entitled *The Expression of the Emotions in Man and Animals*. Most scientists in Darwin's time considered the face a mystery, its expressions having been set at the time of Creation. But Darwin argued that the look of happiness or grief on a person's face was the product of evolution, just as our hands evolved from fish fins.

As evidence, Darwin pointed to the results of his poll. People the world over made faces using the same basic patterns of muscle contraction, starting from infancy. In his book Darwin printed pictures of people getting electric shocks, which were taken by the French physician Guillaume-Benjamin-Amand Duchenne.

Simply by running current through different parts of a person's face, Duchenne could produce expressions of happiness, fear, anger, and disgust. Expressions were reflexes, Darwin argued, instinctive patterns etched in our faces and brains.

To trace the history of our faces, Darwin wrote, we need only look at our fellow animals. Although human faces were unique in some ways, they also bore some striking similarities to those of other species: "He who will look at a dog preparing to attack another dog or a man, and at the same animal when caressing his master, or will watch the countenance of a monkey when insulted, and when fondled by his keeper, will be forced to admit that the movements of their features and their gestures are almost as expressive as those of man."

Darwin described facial expressions as a "language of emotion." They served as a way for us to communicate before we had words. They helped us not only to understand the emotions of others but to share them as well. "The free expression by outward signs of an emotion intensifies it," he wrote. "Even the simulation of an emotion tends to arouse it in our minds."

Darwin's ideas turned out to be prophetic, but when you read *The Expression of Emotions* in the 21st century, you can't help noticing how quaint his scientific research was. Scientists who study faces today do not rely on their pet dogs or letters from friends in Brazil. They trace the development of the face in embryos, scan brains, read the electrical activity of muscles, and record grins and pouts on high-speed video.

Our faces, these scientists have shown, acquired some of their basic form more than half a billion years ago. It was then that early fish evolved muscles on their heads to suck in food and water. All the muscles of our faces develop from a strip of cells at the base of the embryonic head, just as they do in lampreys, which belong to one of the oldest lineages of vertebrates alive today.

The transition to land brought major changes to the faces of our ancestors. They stopped breathing water through gills, and the gill-supporting muscles in the face took on new functions, like controlling the throat to swallow food. At the same time the muscles that moved the jaws became bigger as land vertebrates evolved a more powerful bite.

When our ancestors evolved into mammals, their faces changed again. New muscle attachments spread from the jaws to the skin itself. They boosted the senses of mammals—muscles on the sides of the face could swivel ears, while muscles around the lips controlled whiskers. But mammals could do more with these muscles than sense the world. They could also communicate. A mammal could bare its teeth or turn back its ears to send signals to other mammals.

If the mammal face is an instrument for communication, the primate face is a Stradivarius. When primates evolved about 60 million years ago, big blocks of facial muscles broke into small bits of specialized tissue. Some did nothing but raise eyebrows. Some exclusively puckered lips. Nerves developed new branch patterns across the face to control the new muscles, and the face-controlling regions of the brain grew.

Anne Burrows, a physical anthropologist at Duquesne University, has been dissecting primate faces and finds that they have a lot more in common with ours than anatomists once thought. She has found muscles in the chimpanzee face, for example, that were once believed to be uniquely human.

Not only are the same muscles in the same place, but the primate brain uses them to make many of the same expressions. Bridget Waller, a psychologist at the University of Portsmouth in England, and her colleagues demonstrated this with a new twist on Duchenne's old research. Duchenne could only put electrodes on the skin of his subjects; Waller and her colleagues today can insert fine needles into the muscles themselves. Researchers can also insert those needles into anesthetized chimpanzees. They have found that in most cases, a facial movement produces the same expression whether on the face of a chimpanzee or of a human.

Why did one small group of mammals evolve such sophisticated faces? The answer probably has to do with the intensely social life of primates. Natural selection may have favored primates that could make a wide range of expressions and that could read those expressions in others. The right expression could let a primate stare down a rival or cement a bond. It might even have kept bands of primates from descending into civil war. Seth Dobson, an anthropologist at Dartmouth College, found support for this idea in a study he did on 12 species of monkeys and apes. He found that primates that lived in bigger groups tended to have more mobile faces.

You can see this expressive range not just in the faces of primates, but in their brains, too. Dobson found that primates in bigger groups have larger face-controlling regions in their brains. Primate brains also have impressive networks for reading facial expressions. If a monkey sees a picture of another monkey making a face—an open-mouthed threat, for example, or a submissive lip smack—a network of neurons becomes active in its brain. Some parts of the network process features of the face in order to recognize to whom it belongs. And emotion-processing parts become active as well. Different centers switch on in response to different emotions, allowing the monkey to decode the feelings behind the face.

When we see faces, we don't just recognize them; we also make the same face, if only for a moment. If you see someone wearing a big grin, muscles on your face will start contracting in about a third of a second. The same goes for angry faces and sad ones. We respond this way whether people are looking at us or at someone else.

Mimicking faces is a deep instinct in humans—babies start doing it days after birth. And our ancestors were probably making these faces for millions of years. Earlier this year, Marina Davila Ross of the University of Portsmouth and her colleagues reported the first observation of other apes quickly mimicking faces. When orangutans play with each other, they sometimes open their mouths in the ape equivalent of a smile. Observing 25 orangutans at play, Ross found that when an orangutan sees another orangutan make an open-mouth expression, it tends to do the same in less than half a second.

We do not mimic faces simply as a side-effect of looking at other people. Experiments show that mimicry actually helps us understand what other people are feeling. Harvard University psychologist Lindsay Oberman and her colleagues demonstrated this effect with little more than a pen.

Oberman had volunteers bite down on a pen and then look at a series of faces. They had to pick the emotion they thought the faces were expressing. The volunteers could recognize sad faces and angry ones with the same accuracy as test subjects who did not have pens in their mouths. But they did a worse job of recognizing happy faces.

Biting a pen, it just so happens, requires you to use the same muscles you use to smile. Because the smiling muscles were active throughout the experiment, Oberman's subjects apparently couldn't feel themselves start to mimic happy faces. Without that feedback, they had a more difficult time recognizing when people were happy.

Oberman and a growing number of other psychologists believe that we empathize by mimicking faces. By putting ourselves in other people's places, we understand what they're feeling. To investigate how facial mimicry helps us empathize, Leonhard Schilbach of the University of Cologne and his colleagues recently made a brain-scanning breakthrough. They had volunteers watch movies of computer-animated people turning toward them and smiling while scientists scanned their brain activity and tracked their facial muscles. Later the researchers examined the muscle recordings to pinpoint the precise instant when the volunteers mimicked the faces. Then they looked at how the brains of the volunteers were acting at that instant.

During unconscious facial mimicry, Schilbach discovered, several regions of the brain become active. One of those, the left precentral gyrus, becomes active when people get the urge to move their facial muscles (such as when a song makes them sad). Other regions (the right hippocampus and the posterior cingulate cortex) become active when we have emotional experiences, helping to retrieve emotional memories. Another part of the brain that becomes active during facial mimicry (the dorsal midbrain) relays emotional signals to the rest of the body, bringing on the physical feelings that go along with emotions, like a racing heartbeat.

When humans mimic others' faces, in other words, we don't just go through the motions. We also go through the emotions.

Recently Bernhard Haslinger at the Technical University of Munich realized that he could test the facial feedback theory in a new way. He could temporarily paralyze facial muscles and then scan people's brains as they tried to make faces. To block facial feedback, Haslinger used Dysport, a Botox-like drug available in Europe.

Botox and Dysport are brand names of a toxin made by the spore-forming bacterium *Clostridium botulinum*. Botulinum docks on the surface of neurons, blocking the release of a transmitter called acetylcholine. In small amounts botulinum can be fatal. In far, far smaller amounts, it can simply paralyze a small patch of muscles for a few weeks. Haslinger has used Dysport in people with movement disorders like dystonia to help reduce unwanted muscle movement. But Botox and Dysport are best known as treatments to mask aging. Injections into the muscles that make frowns can slow the growth of lines around the eyebrows.

For his brain experiment, Haslinger and his colleagues gave 19 women Dysport injections. Two weeks later the scientists scanned their brains as they showed the women a series of angry or sad faces and asked them either to imitate or just to observe the expressions. Haslinger then ran the same experiment on 19 women without Dysport and compared the two sets of scans.

When the women made sad faces, the same brain regions became active in both those with Dysport and those without. But making angry faces triggered different patterns. In the Dysport-free women, a region known as the amygdala—a key brain region for processing emotions—became active. In the women with Dysport, who could not use their frown muscles, the amygdala was quieter. Haslinger also found another change, in the connections between the amygdala and the brain stem, where signals can trigger many of the feelings that go along with emotions: Dysport made that connection weaker.

Of course neuroscience labs are not the only place where people get shots of Dysport or Botox. According to the American Society of Plastic Surgeons, in the United States doctors administer millions of injections of Botox each year, many of them to people's faces. Haslinger's research suggests that this is part of a massive, unplanned experiment.

In June 2008 in the *Journal of the American Academy of Dermatology,* a team of cosmetic surgeons suggested this experiment is making all of us happier. People with Botox may be less vulnerable to the angry emotions of other people because they themselves can't make angry or unhappy faces as easily. And because people with Botox can't spread bad feelings to others via their expressions, people without Botox may be happier too. The surgeons grant that this is just speculation for now. Nevertheless, they declare that "we are left with the tantalizing possibility that cosmetic procedures may have beneficial effects that are more than skin deep."

Maybe. But for all the Botox youthfulness plastic surgeons may want to think about, neuroscience raises a darker possibility. Making faces helps us understand how other people are feeling. By altering our faces we're tampering with the ancient lines of communication between face and brain that may change our minds in ways we don't yet understand.

Facial expressions, Darwin argued, were "a language of emotion." They served as a way for us to communicate before we had words.

UNIT 6

Human Diversity

Unit Selections

Key Points to Consider

- Why does skin color vary among humans?

- Are some people born gay?

- Discuss whether the human species can be subdivided into racial categories. Support your position.

- How and why did the concept of race develop?

- To what extent is height a barometer of the health of a society, and why?

Student Website

www.mhcls.com

Internet References

Human Genome Project Information
   http://www.ornl.gov/TechResources/Human_Genome/home.html
OMIM Home Page-Online Mendelian Inheritance in Man
   http://www3.ncbi.nlm.nih.gov/omim/

The field of biological anthropology has come a long way since the days when one of its primary concerns was the classification of human beings according to racial type. Although human diversity is still a matter of major interest in terms of how and why we differ from one another, most anthropologists have concluded that human beings cannot be sorted into sharply distinct entities. (See "How Real is Race?") Without denying the fact of human variation throughout the world, the prevailing view today is that the differences between us exist along geographical gradients, as differences in degree, rather than in terms of separate and discrete entities as perceived in the past.

One of the old ways of looking at human "races" was that each such group was a subspecies of humans that, if left reproductively isolated long enough, would eventually evolve into separate species. While this concept of subspecies, or racial varieties within a species, would seem to apply to some living creatures (such as the dog and wolf or the horse and zebra) and might even be relevant to hominid diversification in the past, the current consensus is that it does not apply today, at least not within the human species.

A more recent attempt to salvage the idea of human races has been to perceive them not so much as reproductively isolated entities, but as many clusters of gene frequencies, separable only by the fact that the proportions of traits (such as skin color, hair form, etc.) differ in each artificially constructed group. Some scientists in the area of forensic physical anthropology appreciate the practical value of this approach. In a similar manner, our ability to reconstruct human prehistory is dependent upon an understanding of human variation (as in "Skin Deep" by Nina G. Jablonski and George Chaplin, "Born Gay?" by Michael Abrams and "The Tall and the Short of It" by Barry Bogin).

Lest anyone think that anthropologists are "in denial" regarding the existence of human races and that some of the viewpoints expressed in this section are merely expressions of contemporary political correctness, it should be pointed out that serious, scholarly attempts to classify people in terms of precise, biological units have been going on now for 200 years, and, so far, nothing of scientific value has come of them.

Complicating the matter is the fact that there are actually two concepts of race: the strictly biological one, as described above, and the one of popular culture, which has been around since time immemorial. These two ways of thinking have resulted not only in fuzzy thinking about racial biology, but they have also

© Creatas/PunchStock

infected the way we think about people and, therefore, the way we treat each other in the social arena.

What we should recognize, claim most anthropologists, is that, despite the superficial physical and biological differences between us, when it comes to intelligence, all human beings are basically the same. The degrees of variation within our species may be accounted for by the subtle, and changing, selective forces experienced as one moves from one geographical area to another. However, no matter what the environmental pressures have been, the same intellectual demands have been made upon all of us. This is not to say, of course, that we do not vary from each other as individuals. Rather, what is being said is that when we look at these artificially created groups of people called "races," we find a varying range of intellectual skills within each group. Indeed, even when we look at traits other than intelligence, we find much greater variation within each group than we find between groups.

It is time, therefore, to put the idea of human races to rest, at least as far as science is concerned. If such notions remain in the realm of social discourse, then so be it. That is where the problems associated with notions of race have to be solved anyway. At least, says Marks, in speaking for the anthropological community: "You may group humans into a small number of races if you want to, but you are denied biology as a support for it."

Skin Deep

Throughout the world, human skin color has evolved to be dark enough to prevent sunlight from destroying the nutrient folate but light enough to foster the production of vitamin D.

NINA G. JABLONSKI AND GEORGE CHAPLIN

Among primates, only humans have a mostly naked skin that comes in different colors. Geographers and anthropologists have long recognized that the distribution of skin colors among indigenous populations is not random: darker peoples tend to be found nearer the equator, lighter ones closer to the poles. For years, the prevailing theory has been that darker skins evolved to protect against skin cancer. But a series of discoveries has led us to construct a new framework for understanding the evolutionary basis of variations in human skin color. Recent epidemiological and physiological evidence suggests to us that the worldwide pattern of human skin color is the product of natural selection acting to regulate the effects of the sun's ultraviolet (UV) radiation on key nutrients crucial to reproductive success.

From Hirsute to Hairless

The evolution of skin pigmentation is linked with that of hairlessness, and to comprehend both these stories, we need to page back in human history. Human beings have been evolving as an independent lineage of apes since at least seven million years ago, when our immediate ancestors diverged from those of our closest relatives, chimpanzees. Because chimpanzees have changed less over time than humans have, they can provide an idea of what human anatomy and physiology must have been like. Chimpanzees' skin is light in color and is covered by hair over most of their bodies. Young animals have pink faces, hands, and feet and become freckled or dark in these areas only as they are exposed to sun with age. The earliest humans almost certainly had a light skin covered with hair. Presumably hair loss occurred first, then skin color changed. But that leads to the question, When did we lose our hair?

The skeletons of ancient humans—such as the well-known skeleton of Lucy, which dates to about 3.2 million years ago—give us a good idea of the build and the way of life of our ancestors. The daily activities of Lucy and other hominids that lived before about three million years ago appear to have been similar to those of primates living on the open savannas of Africa today.

They probably spent much of their day foraging for food over three to four miles before retiring to the safety of trees to sleep.

By 1.6 million years ago, however, we see evidence that this pattern had begun to change dramatically. The famous skeleton of Turkana Boy—which belonged to the species *Homo ergaster*—is that of a long-legged, striding biped that probably walked long distances. These more active early humans faced the problem of staying cool and protecting their brains from overheating. Peter Wheeler of John Moores University in Liverpool, England, has shown that this was accomplished through an increase in the number of sweat glands on the surface of the body and a reduction in the covering of body hair. Once rid of most of their hair, early members of the genus *Homo* then encountered the challenge of protecting their skin from the damaging effects of sunlight, especially UV rays.

Built-In Sunscreen

In chimpanzees, the skin on the hairless parts of the body contains cells called melanocytes that are capable of synthesizing the dark-brown pigment melanin in response to exposure to UV radiation. When humans became mostly hairless, the ability of the skin to produce melanin assumed new importance. Melanin is nature's sunscreen: it is a large organic molecule that Overview/Skin Color Evolution serves the dual purpose of physically and chemically filtering the harmful effects of UV radiation; it absorbs UV rays, causing them to lose energy, and it neutralizes harmful chemicals called free radicals that form in the skin after damage by UV radiation.

Anthropologists and biologists have generally reasoned that high concentrations of melanin arose in the skin of peoples in tropical areas because it protected them against skin cancer. James E. Cleaver of the University of California at San Francisco, for instance, has shown that people with the disease xeroderma pigmentosum, in which melanocytes are destroyed by exposure to the sun, suffer from significantly higher than normal rates of squamous and basal cell carcinomas, which are usually easily treated. Malignant melanomas are more frequently fatal, but

Overview/Skin Color Evolution

- After losing their hair as an adaptation for keeping cool, early hominids gained pigmented skins. Scientists initially thought that such pigmentation arose to protect against skin-cancer-causing ultra-violet [UV] radiation.

- Skin cancers tend to arise after reproductive age, however. An alternative theory suggests that dark skin might have evolved primarily to protect against the breakdown of folate, a nutrient essential for fertility and for fetal development.

- Skin that is too dark blocks the sunlight necessary for catalyzing the production of vitamin D, which is crucial for maternal and fetal bones. Accordingly, humans have evolved to be light enough to make sufficient vitamin B yet dark enough to protect their stores of folate.

- As a result of recent human migrations, many people now live in areas that receive more [or less] UV radiation than is appropriate for their skin color.

The Folate Connection

In 1991 one of US (Jablonski) ran across what turned out to be a critical paper published in 1978 by Richard F. Branda and John W. Eaton, now at the University of Vermont and the University of Louisville, respectively. These investigators showed that light-skinned people who had been exposed to simulated strong sunlight had abnormally low levels of the essential B vitamin folate in their blood. The scientists also observed that subjecting human blood serum to the same conditions resulted in a 50-percent loss of folate content within one hour.

The significance of these findings to reproduction—and hence evolution—became clear when we learned of research being conducted on a major class of birth defects by our colleagues at the University of Western Australia. There Fiona J. Stanley and Carol Bower had established by the late 1980s that folate deficiency in pregnant women is related to an increased risk of neural tube defects such as spina bifida, in which the arches of the spinal vertebrae fail to close around the spinal cord. Many research groups throughout the world have since confirmed this correlation, and efforts to supplement foods with folate and to educate women about the importance of the nutrient have become widespread.

We discovered soon afterward that folate is important not only in preventing neural tube defects but also in a host of other

they are rare (representing 4 percent of skin cancer diagnoses) and tend to strike only light-skinned people. But all skin cancers typically arise later in life, in most cases after the first reproductive years, so they could not have exerted enough evolutionary pressure for skin protection alone to account for darker skin colors. Accordingly, we began to ask what role melanin might play in human evolution.

processes. Because folate is essential for the synthesis of DNA in dividing cells, anything that involves rapid cell proliferation, such as spermatogenesis (the production of sperm cells), requires folate. Male rats and mice with chemically induced folate deficiency have impaired spermatogenesis and are infertile. Although no comparable studies of humans have been conducted, Wai Yee Wong and his colleagues at the University Medical Center of Nijmegen in the Netherlands have recently reported that folic acid treatment can boost the sperm counts of men with fertility problems.

Such observations led us to hypothesize that dark skin evolved to protect the body's folate stores from destruction. Our idea was supported by a report published in 1996 by Argentine pediatrician Pablo Lapunzina, who found that three young and otherwise healthy women whom he had attended gave birth to infants with neural tube defects after using sun beds to tan themselves in the early weeks of pregnancy. Our evidence about the breakdown of folate by UV radiation thus supplements what is already known about the harmful (skin-cancer-causing) effects of UV radiation on DNA.

Human Skin on the Move

The earliest members of *Homo sapiens,* or modern humans, evolved in Africa between 120,000 and 100,000 years ago and had darkly pigmented skin adapted to the conditions of UV radiation and heat that existed near the equator. As modern humans began to venture out of the tropics, however, they encountered environments in which they received significantly less UV radiation during the year. Under these conditions their high concentrations of natural sunscreen probably proved detrimental. Dark skin contains so much melanin that very little UV radiation, and specifically very little of the shorter-wavelength UVB radiation, can penetrate the skin. Although most of the effects of UVB are harmful, the rays perform one indispensable function: initiating the formation of vitamin D in the skin. Dark-skinned people living in the tropics generally receive sufficient UV radiation during the year for UVB to penetrate the skin and allow them to make vitamin D. Outside the tropics this is not the case. The solution, across evolutionary time, has been for migrants to northern latitudes to lose skin pigmentation.

The connection between the evolution of lightly pigmented skin and vitamin D synthesis was elaborated by W. Farnsworth Loomis of Brandeis University in 1967. He established the importance of vitamin D to reproductive success because of its role in enabling calcium absorption by the intestines, which in turn makes possible the normal development of the skeleton and the maintenance of a healthy immune system. Research led by Michael Holick of the Boston University School of Medicine has, over the past 20 years, further cemented the significance of vitamin D in development and immunity. His team also showed that not all sunlight contains enough UVB to stimulate vitamin D production. In Boston, for instance, which is located at about 42 degrees north latitude, human skin cells begin to produce vitamin D only after mid-March. In the wintertime there isn't enough UVB to do the job. We realized that this was another piece of evidence essential to the skin color story.

During the course of our research in the early 1990s, we searched in vain to find sources of data on actual UV radiation levels at the earth's surface. We were rewarded in 1996, when we contacted Elizabeth Weatherhead of the Cooperative Institute for Research in Environmental Sciences at the University of Colorado at Boulder. She shared with us a database of measurements of UV radiation at the earth's surface taken by NASA's Total Ozone Mapping Spectrophotometer satellite between 1978 and 1993. We were then able to model the distribution of UV radiation on the earth and relate the satellite data to the amount of UVB necessary to produce vitamin D.

We found that the earth's surface could be divided into three vitamin D zones: one comprising the tropics, one the subtropics and temperate regions, and the last the circumpolar regions north and south of about 45 degrees latitude. In the first, the dosage of UVB throughout the year is high enough that humans have ample opportunity to synthesize vitamin D all year. In the second, at least one month during the year has insufficient UVB radiation, and in the third area not enough UVB arrives on average during the entire year to prompt vitamin D synthesis. This distribution could explain why indigenous peoples in the tropics generally have dark skin, whereas people in the subtropics and temperate regions are lighter-skinned but have the ability to tan, and those who live in regions near the poles tend to be very light skinned and burn easily.

One of the most interesting aspects of this investigation was the examination of groups that did not precisely fit the predicted skin-color pattern. An example is the Inuit people of Alaska and northern Canada. The Inuit exhibit skin color that is somewhat darker than would be predicted given the UV levels at their latitude. This is probably caused by two factors. The first is that they are relatively recent inhabitants of these climes, having migrated to North America only roughly 5,000 years ago. The second is that the traditional diet of the Inuit is extremely high in foods containing vitamin D, especially fish and marine mammals. This vitamin D-rich diet offsets the problem that they would otherwise have with vitamin D synthesis in their skin at northern latitudes and permits them to remain more darkly pigmented.

Our analysis of the potential to synthesize vitamin D allowed us to understand another trait related to human skin color: women in all populations are generally lighter-skinned than men. (Our data show that women tend to be between 3 and 4 percent lighter than men.) Scientists have often speculated on the reasons, and most have argued that the phenomenon stems from sexual selection—the preference of men for women of lighter color. We contend that although this is probably part of the story, it is not the original reason for the sexual difference. Females have significantly greater needs for calcium throughout their reproductive lives, especially during pregnancy and lactation, and must be able to make the most of the calcium contained in food. We propose, therefore, that women tend to be lighter-skinned than men to allow slightly more UVB rays to penetrate their skin and thereby increase their ability to produce vitamin D. In areas of the world that receive a large amount of UV radiation, women are indeed at the knife's edge of natural selection, needing to maximize the photoprotective function of their skin on the one hand and the ability to synthesize vitamin D on the other.

Where Culture and Biology Meet

As modern humans moved throughout the Old World about 100,000 years ago, their skin adapted to the environmental conditions that prevailed in different regions. The skin color of the indigenous people of Africa has had the longest time to adapt because anatomically modern humans first evolved there. The skin-color changes that modern humans underwent as they moved from one continent to another—first Asia, then Austro-Melanesia, then Europe and, finally, the Americas—can be reconstructed to some extent. It is important to remember, however, that those humans had clothing and shelter to help protect them from the elements. In some places, they also had the ability to harvest foods that were extraordinarily rich in vitamin D, as in the case of the Inuit. These two factors had profound effects on the tempo and degree of skin-color evolution in human populations.

Africa is an environmentally heterogeneous continent. A number of the earliest movements of contemporary humans outside equatorial Africa were into southern Africa. The descendants of some of these early colonizers, the Khoisan (previously known as Hottentots), are still found in southern Africa and have significantly lighter skin than indigenous equatorial Africans do—a clear adaptation to the lower levels of UV radiation that prevail at the southern extremity of the continent.

Interestingly, however, human skin color in southern Africa is not uniform. Populations of Bantu-language speakers who live in southern Africa today are far darker than the Khoisan. We know from the history of this region that Bantu speakers migrated into this region recently—probably within the past 1,000 years—from parts of West Africa near the equator. The skin-color difference between the Khoisan and Bantu speakers such as the Zulu indicates that the length of time that a group has inhabited a particular region is important in understanding why they have the color they do.

Cultural behaviors have probably also strongly influenced the evolution of skin color in recent human history. This effect can be seen in the indigenous peoples who live on the eastern and western banks of the Red Sea. The tribes on the western side, which speak so-called Nilo-Hamitic languages, are thought to have inhabited this region for as long as 6,000 years. These individuals are distinguished by very darkly pigmented skin and long, thin bodies with long limbs, which are excellent biological adaptations for dissipating heat and intense UV radiation. In contrast, modern agricultural and pastoral groups on the eastern bank of the Red Sea, on the Arabian Peninsula, have lived there for only about 2,000 years. These earliest Arab people, of European origin, have adapted to very similar environmental conditions by almost exclusively cultural means—wearing heavy protective clothing and devising portable shade in the form of tents. (Without such clothing, one would have expected their skin to have begun to darken.) Generally speaking, the more recently a group has migrated into an area, the more extensive its cultural, as opposed to biological, adaptations to the area will be.

Perils of Recent Migrations

Despite great improvements in overall human health in the past century, some diseases have appeared or reemerged in populations that had previously been little affected by them. One of these is skin cancer, especially basal and squamous cell carcinomas, among light-skinned peoples. Another is rickets, brought about by severe vitamin D deficiency, in dark-skinned peoples. Why are we seeing these conditions?

As people move from an area with one pattern of UV radiation to another region, biological and cultural adaptations have not been able to keep pace. The light-skinned people of northern European origin who bask in the sun of Florida or northern Australia increasingly pay the price in the form of premature aging of the skin and skin cancers, not to mention the unknown cost in human life of folate depletion. Conversely, a number of dark-skinned people of southern Asian and African origin now living in the northern U.K., northern Europe or the northeastern U.S. suffer from a lack of UV radiation and vitamin D, an insidious problem that manifests itself in high rates of rickets and other diseases related to vitamin D deficiency.

The ability of skin color to adapt over long periods to the various environments to which humans have moved reflects the importance of skin color to our survival. But its unstable nature also makes it one of the least useful characteristics in determining the evolutionary relations between human groups. Early Western scientists used skin color improperly to delineate human races, but the beauty of science is that it can and does correct itself. Our current knowledge of the evolution of human skin indicates that variations in skin color, like most of our physical attributes, can be explained by adaptation to the environment through natural selection. We look ahead to the day when the vestiges of old scientific mistakes will be erased and replaced by a better understanding of human origins and diversity. Our variation in skin color should be celebrated as one of the most visible manifestations of our evolution as a species.

More to Explore

The Evolution of Human Skin Coloration. Nina G. Jablonski and George Chaplin in *Journal of Human Evolution,* Vol. 39, No. 1, pages 57–106; July 1, 2000. An abstract of the article is available online at www.idealibrary.com/links/doi/10.1006/jhev.2000.0403

Why Skin Comes in Colors. Blake Edgar in *California Wild,* Vol. 53, No. 1, pages 6–7; Winter 2000. The article is also available at www.calacademy.org/calwild/winter2000/html/horizons.html

The Biology of Skin Color: Black and White. Gina Kirchweger in *Discover,* Vol. 22, No. 2, pages 32–33; February 2001. The article is also available at www.discover.com/feb_01/featbiology.html

NINA G. JABLONSKI and GEORGE CHAPLIN work at the California Academy of Sciences in San Francisco, where Jablonski is Irvine Chair and curator of anthropology and Chaplin is a research associate in the department of anthropology. Jablonski's research centers on the evolutionary adaptations of monkeys, apes and humans. She is particularly interested in how primates have responded to changes over time in the global environment. Chaplin is a private geographic information systems consultant who specializes in describing and analyzing geographic trends in biodiversity. In 2001 he was awarded the Student of the Year prize by the Association of Geographic Information in London for his master's thesis on the environmental correlates of skin color.

Born Gay?

Is Homosexuality nature or nurture? Science is homing in on the answer.

MICHAEL ABRAMS

Some conservatives argue that homosexuality is a personal choice or the result of environmental influences. Some gay rights activists insist that homosexuality is genetic, hoping that proof from that domain will lead to greater acceptance. Still others, backing the same cause, discourage any investigation into the biological origins of sexual orientation, fearful that positive results will lead to attempts to rid the world of potential homosexuals. A handful of scientists, though, are just curious. For them, the discovery of how an individual becomes gay is likely to shed light on how sexuality-related genes build brains, how people of any persuasion are attracted to each other, and perhaps even how homosexuality evolved.

"Who cares about gay men or lesbian women?" asks geneticist Sven Bocklandt of the David Geffen School of Medicine at UCLA. "Sexual selection defines evolution and creation—such a major player in determining society—and we have no idea how it works. This is much larger than the gay gene; it's about all sexual reproduction."

Bocklandt was once a mere science journalist. It was while producing a documentary for Belgian TV that he first met geneticist Dean Hamer. Hamer had just published a study that claimed not only to have finally proved that male homosexuality was at least partially genetic but also to have pinpointed the stretch of chromosome where one of the genes involved resided. Hamer and his colleagues conducted extensive interviews with 76 pairs of gay brothers and their family members and found that homosexuality seemed to be inherited through the maternal line. This led him to compare the X chromosomes—which can be inherited only from the mother—in those same brothers. There he discovered a shared genetic marker, a patch of DNA called Xq28. Interviews with the subjects also revealed them to be either gay or straight. (In this respect, men are entirely different from women. Studies have shown that women respond to all types of sexual depictions—not only heterosexual and homosexual images but even those of chimpanzees having sex.)

The interview with Hamer fascinated Bocklandt. Not long after, he quit his job and moved to Washington, D.C., to work with Hamer. There he did research on the X chromosome, with hopes of someday finding the gay gene or genes themselves.

Fourteen years later, neither Bocklandt nor any other researcher has pinpointed the precise base pairs that might turn a man gay. Part of this is due to the politics of funding for sex research. For a long period NIH grant proposals that included words like "gay," "condom," or even "sexuality" were turned down, much to the ire of researchers like Hamer. Shortly after he published his gay brothers study, Hamer completed a similarly designed family study looking into a genetic cause for a certain kind of anxiety. Since then there have been more than 400 independent studies looking into those genes. There have been no such studies for the gay gene.

It is not clear if Hamer and his team found the locus of the genetic code that causes men to memorize lines from *A Star Is Born*. Although a follow-up study by the team replicated their findings, a study by George Rice, a neuroscientist at the University of Western Ontario, refuted Hamer's findings completely. In addition, two other researchers told me they don't consider Hamer's study valid. Yet Hamer contends that his results suggest there is a link to Xq28 and that the Rice study was biased because one of the coauthors told Hamer that he didn't believe a gay gene could exist. Hamer also says that, if read correctly, the two other studies confirm his findings. "They didn't even look at the entire X chromosome," says Hamer. "They gave up immediately." For laymen, science journalists, and researchers alike, the question remains unresolved.

Whether or not a gay gene, a set of gay genes, or some other biological mechanism is ever found, one thing is clear: The environment a child grows up in has nothing to do with what makes most gay men gay. Two of the most convincing studies have proved conclusively that sexual orientation in men has a genetic cause.

William Reiner, a psychiatrist at the University of Oklahoma Health Sciences Center, explored the question of environmental influences on sexuality with a group that had been surgically shifted from boys to girls. These boys had been born with certain genital deformities; because it is easier to fashion a vagina than a penis, the boys were surgically made into girls at birth. In many cases they were raised as girls, kept in the dark about the surgery, and thought themselves female long into adulthood. Invariably, Reiner found that the faux females ended up being attracted to women. If societal nudging was what made men gay, at least one of these boys should have grown up to be attracted to men. There is no documented case of that happening.

The second study was an examination of twins by psychologist Michael Bailey of Northwestern University. Among identical twins, he found that if one was gay, the other had a 50 percent chance of also being gay. Among fraternal twins, who do not share the same DNA, there was only a 20 percent chance.

At first glance, those results seem to suggest that at least some homosexuality must not be genetic. Identical twins have the same genes, right? How could one turn out gay and the other not gay as often as 50 percent of the time? There are many other traits that are not always the same in identical twins, however, like eye color and fingerprints. The interesting question is, how do any of these major differences arise between two products of the same code?

The solution to that question is exactly what Bocklandt is trying to find. By looking not at DNA but at where DNA is switched off, he hopes to find the true genetic seat of homosexuality. Hamer looked at broad regions of chromosomes using genetic markers, a low-resolution result that tells little more than "something's going on somewhere around here." Bocklandt is hoping to look with a much stronger magnifying glass at the areas Hamer's research highlighted. If he succeeds, it will be a triumph not only for the genetics of homosexuality but also for genetic research in general.

Bocklandt has collected DNA from two groups of 15 pairs of identical twins. In one group, both twins are gay. In the second, one twin is gay, and the other is straight. Identical twins have the same DNA, but the activity of their genes isn't necessarily the same. The reason is something called methylation.

Methylation turns off certain sections of genetic code. So even though we inherit two copies of every gene—one from our mother, one from our father—whether the gene is methylated often determines which of the two genes will be turned on. Methylation is inherited, just as DNA is. But unlike DNA, which has an enzyme that proofreads both the original and the copy to minimize errors, methylation has no built-in checks. It can change from one generation to the next and may be influenced by diet or environment. It's in this mutability that Bocklandt hopes to find the secret, by seeing which flipped genetic switches correlate with homosexuality.

"For each pair we expect to see a whole lot of things that are random—sometimes someone smoked, or medication was used for long periods of time," Bocklandt says. "But basically we compare the gay results with the straight ones and see if any region shows up multiple times for these subjects."

Bocklandt points out that most likely there is no "gay gene"—no single switch for sexual orientation—but instead a handful of genes that work in ways as yet unexplained.

Bocklandt is quick to point out that most likely there is no single "gay gene"—no single switch for sexual orientation. Instead, there are probably a handful of genes that work in ways as yet unexplained. Still, he is confident that the genes involved are few enough that he can find them. Although sexual attraction between humans has its frills—the social dances, the fetishes, the preferred body types—it is still pretty fundamental. "If you're breeding pigs, you can buy a little spray—spray it on a female and it will stand still as if it's having sex," Bocklandt says. "There's nothing like that for humans. Obviously, the behavior is complex—there's phone sex and of course porn—but genetically it's simple. There are limits to what you can code on a genome." He thinks it is likely that perhaps 5 to 15 genes explain sexual orientation in most people.

Ideally, Bocklandt would scan the genome of each individual, looking for a methylation pattern anywhere on any chromosome that shows up repeatedly in the gay member of each twin pair. Unfortunately, at the moment it costs about $10 million a person to map out every base pair of the 46 chromosomes, so Bocklandt is looking only where he suspects to unearth genetic gold. If he finds a pattern, then he will look at the DNA beneath the methylation.

Actually, the whole genome can be mapped for less than $10 million if you are willing to forfeit the high degree of resolution Bocklandt is after. Alan Sanders, an associate professor of psychiatry at Northwestern, will be looking at the whole genome of about 1,000 gay brothers using the genetic marker technique that Hamer used. A sample that big should eliminate the statistical weaknesses that plagued Hamer. "There are a number of things that go into trying to figure out how much statistical power you have, but the only one that's in your control is sample size—the bigger the better," says Sanders. "So that's what we're doing."

For several years Sanders has been collecting DNA from blood or saliva samples from families with two or more gay brothers. In addition to requesting their spit, Sanders's team asks each individual a set of questions similar to those Hamer used in his study. Then he begins looking at the men's chromosomal markers to see if the brothers are more similar than what chance would predict. Wherever there is a significant increase in sharing, Sanders plans to look at the genes that can be found near that particular marker. (When two brothers come from the same mother and father, about 50 percent of their genes should be identical.) Not only is the sample size bigger than Hamer's, but there are now far more genetic markers available, allowing Sanders to zero in on specific genes much faster.

By setting up a stand at Gay Pride parades and approaching "gay friendly" groups like PFLAG (Parents, Families and Friends of Lesbians and Gays), Sanders has found more than 4,000 gay men with a brother who are interested in participating. He has already started mapping the first 500 and estimates that by mid-2008 the world will know where—if anywhere—to find the gay gene.

"We definitely should be able to put to rest one way or another whether the Xq28 finding is replicable," says Sanders. "We should be able to address that to anyone's satisfaction."

The question of whether there is a gay gene—and if so, where it resides—is hardly the only question about sexual orientation that remains unanswered. If either Bocklandt or Sanders is lucky enough to spot the genes responsible for homosexuality, there will most likely be more questions raised than answered. "Frankly, the biggest problem of the genetic possibilities is the evolutionary problem," says Michael Bailey, the researcher who found that women get turned on by anything, who is now working with Sanders. "And I don't think that Dean [Hamer] has taken that problem seriously enough." Men who like men are obviously less likely to procreate. Even if social pressures through the ages led some gay men to have some children, the significantly lower rate of reproduction would eventually lead to the disappearance of the gene (as Hamer does note in his book, *The Science of Desire: The Search for the Gay Gene and the Biology of Behavior*).

Possible explanations abound, but an ingenious one was recently put to the test. Perhaps, the theory goes, some genes, when found in men, make them more likely to be gay and when found in women make them more likely to have children. ("Fecund" is the word the researchers use.) The increased number of grandchildren that a parent might have through such a superfertile daughter would offset whatever loss of genetic posterity comes from having a gay son.

How such a gene might work is anyone's guess. Perhaps the gene simply increases attraction to men, so a male with the gene comes out liking men, and a female with the gene comes out really liking men. Whatever the mechanism, it turns out that an Italian study found that women with gay family members have more children than women with all straight relatives. Andrea Camperio-Ciani, a professor of ethology and evolutionary psychology at the University of Padua, interviewed 98 gay men and 100 straight men and found that the mothers of gay men had an average of 2.7 children, while the mothers of straight men averaged 2.3.

That study has been criticized in some circles for the same old reason: The sample size was not big enough. But the man with the generous sample size hopes to answer that question too. "We'll look at the offspring of female relatives of gay men—especially of sisters. How many do they have compared to the relatives of straight men?" asks Sanders. "We're also trying to replicate that."

Another way to pass on the seemingly nonreproducing gay gene would be for a nonreproducing gay man to have an extra interest in seeing that the offspring of his siblings survive. Biologist E. O. Wilson first put forward this idea of kin selection as an explanation for homosexuality in 1978, but for some time now it has been considered an unlikely scenario.

Michael Bailey conducted a study in 2001 to find out if gay uncles treat their nephews and nieces any better than straight uncles treat theirs. They did not. Thinking that Bailey did not control for the income level of the uncles surveyed—richer uncles tend to be more generous—Qazi Rahman, a professor of psychobiology at the University of East London, tried to replicate the study in England. In addition to looking at how they spent their money, Rahman tried to see if gay men had some kind of extra psychological generosity by asking questions like, "Assuming you had a million pounds, would you buy gifts for your family?" Again, Rahman found no difference between straight and gay men. He admits that looking at "presents and stuff" might seem a crude measure for an adaptation that was selected for thousands of years ago, but he sees no other way that such an impulse would manifest itself today.

But 21st-century Western society, and the homosexuals therein, could be something of an anomaly in human history, according to Paul Vasey, an associate professor of psychology at the University of Lethbridge in Alberta. "Do I think the social contexts are less representative of our evolutionary past? I'd say yes," Vasey says. "The kind of gay men and lesbian women we are familiar with in Western culture express their homosexuality as egalitarian—they're not differentiated as far as gender." In other times and other places, one partner typically adopts a masculine role, while the other adopts the feminine. Another problem with kinship selection studies that look only in England and, in particular, the United States, is that kinship ties for homosexuals might not be as strong as they would be elsewhere. "The United States is profoundly homophobic," says Vasey, "so you can't be directing altruism at your family members if they've kicked you out and you've moved to the other side of the country."

Vasey has therefore been studying a group of Samoans called *fa'afafine*, whom he describes as more of a third sex than homosexual as commonly construed. These men, who grow up to dress and act like women and are extremely integrated into their society, would be offended to find themselves described as homosexual. They don't have sex with each other, and because their appearance isn't masculine, they don't consider themselves men who sleep with other men. In an initial study, Vasey found that the fa'afafine do exhibit heightened avuncular tendencies with their nieces and nephews. "They babysit, they teach them about the culture, they give them money," he says. To make sure that these traits do not merely reflect a more general fondness for all children, Vasey will soon head back to Samoa to refine and, with luck, replicate the study.

To put the kibosh on the idea that the evolution of a gay gene presents an unsolvable conundrum, Sergey Gavrilets, a theoretical evolutionary biologist at the University of Tennessee, developed a mathematical model of how a set of what he calls "sexually antagonistic" genes might evolve. "Sexuality can be explained as one example of sexual conflict—there may be genes that are beneficial for one sex but detrimental for the other," he says. He didn't put kin selection into the equation. ("I don't think it works, because if you have zero children and compensate for the loss by helping someone else, that help would have to be extremely efficient.") But he did include Camperio-Ciani's results and also assumed that gay genes would be passed down on the mother's side, on the X chromosome, as indicated by Hamer.

The more intolerant the society, the more likely it is to maintain gay genes. The real evolutionary cost of being homosexual isn't too big if you're forced to have kids.

The model shows that over centuries an effect you might call the homophobe's paradox has been at work on the human genome: The more intolerant the society, the more likely it is to maintain gay genes. If a society's conventions keep homosexuals in the closet, then they will be more likely to conform, get married, and have children. This is especially true if gay genes are also responsible for making women more fecund. Imagine, for instance, that for every extra child that such a gay gene–carrying woman has, a gay man can have one fewer and the balance necessary for the survival of the gene is still maintained. The more children he has, thanks to what his contemporaries demand of him, the less evolutionary pressure there is for his female counterpart to have more. "As a society becomes more intolerant, there's more pressure to have offspring," says Gavrilets. "The real [evolutionary] cost of being homosexual isn't too big if you're forced to have kids." On the other hand, the more tolerant the society, the more gay men can be free to be who they are, so the more likely they will be childless—and the more difficult it will be for any female in the family to make up for the loss.

"Bullshit," says Bocklandt. "A mathematical model is a nice exercise, a mental masturbation about how these things could work, but it makes better sense to do that once we know a bit more. One of the problems that none of the mathematical models take into account is that we have no idea what it meant to be gay 10,000 years ago. We have some idea what it meant 200 years ago but not 10,000."

It is also becoming increasingly clear that gay genes are not the only biological factor that influences homosexuality. Some homosexual men appear to have their sexuality oriented not by their DNA but by the environment they experienced in the womb. Ray Blanchard, a psychiatric researcher at the University of Toronto, found in 1996 that men with older brothers were more likely to be gay than those without. His study showed that for every older brother a man has, his odds of being gay go up by 33 percent. If the likelihood that a couple's first son will be gay is 2 percent (a reasonable guess), Blanchard says, the probability that the 5th son will be gay is only 6 percent. But if some poor woman has 14 sons, the 15th would have a 50 percent chance of being gay.

Blanchard's discovery has been replicated more than 20 times. Most recently, in 2006, psychologist Tony Bogaert of Brock University in Ontario quashed the possibility that the older-brother effect results from boys having been teased, beaten, or otherwise affected by their older brothers. Bogaert collected data from gay and heterosexual men who grew up in nonbiological families—in most cases, either adopted or raised in "blended" families. "This allowed me to really pit biological versus nonbiological explanations against each other," Bogaert says. The statistics came back the same as they had in previous studies. "It's not the brother you lived with; it's the environment within the same womb—sharing the same mom."

The older-brother effect accounts for about 15 to 30 percent of gay men, Blanchard estimates. How sharing a biological mother could induce homosexuality in men remains pure guesswork, however. Bogaert and Blanchard hypothesize that with each male child the mother develops an immunity to certain male-specific proteins, like molecules relating to the Y chromosome. Perhaps her body sees them as foreign and mounts an immune attack, which might alter certain structures of the male brain.

Whatever the cause of homosexuality, be it genetic, hormonal, or even sociological, the result is a change somewhere in the brain. Simon LeVay, once a neurobiologist at the Salk Institute, thought he found that part of the brain in 1991. Comparing the gray matter in the cadavers of gay and straight men, he found that an area in the anterior hypothalamus known as INAH-3 was smaller in gay men, about the size it is in women. A study by William Byne of the Mount Sinai School of Medicine in New York City turned up similar results.

Michael Baum, a biologist at Boston University, got a more detailed look by studying ferrets, whose biology is well understood. He has shown that the anterior hypothalamuses of gay and straight ferrets—as well as of male and female ferrets—are also of different sizes. The structural distinctions have clear behavioral consequences. Ferrets find their mates primarily by odor. Using a "reporter gene," Baum proved that a receptor in the anterior hypothalamus responds differently to the same odor depending on the sex of the ferret. Creating a lesion in that part of the brain can make a male ferret approach other males. Baum also finds that administering the right steroids early in life can reverse the animals' sex response: Female ferrets dosed with testosterone early in life act masculine.

Odor does not affect us as much as it does ferrets, but that is not to say that odor doesn't influence our sexual response. Ivanka Savic Berglund, a neuroscientist at the Karolinska Institute in Stockholm, put gay men, straight men, and women in a PET scanner (not all at the same time) and watched how their anterior hypothalamus lit up when presented with an odor similar to one found in men's sweat and one similar to a scent found in women's urine. The gay men's brains responded the way the women's brains did. "I was so pleased when I saw the paper—it kind of made my day," says Baum. "But I think it would have been great if she had used real sweat."

So is brain development the final frontier for seeking the source of homosexuality? "At first blush you might think, 'Well, gosh, maybe gay men didn't get enough testosterone early in life,'" says Marc Breedlove, a neuroscience professor at Michigan State University. "But as we find markers that should tell us about prenatal testosterone, they haven't shown a consistent pattern." Such studies are puzzling for Breedlove, who has spent much of his career proving that for animals things really are that simple. Castrated male rats given ovarian steroids as adults go straight for other male rats, while others given testosterone still flirt with females (however futile their propositions). "We can cause animals to be as masculine or feminine as we want by manipulating their exposure to testosterone," he says. "If I take a female rat pup and I give her just one dose of testosterone, in a few hours that testosterone is gone, and yet for the rest of her life she's masculine."

Lab rats are easier to manipulate than people, however. "I love my rats," says Breedlove, "but they're not very complicated." Apparently, humans are unlike the rest of the animal kingdom. Still, low testosterone or high testosterone could up the chance that a boy would grow up to be gay. No experiment has yet ruled that out.

If researchers do prove that testosterone can alter human sexual orientation—gay gene or no gay gene—the possibility of preventing homosexuality will become a reality. Even a hint of that option is enough to provoke an outcry among activists. Recently word got out that Charles Roselli, a physiologist at Oregon Health and Science University, was trying to find out how hormones affect the brains of gay sheep. PETA roped tennis star and lesbian activist Martina Navratilova into writing a letter to the university, calling the research homophobic and cruel. She accused the researchers of trying to find a "prenatal treatment for various sexual conditions."

What drives the sex researchers (some of whom are openly gay) is most often pure curiosity. They just want to know. "People whose motivations are political don't comprehend that anyone could be interested in why," says Ray Blanchard. And that why isn't just a why for homosexuality but a why for sexuality, period.

"I can't focus enough on how these are not gay genes—these are straight genes," Bocklandt says. "If you want to find a gene that makes you see colors, you compare the genes of people who see colors with the genes of people who are color-blind. They're not genes for color blindness. What we're talking about here is the most basic thing, the most basic question. Why does a crocodile recognize the opposite sex and want to f**k?"

How Real Is Race?

Using Anthropology to Make Sense of Human Diversity

Race is not a scientifically valid biological category, and yet it remains important as a socially constructed category. Once educators grasp this concept, they can use the suggestions and resources the authors offer here to help their students make sense of race.

Carol Mukhopadhyay and Rosemary C. Henze

Surely we've all heard people say there is only one race—the human race. We've also heard and seen overwhelming evidence that would seem to contradict this view. After all, the U.S. Census divides us into groups based on race, and there are certainly observable physical differences among people—skin color, nose and eye shape, body type, hair color and texture, and so on. In the world of education, the message of racial differences as biological "facts" is reinforced when we are told that we should understand specific learning styles and behavior patterns of black, Asian, Native American, white, and Latino children and when books such as *The Bell Curve* make pseudoscientific claims about race and learning.[1]

How can educators make sense of these conflicting messages about race? And why should they bother? Whether we think of all human beings as one race, or as four or five distinct races, or as hundreds of races, does anything really change? If we accept that the concept of race is fundamentally flawed, does that mean that young African Americans are less likely to be followed by security guards in department stores? Are people going to stop thinking of Asians as the "model" minority? Will racism become a thing of the past?

Many educators understandably would like to have clear information to help them teach students about human biological variability. While multicultural education materials are now widely available, they rarely address basic questions about why we look different from one another and what these biological differences do (and do not) mean. Multicultural education emphasizes respecting differences and finding ways to include all students, especially those who have been historically marginalized. Multicultural education has helped us to understand racism and has provided a rich body of literature on antiracist teaching strategies, and this has been all to the good. But it has not helped us understand the two concepts of race: the biological one and the social one.

In this article, we explain what anthropologists mean when they say that "races don't exist" (in other words, when they reject the concept of race as a scientifically valid biological category) and why they argue instead that "race" is a socially constructed category. We'll also discuss why this is such an important understanding and what it means for educators and students who face the social reality of race and racism every day. And finally, we'll offer some suggestions and resources for teachers who want to include teaching about race in their classes.

Why Race Isn't Biologically Real

For the past several decades, biological anthropologists have been arguing that races don't really exist, or, more precisely, that the concept of race has no validity as a biological category. What exactly does this mean?

First, anthropologists are unraveling a deeply embedded ideology, a long-standing European and American racial world view.[2] Historically, the idea of race emerged in Europe in the 17th and 18th centuries, coinciding with the growth of colonialism and the transatlantic slave trade. Attempts were made to classify humans into "natural," geographically distinct "races," hierarchically ordered by their closeness to God's original forms. Europeans were, not surprisingly, at the top, with the most perfect form represented by a female skull from the Caucasus Mountains, near the purported location of Noah's ark and the origin of humans. Hence the origins of the racial term "Caucasian" or "Caucasoid" for those of European ancestry.[3]

In the late 19th century, anthropologists sought to reconstruct human prehistory and trace the evolution of human cultural institutions. Physical and cultural evolution were seen as moving in tandem; "advances" in human mental capacity were thought to be responsible for human cultural inventions, such as marriage, family, law, and agriculture. If cultural "evolution" was propelled by biological evolution, according to this logic, the more "advanced" cultures must be more biologically and intellectually evolved. Physical indicators of evolutionary rank, such as skull size, were sought in order to classify and rank human groups along an evolutionary path from more "primitive" to more "advanced" races.

Nineteenth-century European scientists disagreed on when the "races" began. Theologians had long argued that there was "one human origin," Adam and Eve, and that certain races subsequently "degenerated" (predictably, the non-Europeans). Some evolutionary scientists, however, began to argue for multiple origins, with distinct races evolving in different places and times. By the beginning of the 20th century, European and American science viewed races as natural, long-standing divisions of the human species, evolving at different rates biologically and hence culturally. By such logic was racial inequality naturalized and legitimized.

When contemporary scientists, including anthropologists, assert that races are not scientifically valid, they are rejecting at least three fundamental premises of this old racial ideology: 1) the archaic subspecies concept, 2) the divisibility of contemporary humans into scientifically valid biological groupings, and 3) the link between racial traits and social, cultural, and political status.

1. *There were no distinct, archaic human subspecies.* The first premise anthropologists reject is that humans were originally divided, by nature or God, into a small set of biologically distinct, fixed species, subspecies, or races. Anthropologists now know conclusively, from fossil and DNA evidence, that contemporary humans are one variable species, with our roots in Africa, which moved out of Africa into a wide range of environments around the world, producing hundreds, perhaps thousands, of culturally and genetically distinct populations. Local populations, through natural selection as well as random genetic mutation, acquired some distinctive genetic traits, such as shovel-shaped incisor teeth, hairy ears, or red hair. Adaptation to human cultural inventions—such as agriculture, which creates concentrations of water that allow malaria-carrying mosquitoes to breed—also produced higher frequencies of sickle-cell genes (related to malaria resistance) in human populations in some parts of Africa, India, Arabia, and the Mediterranean.[4] At the same time, continuous migration and intermating between local populations prevented us from branching off into distinct subspecies or species and instead created a richer and more variable gene pool, producing new combinations and permutations of the human genome.

Human prehistory and history, then, are a continuing story of fusion and fission, of a myriad of populations, emerging and shifting over time and space, sometimes isolated temporarily, then fusing and producing new formations. There have been thousands and thousands of groups throughout human history, marrying in and, more often, out; they have disappeared and reemerged in new forms over time.

In short, there are no "basic" or "ancient" races; there are no stable, "natural," permanent, or even long-standing groupings

called races. There have never have been any "pure" races. All human populations are historically specific mixtures of the human gene pool. This is human evolution, and we see these same processes at work in the 19th and 20th centuries and today. "Races" are ephemeral—here today, gone tomorrow.

2. *Contemporary humans are not divisible into biological races.* When anthropologists say races aren't biologically real, they also reject the idea that *modern* humans can be divided into scientifically valid, biologically distinct groupings or races. For races to be real as biological categories, the classification must be based on objective, consistent, and reliable biological criteria. The classification system must also have predictive value that will make it useful in research.

Scientists have demonstrated that both the concept of race and racial criteria are subjective, arbitrary, and inconsistently applied.[5] U.S. racial categories, such as the ones used in the Census, aren't valid in part because the biological attributes used to define races and create racial classifications rely on only a few visible, superficial, genetic traits—such as skin color and hair texture—and ignore the remaining preponderance of human variation. Alternative, equally visible racial classifications could be constructed using such criteria as hair color, eye color, height, weight, ear shape, or hairiness. However, there are less visible genetic traits that have far greater biological significance. For example, there are at least 13 genetic factors related to hemoglobin, the protein that helps carry oxygen to tissues, and there is also significant variation in the ABO, RH, and other blood systems. We could create racial classifications based on genetic factors that affect susceptibility to diabetes or to certain kinds of breast cancer or to the ability to digest milk. In sum, given the variety of possible biologically based traits for classifying human beings, the criteria used in U.S. racial categorizations are highly arbitrary and subjective. Our discussion here focuses on the U.S. concept of race. While racial concepts are no doubt similar in Canada and Europe, this is not true in other parts of the Americas.[6]

The number of potential biologically based racial groupings is enormous. Not only are there millions of genetic traits, but most genetic traits—even culturally salient but superficial traits such as skin color, hair texture, eye shape, and eye color—do not cluster together. Darker skin can cluster with straight hair as well as with very curly hair or with hairy or nonhairy bodies; paler skin can cluster with straight or curly hair or with black or blond hair or with lighter to darker eyes. Each trait could produce a different racial classification. For example, if one used height as a criterion rather than skin pigmentation, then the Northern Afghan population would be in the same racial category as the Swedes and the Tutsi of Rwanda. There are huge numbers of genetically influenced traits, visible and nonvisible, which could be used to classify humans into biologically distinct groups. There is no "natural" classification—no co-occurring clusters of racial traits. There are just alternatives, with different implications and uses.

Racial classifications are also unscientific because they are unreliable and unstable over time. Individuals cannot reliably be "raced," partly because the criteria are so subjective and unscientific. Robert Hahn, a medical anthropologist, found that 37% of babies described as Native American on their birth certificates ended up in a different racial category on their death certificates.[7] Racial identifications by forensic anthropologists, long touted as accurate, have been shown to be disturbingly unreliable, even in relatively ethnically homogeneous areas, such as Missouri and Ohio.[8] Forensic evidence from such urban areas as San Jose, California, or New York City is even more problematic.

Racial categories used by the U.S. Census Bureau have changed over time. In 1900, races included "mulatto, quadroon, or octoroon" in addition to "black." Southern Europeans and Jews were deemed to be separate races before World War II. Asian Indians ("Hindus") were initially categorized as "Caucasoid"—except for voting rights. The number and definitions of races in the most recent U.S. Census reflect the instability—and hence unreliability—of the concept of race. And U.S. racial classifications simply don't work in much of the rest of the world. Brazil is a classic, often-studied example, but they also don't work in South Asia, an area that includes over one-fifth of the world's population.

Historical and contemporary European and American racial categories are huge, biologically diverse macro-categories. Members of the same racial group tend to be similar in a few genetic ways that are often biologically irrelevant. Moreover, the genetic variability found within each racial grouping is far greater than the genetic similarity. Africa, by itself, is home to distinct populations whose average height ranges from less than five feet (the Mbuti) to over six feet (the Tutsi). Estimates suggest that contemporary racial variation accounts for less than 7% of all human genetic variation.[9] U.S. races, then, are not biologically distinct or biologically meaningful, scientifically based groupings of the human species.

3. *Race as biology has no scientific value.* An additional critique of the concept of race is that racial categories, as defined biologically, are not very useful in understanding other phenomena, whether biological or cultural.

There is no substantial evidence that race, as a biological category, and "racial" characteristics, such as skin color, hair texture, and eye shape, are causally linked to behavior, to capacities, to individual and group accomplishments, to cultural institutions, or to propensities to engage in any specific activities. In the area of academic achievement, the focus on race as biology can lead researchers to ignore underlying nonbiological causal factors. One classic study found that controlling for socioeconomic and other environmental variables eliminated purported "racial" differences in I.Q. scores and academic achievement between African American, Mexican American, and European American students.[10]

Health professionals have also critiqued the concept of race. Alan Goodman and others have shown that race does not help physicians with diagnosis, prevention, or treatment of medical diseases.[11] Racial categories and a false ideology of race as "biology" encourage both doctors and their patients to view medical conditions as necessarily genetic, ignoring possible environmental sources. Hypertension, infant birthweights, osteoporosis, ovarian cysts—all traditionally viewed as "racial" (i.e., genetically based)—now seem to reflect environmental rather than racially linked genetic factors. The Centers for Disease Control concluded in 1993 that most associations between race and disease have no genetic or biological basis and that the concept of "race" is therefore not useful in public health.

As a result of recent evolution and constant interbreeding between groups of humans, two individuals from different "races" are just as likely to be more similar to one another genetically than two individuals from the same "race." This being so, race-as-biology has no predictive value.

If Not Race, Then What?

Classifications are usually created for some purpose. Alan Goodman and other biological anthropologists suggest that investigators focus on using traits relevant to the problem at hand. For example, if a particular blood factor puts an individual at risk for a disease, then classify individuals on that basis for that purpose.

Some suggest using the term "population" or "breeding population" to refer to the multitude of small, often geographically localized, groups that have developed high frequencies of one or more somewhat distinctive biological traits (e.g., shovel-shaped incisors) in response to biological, historical, and cultural factors. But others point out that there could be thousands of such groups, depending on the classifying criteria used, and that the groups would be merging and recombining over time and space. Moreover, the variability "captured" would reflect only a fraction of the variability in the human species.

Most anthropologists now use the concept of "clines" to help understand how genetic traits are distributed.[12] New data indicate that biological traits, such as blood type or skin color, are distributed in geographic gradations or "clines"; that is, the frequency of a trait varies continuously over a geographic area. For example, the genes for type B blood increase in frequency in an east-to-west direction (reflecting, in part, the travels of Genghis Khan and his army). In contrast, skin pigmentation grades from north to south, with increasing pigmentation as one gets closer to the equator. The frequency of the gene for sickle cell decreases from West Africa moving northeast.

Virtually all traits have distinct geographic distributions. Genes controlling skin color, body size and shape (head, limbs, lips, fingers, nose, ears), hairiness, and blood type are each distributed in different patterns over geographic space. Once again, for biological races to exist, these traits would have to co-vary, but they don't. Instead, biological traits produce a nearly infinite number of potential races. This is why anthropologists conclude that there are no scientifically distinguishable biological races—only thousands of clines!

So What Is Race Then?

We hope we have made the point that the concept of separate, biologically distinct human races is not scientifically defensible. Unfortunately, racial ideology, by focusing on a few physical attributes, traps us into a discourse about race as biology rather than race as a cultural construction. The concept of race is a cultural invention, a culturally and historically specific way of thinking about, categorizing, and treating human beings.[13] It is about social divisions within society, about social categories and identities, about power and privilege. It has been and remains a particular type of ideology for legitimizing social inequality between groups with different ancestries, national origins, and histories. Indeed, the concept of race is also a major system of social identity, affecting one's own self-perception and how one is perceived and treated by others.

But race does have a biological component, one that can trick us into thinking that races are scientifically valid, biological subdivisions of the human species. As noted earlier, geographically localized populations—as a result of adaptation, migration, and chance—tend to have some characteristic physical traits. While these may be traits that characterize an entire population, such as hairy ears, it is more accurate to talk about the relative frequency of a particular trait, such as blood type O, in one population as compared to another, or the relative amount of pigmentation of individuals in a population, relative to other populations. Some traits, such as skin color, reflect climatic conditions; others, such as eye color and shape, probably reflect random, historical processes and migration patterns. The U.S. was peopled by populations from geographically distinct regions of the world—voluntary immigrants, forced African slaves, and indigenous American groups. Therefore, dominant northwestern European ethnic groups, such as the English and Germans, were able to exploit certain visually salient biological traits, especially skin color, as markers of race.

The effectiveness of these physical traits as markers of one's race depended, of course, on their being preserved in future generations. So dominant cultural groups created elaborate social and physical barriers to mating, reproduction, and marriage that crossed racial lines. The most explicit were the so-called anti-miscegenation laws, which outlawed sex between members of different races, whether married or not. These laws were not declared unconstitutional by the U.S. Supreme Court until the 1967 case of *Loving v. Virginia*.[14] Another vehicle was the cultural definition of kinship, whereby children of interracial (often forced) matings acquired the racial status of their lower-ranking parent; this was the so-called one-drop rule or hypodescent. Especially during the time of slavery, the lower-ranking parent was generally the mother, and thus the long-standing European cultural tradition of affiliating socially "legitimate" children with the father's kinship group was effectively reversed.

In contrast, there have been fewer social or legal barriers in the U.S. to mating and marriage between Italians, British, Germans, Swedes, and others of European ancestry. Consequently, the physical and cultural characteristics of European regional populations are less evident in the U.S. With intermarriage, distinct European identities were submerged in the culturally relevant macroracial category of "white"—more accurately, European American.

Thus even the biological dimension of contemporary racial groupings is the result of sociocultural processes. That is, humans as cultural beings first gave social significance to some physical differences between groups and then tried to perpetuate these "racial markers" by preventing social and physical intercourse between members of the groups. Although the dominant racial ideology was about maintaining racial "purity," the issue was not about biology; it was about maintaining social, political, and economic privilege.[15]

Why Is This Understanding Important for Educators?

We hope we've convinced you that race isn't biologically "real" and that race in the U.S. and elsewhere is a historical, social, and cultural creation. But so what? What is the significance of this way of viewing race for teachers, students, and society?

1. *The potential for change.* First, it is important to understand that, while races are biological fictions, they are social realities. Race may not be "real" in a biological sense, but it surely is "real" socially, politically, economically, and psychologically. Race and racism profoundly structure who we are, how we are treated, how we treat others, and our access to resources and rights.

Perhaps the most important message educators can take from the foregoing discussion is that race, racial classifications, racial stratification, and other forms of racism, including racial ideology, rather than being part of our biology, are part of our culture. Like other cultural forms, both the concept of race and our racial classifications are part of a system we have created. This means that we have the ability to change the system, to transform it, and even to totally eradicate it. Educators, in their role as transmitters of official culture, are particularly well poised to be active change agents in such a transformation.

But how, you may well ask, can teachers or anybody else make people stop classifying by race? And are there any good reasons to do so? These familiar categories—black, white, Asian, Native American, and so on—seem so embedded in U.S. society. They seem so "natural." Of course, that's how culture works. It seems "natural" to think of chicken, but not rats, as food. But, as we have shown above, the labels and underlying constructs that we use to talk about human diversity are unstable, depending on particular social, political, and historical contexts. Individuals in positions of authority, of course, have the ability to change them institutionally. But ordinary people also have the ability to change how they classify and label people in their everyday lives.

Several questions arise at this point. Do we as educators consciously want to change our way of conceptualizing and discussing human biological variation? What makes the "race as biology" assumption so dangerous? Are we going to continue to classify people by race, even while recognizing that it is a social construct? What vested interests do people have in holding onto—or rejecting—racial categories? How can we become more sophisticated in our understanding of how systems of classification work while also becoming more critical of our own ways of classifying people? Are there alternative ways of thinking about, classifying, and labeling human beings that might be more empowering for students, teachers, and community members? By eliminating or changing labels, will we change the power structures that perpetuate privilege and entitlement? Moving beyond race as biology forces us to confront these and other issues.

2. *The dangers of using racial classifications.* Categories and classifications are not intrinsically good or bad. People have always grouped others in ways that were important within a given society. However, the myth of race as biology is dangerous because it conflates physical attributes, such as skin color, with unrelated qualities, such as intelligence. Racial labels delude people into thinking that race predicts such other outcomes and behaviors as achievement in sports, music, or school; rates of employment; pregnancies outside marriage; or drug use. Race was historically equated with intelligence and, on that basis, was used to justify slavery and educational discrimination; it later provided the rationale that supported the genocide of Jews, blacks, Gypsies, and other "inferior" races under Hitler. So using racial categories brings along this history, like unwanted baggage.

Macroracial categories are dangerous in that the categories oversimplify and mask complex human differences. Saying that someone is Asian tells us virtually nothing concrete, but it brings with it a host of stereotypes, such as "model minority," "quiet," "good at math," "inscrutable," and so on. Yet the Asian label includes a wide range of groups, such as Koreans, Filipinos, and Vietnamese, with distinct histories and languages. The same is true for "white," a term that homogenizes the multiple nationalities, languages, and cultures that constitute Europe. The label "African American" ignores the enormous linguistic, physical, and cultural diversity of the peoples of Africa. The term "black" conflates people of African descent who were brought to the U.S. as slaves with recent immigrants from Africa and the Caribbean. These macroracial labels oversimplify and reduce human diversity to four or five giant groups. Apart from being bad science, these categories don't predict anything helpful—yet they have acquired a life of their own.

Macroracial categories, such as those used in the U.S. Census and other institutional data-collection efforts, force people to use labels that may not represent their own self-identity or classifying system. They must either select an existing category or select "other"—by definition, a kind of nonidentity. The impossibility, until recently, of selecting more than one ethnic/racial category implicitly stigmatizes multiracial individuals. And the term "mixed" wrongly implies that there are such things as "pure" races, an ideology with no basis in science. The recent expansion of the number of U.S. Census categories still cannot accommodate the diversity of the U.S. population, which includes people whose ancestry ranges from Egypt, Brazil, Sri Lanka, Ghana, and the Dominican Republic to Iceland and Korea.

3. *How macroracial categories have served people in positive ways.* Having noted some negative aspects, it is equally important to discuss how macroracial categories also serve society. Recall that labels are not intrinsically "good" or "bad." It depends on what people do with them. During the 1960s, the U.S. civil rights movement helped bring about consciousness and pride in being African American. This consciousness— known by terms such as ethnic pride and black power—united people who had been the victims of racism and oppression. From that consciousness sprang such educational interventions as black and Chicano history classes, ethnic studies departments, Afrocentric schools, and other efforts to empower young people. The movement to engender pride in and knowledge of one's ancestry has had a powerful impact. Many individuals are deeply attached to these racial labels as part of a positive identity. As one community activist put it, "Why should I give up being a race? I like being a race."

Racial classification can also have positive impact by allowing educators to monitor how equitably our institutions are serving the public. Racial categories are used by schools to disaggregate data on student outcomes, including achievement, attendance, discipline, course placements, college attendance rates, and other areas of school and student performance. These data are then used to examine whether certain groups of students are disproportionately represented in any outcome areas. For example, a school might discover that the percentage of Latino students who receive some type of disciplinary intervention is higher than that for other school populations. The school can then consider what it can do to change this outcome. Teachers might ask, Is there something about the way Latino students are treated in the school that leads to higher disciplinary referral rates? What other factors might be involved?

The racial classifications that educators use to monitor student outcome data reflect our society's social construction of race. As such, the categories represent groups that have been historically disenfranchised, oppressed, or marginalized. Without data disaggregated by race, gender, and other categories, it would be difficult to identify problems stemming from race-based institutional and societal factors that privilege certain groups, such as the widespread U.S. practice of tracking by so-called ability. Without data broken out according to racial, gender, and ethnic categories, schools would not be able to assess the positive impact intervention programs have had on different groups of students.

4. *Shifting the conversation from biology to culture.* One function of the myth of race as biology has been to distract us from the underlying causes of social inequality in the United States. Dismantling the myth of race as biology means that we must now shift our focus to analyzing the social, economic, political, and historical conditions that breed and serve to perpetuate social inequality. For educators, this means helping students to recognize and understand socioeconomic stratification, who benefits and who is harmed by racial discrimination, and how we as individuals and institutional agents can act to dismantle ideologies, institutions, and practices that harm young people.

There is another, more profound implication of the impermanence of race. Culture, acting collectively, and humans, acting individually, can make races disappear. That is, we can mate and marry across populations, thus destroying the racial "markers" that have been used to facilitate categorization and differential treatment of people of different ancestry and social rank. An understanding of human biological variation reveals the positive, indeed essential, role that intermating and intermarriage have played in human evolution and human adaptation. Rather than "mongrelizing" a "pure species," mating between different populations enriches the genetic pool. It is society, rather than nature—and socially and economically stratified societies, for the most part—that restricts social and sexual intercourse and severely penalizes those who mate across racial and other socially created lines.

Suggestions and Resources for Educators

Anthropological knowledge about race informs us about what race is and is not, but it cannot guide educational decision making. The underlying goal of social justice can help educators in making policy decisions, such as whether to use racial and ethnic categories to monitor educational outcomes. As long as we continue to see racially based disparities in young peoples' school achievement, then we must monitor and investigate the social conditions that produce these disparities. We must be careful, however, to avoid "biologizing" the classification; that is, we must avoid assuming genetic explanations for racial differences in behaviors and educational outcomes or even diseases.

As we pursue a more socially just world, educators should also continue to support young people's quest for knowledge about the history and struggles of their own people, as well as those of other groups, so that students in the future will not be able to point to their textbooks and say, "My people are not included in the curriculum." In the process, we can encourage both curiosity about and respect for human diversity, and we can emphasize the importance that historical and social context plays in creating social inequality. We can also encourage comparative studies of racial and other forms of social stratification, further challenging the notion that there is a biological explanation for oppression and inequality. In short, students will understand that there is no biological explanation for a group's historical position as either oppressed—or oppressor. We can encourage these studies to point out variations and fine distinctions within human racial groupings.

In addition to viewing the treatment of race and racial categories through a social-justice lens, we would apply another criterion that we call "depth of knowledge." We believe that it is important to challenge and inspire young people by exposing them to the best of our current knowledge in the sciences, social sciences, and other disciplines. Until now, most students in our education system have not been exposed to systematic, scientifically based teaching about race and human biological variation. One reason is that many social studies teachers may think they lack sufficient background in genetics and human biology. At the same time, many biology teachers may feel uncomfortable teaching about race as a social construct. The null move for teachers seems to be to say that we should all be "color blind." However, this does not help educate students about human diversity, both biological and social. In rare cases when students have the opportunity to engage in studies of race, ethnicity, culture, and ways to end racism, they are both interested and intellectually challenged.[16] One high school teacher who teaches students about race said he wants to dispel the notion that teaching about diversity is "touchy feely." "We don't just want to touch diversity; we want to approach it academically. . . . We feel we have a definite discipline."[17]

Rather than shield students and ourselves from current scientific knowledge about race, including its contradictions and controversies, we submit that educators should be providing opportunities for students to learn what anthropologists, geneticists, and other scientists, including social scientists, have to say about human biological variation and the issue of race. Particularly in middle schools, high schools, and beyond, students should be involved in inquiry projects and social action projects, in critical examination of the labels we currently use, and in analysis of the reasons for and against using them in particular contexts. Rather than tell students that they should or should not use racial labels (except for slurs), educators should be creating projects in which students explore together the range of possible ways of classifying people and the implications and political significance of alternative approaches in different contexts.

We would like to conclude by offering readers some ideas for student inquiry and by suggesting some resources that can serve to get teachers in all subject areas started on the quest to learn about human biological variation and ways to teach about it.

1. *Ideas for student inquiry.* Here are some examples of how teachers might engage students in critically examining the social, historical, and cultural construction of racial categories.

- Have students create and employ alternative "racial" classification schemes using as many observable and nonobservable physical differences as they can think of (e.g., foot size, height, ear shape, eyebrow shape, waist/shoulder ratio, hairiness). What do the groups look like? What does this tell us about macroracial classifications based on skin pigmentation and other surface features?
- Show students U.S. Census forms from 1870, 1950, and 2000, and ask them to place themselves in the most appropriate category.[18] Or show a photograph of a person of multiple ethnic ancestry and ask students to place this person in one of the categories from these three censuses. Ask them why they think the census form has changed over time and what that says about the meaning of "race."
- Ask immigrant students to investigate the racial/ethnic categories used in their country of origin and to reflect on how well they mesh with the U.S. categories. For example, have students from Mexico taken on an identity as Latino or Hispanic? And what does it mean for them to become part of a larger "macro" race in the U.S.?[19]
- Ask students how they feel when someone asks them to "represent their race." For example, how do students who identify themselves as African Americans feel when someone asks, "How do African Americans feel about this issue?" or "What's the African American perspective on this?"
- Discuss "reverse discrimination." When did this term come into use and why? Who is being discriminated against when discrimination is reversed?

- Discuss "political correctness." Where did this term come from? Who uses it and for what purposes? And why did it emerge?

2. *Resources for teachers.* The following examples will give readers a place to start in compiling resources available for teaching about race.

- Two major anthropological associations have produced highly readable position statements on the topic of race and human biological variation. First, the American Anthropological Association website features both the AAA position and a summary of testimony given in conjunction with the debates on the 2000 census categories. Second, the official statement of the American Association of Physical Anthropologists has appeared in that organization's journal.[20]

- The American Anthropological Association is making a special effort to disseminate understandings about race and human variation to the broader public. *AnthroNotes,* designed for precollege teachers, is a superb resource that offers concrete approaches to teaching about race, human diversity, and human evolution. It is available at no charge from the Anthropology Outreach Office (anthroutreach.@nmnh.si.edu). Several past issues of *AnthroNotes* treat race and ethnicity.[21] Anthropologists have produced materials for precollege teachers and teacher educators that deal with cultural diversity; some include strategies for teaching about culture and human diversity.[22] Others provide useful overviews of relevant topics.[23]

- The AAA is currently engaged in a public education initiative called Understanding Race and Human Variation, which will involve a traveling museum exhibit and a website. The Ford Foundation has contributed one million dollars to this project.

- In 1999, the AAA created a special commission called the Anthropology Education Commission (AEC) to "help achieve significant progress towards the integration of anthropological concepts, methods, and issues into pre-K through community college and adult education as a means of increasing public understanding of anthropology." The two teaching modules by Leonard Lieberman and by Lieberman and Patricia Rice, which we cited above, are available at no charge on the AEC website (www.aaanet.org/committees/commissions/aec). The AEC webpage contains extensive resources that teachers can use to teach anthropological concepts and methods, including some that address race.

Anthropologists recognize an obligation to disseminate their knowledge of human biological variation and the social construction of race to the wider public. We hope that this article and the resources we have provided will contribute to this effort.

Notes

1. Richard Herrnstein and Charles Murray, *The Bell Curve: Intelligence and Class Structure in American Life* (New York: Free Press, 1994).

2. Audrey Smedley, *Race in North America: Origin and Evolution of a Worldview* (Boulder, Colo.: Westview Press, 1998).

3. Jonathan Marks, *Human Biodiversity: Genes, Race, and History* (New York: Aldine de Gruyter, 1995).

4. Leonard Lieberman and Patricia Rice, "Races or Clines?," p. 7, available on the Anthropology Education Commission page of the American Anthropological Association website, www.aaanet.org/committees/commissions/aec—click on Teaching About Race.

5. George J. Armelagos and Alan H. Goodman, "Race, Racism, and Anthropology," in Alan H. Goodman and Thomas L. Leatherman, eds., *Building a New Biocultural Synthesis: Political-Economic Perspectives on Human Biology* (Ann Arbor: University of Michigan Press, 1998).

6. Jeffrey M. Fish, "Mixed Blood," in James Spradley and William McCurdy, eds., *Conformity and Conflict,* 11th ed. (New York: Allyn & Bacon, 2002), pp. 270–80.

7. Alan Goodman, "Bred in the Bone?," *Sciences,* vol. 37, no. 2, 1997, p. 24.

8. Ibid., p. 22.

9. Leonard Lieberman, "'Race' 1997 and 2001: A Race Odyssey," available on the Anthropology Education Commission page of the American Anthropological Association website, www.aaanet.org/committees/commissions/aec—click on Teaching About Race.

10. Jane Mercer, "Ethnic Differences in IQ Scores: What Do They Mean? (A Response to Lloyd Dunn)," *Hispanic Journal of Behavioral Sciences,* vol. 10, 1988, pp. 199–218.

11. Goodman, op. cit.

12. Lieberman and Rice, op. cit.

13. Carol Mukhopadhyay and Yolanda Moses, "Reestablishing 'Race' in Anthropological Discourse," *American Anthropologist,* vol. 99, 1997, pp. 517–33.

14. Janet Hyde and John DeLamater, *Understanding Human Sexuality,* 6th ed. (New York: McGraw-Hill, 1997).

15. Smedley, op. cit.

16. Karen Donaldson, *Through Students' Eyes: Combating Racism in United States Schools* (Westport, Conn.: Praeger, 1996); and Rosemary C. Henze, "Curricular Approaches to Developing Positive Interethnic Relations," *Journal of Negro Education,* vol. 68, 2001, pp. 529–49.

17. Henze, p. 539.

18. American Anthropological Association. (2002). Front End Evaluation of *Understanding Race and Human Variability.* Arlington, VA: American Anthropological Association.

19. Clara Rodriguez, *Changing Race: Latinos, the Census, and the History of Ethnicity in the United States* (New York: New York University Press, 2000); and Gilberto Arriaza, "The School Yard as a Stage: Missing Culture Clues in Symbolic Fighting," *Multicultural Education Journal,* Spring 2003, in press.

20. American Anthropological Association, "AAA Statement on Race," www.aaanet.org/stmts/racepp.htm; and American Association of Physical Anthropologists, "AAPA Statement on Biological Aspects of Race," *American Journal of Physical Anthropology,* vol. 101, 1996, pp. 569–70.

21. Alison S. Brooks et al., "Race and Ethnicity in America," in Ruth O. Selig and Marilyn R. London, eds., *Anthropology Explored: The Best of Smithsonian AnthroNotes* (Washington, D.C.: Smithsonian Institution Press), pp. 315–26; E. L. Cerrini-Long, "Ethnicity in the U.S.A.: An Anthropological Model," *AnthroNotes,* vol. 15, no. 3, 1993; William L. Merrill, "Identity Transformation in Colonial Northern Mexico," *AnthroNotes,* vol. 19, no. 2, 1997, pp. 1–8; and Boyce Rensberger, "Forget the Old Labels: Here's a New Way to Look at Race," *AnthroNotes,* vol. 18, no. 1, 1996, pp. 1–7.

22. Hilda Hernandez and Carol C. Mukhopadhyay, *Integrating Multicultural Perspectives in Teacher Education: A Curriculum Resource Guide* (Chico: California State University, 1985); and Conrad P. Kottak, R. Furlow White, and Patricia Rice, eds. *The Teaching of Anthropology: Problems, Issues, and Decisions* (Mountain View, Calif.: Mayfield Publishing, 1996).

23. Faye Harrison, "The Persistent Power of 'Race' in the Cultural and Political Economy of Racism," *Annual Review of Anthropology,* vol. 24, 1995, pp. 47–74; and Ida Susser and Thomas Patterson, eds., *Cultural Diversity in the United States: A Critical Reader* (Malden, Mass.: Blackwell, 2001).

CAROL MUKHOPADHYAY is a professor in the Department of Anthropology, San José State University, San José, Calif., where **ROSEMARY C. HENZE** is an associate professor in the Department of Linguistics and Language Development. They wish to thank Gilberto Arriaza, Paul Erickson, Alan Goodman, and Yolanda Moses for their comments on this article.

The Tall and the Short of It

BARRY BOGIN

Baffled by your future prospects? As a biological anthropologist, I have just one word of advice for you: plasticity. *Plasticity* refers to the ability of many organisms, including humans, to alter themselves—their behavior or even their biology—in response to changes in the environment. We tend to think that our bodies get locked into their final form by our genes, but in fact we alter our bodies as the conditions surrounding us shift, particularly as we grow during childhood. Plasticity is as much a product of evolution's fine-tuning as any particular gene, and it makes just as much evolutionary good sense. Rather than being able to adapt to a single environment, we can, thanks to plasticity, change our bodies to cope with a wide range of environments. Combined with the genes we inherit from our parents, plasticity accounts for what we are and what we can become.

Anthropologists began to think about human plasticity around the turn of the century, but the concept was first clearly defined in 1969 by Gabriel Lasker, a biological anthropologist at Wayne State University in Detroit. At that time scientists tended to consider only those adaptations that were built into the genetic makeup of a person and passed on automatically to the next generation. A classic example of this is the ability of adults in some human societies to drink milk. As children, we all produce an enzyme called lactase, which we need to break down the sugar lactose in our mother's milk. In many of us, however, the lactase gene slows down dramatically as we approach adolescence—probably as the result of another gene that regulates its activity. When that regulating gene turns down the production of lactase, we can no longer digest milk.

Lactose intolerance—which causes intestinal gas and diarrhea—affects between 70 and 90 percent of African Americans, Native Americans, Asians, and people who come from around the Mediterranean. But others, such as people of central and western European descent and the Fulani of West Africa, typically have no problem drinking milk as adults. That's because they are descended from societies with long histories of raising goats and cattle. Among these people there was a clear benefit to being able to drink milk, so natural selection gradually changed the regulation of their lactase gene, keeping it functioning throughout life.

That kind of adaptation takes many centuries to become established, but Lasker pointed out that there are two other kinds of adaptation in humans that need far less time to kick in. If people have to face a cold winter with little or no heat, for example, their metabolic rates rise over the course of a few weeks and they produce more body heat. When summer returns, the rates sink again.

Lasker's other mode of adaptation concerned the irreversible, lifelong modification of people as they develop—that is, their plasticity. Because we humans take so many years to grow to adulthood, and because we live in so many different environments, from forests to cities and from deserts to the Arctic, we are among the world's most variable species in our physical form and behavior. Indeed, we are one of the most plastic of all species.

In an age when DNA is king, it's worth considering why Americans are no longer the world's tallest people, and some Guatemalans no longer pygmies.

One of the most obvious manifestations of human malleability is our great range of height, and it is a subject I've made a special study of for the last 25 years. Consider these statistics: in 1850 Americans were the tallest people in the world, with American men averaging 5'6". Almost 150 years later, American men now average 5'8", but we have fallen in the standings and are now only the third tallest people in the world. In first place are the Dutch. Back in 1850 they averaged only 5'4"—the shortest men in Europe—but today they are a towering 5'10". (In these two groups, and just about everywhere else, women average about five inches less than men at all times.)

So what happened? Did all the short Dutch sail over to the United States? Did the Dutch back in Europe get an infusion of "tall genes"? Neither. In both America and the Netherlands life got better, but more so for the Dutch, and height increased as a result. We know this is true thanks in part to studies on how height is determined. It's the product of plasticity in our childhood and in our mothers' childhood as well. If a girl is undernourished and suffers poor health, the growth of her body, including her reproductive system, is usually reduced. With a shortage of raw materials, she can't build more cells to construct a bigger body; at the same time, she has to invest what materials she can get into repairing already existing cells and tissues from the damage caused by disease. Her shorter stature as an adult is the result of a compromise her body makes while growing up.

Such a woman can pass on her short stature to her child, but genes have nothing to do with it for either of them. If she becomes pregnant, her small reproductive system probably won't be able to supply a normal level of nutrients and oxygen to her fetus. This harsh environment reprograms the fetus to grow more slowly than it would if the woman was healthier, so she is more likely to give birth to a smaller baby. Low-birth-weight babies (weighing less than 5.5 pounds) tend to continue their prenatal program of slow growth through childhood. By the time they are teenagers, they are usually significantly shorter than people of normal birth weight. Some particularly striking evidence of this reprogramming comes from studies on monozygotic twins, which develop from a single fertilized egg cell and are therefore identical genetically. But in certain cases, monozygotic twins end up being nourished by unequal portions of the placenta. The twin with the smaller fraction of the placenta is often born with low birth weight, while the other one is normal. Follow-up studies show that this difference between the twins can last throughout their lives.

As such research suggests, we can use the average height of any group of people as a barometer of the health of their society. After the turn of the century both the United States and the Netherlands began to protect the health of their citizens by purifying drinking water, installing sewer systems, regulating the safety of food, and, most important, providing better health care and diets to children. The children responded to their changed environment by growing taller. But the differences in Dutch and American societies determined their differing heights today. The Dutch decided to provide public health benefits to all the public, including the poor. In the United States, meanwhile, improved health is enjoyed most by those who can afford it. The poor often lack adequate housing, sanitation, and health care. The difference in our two societies can be seen at birth: in 1990 only 4 percent of Dutch babies were born at low birth weight, compared with 7 percent in the United States. For white Americans the rate was 5.7 percent, and for black Americans the rate was a whopping 13.3 percent. The disparity between rich and poor in the United States carries through to adulthood: poor Americans are shorter than the better-off by about one inch. Thus, despite great affluence in the United States, our average height has fallen to third place.

People are often surprised when I tell them the Dutch are the tallest people in the world. Aren't they shrimps compared with the famously tall Tutsi (or "Watusi," as you probably first encountered them) of Central Africa? Actually, the supposed great height of the Tutsi is one of the most durable myths from the age of European exploration. Careful investigation reveals that today's Tutsi men average 5'7" and that they have maintained that average for more than 100 years. That means that back in the 1800s, when puny European men first met the Tutsi, the Europeans suffered strained necks from looking up all the time. The two-to-three-inch difference in average height back then could easily have turned into fantastic stories of African giants by European adventures and writers.

The Tutsi could be as tall or taller than the Dutch if equally good health care and diets were available in Rwanda and Burundi, where the Tutsi live. But poverty rules the lives of most African people, punctuated by warfare, which makes the conditions for growth during childhood even worse. And indeed, it turns out that the Tutsi and other Africans who migrate to Western Europe or North America at young ages end up taller than Africans remaining in Africa.

At the other end of the height spectrum, Pygmies tell a similar story. The shortest people in the world today are the Mbuti, the Efe, and other Pygmy peoples of Central Africa. Their average stature is almost 4'9" for adult men and 4'6" for women. Part of the reason Pygmies are short is indeed genetic: some evidently lack the genes for producing the growth-promoting hormones that course through other people's bodies, while others are genetically incapable of using these hormones to trigger the cascade of reactions that lead to growth. But another important reason for their small size is environmental. Pygmies living as hunter-gatherers in the forests of Central African countries appear to be undernourished, which further limits their growth. Pygmies who live on farms and ranches outside the forest are better fed than their hunter-gatherer relatives and are taller as well. Both genes and nutrition thus account for the size of Pygmies.

Peoples in other parts of the world have also been labeled pygmies, such as some groups in Southeast Asia and the Maya of Guatemala. Well-meaning explorers and scientists have often claimed that they are genetically short, but here we encounter another myth of height. A group of extremely short people in New Guinea, for example, turned out to eat a diet deficient in iodine and other essential nutrients. When they were supplied with cheap mineral and vitamin supplements, their supposedly genetic short stature vanished in their children, who grew to a more normal height.

A nother way for these so-called pygmies to stop being pygmies is to immigrate to the United States. In my own research, I study the growth of two groups of Mayan children. One group lives in their homeland of Guatemala, and the other is a group of refugees living in the United States. The Maya in Guatemala live in the village of San Pedro, which has no safe source of drinking water. Most of the water is contaminated with fertilizers and pesticides used on nearby agricultural fields. Until recently, when a deep well was dug, the townspeople depended on an unreliable supply of water from rain-swollen streams. Most homes still lack running water and have only pit toilets. The parents of the Mayan children work mostly at clothing factories and are paid only a few dollars a day.

One way for the so-called pygmies of Guatemala to stop being pygmies is to immigrate to the United States.

I began working with the schoolchildren in this village in 1979, and my research shows that most of them eat only 80 percent of the food they need. Other research shows that almost 30 percent of the girls and 20 percent of the boys are deficient in iodine, that most of the children suffer from intestinal parasites, and that many have persistent ear and eye infections. As a consequence, their health is poor and their height reflects it: they average about three inches shorter than better-fed Guatemalan children.

The Mayan refugees I work with in the United States live in Los Angeles and in the rural agricultural community of Indiantown in central Florida. Although the adults work mostly in minimum-wage jobs, the children in these communities are generally better off than their counterparts in Guatemala. Most Maya arrived in the 1980s as refugees escaping a civil war as well as a political system that threatened them and their children. In the United States they found security and started new lives, and before long their children began growing faster and bigger. My data show that the average increase in height among the first generation of these immigrants was 2.2 inches, which means that these so-called pygmies have undergone one of the largest single-generation increases in height ever recorded. When people such as my own grandparents migrated from the poverty of rural life in Eastern Europe to the cities of the United States just after World War I, the increase in height of the next generation was only about one inch.

One reason for the rapid increase in stature is that in the United States the Maya have access to treated drinking water and to a reliable supply of food. Especially critical are school breakfast and lunch programs for children from low-income families, as well as public assistance programs such as the federal Woman, Infants, and Children (WIC) program and food stamps. That these programs improve health and growth is no secret. What is surprising is how fast they work. Mayan mothers in the United States tell me that even their babies are bigger and healthier than the babies they raised in Guatemala, and hospital statistics bear them out. These women must be enjoying a level of health so improved from that of their lives in Guatemala that their babies are growing faster in the womb. Of course, plasticity means that such changes are dependent on external conditions, and unfortunately the rising height—and health—of the Maya is in danger from political forces that are attempting to cut funding for food stamps and the WIC program. If that funding is cut, the negative impact on the lives of poor Americans, including the Mayan refugees, will be as dramatic as were the former positive effects.

Height is only the most obvious example of plasticity's power; there are others to be found everywhere you look. The Andes-dwelling Quechua people of Peru are well-adapted to their high-altitude homes. Their large, barrel-shaped chests house big lungs that inspire huge amounts of air with each breath, and they manage to survive on the lower pressure of oxygen they breathe with an unusually high level of red blood cells. Yet these secrets of mountain living are not hereditary. Instead the bodies of young Quechua adapt as they grow in their particular environment, just as those of European children do when they live at high altitudes.

Plasticity may also have a hand in determining our risks for developing a number of diseases. For example, scientists have long been searching for a cause for Parkinson's disease. Because Parkinson's tends to run in families, it is natural to think there is a genetic cause. But while a genetic mutation linked to some types of Parkinson's disease was reported in mid-1997, the gene accounts for only a fraction of people with the disease. Many more people with Parkinson's do not have the gene, and not all people with the mutated gene develop the disease.

Ralph Garruto, a medical researcher and biological anthropologist at the National Institutes of Health, is investigating the role of the environment and human plasticity not only in Parkinson's but in Lou Gehrig's disease as well. Garruto and his team traveled to the islands of Guam and New Guinea, where rates of both diseases are 50 to 100 times higher than in the United States. Among the native Chamorro people of Guam these diseases kill one person out of every five over the age of 25. The scientists found that both diseases are linked to a shortage of calcium in the diet. This shortage sets off a cascade of events that result in the digestive system's absorbing too much of the aluminum present in the diet. The aluminum wreaks havoc on various parts of the body, including the brain, where it destroys neurons and eventually causes paralysis and death.

The most amazing discovery made by Garruto's team is that up to 70 percent of the people they studied in Guam had some brain damage, but only 20 percent progressed all the way to Parkinson's or Lou Gehrig's disease. Genes and plasticity seem to be working hand in hand to produce these lower-than-expected rates of disease. There is a certain amount of genetic variation in the ability that all people have in coping with calcium shortages—some can function better than others. But thanks to plasticity, it's also possible for people's bodies to gradually develop ways to protect themselves against aluminum poisoning. Some people develop biochemical barriers to the aluminum they eat, while others develop ways to prevent the aluminum from reaching the brain.

An appreciation of plasticity may temper some of our fears about these diseases and even offer some hope. For if Parkinson's and Lou Gehrig's diseases can be prevented among the Chamorro by plasticity, then maybe medical researchers can figure out a way to produce the same sort of plastic changes in you and me. Maybe Lou Gehrig's disease and Parkinson's disease—as well as many other, including some cancers—aren't our genetic doom but a product of our development, just like variations in human height. And maybe their danger will in time prove as illusory as the notion that the Tutsi are giants, or the Maya pygmies—or Americans still the tallest of the tall.

BARRY BOGIN is a professor of anthropology at the University of Michigan in Dearborn and the author of *Patterns of Human Growth*.

UNIT 7

Living with the Past

Unit Selections

Key Points to Consider

- What are the ways to prevent epidemics in the human species?

- Does the concept of natural selection have any relevance to the treatment of disease? Defend your answer.

- What healthful habits can we learn by studying hunter-gatherers?

- What is "Darwinian medicine?"

- Why is Tay-Sachs disease so common among East European Jews?

- Why would such a deadly disease as hemochromatosis be bred into our genetic code?

Student Website
www.mhcls.com

Internet References

Evolution and Medicine Network
   http://www.evolutionandmedicine.org/
Forensic Science Reference Page
   http://www.lab.fws.gov
The Paleolithic Diet Page
   http://www.paleodiet.com/
Zeno's Forensic Page
   http://www.forensic.to/forensic.html

Anthropology continues to evolve as a discipline, not only with respect to the tools and techniques of the trade, but also in the application of whatever knowledge we stand to gain about ourselves. Sometimes an awareness of our biological and behavioral past may help us to better understand the present. For instance, in showing how our evolutionary past may make a difference in bodily health, Patricia Gadsby (in "The Inuit Paradox") deals with the question of how traditional hunters, such as the Inuit, gorged themselves on fat, rarely saw a vegetable and was still healthier than we are. Lori Oliwenstein (in "Dr. Darwin") then talks about how the symptoms of disease must first be interpreted as to whether they represent part of the aggressive strategy of microbes or the defensive mechanisms of the patient before treatment can be applied. Jared Diamond, in "Curse and Blessing of the Ghetto" and Sharon Moalem in "Ironing It Out" show that, while many deleterious genes do get weeded out of the population by means of natural selection, there are other harmful ones that may actually have a good side to them and will therefore be perpetuated.

As we reflect upon where we have been and how we came to be as we are in the evolutionary sense, the inevitable question arises as to what will happen next. This is the most difficult issue of all, because our biological future depends so much on long-range environmental trends that no one seems to be able to predict. Take, for example, the sweeping effects of ecological change upon the viruses of the world, which in turn seem to be paving the way for new waves of human epidemics. There is no better example of this problem than the recent explosion of new diseases, as described in "The Viral Superhighway" by George Armelagos. As we gain a better understanding of the processes of mutation and natural selection, and their relevance to human beings, we might even gain some control over the evolutionary direction of our species. However, the issue of what is a beneficial application of scientific knowledge becomes a subject for debate. Who will have the final word as to how these technological breakthroughs are to be employed in the future? Even with the best of intentions, how can we be certain of the long-range consequences of our actions in such a complicated field?

Knowledge in itself, of course, is neutral—its potential for good or ill being determined by those who happen to be in the position to use it. Consider, for example, that some men may be dying from a genetically caused overabundance of iron in their blood systems in a trade-off that allows some women to absorb sufficient amounts of the element to guarantee their own survival.

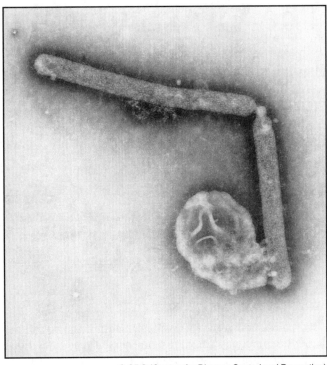

© CDC (Centers for Disease Control and Prevention)

The question of whether we should eliminate such a gene that brings about this situation would seem to depend on which sex we decide should reap the benefit.

As we read the essays in this unit and contemplate the significance of "Darwinian medicine" for human evolution, we can hope that a better understanding of the diseases that afflict our species will lead to a reduction of human suffering. At the same time, we must remain aware that someone, at some time, may actually use the same knowledge to increase rather than reduce the misery that exists in the world.

Since it has been our conscious decision making (and not the genetically predetermined behavior that characterizes some species) that has gotten us into this mess, then it is the conscious will of our generation and future generations that will get us out of it. But, can we wait much longer for humanity to collectively come to its senses? Or is it too late already?

The Viral Superhighway

Environmental disruptions and international travel have brought on a new era in human illness, one marked by diabolical new diseases.

GEORGE J. ARMELAGOS

So the Lord sent a pestilence upon Israel from the morning until the appointed time; and there died of the people from Dan to Beer-sheba seventy thousand men.

—2 Sam. 24:15

Swarms of crop-destroying locusts, rivers fouled with blood, lion-headed horses breathing fire and sulfur: the Bible presents a lurid assortment of plagues, described as acts of retribution by a vengeful God. Indeed, real-life epidemics—such as the influenza outbreak of 1918, which killed 21 million people in a matter of months—can be so sudden and deadly that it is easy, even for nonbelievers, to view them as angry messages from the beyond.

How reassuring it was, then, when the march of technology began to give people some control over the scourges of the past. In the 1950s the Salk vaccine, and later, the Sabin vaccine, dramatically reduced the incidence of polio. And by 1980 a determined effort by health workers worldwide eradicated smallpox, a disease that had afflicted humankind since earliest times with blindness, disfigurement and death, killing nearly 300 million people in the twentieth century alone.

But those optimistic years in the second half of our century now seem, with hindsight, to have been an era of inflated expectations, even arrogance. In 1967 the surgeon general of the United States, William H. Stewart, announced that victory over infectious diseases was imminent—a victory that would close the book on modern plagues. Sadly, we now know differently. Not only have deadly and previously unimagined new illnesses such as AIDS and Legionnaires' disease emerged in recent years, but historical diseases that just a few decades ago seemed to have been tamed are returning in virulent, drug-resistant varieties. Tuberculosis, the ancient lung disease that haunted nineteenth-century Europe, afflicting, among others, Chopin, Dostoyevski and Keats, is aggressively mutating into strains that defy the standard medicines; as a result, modern TB victims must undergo a daily drug regimen so elaborate that health-department workers often have to personally monitor

patients to make sure they comply [see "A Plague Returns," by Mark Earnest and John A. Sbarbaro, September/October 1993]. Meanwhile, bacteria and viruses in foods from chicken to strawberries to alfalfa sprouts are sickening as many as 80 million Americans each year.

And those are only symptoms of a much more general threat. Deaths from infectious diseases in the United States rose 58 percent between 1980 and 1992. Twenty-nine new diseases have been reported in the past twenty-five years, a few of them so bloodcurdling and bizarre that descriptions of them bring to mind tacky horror movies. Ebola virus, for instance, can in just a few days reduce a healthy person to a bag of teeming flesh spilling blood and organ parts from every orifice. Creutzfeldt-Jakob disease, which killed the choreographer George Balanchine in 1983, eats away at its victims' brains until they resemble wet sponges. Never slow to fan mass hysteria, Hollywood has capitalized on the phenomenon with films such as *Outbreak,* in which a monkey carrying a deadly new virus from central Africa infects unwitting Californians and starts an epidemic that threatens to annihilate the human race.

The reality about infectious disease is less sensational but alarming nonetheless. Gruesome new pathogens such as Ebola are unlikely to cause a widespread epidemic because they sicken and kill so quickly that victims can be easily identified and isolated; on the other hand, the seemingly innocuous practice of overprescribing antibiotics for bad colds could ultimately lead to untold deaths, as familiar germs evolve to become untreatable. We are living in the twilight of the antibiotic era: within our lifetimes, scraped knees and cut fingers may return to the realm of fatal conditions.

Through international travel, global commerce and the accelerating destruction of ecosystems worldwide, people are inadvertently exposing themselves to a Pandora's box of emerging microbial threats. And the recent rumblings of biological terrorism from Iraq highlight the appalling potential of disease organisms for being manipulated to vile ends. But although it may appear that the apocalypse has arrived, the truth is that people today are not facing a unique predicament. Emerging diseases have long loomed like a shadow over the human race.

eople and pathogens have a long history together. Infections have been detected in the bones of human ancestors more than a million years old, and evidence from the mummy of the Egyptian pharaoh Ramses V suggests that he may have died from smallpox more than 3,000 years ago. Widespread outbreaks of disease are also well documented. Between 1347 and 1351 roughly a third of the population of medieval Europe was wiped out by bubonic plague, which is carried by fleas that live on rodents. In 1793, 10 percent of the population of Philadelphia succumbed to yellow fever, which is spread by mosquitoes. And in 1875 the son of a Fiji chief came down with measles after a ceremonial trip to Australia. Within four months more than 20,000 Fijians were dead from the imported disease, which spreads through the air when its victims cough or sneeze.

According to conventional wisdom in biology, people and invading microorganisms evolve together: people gradually become more resistant, and the microorganisms become less virulent. The result is either mutualism, in which the relation benefits both species, or commensalism, in which one species benefits without harming the other. Chicken pox and measles, once fatal afflictions, now exist in more benign forms. Logic would suggest, after all, that the best interests of an organism are not served if it kills its host; doing so would be like picking a fight with the person who signs your paycheck.

But recently it has become clear to epidemiologists that the reverse of that cooperative paradigm of illness can also be true: microorganisms and their hosts sometimes exhaust their energies devising increasingly powerful weaponry and defenses. For example, several variants of human immunodeficiency virus (HIV) may compete for dominance within a person's body, placing the immune system under ever-greater siege. As long as a virus has an effective mechanism for jumping from one person to another, it can afford to kill its victims [see "The Deadliest Virus," by Cynthia Mills, January/February 1997].

If the competition were merely a question of size, humans would surely win: the average person is 10^{17} times the size of the average bacterium. But human beings, after all, constitute only one species, which must compete with 5,000 kinds of viruses and more than 300,000 species of bacteria. Moreover, in the twenty years it takes humans to produce a new generation, bacteria can reproduce a half-million times. That disparity enables pathogens to evolve ever more virulent adaptations that quickly outstrip human responses to them. The scenario is governed by what the English zoologist Richard Dawkins of the University of Oxford and a colleague have called the "Red Queen Principle." In Lewis Carroll's *Through the Looking Glass* the Red Queen tells Alice she will need to run faster and faster just to stay in the same place. Staving off illness can be equally elusive.

The Centers For Disease Control and Prevention (CDC) in Atlanta, Georgia, has compiled a list of the most recent emerging pathogens. They include:

- *Campylobacter,* a bacterium widely found in chickens because of the commercial practice of raising them in cramped, unhealthy conditions. It causes between two

million and eight million cases of food poisoning a year in the United States and between 200 and 800 deaths.
- *Escherichia coli* 0157:H7, a dangerously mutated version of an often harmless bacterium. Hamburger meat from Jack in the Box fast-food restaurants that was contaminated with this bug led to the deaths of at least four people in 1993.
- Hantaviruses, a genus of fast-acting, lethal viruses, often carried by rodents, that kill by causing the capillaries to leak blood. A new hantavirus known as *sin nombre* (Spanish for "nameless") surfaced in 1993 in the southwestern United States, causing the sudden and mysterious deaths of thirty-two people.
- HIV, the deadly virus that causes AIDS (acquired immunodeficiency syndrome). Although it was first observed in people as recently as 1981, it has spread like wildfire and is now a global scourge, affecting more than 30 million people worldwide.
- The strange new infectious agent that causes bovine spongiform encephalopathy, or mad cow disease, which recently threw the British meat industry and consumers into a panic. This bizarre agent, known as a prion, or "proteinaceous infectious particle," is also responsible for Creutzfeldt-Jakob disease, the brain-eater I mentioned earlier. A Nobel Prize was awarded last year to the biochemist Stanley B. Prusiner of the University of California, San Francisco, for his discovery of the prion.
- *Legionella pneumophila,* the bacterium that causes Legionnaires' disease. The microorganism thrives in wet environments; when it lodges in air-conditioning systems or the mist machines in supermarket produce sections, it can be expelled into the air, reaching people's lungs. In 1976 thirty-four participants at an American Legion convention in Philadelphia died—the incident that led to the discovery and naming of the disease.
- *Borrelia burgdorferi,* the bacterium that causes Lyme disease. It is carried by ticks that live on deer and white-footed mice. Left untreated, it can cause crippling, chronic problems in the nerves, joints and internal organs.

How ironic, given such a rogues' gallery of nasty characters, that just a quarter-century ago the Egyptian demographer Abdel R. Omran could observe that in many modern industrial nations the major killers were no longer infectious diseases. Death, he noted, now came not from outside but rather from within the body, the result of gradual deterioration. Omran traced the change to the middle of the nineteenth century, when the industrial revolution took hold in the United States and parts of Europe. Thanks to better nutrition, improved public-health measures and medical advances such as mass immunization and the introduction of antibiotics, microorganisms were brought under control. As people began living longer, their aging bodies succumbed to "diseases of civilization": cancer, clogged arteries, diabetes, obesity and osteoporosis. Omran was the first to formally recognize that shift in the disease environment. He called it an "epidemiological transition."

Like other anthropologists of my generation, I learned of Omran's theory early in my career, and it soon became a basic tenet—a comforting one, too, implying as it did an end to the supremacy of microorganisms. Then, three years ago, I began working with the anthropologist Kathleen C. Barnes of Johns Hopkins University in Baltimore, Maryland, to formulate an expansion of Omran's ideas. It occurred to us that his epidemiological transition had not been a unique event. Throughout history human populations have undergone shifts in their relations with disease—shifts, we noted, that are always linked to major changes in the way people interact with the environment. Barnes and I, along with James Lin, a master's student at Johns Hopkins University School of Hygiene and Public Health, have since developed a new theory: that there have been not one but three major epidemiological transitions; that each one has been sparked by human activities; and that we are living through the third one right now.

The first epidemiological transition took place some 10,000 years ago, when people abandoned their nomadic existence and began farming. That profoundly new way of life disrupted ecosystems and created denser living conditions that led, as I will soon detail, to new diseases. The second epidemiological transition was the salutary one Omran singled out in 1971, when the war against infectious diseases seemed to have been won. And in the past two decades the emergence of illnesses such as hepatitis C, cat scratch disease (caused by the bacterium *Bartonella henselae*), Ebola and others on CDC's list has created a third epidemiological transition, a disheartening set of changes that in many ways have reversed the effects of the second transition and coincide with the shift to globalism. Burgeoning population growth and urbanization, widespread environmental degradation, including global warming and tropical deforestation, and radically improved methods of transportation have given rise to new ways of contracting and spreading disease.

We are, quite literally, making ourselves sick.

When early human ancestors moved from African forests onto the savanna millions of years ago, a few diseases came along for the ride. Those "heirloom" species—thus designated by the Australian parasitologist J. F. A. Sprent because they had afflicted earlier primates—included head and body lice; parasitic worms such as pinworms, tapeworms and liver flukes; and possibly herpes virus and malaria.

For 99.8 percent of the five million years of human existence, hunting and gathering was the primary mode of subsistence. Our ancestors lived in small groups and relied on wild animals and plants for their survival. In their foraging rounds, early humans would occasionally have contracted new kinds of illnesses through insect bites or by butchering and eating disease-ridden animals. Such events would not have led to widespread epidemics, however, because groups of people were so sparse and widely dispersed.

About 10,000 years ago, at the end of the last ice age, many groups began to abandon their nomadic lifestyles for a more efficient and secure way of life. The agricultural revolution first appeared in the Middle East; later, farming centers developed independently in China and Central America. Permanent villages grew up, and people turned their attention to crafts such as toolmaking and pottery. Thus when people took to cultivating wheat and barley, they planted the seeds of civilization as well.

With the new ways, however, came certain costs. As wild habitats were transformed into urban settings, the farmers who brought in the harvest with their flint-bladed sickles were assailed by grim new ailments. Among the most common was scrub typhus, which is carried by mites that live in tall grasses, and causes a potentially lethal fever. Clearing vegetation to create arable fields brought farmers frequently into mite-infested terrain.

Irrigation brought further hazards. Standing thigh-deep in watery canals, farm workers were prey to the worms that cause schistosomiasis. After living within aquatic snails during their larval stage, those worms emerge in a free-swimming form that can penetrate human skin, lodge in the intestine or urinary tract, and cause bloody urine and other serious maladies. Schistosomiasis was well known in ancient Egypt, where outlying fields were irrigated with water from the Nile River; descriptions of its symptoms and remedies are preserved in contemporary medical papyruses.

The domestication of sheep, goats and other animals cleared another pathway for microorganisms. With pigs in their yards and chickens roaming the streets, people in agricultural societies were constantly vulnerable to pathogens that could cross interspecies barriers. Many such organisms had long since reached commensalism with their animal hosts, but they were highly dangerous to humans. Milk from infected cattle could transmit tuberculosis, a slow killer that eats away at the lungs and causes its victims to cough blood and pus. Wool and skins were loaded with anthrax, which can be fatal when inhaled and, in modern times, has been developed by several nations as a potential agent of biological warfare. Blood from infected cattle, injected into people by biting insects such as the tsetse fly, spread sleeping sickness, an often-fatal disease marked by tremors and protracted lethargy.

A second major effect of agriculture was to spur population growth and, perhaps more important, density. Cities with populations as high as 50,000 had developed in the Near East by 3000 B.C. Scavenger species such as rats, mice and sparrows, which congregate wherever large groups of people live, exposed city dwellers to bubonic plague, typhus and rabies. And now that people were crowded together, a new pathogen could quickly start an epidemic. Larger populations also enabled diseases such as measles, mumps, chicken pox and smallpox to persist in an endemic form—always present, afflicting part of the population while sparing those with acquired immunity.

Thus the birth of agriculture launched humanity on a trajectory that has again and again brought people into contact with new pathogens. Tilling soil and raising livestock led to more energy-intensive ways of extracting resources from the earth—to lumbering, coal mining, oil drilling. New resources led to increasingly complex social organization, and to new and more frequent contacts between various societies. Loggers today who venture into the rain forest disturb previously untouched creatures and give them, for the first time, the chance to attack humans. But there is nothing new about this drama; only the players have changed. Some 2,000 years ago the introduction of iron tools to sub-Saharan Africa led to a slash-and-burn style of agriculture that brought people into contact with *Anopheles gambiae,* a mosquito that transmits malaria.

Improved transportation methods also help diseases extend their reach: microorganisms cannot travel far on their own, but they are expert hitchhikers. When the Spanish invaded Mexico in the early 1500s, for instance, they brought with them diseases that quickly raged through Tenochtitlán, the stately, temple-filled capital of the Aztec Empire. Smallpox, measles and influenza wiped out millions of Central America's original inhabitants, becoming the invisible weapon in the European conquest.

I n the past three decades people and their inventions have drilled, polluted, engineered, paved, planted and deforested at soaring rates, changing the biosphere faster than ever before. The combined effects can, without hyperbole, be called a global revolution. After all, many of them have worldwide repercussions: the widespread chemical contamination of waterways, the thinning of the ozone layer, the loss of species diversity. And such global human actions have put people at risk for infectious diseases in newly complex and devastating ways. Global warming, for instance, could expose millions of people for the first time to malaria, sleeping sickness and other insect-borne illnesses; in the United States, a slight overall temperature increase would allow the mosquitoes that carry dengue fever to survive as far north as New York City.

Global Warming could allow the mosquitoes that carry dengue fever to survive as far north as New York City.

Major changes to the landscape that have become possible in the past quarter-century have also triggered new diseases. After the construction of the Aswan Dam in 1970, for instance, Rift Valley fever infected 200,000 people in Egypt, killing 600. The disease had been known to affect livestock, but it was not a major problem in people until the vast quantities of dammed water became a breeding ground for mosquitoes. The insects bit both cattle and humans, helping the virus jump the interspecies barrier.

In the eastern United States, suburbanization, another relatively recent phenomenon, is a dominant factor in the emergence of Lyme disease—10,000 cases of which are reported annually. Thanks to modern earth-moving equipment, a soaring economy and population pressures, many Americans have built homes in formerly remote, wooded areas. Nourished by lawns and gardens and unchecked by wolves, which were exterminated by settlers long ago, the deer population has exploded, exposing people to the ticks that carry Lyme disease.

Meanwhile, widespread pollution has made the oceans a breeding ground for microorganisms. Epidemiologists have suggested that toxic algal blooms—fed by the sewage, fertilizers and other contaminants that wash into the oceans—harbor countless viruses and bacteria. Thrown together into what amounts to a dirty genetic soup, those pathogens can undergo gene-swapping and mutations, engendering newly antibiotic-resistant strains. Nautical traffic can carry ocean pathogens far and wide: a devastating outbreak of cholera hit Latin America in 1991 after a ship from Asia unloaded its contaminated ballast water into the harbor of Callao, Peru. Cholera causes diarrhea so severe its victims can die in a few days from dehydration; in that outbreak more than 300,000 people became ill, and more than 3,000 died.

The modern world is becoming—to paraphrase the words of the microbiologist Stephen S. Morse of Columbia University—a viral superhighway. Everyone is at risk.

Our newly global society is characterized by huge increases in population, international travel and international trade—factors that enable diseases to spread much more readily than ever before from person to person and from continent to continent. By 2020 the world population will have surpassed seven billion, and half those people will be living in urban centers. Beleaguered third-world nations are already hard-pressed to provide sewers, plumbing and other infrastructure; in the future, clean water and adequate sanitation could become increasingly rare. Meanwhile, political upheavals regularly cause millions of people to flee their homelands and gather in refugee camps, which become petri dishes for germs.

More than 500 million people cross international borders each year on commercial flights. Not only does that traffic volume dramatically increase the chance a sick person will infect the inhabitants of a distant area when she reaches her destination; it also exposes the sick person's fellow passengers to the disease, because of poor air circulation on planes. Many of those passengers can, in turn, pass the disease on to others when they disembark.

T he global economy that has arisen in the past two decades has established a myriad of connections between far-flung places. Not too long ago bananas and oranges were rare treats in northern climes. Now you can walk into your neighborhood market and find food that has been flown and trucked in from all over the world: oranges from Israel, apples from New Zealand, avocados from California. Consumers in affluent nations expect to be able to buy whatever they want whenever they want it. What people do not generally realize, however, is that this global network of food production and delivery provides countless pathways for pathogens. Raspberries from Guatemala, carrots from Peru and coconut milk from Thailand have been responsible for recent outbreaks of food poisoning in the United States. And the problem cuts both ways: contaminated radish seeds and frozen beef from the United States have ended up in Japan and South Korea.

Finally, the widespread and often indiscriminate use of antibiotics has played a key role in spurring disease. Forty million pounds of antibiotics are manufactured annually in the United States, an eightyfold increase since 1954. Dangerous microorganisms have evolved accordingly, often developing antibiotic-resistant strains. Physicians are now faced with penicillin-resistant gonorrhea, multiple-drug-resistant tuberculosis and E. coli variants such as 0157:H7. And frighteningly, some enterococcus bacteria have become resistant to all known antibiotics. Enterococcus infections are rare, but staphylococcus infections are not, and many strains of staph bacteria now respond to just one antibiotic, vancomycin. How long will it be before run-of-the-mill staph infections—in a boil, for instance, or in a surgical incision—become untreatable?

Although civilization can expose people to new pathogens, cultural progress also has an obvious countervailing effect: it can provide tools—medicines, sensible city planning, educational campaigns about sexually transmitted diseases—to fight the encroachments of disease. Moreover, since biology seems to side with microorganisms anyway, people have little choice but to depend on protective cultural practices to keep pace: vaccinations, for instance, to confer immunity, combined with practices such as hand-washing by physicians between patient visits, to limit contact between people and pathogens.

All too often, though, obvious protective measures such as using only clean hypodermic needles or treating urban drinking water with chlorine are neglected, whether out of ignorance or a wrongheaded emphasis on the short-term financial costs. The worldwide disparity in wealth is also to blame: not surprisingly, the advances made during the second epidemiological transition were limited largely to the affluent of the industrial world.

Such lapses are now beginning to teach the bitter lesson that the delicate balance between humans and invasive microorganisms can tip the other way again. Overconfidence—the legacy of the second epidemiological transition—has made us especially vulnerable to emerging and reemerging diseases. Evolutionary principles can provide this useful corrective: in spite of all our medical and technological hubris, there is no quick fix. If human beings are to overcome the current crisis, it will be through sensible changes in behavior, such as increased condom use and improved sanitation, combined with a commitment to stop disturbing the ecological balance of the planet.

The Bible, in short, was not far from wrong: We do bring plagues upon ourselves—not by sinning, but by refusing to heed our own alarms, our own best judgment. The price of peace—or at least peaceful coexistence—with the microorganisms on this planet is eternal vigilance.

GEORGE J. ARMELAGOS is a professor of anthropology at Emory University in Atlanta, Georgia. He has coedited two books on the evolution of human disease: *Paleopathology at the Origins of Agriculture,* which deals with prehistoric populations, and *Disease in Populations in Transition,* which focuses on contemporary societies.

The Perfect Plague

The next killer germ could burst from the African rain forest—or from your family pet.

JARED DIAMOND AND NATHAN WOLFE

Shortly after one of us (Jared Diamond) boarded a flight from Hong Kong back to Los Angeles, the passenger in the next seat sneezed. She sneezed again—and again— and then she began coughing. Finally she gagged, pulled out the vomit bag from the seat back in front of her, threw up into the bag, stood up, squeezed past, and lurched to the toilet at the front of the plane. The woman was obviously miserable, but sympathy for her pain was not what I felt. Instead I was frightened and asked the flight attendant to move me to a seat as far from her as possible.

All I could think of was another sick person, a man from Guangdong province in southern China, who spent the night of February 21, 2003, at the Metropole Hotel in Hong Kong, an upscale establishment with a swimming pool, fitness center, restaurants, a bar, and all kinds of areas where visitors could socialize and connect. The man stayed a single night in room 911. Unfortunately for him and for many other people, he had picked up severe acute respiratory syndrome, or SARS— perhaps directly from an infected bat or from a small, arboreal mammal called a civet, common in one of Guangdong's famous "wet markets" that sell wild animals for food, or else from a person or chain of people ultimately infected from one of those animal sources.

In the course of his brief stay, the man initiated a SARS "super spreader" event that led to at least 16 more SARS cases among the hotel's guests and visitors and then to hundreds of other cases throughout Asia, Europe, and North America as those guests and visitors continued on their travels—just as my neighbor was now traveling to L.A. The infectiousness of room 911's guest can be gauged from the fact that three months later, the carpet right outside the door and near the hotel elevator yielded genetic evidence of the SARS virus, presumably spewed out in his own sneezing, coughing, or vomiting.

I didn't end up with SARS, but my experience drives home the terrifying prospect of a novel, unstoppable infectious disease. Globalization, changing climate, and the threat of drug resistance have conspired to set the stage for that perfect microbial storm: a situation in which an emerging pathogen—another HIV or smallpox, perhaps—might burst on the scene and kill millions before we can respond.

Pathogen Paradox

To grasp the risk, we first must understand why *any* microbe would evolve to sicken or kill us. In evolutionary terms, how does destroying its host help a microbe to survive?

Think of your body as a potential "habitat" for tiny microbes, just as a forest provides a habitat for bigger creatures like birds and squirrels. The species living in the forests of our bodies include lice, worms, bacteria, viruses, and amoebas. Many of those denizens are benign and cause us no harm. But some microbes seem to go out of their way to make us sick—either mildly sick, as in the case of the common cold, or else sick to the point of killing us, as in the case of smallpox.

Killer microbes have long posed a paradox for evolutionary biologists. Why would a microbe evolve to devastate the very habitat on which it depends? By analogy, you might reason that there should be no squirrels that destroy the forest they live in, because such a species would quickly go extinct.

The answer stems from the fact that in order to survive over the long haul, any microbe restricted to humans must be able to spread from one victim to the next. There is a simple mathematical requirement here: On average, the germ must infect at least one new victim for every old one who either dies or recovers and purges himself of the microbe. If the average number of new victims per old drops to fewer than one, then the spread of the microbe is doomed.

A microbe can't walk or fly from one host to the next. Instead it must resort to a range of nefarious tricks. What from our point of view is simply a disease symptom can, from the bug's perspective, be an all-important means of enlisting our help to move around. Common microbe tricks are to make us cough or sneeze, suffer from diarrhea, or develop open sores on our skin. Respectively, these symptoms spread the microbe into our exhaled breath, into the local water supply via our feces, and onto the skin of those who touch us, explaining why a microbe might want to induce unpleasant symptoms in its victims.

Evolutionary biologists reason that keeping us alive and pumping out new microbes would be an excellent strategy for such a bug, which might therefore evolve to be less, not more, virulent over time. An example comes from the history of syphilis. When it first appeared in Europe in 1495, it caused severe and painful symptoms within a few months, but by 1546 it had begun evolving into the slowly progressing disease that we know today.

Yet if keeping us alive is strategically sound, why do some pathogens go so far as to actually kill us?

Sometimes a microbe's deadly rampage through a human population stems from an accident of nature. For instance, the microbe could be comfortably adapted to some animal host that it routinely inhabits without deadly consequences, but it could be maladapted to the human environment. The microbe may rarely infect people, but when it does, it may kill the human host, who becomes a literal dead end for the virus as well.

A microbe's deadly rampage through humans might stem from an accident of nature.

But what of those killer microbes that target humans, making us their primary host? Their survival strategy, evolutionary biologists now realize, differs from that of a disease like syphilis but works just as well. Take the cholera bacterium that gives us diarrhea or the smallpox virus that makes us develop skin sores; both of these can kill us in days to weeks. Such virulence may be evolutionary favored if, in the brief time between our becoming infected and dying, the fatal symptoms spread trillions of microbes to potential new victims. The fact that we may die is unfortunate for us but an acceptable cost for the microbe. In the world of evolution and natural selection, anything that the microbe does to us is fair—just as long as at least one new victim gets infected for each old one.

Hence the recipe for a killer disease is for the microbe to achieve a balance between two things: the probability of its killing us quickly once we become infected and its efficiency in leading our bodies to transmit the microbe to new victims.

Humanity's greatest predators can be seen only with the aid of a microscope. The virus responsible for AIDS; the SARS virus; *Vibrio cholerae* bacteria, responsible for cholera; and spores of anthrax.

Those two things are connected. The greater its efficiency in inducing lethal, bug-spreading syndromes (good for the microbe), the faster the microbe kills us (bad for the microbe). Following this logic, a pathogen may end up killing lots of people by one of two routes. In the style of HIV, it can keep the disease carrier alive for a long time, infecting new victims over the course of months or years. Or in the style of smallpox and cholera, it might kill quickly with explosive symptoms that can spread an infection to dozens of new victims within a day.

Searching for the Source

For epidemiologists hoping to stanch such outbreaks, tracking killer germs to the source is key. Do deadly pandemics arise spontaneously in human populations? Or are they "gifts" from other species, mutating and then crossing over to make us ill? Which ecosystems are spawning them, and can we catch them at the start, before they cause too much damage?

Some answers can be found in the history of yellow fever, a virus spread by mosquitoes. The cause of devastating human epidemics throughout history, yellow fever is still rife in tropical South America and Africa. Biologists now understand that yellow fever arose in tropical African monkeys, which, through the mosquito vector, infected (and continue to infect) tropical African people, some of whom unintentionally carried yellow fever with them on slave ships several hundred years ago to South America.

Mosquitoes bit the infected slaves and in turn carried the virus to South American monkeys. In due course, mosquitoes bit infected monkeys and transmitted yellow fever right back to the human population there.

In Venezuela today, the Ministry of Health keeps a lookout for the appearance of unusual numbers of dead wild monkeys, such as howler monkeys. Because the monkeys are so susceptible to yellow fever and can act as a reservoir from which the virus leaps to the human population, an explosion of monkey deaths serves as an advance warning system, signaling the need to vaccinate humans in the vicinity.

This pattern of cross-infection from animals to humans is par for the course in emerging infectious disease. In fact, the big killer diseases of history all came to us from microbes living in other species, overwhelmingly from other warm-blooded mammals and, to a lesser extent, from birds.

On reflection, this all makes sense. Each new animal host to which a microbe adapts represents a new habitat. It is easiest for a microbe to jump between closely related habitats, from an animal species with one sort of body chemistry to a closely related animal species with very similar body chemistry.

In the tropics, disease sources have included a host of wild animals, most notably the nonhuman primates. We can thank our primate cousins not just for yellow fever but also for HIV, dengue fever, hepatitis B, and vivax malaria. Other wild animal disease donors include rats, the source of the plague and typhus.

In temperate regions like the United States, meanwhile, ticks in suburban neighborhoods and domestic livestock living in proximity to humans have posed threats. Mammalian reservoirs like mice and chipmunks carry Lyme disease and tularemia; ticks transmit these diseases to humans. Cattle probably gave rise to the measles and tuberculosis. Smallpox is likely to have come from camels, biologists say, and flu from pigs and ducks.

The Next Wave

Today, with fewer people tending farms and more living in the suburbs, things have certainly changed. The principles of infectious disease are the same as they have always been, but modern conditions, including life in proximity to pets and mammal-filled woods, are exposing us to new pathogen reservoirs and new modes of transmitting disease.

One of us (Nathan Wolfe) has spent much of the last six years in the tropical African country of Cameroon, studying the kinds of interspecies jumps that such conditions might spawn. To examine the mechanisms, I worked with rural hunters who butchered wild animals for food. I collected blood samples from the hunters, from other people in their community, and from their animal prey. By testing all those samples, I identified microbes inhabiting the animal reservoirs and focused on those that showed up in the hunters' blood, making them candidates for firing up human disease.

Three strains of influenza virus, including H5N1, better known as the avian flu virus. The influenza virus frequently mutates, creating new strains. This makes it difficult to produce vaccines and opens the door to another global influenza pandemic, such as the one that struck in 1918 and eventually killed more than 20 million people.

One evening I asked a group of hunters if they had ever cut themselves while butchering wild monkeys or apes. The response was incredulous laughter: "You don't know the answer to that?" Of course, they said. All of them had cut themselves once or more, thereby giving themselves ample opportunity to get infected from animal blood.

On reflection, I shouldn't have been surprised. I can't count all the times I have cut myself while chopping onions. The difference is that onions aren't closely related to us humans, and an onion virus has far less chance of taking hold in us than does a monkey virus.

The statistics are telling. Researchers like Mark Woolhouse, professor of infectious disease epidemiology at the University of Edinburgh in Scotland, have found at least 868 human pathogens that infect both animals and humans, although some are not as fearsome as they seem.

Overhyped microbes include anthrax (famous for the U.S. mail attacks in 2000), the Ebola and Marburg viruses (which can cause dramatic bleeding and high fever in their victims), and the prion agent of mad cow disease (otherwise known as bovine spongiform encephalopathy, or BSE), which kills people by making their nervous systems degenerate. These bugs arouse terror because they kill so many of their victims. For example, in the 2000 Ebola outbreak, which struck the Gulu district of

Uganda, 53 percent of the 425 people who contracted the disease died. The case fatality rate for BSE is 100 percent.

Although spectacularly lethal, these pathogens generally kill just a few hundred people at a time and then burn themselves out. They transmit from human to human too inefficiently to spread very widely; 100 percent of a small number of victims is still a small number of fatalities.

There are many reasons why an agent leaping from animals to humans might not affect more individuals. For example, humans do not normally bite, scratch, hunt, or eat each other. This surely contributes to the rarity or nonexistence of human-to-human transmission of rabies (acquired by the bite of an infected dog or bat); cat-scratch disease (which causes skin lesions and swollen lymph nodes); tularemia (a disease, often acquired when hunting and cutting up an infected rabbit, that can cause skin ulcers, swollen lymph nodes, and fever); and BSE (probably acquired by eating the nervous system tissue of infected cows).

Some outbreaks, once recognized, are relatively easy to control. Anthrax is treatable with antibiotics; after an initial malaria-like stage, the rapid onset and severity of Ebola and Marburg symptoms have made identification and containment straightforward.

In fact, within the last 40 years, only HIV (derived from chimpanzees) has taken off to cause a pandemic.

Back to the Future

If not anthrax or Ebola, which pathogens might spawn the next deadly pandemic in our midst?

New pandemics are most likely to be triggered by mutant strains of familiar microbe species, especially those that have caused plagues by churning out mutant strains in the past. For example, the highest known epidemic death toll in history was caused by a new strain of influenza virus that killed more than 20 million people in 1918 and 1919. Unfairly named Spanish influenza, it apparently emerged in Kansas during World War I, was carried by American troops to Europe, arid then spread around the world in three waves before ebbing in outbreaks of declining virulence in the 1920s. Mutant strains of influenza or cholera remain prime candidates for another deadly outbreak. Both can persist in animal reservoirs or the environment, and both are adept at spawning new strains. Both pathogens also transmit efficiently, and it is possible that these two important diseases of the past could become important diseases of the future.

Attention often focuses on exotic diseases like that caused by the Ebola virus, but we should be more worried about familiar foes, such as the strain of influenza known as Russian flu, which caused an epidemic in 1977, or the bacteria (bottom) that cause tuberculosis.

A future pandemic could also come from tuberculosis. New mutants have already arisen through the mechanism of drug resistance. And the disease lives on in the human population, especially among those with weakened immunity, including patients with HIV.

Also of concern are emerging sexually transmitted diseases, which, once introduced, may be difficult to control because it is hard to persuade humans to change sexual behavior or to abstain from sex. HIV offers a grim warning: Despite its huge global impact, the AIDS epidemic would have been far worse if the sexual transmissibility of HIV (which is actually rather modest) had equaled that of some other sexually transmitted agents, such as human papilloma virus (HPV). While the probability of HIV transmission varies with the stage of the disease and the type of sexual contact, it appears to pass from infected to uninfected individuals in less than 1 percent of acts of unprotected heterosexual intercourse, while the corresponding probability of HPV transmission is thought to be higher than 5 percent—probably much higher.

Similarly, it could be difficult to control emerging pathogens transmitted by pets, which increasingly include exotic species along with traditional domestic animals like dogs and cats. Already we are at risk of catching rabies from our dogs, toxoplasmosis and cat-scratch disease from our cats, and psittacosis from our parrots. Most people now accept the need to cull millions of farmyard animals in the face of epidemics like mad cow disease, but it is hard to imagine killing beloved puppies, bunnies, and kittens, even if those pets do turn out to offer a pathway for a dangerous new disease.

Have Plague, Will Travel

Once a killer disease has emerged, modern societies offer new ways for it to flourish and spread. Global travel, the close quarters of the urban environment, climate change, the evolution of drug-resistant microbes, and increasing numbers of the elderly or antibiotic-treated immunosuppressed could all aid the next great plague.

For example, rapid urbanization in Africa could transform yellow fever, Chikungunya fever (which causes severe joint pain and fever), and other rural African arboviruses (viruses, including yellow fever, spread by bloodsucking insects) into plagues of African cities, as has already happened with dengue hemorrhagic fever. One of us (Wolfe) theorizes that this might follow increasing demand in those cities for bush meat. Like urban people everywhere, urban Africans love to eat the foods enjoyed by their village-dwelling ancestors, and in tropical Africa this means bush meat. In that respect it's similar to the smoked fish and bagels that I eat in the United States, which give me some comforting memory of my Eastern European roots. But there's an important difference: The wild game that I see served in fancy restaurants in the capital of Cameroon is much more likely to transmit a dangerous virus to the person who hunted and butchered it, or to the cook who prepared it, or to the restaurant patron who ate the meat undercooked, than is my brunch of smoked fish and bagels.

By connecting distant places, meanwhile, globalization permits the long-distance transfer of microbes along with their insect vectors and their human victims, as evidenced not only by the spread of HIV around the world, but also by North American cases of cholera and SARS brought by infected passengers on jet flights from South America and Asia, respectively. Indeed, when a flight from Buenos Aires to Los Angeles stopped in Lima in 1992, it picked up some seafood infected with the cholera then making the rounds in Peru. As a result, dozens of passengers who arrived in Los Angeles, some of whom then changed planes and flew on to Nevada and even as far as Japan, found that they had contracted cholera. Within days that single airplane spread cholera 10,000 miles around the whole rim of the Pacific Basin.

The tuberculosis bacterium, *Mycobacterium tuberculosis,* has developed a resistance to antibiotics in many regions of the world, fueling a resurgence of this disease.

Consider as well those diseases thought of as "just" tropical because they are transmitted by tropical vectors: malaria transmitted by mosquitoes, sleeping sickness spread by tsetse flies, and Chagas' disease (associated with edema, fever, and heart disease) spread by kissing bugs. How will we feel about those tropical diseases if global warming enables their vectors to spread into temperate zones? While microbe and vector movement can be difficult to detect, modeling suggests that global warming will expand the reach of malaria to higher latitudes and into tropical mountain regions.

The transmission of emerging diseases has also been enhanced by a host of modern practices and technologies. The commercial bush meat trade has introduced retroviruses into human populations. Ecotourism has exposed first-world tourists to cutaneous leishmaniasis and other third-world diseases. Underequipped rural hospitals have facilitated Ebola virus outbreaks in Africa. Air conditioners and water circulation systems have spread Legionnaires' disease. Industrial food production was responsible in Europe for the spread of BSE. And intravenous drug use and blood transfusion have both spread HIV and hepatitis B and C.

We have the potential to avert the next HIV, saving millions of lives and billions of dollars.

All this shows that disease prevention and treatment need to be supplemented by a new effort: disease forecasting. This refers to the early detection of potential pandemics at a stage when we might still be able to localize them, before they have had the opportunity to infect a high percentage of the local population and thereby spread around the world, as happened with HIV. Already one of us (Wolfe) is working through a new initiative, the Global Viral Forecasting Initiative (GVFI), to do just that. GVFI works in countries throughout the world to monitor the entry and movement of new agents before they become pandemics. By studying emerging agents at the interface between humans and animals, GVFI hopes to stop new epidemics before they explode. Monitoring for the emergence of both new sexually transmitted diseases and pet-associated diseases would be good investments.

The predictions here are admittedly educated guesses—but they are educated by some of the best science available. The time to act is now. If we don't, then we will continue to be like the cardiologists of the 1950s, waiting for their patients' heart attacks and doing little to prevent them. If we do act, we have the potential to avert the next HIV, saving millions of lives and billions of dollars. The choice seems obvious.

The Inuit Paradox

How can people who gorge on fat and rarely see a vegetable be healthier than we are?

Patricia Gadsby

Patricia Cochran, an Inupiat from Northwestern Alaska, is talking about the native foods of her childhood: "We pretty much had a subsistence way of life. Our food supply was right outside our front door. We did our hunting and foraging on the Seward Peninsula and along the Bering Sea."

"Our meat was seal and walrus, marine mammals that live in cold water and have lots of fat. We used seal oil for our cooking and as a dipping sauce for food. We had moose, caribou, and reindeer. We hunted ducks, geese, and little land birds like quail, called ptarmigan. We caught crab and lots of fish—salmon, whitefish, tomcod, pike, and char. Our fish were cooked, dried, smoked, or frozen. We ate frozen raw whitefish, sliced thin. The elders liked stinkfish, fish buried in seal bags or cans in the tundra and left to ferment. And fermented seal flipper, they liked that too."

Cochran's family also received shipments of whale meat from kin living farther north, near Barrow. Beluga was one she liked; raw muktuk, which is whale skin with its underlying blubber, she definitely did not. "To me it has a chew-on-a-tire consistency," she says, "but to many people it's a mainstay." In the short subarctic summers, the family searched for roots and greens and, best of all from a child's point of view, wild blueberries, crowberries, or salmonberries, which her aunts would mix with whipped fat to make a special treat called *akutuq*—in colloquial English, Eskimo ice cream.

Now Cochran directs the Alaska Native Science Commission, which promotes research on native cultures and the health and environmental issues that affect them. She sits at her keyboard in Anchorage, a bustling city offering fare from Taco Bell to French cuisine. But at home Cochran keeps a freezer filled with fish, seal, walrus, reindeer, and whale meat, sent by her family up north, and she and her husband fish and go berry picking—"sometimes a challenge in Anchorage," she adds, laughing. "I eat fifty-fifty," she explains, half traditional, half regular American.

No one, not even residents of the northernmost villages on Earth, eats an entirely traditional northern diet anymore. Even the groups we came to know as Eskimo—which include the Inupiat and the Yupiks of Alaska, the Canadian Inuit and Inuvialuit, Inuit Greenlanders, and the Siberian Yupiks—have probably seen more changes in their diet in a lifetime than their ancestors did over thousands of years. The closer people live to towns and the more access they have to stores and cash-paying jobs, the more likely they are to have westernized their eating. And with westernization, at least on the North American continent, comes processed foods and cheap carbohydrates—Crisco, Tang, soda, cookies, chips, pizza, fries. "The young and urbanized," says Harriet Kuhnlein, director of the Centre for Indigenous Peoples' Nutrition and Environment at McGill University in Montreal, "are increasingly into fast food." So much so that type 2 diabetes, obesity, and other diseases of Western civilization are becoming causes for concern there too.

Today, when diet books top the best-seller list and nobody seems sure of what to eat to stay healthy, it's surprising to learn how well the Eskimo did on a high-protein, high-fat diet. Shaped by glacial temperatures, stark landscapes, and protracted winters, the traditional Eskimo diet had little in the way of plant food, no agricultural or dairy products, and was unusually low in carbohydrates. Mostly people subsisted on what they hunted and fished. Inland dwellers took advantage of caribou feeding on tundra mosses, lichens, and plants too tough for humans to stomach (though predigested vegetation in the animals' paunches became dinner as well). Coastal people exploited the sea. The main nutritional challenge was avoiding starvation in late winter if primary meat sources became too scarce or lean.

These foods hardly make up the "balanced" diet most of us grew up with, and they look nothing like the mix of grains, fruits, vegetables, meat, eggs, and dairy we're accustomed to seeing in conventional food pyramid diagrams. How could such a diet possibly be adequate? How did people get along on little else but fat and animal protein?

The diet of the far north shows that there are no essential foods—only essential nutrients.

What the diet of the Far North illustrates, says Harold Draper, a biochemist and expert in Eskimo nutrition, is that there are no essential foods—only essential nutrients. And humans can get those nutrients from diverse and eye-opening sources.

One might, for instance, imagine gross vitamin deficiencies arising from a diet with scarcely any fruits and vegetables. What furnishes vitamin A, vital for eyes and bones? We derive much of ours from colorful plant foods, constructing it from pigmented plant precursors called carotenoids (as in carrots). But vitamin A, which is oil soluble, is also plentiful in the oils of cold-water fishes and sea mammals, as well as in the animals' livers, where fat is processed. These dietary staples also provide vitamin D, another oil-soluble vitamin needed for bones. Those of us living in temperate and tropical climates, on the other hand, usually make vitamin D indirectly by exposing skin to strong sun—hardly an option in the Arctic winter—and by consuming fortified cow's milk, to which the indigenous northern groups had little access until recent decades and often don't tolerate all that well.

As for vitamin C, the source in the Eskimo diet was long a mystery. Most animals can synthesize their own vitamin C, or ascorbic acid, in their livers, but humans are among the exceptions, along with other primates and oddballs like guinea pigs and bats. If we don't ingest enough of it, we fall apart from scurvy, a gruesome connective-tissue disease. In the United States today we can get ample supplies from orange juice, citrus fruits, and fresh vegetables. But vitamin C oxidizes with time; getting enough from a ship's provisions was tricky for early 18th- and 19th-century voyagers to the polar regions. Scurvy—joint pain, rotting gums, leaky blood vessels, physical and mental degeneration—plagued European and U.S. expeditions even in the 20th century. However, Arctic peoples living on fresh fish and meat were free of the disease.

Impressed, the explorer Vilhjalmur Stefansson adopted an Eskimo-style diet for five years during the two Arctic expeditions he led between 1908 and 1918. "The thing to do is to find your antiscorbutics where you are," he wrote. "Pick them up as you go." In 1928, to convince skeptics, he and a young colleague spent a year on an Americanized version of the diet under medical supervision at Bellevue Hospital in New York City. The pair ate steaks, chops, organ meats like brain and liver, poultry, fish, and fat with gusto. "If you have

some fresh meat in your diet every day and don't overcook it," Stefansson declared triumphantly, "there will be enough C from that source alone to prevent scurvy."

In fact, all it takes to ward off scurvy is a daily dose of 10 milligrams, says Karen Fediuk, a consulting dietitian and former graduate student of Harriet Kuhnlein's who did her master's thesis on vitamin C. (That's far less than the U.S. recommended daily allowance of 75 to 90 milligrams—75 for women, 90 for men.) Native foods easily supply those 10 milligrams of scurvy prevention, especially when organ meats—preferably raw—are on the menu. For a study published with Kuhnlein in 2002, Fediuk compared the vitamin C content of 100-gram (3.55-ounce) samples of foods eaten by Inuit women living in the Canadian Arctic: Raw caribou liver supplied almost 24 milligrams, seal brain close to 15 milligrams, and raw kelp more than 28 milligrams. Still higher levels were found in whale skin and muktuk.

As you might guess from its antiscorbutic role, vitamin C is crucial for the synthesis of connective tissue, including the matrix of skin. "Wherever collagen's made, you can expect vitamin C," says Kuhnlein. Thick skinned, chewy, and collagen rich, raw muktuk can serve up an impressive 36 milligrams in a 100-gram piece, according to Fediuk's analyses. "Weight for weight, it's as good as orange juice," she says. Traditional Inuit practices like freezing meat and fish and frequently eating them raw, she notes, conserve vitamin C, which is easily cooked off and lost in food processing.

Hunter-gatherer diets like those eaten by these northern groups and other traditional diets based on nomadic herding or subsistence farming are among the older approaches to human eating. Some of these eating plans might seem strange to us— diets centered around milk, meat, and blood among the East African pastoralists, enthusiastic tuber eating by the Quechua living in the High Andes, the staple use of the mongongo nut in the southern African !Kung—but all proved resourceful adaptations to particular eco-niches. No people, though, may have been forced to push the nutritional envelope further than those living at Earth's frozen extremes. The unusual makeup of the far-northern diet led Loren Cordain, a professor of evolutionary nutrition at Colorado State University at Fort Collins, to make an intriguing observation.

Four years ago, Cordain reviewed the macronutrient content (protein, carbohydrates, fat) in the diets of 229 hunter-gatherer groups listed in a series of journal articles collectively known as the Ethnographic Atlas. These are some of the oldest surviving human diets. In general, hunter-gatherers tend to eat more animal protein than we do in our standard Western diet, with its reliance on agriculture and carbohydrates derived from grains and starchy plants. Lowest of all in carbohydrate, and highest in combined fat and protein, are the diets of peoples living in the Far North, where they make up for fewer plant foods with extra fish. What's equally striking, though, says Cordain, is that these meat-and-fish diets also exhibit a natural "protein ceiling." Protein accounts for no more than 35 to 40 percent of their total calories, which suggests to him that's all the protein humans can comfortably handle.

Wild-animal fats are different from other fats. Farm animals typically have lots of highly saturated fat.

This ceiling, Cordain thinks, could be imposed by the way we process protein for energy. The simplest, fastest way to make energy is to convert carbohydrates into glucose, our body's primary fuel. But if the body is out of carbs, it can burn fat, or if necessary, break down protein. The name given to the convoluted business of making glucose from protein is gluconeogenesis. It takes place in the liver, uses a dizzying slew of enzymes, and creates nitrogen waste that has to be converted into urea and disposed of through the kidneys. On a truly traditional diet, says Draper, recalling his studies in the 1970s, Arctic people had plenty of protein but little carbohydrate, so they often relied on gluconeogenesis. Not only did they have bigger livers to handle the additional work but their urine volumes were also typically larger to get rid of the extra urea. Nonetheless, there appears to be a limit on how much protein the human liver can safely cope with: Too much overwhelms the liver's waste-disposal system, leading to protein poisoning—nausea, diarrhea, wasting, and death.

Whatever the metabolic reason for this syndrome, says John Speth, an archaeologist at the University of Michigan's Museum of Anthropology, plenty of evidence shows that hunters through the ages avoided protein excesses, discarding fat-depleted animals even when food was scarce. Early pioneers and trappers in North America encountered what looks like a similar affliction, sometimes referred to as rabbit starvation because rabbit meat is notoriously lean. Forced to subsist on fat-deficient meat, the men would gorge themselves, yet wither away. Protein can't be the sole source of energy for humans, concludes Cordain. Anyone eating a meaty diet that is low in carbohydrates must have fat as well.

Stefansson had arrived at this conclusion, too, while living among the Copper Eskimo. He recalled how he and his Eskimo companions had become quite ill after weeks of eating "caribou so skinny that there was no appreciable fat behind the eyes or in the marrow." Later he agreed to repeat the miserable experience at Bellevue Hospital, for science's sake, and for a while ate nothing but defatted meat. "The symptoms brought on at Bellevue by an incomplete meat diet [lean without fat] were exactly the same as in the Arctic

. . . diarrhea and a feeling of general baffling discomfort," he wrote. He was restored with a fat fix but "had lost considerable weight." For the remainder of his year on meat, Stefansson tucked into his rations of chops and steaks with fat intact. "A normal meat diet is not a high-protein diet," he pronounced. "We were really getting three-quarters of our calories from fat." (Fat is more than twice as calorie dense as protein or carbohydrate, but even so, that's a lot of lard. A typical U.S diet provides about 35 percent of its calories from fat.)

Stefansson dropped 10 pounds on his meat-and-fat regimen and remarked on its "slenderizing" aspect, so perhaps it's no surprise he's been co-opted as a posthumous poster boy for Atkins-type diets. No discussion about diet these days can avoid Atkins. Even some researchers interviewed for this article couldn't resist referring to the Inuit way of eating as the "original Atkins." "Superficially, at a macro-nutrient level, the two diets certainly look similar," allows Samuel Klein, a nutrition researcher at Washington University in St. Louis, who's attempting to study how Atkins stacks up against conventional weight-loss diets. Like the Inuit diet, Atkins is low in carbohydrates and very high in fat. But numerous researchers, including Klein, point out that there are profound differences between the two diets, beginning with the type of meat and fat eaten.

Fats have been demonized in the United States, says Eric Dewailly, a professor of preventive medicine at Laval University in Quebec. But all fats are not created equal. This lies at the heart of a paradox—the Inuit paradox, if you will. In the Nunavik villages in northern Quebec, adults over 40 get almost half their calories from native foods, says Dewailly, and they don't die of heart attacks at nearly the same rates as other Canadians or Americans. Their cardiac death rate is about half of ours, he says. As someone who looks for links between diet and cardiovascular health, he's intrigued by that reduced risk. Because the traditional Inuit diet is "so restricted," he says, it's easier to study than the famously heart-healthy Mediterranean diet, with its cornucopia of vegetables, fruits, grains, herbs, spices, olive oil, and red wine.

A key difference in the typical Nunavik Inuit's diet is that more than 50 percent of the calories in Inuit native foods come from fats. Much more important, the fats come from wild animals.

Wild-animal fats are different from both farm-animal fats and processed fats, says Dewailly. Farm animals, cooped up and stuffed with agricultural grains (carbohydrates) typically have lots of solid, highly saturated fat. Much of our processed food is also riddled with solid fats, or so-called trans fats, such as the reengineered vegetable oils and shortenings cached in baked goods and snacks. "A lot of the packaged food on supermarket shelves contains them. So do commercial french fries," Dewailly adds.

Trans fats are polyunsaturated vegetable oils tricked up to make them more solid at room temperature. Manufacturers do this by hydrogenating the oils—adding extra hydrogen atoms to their molecular structures—which "twists" their shapes. Dewailly makes twisting sound less like a chemical transformation than a perversion, an act of public-health sabotage: "These man-made fats are dangerous, even worse for the heart than saturated fats." They not only lower high-density lipoprotein cholesterol (HDL, the "good" cholesterol) but they also raise low-density lipoprotein cholesterol (LDL, the "bad" cholesterol) and triglycerides, he says. In the process, trans fats set the stage for heart attacks because they lead to the increase of fatty buildup in artery walls.

Wild animals that range freely and eat what nature intended, says Dewailly, have fat that is far more healthful. Less of their fat is saturated, and more of it is in the mono-unsaturated form (like olive oil). What's more, cold-water fishes and sea mammals are particularly rich in polyunsaturated fats called n-3 fatty acids or omega-3 fatty acids. These fats appear to benefit the heart and vascular system. But the polyunsaturated fats in most Americans' diets are the omega-6 fatty acids supplied by vegetable oils. By contrast, whale blubber consists of 70 percent monounsaturated fat and close to 30 percent omega-3s, says Dewailly.

Dieting is the price we pay for too little exercise and too much mass-produced food.

Omega-3s evidently help raise HDL cholesterol, lower triglycerides, and are known for anticlotting effects. (Ethnographers have remarked on an Eskimo propensity for nosebleeds.) These fatty acids are believed to protect the heart from life-threatening arrhythmias that can lead to sudden cardiac death. And like a "natural aspirin," adds Dewailly, omega-3 polyunsaturated fats help put a damper on runaway inflammatory processes, which play a part in atherosclerosis, arthritis, diabetes, and other so-called diseases of civilization.

You can be sure, however, that Atkins devotees aren't routinely eating seal and whale blubber. Besides the acquired taste problem, their commerce is extremely restricted in the United States by the Marine Mammal Protection Act, says Bruce Holub, a nutritional biochemist in the department of human biology and nutritional sciences at the University of Guelph in Ontario.

"In heartland America it's probable they're not eating in an Eskimo-like way," says Gary Foster, clinical director of the Weight and Eating Disorders Program at the Pennsylvania School of Medicine. Foster, who describes himself as open-minded about Atkins, says he'd nonetheless worry if people saw the diet as a green light to eat all the butter and bacon—saturated fats—they want. Just before rumors

surfaced that Robert Atkins had heart and weight problems when he died, Atkins officials themselves were stressing saturated fat should account for no more than 20 percent of dieters' calories. This seems to be a clear retreat from the diet's original don't-count-the-calories approach to bacon and butter and its happy exhortations to "plow into those prime ribs." Furthermore, 20 percent of calories from saturated fats is *double* what most nutritionists advise. Before plowing into those prime ribs, readers of a recent edition of the *Dr. Atkins' New Diet Revolution* are urged to take omega-3 pills to help protect their hearts. "If you watch carefully," says Holub wryly, "you'll see many popular U.S. diets have quietly added omega-3 pills, in the form of fish oil or flaxseed capsules, as supplements."

Needless to say, the subsistence diets of the Far North are not "dieting." Dieting is the price we pay for too little exercise and too much mass-produced food. Northern diets were a way of life in places too cold for agriculture, where food, whether hunted, fished, or foraged, could not be taken for granted. They were about keeping weight on.

This is not to say that people in the Far North were fat: Subsistence living requires exercise—hard physical work. Indeed, among the good reasons for native people to maintain their old way of eating, as far as it's possible today, is that it provides a hedge against obesity, type 2 diabetes, and heart disease. Unfortunately, no place on Earth is immune to the spreading taint of growth and development. The very well-being of the northern food chain is coming under threat from global warming, land development, and industrial pollutants in the marine environment. "I'm a pragmatist," says Cochran, whose organization is involved in pollution monitoring and disseminating food-safety information to native villages. "Global warming we don't have control over. But we can, for example, do cleanups of military sites in Alaska or of communication cables leaching lead into fish-spawning areas. We can help communities make informed food choices. A young woman of childbearing age may choose not to eat certain organ meats that concentrate contaminants. As individuals, we do have options. And eating our salmon and our seal is still a heck of a better option than pulling something processed that's full of additives off a store shelf."

Not often in our industrial society do we hear someone speak so familiarly about "our" food animals. We don't talk of "our pig" and "our beef." We've lost that creature feeling, that sense of kinship with food sources. "You're taught to think in boxes," says Cochran. "In our culture the connectivity between humans, animals, plants, the land they live on, and the air they share is ingrained in us from birth.

"You truthfully can't separate the way we get our food from the way we live," she says. "How we get our food is intrinsic to our culture. It's how we pass on our values and knowledge to the young. When you go out with your aunts and uncles to hunt or to gather, you learn to smell the air, watch the wind, understand the way the ice moves, know the land. You get to know where to pick which plant and what animal to take."

"It's part, too, of your development as a person. You share food with your community. You show respect to your elders by offering them the first catch. You give thanks to the animal that gave up its life for your sustenance. So you get all the physical activity of harvesting your own food, all the social activity of sharing and preparing it, and all the spiritual aspects as well," says Cochran. "You certainly don't get all that, do you, when you buy prepackaged food from a store."

"That's why some of us here in Anchorage are working to protect what's ours, so that others can continue to live back home in the villages," she adds. "Because if we don't take care of our food, it won't be there for us in the future. And if we lose our foods, we lose who we are." The word Inupiat means "the real people." "That's who we are," says Cochran.

From *Discover*, October 2004, pp. 48, 50, 52, 54. Copyright © 2004 by Patricia Gadsby. Reprinted by permission of the author.

Dr. Darwin

With a nod to evolution's god, physicians are looking at illness through the lens of natural selection to find out why we get sick and what we can do about it.

Lori Oliwenstein

Paul Ewald knew from the beginning that the Ebola virus outbreak in Zaire would fizzle out. On May 26, after eight days in which only six new cases were reported, that fizzle became official. The World Health Organization announced it would no longer need to update the Ebola figures daily (though sporadic cases continued to be reported until June 20).

The virus had held Zaire's Bandundu Province in its deadly grip for weeks, infecting some 300 people and killing 80 percent of them. Most of those infected hailed from the town of Kikwit. It was all just as Ewald predicted. "When the Ebola outbreak occurred," he recalls, "I said, as I have before, these things are going to pop up, they're going to smolder, you'll have a bad outbreak of maybe 100 or 200 people in a hospital, maybe you'll have the outbreak slip into another isolated community, but then it will peter out on its own."

Ewald is no soothsayer. He's an evolutionary biologist at Amherst College in Massachusetts and perhaps the world's leading expert on how infectious diseases—and the organisms that cause them—evolve. He's also a force behind what some are touting as the next great medical revolution: the application of Darwin's theory of natural selection to the understanding of human diseases.

A Darwinian view can shed some light on how Ebola moves from human to human once it has entered the population. (Between human outbreaks, the virus resides in some as yet unknown living reservoir.) A pathogen can survive in a population, explains Ewald, only if it can easily transmit its progeny from one host to another. One way to do this is to take a long time to disable a host, giving him plenty of time to come into contact with other potential victims. Ebola, however, kills quickly, usually in less than a week. Another way is to survive for a long time outside the human body, so that the pathogen can wait for new hosts to find it. But the Ebola strains encountered thus far are destroyed almost at once by sunlight, and even if no rays reach them, they tend to lose their infectiousness outside the human body within a day. "If you look at it from an evolutionary point of view, you can sort out the 95 percent of disease

organisms that aren't a major threat from the 5 percent that are," says Ewald. "Ebola really isn't one of those 5 percent."

> **If you look at it from an evolutionary point of view, you can sort out the 95 percent of disease organisms that aren't a major threat from the 5 percent that are.**

The earliest suggestion of a Darwinian approach to medicine came in 1980, when George Williams, an evolutionary biologist at the State University of New York at Stony Brook, read an article in which Ewald discussed using Darwinian theory to illuminate the origins of certain symptoms of infectious disease—things like fever, low iron counts, diarrhea. Ewald's approach struck a chord in Williams. Twenty-three years earlier he had written a paper proposing an evolutionary framework for senescence, or aging. "Way back in the 1950s I didn't worry about the practical aspects of senescence, the medical aspects," Williams notes. "I was pretty young then." Now, however, he sat up and took notice.

While Williams was discovering Ewald's work, Randolph Nesse was discovering Williams's. Nesse, a psychiatrist and a founder of the University of Michigan Evolution and Human Behavior Program, was exploring his own interest in the aging process, and he and Williams soon got together. "He had wanted to find a physician to work with on medical problems," says Nesse, "and I had long wanted to find an evolutionary biologist, so it was a very natural match for us." Their collaboration led to a 1991 article that most researchers say signaled the real birth of the field.

Nesse and Williams define Darwinian medicine as the hunt for evolutionary explanations of vulnerabilities to disease. It can, as Ewald noted, be a way to interpret the body's defenses, to try to figure out, say, the reasons we feel pain or get runny noses when we have a cold, and to determine what we should—or shouldn't—be doing about those defenses. For instance, Darwinian researchers like physiologist Matthew Kluger of the Lovelace Institute in Albuquerque now say that a moderate rise in body temperature is more than just a symptom of disease; it's an evolutionary adaptation the body uses to fight infection by making itself inhospitable to invading microbes. It would seem, then, that if you lower the fever, you may prolong the infection. Yet no one is ready to say whether we should toss out our aspirin bottles. "I would love to see a dozen proper studies of whether it's wise to bring fever down when someone has influenza," says Nesse. "It's never been done, and it's just astounding that it's never been done."

Diarrhea is another common symptom of disease, one that's sometimes the result of a pathogen's manipulating your body for its own good purposes, but it may also be a defense mechanism mounted by your body. Cholera bacteria, for example, once they invade the human body, induce diarrhea by producing toxins that make the intestine's cells leaky. The resultant diarrhea then both flushes competing beneficial bacteria from the gut and gives the cholera bacteria a ride into the world, so that they can find another hapless victim. In the case of cholera, then, it seems clear that stopping the diarrhea can only do good.

But the diarrhea that results from an invasion of shigella bacteria—which cause various forms of dysentery—seems to be more an intestinal defense than a bacterial offense. The infection causes the muscles surrounding the gut to contract more frequently, apparently in an attempt to flush out the bacteria as quickly as possible. Studies done more than a decade ago showed that using drugs like Lomotil to decrease the gut's contractions and cut down the diarrheal output actually prolong infection. On the other hand, the ingredients in over-the-counter preparations like Pepto Bismol, which don't affect how frequently the gut contracts, can be used to stem the diarrheal flow without prolonging infection.

Seattle biologist Margie Profet points to menstruation as another "symptom" that may be more properly viewed as an evolutionary defense. As Profet points out, there must be a good reason for the body to engage in such costly activities as shedding the uterine lining and letting blood flow away. That reason, she claims, is to rid the uterus of any organisms that might arrive with sperm in the seminal fluid. If an egg is fertilized, infection may be worth risking. But if there is no fertilized egg, says Profet, the body defends itself by ejecting the uterine cells, which might have been infected. Similarly, Profet has theorized that morning sickness during pregnancy causes the mother to avoid foods that might contain chemicals harmful to a developing fetus. If she's right, blocking that nausea with drugs could result in higher miscarriage rates or more birth defects.

Darwinian medicine isn't simply about which symptoms to treat and which to ignore. It's a way to understand microbes—which, because they evolve so much more quickly than we do, will probably always beat us unless we figure out how to harness their evolutionary power for our own benefit. It's also a way to realize how disease-causing genes that persist in the population are often selected for, not against, in the long run.

Sickle-cell anemia is a classic case of how evolution tallies costs and benefits. Some years ago, researchers discovered that people with one copy of the sickle-cell gene are better able to resist the protozoans that cause malaria than are people with no copies of the gene. People with two copies of the gene may die, but in malaria-plagued regions such as tropical Africa, their numbers will be more than made up for by the offspring left by the disease-resistant kin.

Cystic fibrosis may also persist through such genetic logic. Animal studies indicate that individuals with just one copy of the cystic fibrosis gene may be more resistant to the effects of the cholera bacterium. As is the case with malaria and sickle-cell, cholera is much more prevalent than cystic fibrosis; since there are many more people with a single, resistance-conferring copy of the gene than with a disease-causing double dose, the gene is stably passed from generation to generation.

"With our power to do gene manipulations, there will be temptations to find genes that do things like cause aging, and get rid of them," says Nesse. "If we're sure about everything a gene does, that's fine. But an evolutionary approach cautions us not to go too fast, and to expect that every gene might well have some benefit as well as costs, and maybe some quite unrelated benefit."

Darwinian medicine can also help us understand the problems encountered in the New Age by a body designed for the Stone Age. As evolutionary psychologist Charles Crawford of Simon Fraser University in Burnaby, British Columbia, put it: "I used to hunt saber-toothed tigers all the time, thousands of years ago. I got lots of exercise and all that sort of stuff. Now I sit in front of a computer, and all I do is play with a mouse, and I don't get exercise. So I've changed my body biochemistry in all sorts of unknown ways, and it could affect me in all sorts of ways, and we have no idea what they are."

> I used to hunt saber-toothed tigers all the time, thousands of years ago. I got lots of exercise and all that sort of stuff. Now I sit in front of a computer and don't get exercise, so I've changed my body chemistry.

Radiologist Boyd Eaton of Emory University and his colleagues believe such biochemical changes are behind today's breast cancer epidemic. While it's impossible to study a Stone Ager's biochemistry, there are still groups of hunter-gatherers around—such as the San of Africa—who make admirable stand-ins. A foraging life-style, notes Eaton, also means a lifestyle in which menstruation begins later, the first child is born earlier, there are more children altogether, they are breast-fed for years rather than months, and menopause comes somewhat earlier. Overall, he says, American women today probably experience 3.5 times more menstrual cycles than our ancestors did 10,000 years ago. During each cycle a woman's body is flooded with the hormone estrogen, and breast cancer, as research has found, is very much estrogen related. The more frequently the breasts are exposed to the hormone, the greater the chance that a tumor will take seed.

Depending on which data you choose, women today are somewhere between 10 and 100 times more likely to be stricken with breast cancer than our ancestors were. Eaton's proposed solutions are pretty radical, but he hopes people will at least entertain them; they include delaying puberty with hormones and using hormones to create pseudopregnancies, which offer a woman the biochemical advantages of pregnancy at an early age without requiring her to bear a child.

In general, Darwinian medicine tells us that the organs and systems that make up our bodies result not from the pursuit of perfection but from millions of years of evolutionary compromises designed to get the greatest reproductive benefit at the lowest cost. We walk upright with a spine that evolved while we scampered on four limbs; balancing on two legs leaves our hands free, but we'll probably always suffer some back pain as well.

"What's really different is that up to now people have used evolutionary theory to try to explain why things work, why they're normal," explains Nesse. "The twist—and I don't know if it's simple or profound—is to say we're trying to understand the abnormal, the vulnerability to disease. We're trying to understand why natural selection has not made the body better, why natural selection has left the body with vulnerabilities. For every single disease, there is an answer to that question. And for very few of them is the answer very clear yet."

One reason those answers aren't yet clear is that few physicians or medical researchers have done much serious surveying from Darwin's viewpoint. In many cases, that's because evolutionary theories are hard to test. There's no way to watch human evolution in progress—at best it works on a time scale involving hundreds of thousands of years. "Darwinian medicine is mostly a guessing game about how we think evolution worked in the past on humans, what it designed for us," say evolutionary biologist James Bull of the University of Texas at Austin. "It's almost impossible to test ideas that we evolved to respond to this or that kind of environment. You can make educated guesses, but no one's going to go out and do an experiment to show that yes, in fact humans will evolve this way under these environmental conditions."

Yet some say that these experiments can, should, and will be done. Howard Howland, a sensory physiologist at Cornell, is setting up just such an evolutionary experiment, hoping to interfere with the myopia, or nearsightedness, that afflicts a full quarter of all Americans. Myopia is thought to be the result of a delicate feedback loop that tries to keep images focused on the eye's retina. There's not much room for error: if the length of your eyeball is off by just a tenth of a millimeter, your vision will be blurry. Research has shown that when the eye perceives an image as fuzzy, it compensates by altering its length.

This loop obviously has a genetic component, notes Howland, but what drives it is the environment. During the Stone Age, when we were chasing buffalo in the field, the images we saw were usually sharp and clear. But with modern civilization came a lot of close work. When your eye focuses on something

nearby, the lens has to bend, and since bending that lens is hard work, you do as little bending as you can get away with. That's why, whether you're conscious of it or not, near objects tend to be a bit blurry. "Blurry image?" says the eye. "Time to grow." And the more it grows, the fuzzier those buffalo get. Myopia seems to be a disease of industrial society.

To prevent that disease, Howland suggests going back to the Stone Age—or at least convincing people's eyes that that's where they are. If you give folks with normal vision glasses that make their eyes think they're looking at an object in the distance when they're really looking at one nearby, he says, you'll avoid the whole feedback loop in the first place. "The military academies induct young men and women with twenty-twenty vision who then go through four years of college and are trained to fly an airplane or do some difficult visual task. But because they do so much reading, they come out the other end nearsighted, no longer eligible to do what they were hired to do," Howland notes. "I think these folks would very much like not to become nearsighted in the course of their studies." He hopes to be putting glasses on them within a year.

The numbing pace of evolution is a much smaller problem for researchers interested in how the bugs that plague us do their dirty work. Bacteria are present in such large numbers (one person can carry around more pathogens than there are people on the planet) and evolve so quickly (a single bacterium can reproduce a million times in one human lifetime) that experiments we couldn't imagine in humans can be carried out in microbes in mere weeks. We might even, says Ewald, be able to use evolutionary theory to tame the human immunodeficiency virus.

"HIV is mutating so quickly that surely we're going to have plenty of sources of mutants that are mild as well as severe," he notes. "So now the question is, which of the variants will win?" As in the case of Ebola, he says, it will all come down to how well the virus manages to get from one person to another.

"If there's a great potential for sexual transmission to new partners, then the viruses that reproduce quickly will spread," Ewald says. "And since they're reproducing in a cell type that's critical for the well-being of the host—the helper T cell—then that cell type will be decimated, and the host is likely to suffer from it." On the other hand, if you lower the rate of transmission—through abstinence, monogamy, condom use—then the more severe strains might well die out before they have a chance to be passed very far. "The real question," says Ewald, "is, exactly how mild can you make this virus as a result of reducing the rate at which it could be transmitted to new partners, and how long will it take for this change to occur?" There are already strains of HIV in Senegal with such low virulence, he points out, that most people infected will die of old age. "We don't have all the answers. But I think we're going to be living with this virus for a long time, and if we have to live with it, let's live with a really mild virus instead of a severe virus."

Though condoms and monogamy are not a particularly radical treatment, that they might be used not only to stave off the virus but to tame it is a radical notion—and one that some researchers find suspect. "If it becomes too virulent, it will end up cutting off its own transmission by killing its host too quickly," notes James Bull. "But the speculation is that people transmit HIV primarily within one to five months of infection, when they spike a high level of virus in the blood. So with HIV, the main period of transmission occurs a few months into the infection, and yet the virulence—the death from it—occurs years later. The major stage of transmission is decoupled from the virulence." So unless the protective measures are carried out by everyone, all the time, we won't stop most instances of transmission; after all, most people don't even know they're infected when they pass the virus on.

But Ewald thinks these protective measures are worth a shot. After all, he says, pathogen taming has occurred in the past. The forms of dysentery we encounter in the United States are quite mild because our purified water supplies have cut off the main route of transmission for virulent strains of the bacteria. Not only did hygienic changes reduce the number of cases, they selected for the milder shigella organisms, those that leave their victim well enough to get out and about. Diphtheria is another case in point. When the diphtheria vaccine was invented, it targeted only the most severe form of diphtheria toxin, though for economic rather than evolutionary reasons. Over the years, however, that choice has weeded out the most virulent strains of diphtheria, selecting for the ones that cause few or no symptoms. Today those weaker strains act like another level of vaccine to protect us against new, virulent strains.

"You're doing to these organisms what we did to wolves," says Ewald. "Wolves were dangerous to us, we domesticated them into dogs, and then they helped us, they warned us against the wolves that were out there ready to take our babies. And by doing that, we've essentially turned what was a harmful organism into a helpful organism. That's the same thing we did with diphtheria; we took an organism that was causing harm, and without knowing it, we domesticated it into an organism that is protecting us against harmful ones."

We did with diphtheria what we did with wolves. We took an organism that caused harm, and unknowingly, we domesticated it into an organism that protects us.

Putting together a new scientific discipline—and getting it recognized—is in itself an evolutionary process. Though Williams and Neese say there are hundreds of researchers working (whether they know it or not) within this newly built framework, they realize the field is still in its infancy. It may take some time before *Darwinian medicine* is a household term. Nesse tells how the editor of a prominent medical journal, when asked about the field, replied, "Darwinian medicine? I haven't heard of it, so it can't be very important."

But Darwinian medicine's critics don't deny the field's legitimacy; they point mostly to its lack of hard-and-fast answers, its lack of clear clinical guidelines. "I think this idea will eventually establish itself as a basic science for medicine," answers Nesse. "What did people say, for instance, to the biochemists back in 1900 as they were playing out the Krebs cycle? People would say, 'So what does biochemistry really have to do with medicine? What can you cure now that you couldn't before you knew about the Krebs cycle?' And the biochemists could only say, 'Well, gee, we're not sure, but we know what we're doing is answering important scientific questions, and eventually this will be useful.' And I think exactly the same applies here."

LORI OLIWENSTEIN, a former *Discover* senior editor, is now a freelance journalist based in Los Angeles.

Curse and Blessing of the Ghetto

Tay-Sachs disease is a choosy killer, one that for centuries targeted Eastern European Jews above all others. By decoding its lethal logic, we can learn a lot about how genetic diseases evolve—and how they can be conquered.

JARED DIAMOND

Marie and I hated her at first sight, even though she was trying hard to be helpful. As our obstetrician's genetics counselor, she was just doing her job, explaining to us the unpleasant results that might come out of the genetic tests we were about to have performed. As a scientist, though, I already knew all I wanted to know about Tay-Sachs disease, and I didn't need to be reminded that the baby sentenced to death by it could be my own.

Fortunately, the tests would reveal that my wife and I were not carriers of the Tay-Sachs gene, and our preparenthood fears on that matter at least could be put to rest. But at the time I didn't yet know that. As I glared angrily at that poor genetics counselor, so strong was my anxiety that now, four years later, I can still clearly remember what was going through my mind: If I were an evil deity, I thought, trying to devise exquisite tortures for babies and their parents, I would be proud to have designed Tay-Sachs disease.

Tay-Sachs is completely incurable, unpreventable, and preprogrammed in the genes. A Tay-Sachs infant usually appears normal for the first few months after birth, just long enough for the parents to grow to love him. An exaggerated "startle reaction" to sounds is the first ominous sign. At about six months the baby starts to lose control of his head and can't roll over or sit without support. Later he begins to drool, breaks out into unmotivated bouts of laughter, and suffers convulsions. Then his head grows abnormally large, and he becomes blind. Perhaps what's most frightening for the parents is that their baby loses all contact with his environment and becomes virtually a vegetable. By the child's third birthday, if he's still alive, his skin will turn yellow and his hands pudgy. Most likely he will die before he's four years old.

My wife and I were tested for the Tay-Sachs gene because at the time we rated as high-risk candidates, for two reasons. First, Marie was carrying twins, so we had double the usual chance to bear a Tay-Sachs baby. Second, both she and I are of Eastern European Jewish ancestry, the population with by far the world's highest Tay-Sachs frequency.

In peoples around the world Tay-Sachs appears once in every 400,000 births. But it appears a hundred times more frequently—about once in 3,600 births—among descendants of Eastern European Jews, people known as Ashkenazim. For descendants of most other groups of Jews—Oriental Jews, chiefly from the Middle East, or Sephardic Jews, from Spain and other Mediterranean countries—the frequency of Tay-Sachs disease is no higher than in non-Jews. Faced with such a clear correlation, one cannot help but wonder: What is it about this one group of people that produces such an extraordinarily high risk of this disease?

Finding the answer to this question concerns all of us, regardless of our ancestry. Every human population is especially susceptible to certain diseases, not only because of its life-style but also because of its genetic inheritance. For example, genes put European whites at high risk for cystic fibrosis, African blacks for sickle-cell disease, Pacific Islanders for diabetes—and Eastern European Jews for ten different diseases, including Tay-Sachs. It's not that Jews are notably susceptible to genetic diseases in general; but a combination of historical factors has led to Jews' being intensively studied, and so their susceptibilities are far better known than those of, say, Pacific Islanders.

Tay-Sachs exemplifies how we can deal with such diseases; it has been the object of the most successful screening program to date. Moreover, Tay-Sachs is helping us understand how ethnic diseases evolve. Within the past couple of years discoveries by molecular biologists have provided tantalizing clues to precisely how a deadly gene can persist and spread over the centuries. Tay-Sachs may be primarily a disease of Eastern European Jews, but through this affliction of one group of people, we gain a window on how our genes simultaneously curse and bless us all.

The disease's hyphenated name comes from the two physicians—British ophthalmologist W. Tay and New York neurologist B. Sachs—who independently first recognized the disease, in 1881 and 1887, respectively. By 1896 Sachs had seen enough cases to realize that the disease was most common among Jewish children.

Not until 1962, however, were researchers able to trace the cause of the affliction to a single biochemical abnormality: the excessive accumulation in nerve cells of a fatty substance called G_{M2} ganglioside. Normally G_{M2} ganglioside is present at only modest levels in cell membranes, because it is constantly being broken down as well as synthesized. The breakdown depends on the enzyme hexosaminidase A, which is found in the tiny structures within our cells known as lysosomes. In the unfortunate Tay-Sachs victims this enzyme is lacking, and without it the ganglioside piles up and produces all the symptoms of the disease.

We have two copies of the gene that programs our supply of hexosaminidase A, one inherited from our father, the other from our mother; each of our parents, in turn, has two copies derived from their own parents. As long as we have one good copy of the gene, we can produce enough hexosaminidase A to prevent a buildup of G_{M2} ganglioside and we won't get Tay-Sachs. This genetic disease is of the sort termed recessive rather than dominant—meaning that to get it, a child must inherit a defective gene not just from one parent but from both of them. Clearly, each parent must have had one good copy of the gene along with the defective copy—if either had had two defective genes, he or she would have died of the disease long before reaching the age of reproduction. In genetic terms the diseased child is homozygous for the defective gene and both parents are heterozygous for it.

None of this yet gives any hint as to why the Tay-Sachs gene should be most common among Eastern European Jews. To come to grips with that question, we must take a short detour into history.

From their biblical home of ancient Israel, Jews spread peacefully to other Mediterranean lands, Yemen, and India. They were also dispersed violently through conquest by Assyrians, Babylonians, and Romans. Under the Carolingian kings of the eighth and ninth centuries Jews were invited to settle in France and Germany as traders and financiers. In subsequent centuries, however, persecutions triggered by the Crusades gradually drove Jews out of Western Europe; the process culminated in their total expulsion from Spain in 1492. Those Spanish Jews—called Sephardim—fled to other lands around the Mediterranean. Jews of France and Germany—the Ashkenazim—fled east to Poland and from there to Lithuania and western Russia, where they settled mostly in towns, as businessmen engaged in whatever pursuit they were allowed.

There the Jews stayed for centuries, through periods of both tolerance and oppression. But toward the end of the nineteenth century and the beginning of the twentieth, waves of murderous anti-Semitic attacks drove millions of Jews out of Eastern Europe, with most of them heading for the United States. My mother's parents, for example, fled to New York from Lithuanian pogroms of the 1880s, while my father's parents fled from the Ukrainian pogroms of 1903–6. The more modern history of Jewish migration is probably well known to you all: most Jews who remained in Eastern Europe were exterminated during World War II, while most the survivors immigrated to the United States and Israel. Of the 13 million Jews alive today, more than three-quarters are Ashkenazim, the descendants of the Eastern European Jews and the people most at risk for Tay-Sachs.

Have these Jews maintained their genetic distinctness through the thousands of years of wandering? Some scholars claim that there has been so much intermarriage and conversion that Ashkenazic Jews are now just Eastern Europeans who adopted Jewish culture. However, modern genetic studies refute that speculation.

First of all, there are those ten genetic diseases that the Ashkenazim have somehow acquired, by which they differ both from other Jews and from Eastern European non-Jews. In addition, many Ashkenazic genes turn out to be ones typical of Palestinian Arabs and other peoples of the Eastern Mediterranean areas where Jews originated. (In fact, by genetic standards the current Arab-Israeli conflict is an internecine civil war.) Other Ashkenazic genes have indeed diverged from Mediterranean ones (including genes of Sephardic and Oriental Jews) and have evolved to converge on genes of Eastern European non-Jews subject to the same local forces of natural selection. But the degree to which Ashkenazim prove to differ genetically from Eastern European non-Jews implies an intermarriage rate of only about 15 percent.

Can history help explain why the Tay-Sachs gene in particular is so much more common in Ashkenazim than in their non-Jewish neighbors or in other Jews? At the risk of spoiling a mystery, I'll tell you now that the answer is yes, but to appreciate it, you'll have to understand the four possible explanations for the persistence of the Tay-Sachs gene.

First, new copies of the gene might be arising by mutation as fast as existing copies disappear with the death of Tay-Sachs children. That's the most likely explanation for the gene's persistence in most of the world, where the disease frequency is only one in 400,000 births—that frequency reflects a typical human mutation rate. But for this explanation to apply to the Ashkenazim would require a mutation rate of at least one per 3,600 births—far above the frequency observed for any human gene. Furthermore, there would be no precedent for one particular gene mutating so much more often in one human population than in others.

As a second possibility, the Ashkenazim might have acquired the Tay-Sachs gene from some other people who already had the gene at high frequency. Arthur Koestler's controversial book *The Thirteenth Tribe,* for example, popularized the view that the Ashkenazim are really not a Semitic people but are instead descended from the Khazar, a Turkic tribe whose rulers converted to Judaism in the eighth century. Could the Khazar have brought the Tay-Sachs gene to Eastern Europe? This speculation makes good romantic reading, but there is no good evidence to support it. Moreover, it fails to explain why deaths of Tay-Sachs children didn't eliminate the gene by natural selection in the past 1,200 years, nor how the Khazar acquired high frequencies of the gene in the first place.

The third hypothesis was the one preferred by a good many geneticists until recently. It invokes two genetic processes, termed the founder effect and genetic drift, that may operate in small populations. To understand these concepts, imagine that 100 couples settle in a new land and found a population that then increases. Imagine further that one parent among those original 100 couples happens to have some rare gene, one, say, that normally occurs at a frequency of one in a million. The gene's frequency in the new population will now be one in 200 as a result of the accidental presence of that rare founder.

Or suppose again that 100 couples found a population, but that one of the 100 men happens to have lots of kids by his wife or that he is exceptionally popular with other women, while the other 99 men are childless or have few kids or are simply less popular. That one man may thereby father 10 percent rather than a more representative one percent of the next generation's babies, and their genes will disproportionately reflect that man's genes. In other words, gene frequencies will have drifted between the first and second generation.

Through these two types of genetic accidents a rare gene may occur with an unusually high frequency in a small expanding population. Eventually, if the gene is harmful, natural selection will bring its frequency back to normal by killing off gene bearers. But if the resultant disease is recessive—if heterozygous individuals don't get the disease and only the rare, homozygous individuals die of it—the gene's high frequency may persist for many generations.

These accidents do in fact account for the astonishingly high Tay-Sachs gene frequency found in one group of Pennsylvania Dutch: out of the 333 people in this group, 98 proved to carry the Tay-Sachs gene. Those 333 are all descended from one couple who settled in the United States in the eighteenth century and had 13 children. Clearly, one of that founding couple must have carried the gene. A similar accident may explain why Tay-Sachs is also relatively common among French Canadians, who number 5 million today but are descended from fewer than 6,000 French immigrants who arrived in the New World between 1638 and 1759. In the two or three centuries since both these founding events, the high Tay-Sachs gene frequency among Pennsylvania Dutch and French Canadians has not yet had enough time to decline to normal levels.

The same mechanisms were one proposed to explain the high rate of Tay-Sachs disease among the Ashkenazim. Perhaps, the reasoning went, the gene just happened to be overrepresented in the founding Jewish population that settled in Germany or Eastern Europe. Perhaps the gene just happened to drift up in frequency in the Jewish populations scattered among the isolated towns of Eastern Europe.

But geneticists have long questioned whether the Ashkenazim population's history was really suitable for these genetic accidents to have been significant. Remember, the founder effect and genetic drift become significant only in small populations, and the founding populations of Ashkenazim may have been quite large. Moreover, Ashkenazic communities were considerably widespread; drift would have sent gene frequencies up in some towns but down in others. And, finally, natural selection has by now had a thousand years to restore gene frequencies to normal.

Granted, those doubts are based on historical data, which are not always as precise or reliable as one might want. But within the past several years the case against those accidental explanations for Tay-Sachs disease in the Ashkenazim has been bolstered by discoveries by molecular biologists.

Like all proteins, the enzyme absent in Tay-Sachs children is coded for by a piece of our DNA. Along that particular stretch of DNA there are thousands of different sites where a mutation could occur that would result in no enzyme and hence in the same set of symptoms. If molecular biologists had discovered that all cases of Tay-Sachs in Ashkenazim involved damage to DNA at the same site, that would have been strong evidence that in Ashkenazim the disease stems from a single mutation that has been multiplied by the founder effect or genetic drift—in other words, the high incidence of Tay-Sachs among Eastern European Jews is accidental.

In reality, though, several different mutations along this stretch of DNA have been identified in Ashkenazim, and two of them occur much more frequently than in non-Ashkenazim populations. It seems unlikely that genetic accidents would have pumped up the frequency of the same gene not once but twice in the same population.

It seems unlikely that genetic accidents would have pumped up the frequency of the same gene not once but twice in the same population.

And that's not the sole unlikely coincidence arguing against accidental explanations. Recall that Tay-Sachs is caused by the excessive accumulation of one fatty substance, G_{M2} ganglioside, from a defect in one enzyme, hexosaminidase A. But Tay-Sachs is one of ten genetic diseases characteristic of Ashkenazim. Among those other nine, two—Gaucher's disease and Niemann-Pick disease—result from the accumulation of two other fatty substances similar to G_{M2} ganglioside, as a result of defects in two other enzymes similar to hexosaminidase A. Yet our bodies contain thousands of different enzymes. It would have been an incredible roll of the genetic dice if, by nothing more than chance, Ashkenazim had independently acquired mutations in three closely related enzymes—and had acquired mutations in one of those enzymes twice.

All these facts bring us to the fourth possible explanation of why the Tay-Sachs gene is so prevalent among Ashkenazim: namely, that something about them favored accumulation of G_{M2} ganglioside and related fats.

For comparison, suppose that a friend doubles her money on one stock while you are getting wiped out with your investments. Taken alone, that could just mean she was lucky on that one occasion. But suppose that she doubles her money on each of two different stocks and at the same time rings up big profits in real estate while also making a killing in bonds. That implies more than lady luck; it suggests that something about your friend—like shrewd judgment—favors financial success.

What could be the blessings of fat accumulation in Eastern European Jews? At first this question sounds weird. After all, that fat accumulation was noticed only because of the curses it bestows: Tay-Sachs, Gaucher's, or Niemann-Pick disease. But many of our common genetic diseases may persist because they bring both blessings and curses (see "The Cruel Logic of Our Genes," *Discover*, November 1989). They kill or impair individuals who inherit two copies of the faulty gene, but they help those who receive only one defective gene by protecting them against other diseases. The best understood example is the sickle-cell gene of African blacks, which often kills homo-zygotes but protects heterozygotes against malaria. Natural selection sustains such genes because more heterozygotes than normal individuals survive to pass on their genes, and those extra gene copies offset the copies lost through the deaths of homozygotes.

So let us refine our question and ask, What blessing could the Tay-Sachs gene bring to those individuals who are heterozygous for it? A clue first emerged back in 1972, with the publication of the results of a questionnaire that had asked U.S. Ashkenazic parents of Tay-Sachs children what their own Eastern European-born parents had died of. Keep in mind that since these unfortunate children had to be homozygotes, with two copies of the Tay-Sachs gene, all their parents had to be heterozygotes, with one copy, and half of the parents' parents also had to be heterozygotes.

As it turned out, most of those Tay-Sachs grandparents had died of the usual causes: heart disease, stroke, cancer, and diabetes. But strikingly, only one of the 306 grandparents had died of tuberculosis, even though TB was generally one of the big killers in these grandparents' time. Indeed, among the general population of large Eastern European cities in the early twentieth century, TB caused up to 20 percent of all deaths.

This big discrepancy suggested that Tay-Sachs heterozygotes might somehow have been protected against TB. Interestingly, it was already well known that Ashkenazim in general had some such protection: even when Jews and non-Jews were compared within the same European city, class, and occupational group (for example, Warsaw garment workers), Jews had only half the TB death rate of non-Jews, despite their being equally susceptible to infection. Perhaps, one could reason, the Tay-Sachs gene furnished part of that well-established Jewish resistance.

A second clue to a heterozygote advantage conveyed by the Tay-Sachs gene emerged in 1983, with a fresh look at the data concerning the distributions of TB and the Tay-Sachs gene within Europe. The statistics showed that the Tay-Sachs gene was nearly three times more frequent among Jews originating from Austria, Hungary, and Czechoslovakia—areas where an amazing 9 to 10 percent of the population were heterozygotes—than among Jews from Poland, Russia, and Germany. At the same time records from an old Jewish TB sanatorium in Denver in 1904 showed that among patients born in Europe between 1860 and 1910, Jews from Austria and Hungary were overrepresented.

Initially, in putting together these two pieces of information, you might be tempted to conclude that because the highest frequency of the Tay-Sachs gene appeared in the same geographic region that produced the most cases of TB, the gene in fact offers no protection whatsoever. Indeed, this was precisely the mistaken conclusion of many researchers who had looked at these data before. But you have to pay careful attention to the numbers here: even at its highest frequency the Tay-Sachs gene

was carried by far fewer people than would be infected by TB. What the statistics really indicate is that where TB is the biggest threat, natural selection produces the biggest response.

Think of it this way: You arrive at an island where you find that all the inhabitants of the north end wear suits of armor, while all the inhabitants of the south end wear only cloth shirts. You'd be pretty safe in assuming that warfare is more prevalent in the north—and that war-related injuries account for far more deaths there than in the south. Thus, if the Tay-Sachs gene does indeed lend heterozygotes some protection against TB, you would expect to find the gene most often precisely where you find TB most often. Similarly, the sickle-cell gene reaches its highest frequencies in those parts of Africa where malaria is the biggest risk.

But you may believe there's still a hole in the argument: If Tay-Sachs heterozygotes are protected against TB, you may be asking, why is the gene common just in the Ashkenazim? Why did it not become common in the non-Jewish populations also exposed to TB in Austria, Hungary, and Czechoslovakia?

At this point we must recall the peculiar circumstances in which the Jews of Eastern Europe were forced to live. They were unique among the world's ethnic groups in having been virtually confined to towns for most of the past 2,000 years. Being forbidden to own land, Eastern European Jews were not peasant farmers living in the countryside, but businesspeople forced to live in crowded ghettos, in an environment where tuberculosis thrived.

Of course, until recent improvements in sanitation, these towns were not very healthy places for non-Jews either. Indeed, their populations couldn't sustain themselves: deaths exceeded births, and the number of dead had to be balanced by continued emigration from the countryside. For non-Jews, therefore, there was no genetically distinct urban population. For ghetto-bound Jews, however, there could be no emigration from the countryside; thus the Jewish population was under the strongest selection to evolve genetic resistance to TB.

Those are the conditions that probably led to Jewish TB resistance, whatever particular genetic factors prove to underlie it. I'd speculate that G_{M2} and related fats accumulate at slightly higher-than-normal levels in heterozygotes, although not at the lethal levels seen in homozygotes. (The fat accumulation in heterozygotes probably takes place in the cell membrane, the cell's "armor.") I'd also speculate that the accumulation provides heterozygotes with some protection against TB, and that that's why the genes for Tay-Sachs, Gaucher's, and Niemann-Pick disease reached high frequencies in the Ashkenazim.

Having thus stated the case, let me make clear that I don't want to overstate it. The evidence is still speculative. Depending on how you do the calculation, the low frequency of TB deaths in Tay-Sachs grandparents either barely reaches or doesn't quite reach the level of proof that statisticians require to accept an effect as real rather than as one that's arisen by chance. Moreover, we have no idea of the biochemical mechanism by which fat accumulation might confer resistance against TB. For the moment, I'd say that the evidence points to some selective advantage of Tay-Sachs heterozygotes among the Ashkenazim, and that TB resistance is the only plausible hypothesis yet proposed.

For now Tay-Sachs remains a speculative model for the evolution of ethnic diseases. But it's already a proven model of what to do about them. Twenty years ago a test was developed to identify Tay-Sachs heterozygotes, based on their lower-than-normal levels of hexosaminidase A. The test is simple, cheap, and accurate: all I did was to donate a small sample of my blood, pay $35, and wait a few days to receive the results.

If that test shows that at least one member of a couple is not a Tay-Sachs heterozygote, then any child of theirs can't be a Tay-Sachs homozygote. If both parents prove to be heterozygotes, there's a one-in-four chance of their child being a homozygote; that can then be determined by other tests performed on the mother early in pregnancy. If the results are positive, it's early enough for her to abort, should she choose to. That critical bit of knowledge has enabled parents who had gone through the agony of bearing a Tay-Sachs baby and watching him die to find the courage to try again.

The Tay-Sachs screening program launched in the United States in 1971 was targeted at the high-risk population: Ashkenazic Jewish couples of childbearing age. So successful has this approach been that the number of Tay-Sachs babies born each year in this country has declined tenfold. Today, in fact, more Tay-Sachs cases appear here in non-Jews than in Jews, because only the latter couples are routinely tested. Thus, what used to be the classic genetic disease of Jews is so no longer.

There's also a broader message to the Tay-Sachs story. We commonly refer to the United States as a melting pot, and in many ways that metaphor is apt. But in other ways we're not a melting pot, and we won't be for a long time. Each ethnic group has some characteristic genes of its own, a legacy of its distinct history. Tuberculosis and malaria are not major causes of death in the United States, but the genes that some of us evolved to protect ourselves against them are still frequent. Those genes are frequent only in certain ethnic groups, though, and they'll be slow to melt through the population.

We're not a melting pot, and we won't be for a long time. Each ethnic group has some characteristic genes of its own, a legacy of its distinct history.

With modern advances in molecular genetics, we can expect to see more, not less, ethnically targeted practice of medicine. Genetic screening for cystic fibrosis in European whites, for example, is one program that has been much discussed recently; when it comes, it will surely be based on the Tay-Sachs experience. Of course, what that may mean someday is more anxiety-ridden parents-to-be glowering at more dedicated genetics counselors. It will also mean fewer babies doomed to the agonies of diseases we may understand but that we'll never be able to accept.

Contributing editor **JARED DIAMOND** is a professor of physiology at the UCLA School of Medicine.

Ironing It Out

SHARON MOALEM

A ran Gordon is a born competitor. He's a top financial executive, a competitive swimmer since he was six years old, and a natural long-distance runner. A little more than a dozen years after he ran his first marathon in 1984 he set his sights on the Mount Everest of marathons—the Marathon des Sables, a 150-mile race across the Sahara Desert, all brutal heat and endlesss sand that test endurance runners like nothing else.

As he began to train he experienced something he'd never really had to deal with before—physical difficulty. He was tired all the time. His joints hurt. His heart seemed to skip a funny beat. He told his running partner he wasn't sure he could go on with training, with running at all. And he went to the doctor.

Actually, he went to *doctors*. Doctor after doctor—they couldn't account for his symptoms, or they drew the wrong conclusion. When his illness left him depressed, they told him it was stress and recommended he talk to a therapist. When blood tests revealed a liver problem, they told him he was drinking too much. Finally, after three years, his doctors uncovered the real problem. New tests revealed massive amounts of iron in his blood and liver—off-the-charts amounts of iron.

Aran Gordon was rusting to death.

H emochromatosis is a hereditary disease that disrupts the way the body metabolizes iron. Normally, when your body detects that it has sufficient iron in the blood, it reduces the amount of iron absorbed by your intestines from the food you eat. So even if you stuffed yourself with iron supplements you wouldn't load up with excess iron. Once your body is satisfied with the amount of iron it has, the excess will pass through you instead of being absorbed. But in a person who has hemochromatosis, the body always thinks that it doesn't have enough iron and continues to absorb iron unabated. This iron loading has deadly consequences over time. The excess iron is deposited throughout the body, ultimately damaging the joints, the major organs, and overall body chemistry. Unchecked, hemochromatosis can lead to liver failure, heart failure, diabetes, arthritis, infertility, psychiatric disorders, and even cancer. Unchecked, hemochromatosis will lead to death.

For more than 125 years after Armand Trousseau first described it in 1865, hemochromatosis was thought to be extremely rare. Then, in 1996, the primary gene that causes the condition was isolated for the first time. Since then, we've discovered that the gene for hemochromatosis is the most common genetic variant in people of Western European descent. If your ancestors are Western European, the odds are about one in three, or one in four, that you carry at least one copy of the hemochromatosis gene. Yet only one in two hundred people of Western European ancestry actually have hemochromatosis disease with all of its assorted symptoms. In genetics parlance, the degree that a given gene manifests itself in an individual is called penetrance. If a single gene means everyone who carries it will have dimples, that gene has very high or complete penetrance. On the other hand, a gene that requires a host of other circumstances to really manifest, like the gene for hemochromatosis, is considered to have low penetrance.

Aran Gordon had hemochromatosis. His body had been accumulating iron for more than thirty years. If it were untreated, doctors told him, it would kill him in another five. Fortunately for Aran, one of the oldest medical therapies known to man would soon enter his life and help him manage his iron-loading problem. But to get there, we have to go back.

W hy would a disease so deadly be bred into our genetic code? You see, hemochromatosis isn't an infectious disease like malaria, related to bad habits like lung cancer caused by smoking, or a viral invader like smallpox. Hemochromatosis is inherited—and the gene for it is very common in certain populations. In evolutionary terms, that means we asked for it.

Remember how natural selection works. If a given genetic trait makes you stronger—especially if it makes you stronger before you have children—then you're more likely to survive, reproduce, and pass that trait on. If a given trait makes you weaker, you're less likely to survive, reproduce, and pass that trait on. Over time, species "select" those traits that make them stronger and eliminate those traits that make them weaker.

So why is a natural-born killer like hemochromatosis swimming in our gene pool? To answer that, we have to examine the relationship between life—not just human life, but pretty much all life—and iron. But before we do, think about this—why would you take a drug that is guaranteed to kill you in forty years? One reason, right? It's the only thing that will stop you from dying tomorrow.

Just about every form of life has a thing for iron. Humans need iron for nearly every function of our metabolism. Iron carries oxygen from our lungs through the bloodstream and releases it in the body where it's needed. Iron is built into the enzymes that do most of the chemical heavy lifting in our bodies, where it helps us to detoxify poisons and to convert sugars into energy. Iron-poor diets and other iron deficiencies are the most common cause of anemia, a lack of red blood cells that can cause fatigue, shortness of breath, and even heart failure. (As many as 20 percent of menstruating women may have iron-related anemia because their monthly blood loss produces an iron deficiency. That may be the case in as much as half of all pregnant women as well—they're not menstruating, but the passenger they're carrying is hungry for iron too!) Without enough iron our immune system functions poorly, the skin gets pale, and people can feel confused, dizzy, cold, and extremely fatigued.

Iron even explains why some areas of the world's ocean are crystal clear blue and almost devoid of life, while others are bright green and teeming with it. It turns out that oceans can be seeded with iron when dust from land is blown across them. Oceans, like parts of the Pacific, that aren't in the path of these iron-bearing winds develop smaller communities of phytoplankton, the single-celled creatures at the bottom of the ocean's food chain. No phytoplankton, no zooplankton. No zooplankton, no anchovies. No anchovies, no tuna. But an ocean area like the North Atlantic, straight in the path of iron-rich dust from the Sahara Desert, is a green-hued aquatic metropolis. (This has even given rise to an idea to fight global warming that its originator calls the Geritol Solution. The notion is basically this—dumping billions of tons of iron solution into the ocean will stimulate massive plant growth that will suck enough carbon dioxide out of the atmosphere to counter the effects of all the CO_2 humans are releasing into the atmosphere by burning fossil fuels. A test of the theory in 1995 transformed a patch of ocean near the Galápagos Islands from sparkling blue to murky green overnight, as the iron triggered the growth of massive amounts of phytoplankton.)

Because iron is so important, most medical research has focused on populations who don't get enough iron. Some doctors and nutritionists have operated under the assumption that more iron can only be better. The food industry currently supplements everything from flour to breakfast cereal to baby formula with iron.

You know what they say about too much of a good thing?

Our relationship with iron is much more complex than it's been considered traditionally. It's essential—but it also provides a proverbial leg up to just about every biological threat to our lives. With very few exceptions in the form of a few bacteria that use other metals in its place, almost all life on earth needs iron to survive. Parasites hunt us for our iron; cancer cells thrive on our iron. Finding, controlling, and using iron is the game of life. For bacteria, fungi, and protozoa, human blood and tissue are an iron gold mine. Add too much iron to the human system and you may just be loading up the buffet table.

In 1952, Eugene D. Weinberg was a gifted microbial researcher with a healthy curiosity and a sick wife. Diagnosed with a mild infection, his wife was prescribed tetracycline, an antibiotic. Professor Weinberg wondered whether anything in her diet could interfere with the effectiveness of the antibiotic. We've only scratched the surface of our understanding of bacterial interactions today; in 1952, medical science had only scratched the surface of the scratch. Weinberg knew how little we knew, and he knew how unpredictable bacteria could be, so he wanted to test how the antibiotic would react to the presence or absence of specific chemicals that his wife was adding to her system by eating.

In his lab, at Indiana University, he directed his assistant to load up dozens of petri dishes with three compounds: tetracycline, bacteria, and a third organic or elemental nutrient, which varied from dish to dish. A few days later, one dish was so loaded with bacteria that Professor Weinberg's assistant assumed she had forgotten to add the antibiotic to that dish. She repeated the test for that nutrient and got the same result—massive bacteria growth. The nutrient in this sample was providing so much booster fuel to the bacteria that it effectively neutralized the antibiotic. You guessed it—it was iron.

Weinberg went on to prove that access to iron helps nearly all bacteria multiply almost unimpeded. From that point on, he dedicated his life's work to understanding the negative effect that the ingestion of excess iron can have on humans and the relationship other life-forms have to it.

Human iron regulation is a complex system that involves virtually every part of the body. A healthy adult usually has between three and four grams of iron in his or her body. Most of this iron is in the bloodstream within hemoglobin, distributing oxygen, but iron can also be found throughout the body. Given that iron is not only crucial to our survival but can be a potentially deadly liability, it shouldn't be surprising that we have iron-related defense mechanisms as well.

We're most vulnerable to infection where infection has a gateway to our bodies. In an adult without wounds or broken skin, that means our mouths, eyes, noses, ears, and genitals. And because infectious agents need iron to survive, all those openings have been declared iron no-fly-zones by our bodies. On top of that, those openings are patrolled by chelators—proteins that lock up iron molecules and prevent them from being used. Everything from tears to saliva to mucus—all the fluids found in those bodily entry points—are rich with chelators.

There's more to our iron defense system. When we're first beset by illness, our immune system kicks into high gear and fights back with what is called the *acute phase response*. The bloodstream is flooded with illness-fighting proteins, and, at the same time, iron is locked away to prevent biological invaders from using it against us. It's the biological equivalent of a prison lockdown—flood the halls with guards and secure the guns.

A similar response appears to occur when cells become cancerous and begin to spread without control. Cancer cells require iron to grow, so the body attempts to limit its availability. New pharmaceutical research is exploring ways to mimic this response by developing drugs to treat cancer and infections by limiting their access to iron.

Even some folk cures have regained respect as our understanding of bacteria's reliance on iron has grown. People used to cover wounds with egg-white-soaked straw to protect them from infection. It turns out that wasn't such a bad idea—preventing infection is what egg whites are made for. Egg shells are porous so that the chick embryo inside can "breathe." The problem with a porous shell, of course, is that air isn't the only thing that can get through it—so can all sorts of nasty microbes. The egg white's there to stop them. Egg whites are chock-full of chelators (those iron locking proteins that patrol our bodies' entry points) like ovoferrin in order to protect the developing chicken embryo—the yolk—from infection.

The relationship between iron and infection also explains one of the ways breast-feeding helps to prevent infections in newborns. Mother's milk contains lactoferrin—a chelating protein that binds with iron and prevents bacteria from feeding on it.

Before we return to Aran Gordon and hemochromatosis, we need to take a side trip, this time to Europe in the middle of the fourteenth century—not the best time to visit.

From 1347 through the next few years, the bubonic plague swept across Europe, leaving death, death, and more death in its wake. Somewhere between one-third and one-half of the population was killed—more than 25 million people. No recorded pandemic, before or since, has come close to touching the plague's record. We hope none ever will.

It was a gruesome disease. In its most common form the bacterium that's thought to have caused the plague (*Yersinia pestis,* named after Alexander Yersin, one of the bacteriologists who first isolated it in 1894) finds a home in the body's lymphatic system, painfully swelling the lymph nodes in the armpits and groin until those swollen lymph nodes literally burst through the skin. Untreated, the survival rate is about one in three. (And that's just the bubonic form, which infects the lymphatic system; when *Y. pestis* makes it into the lungs and becomes airborne, it kills nine out of ten—and not only is it more lethal when it's airborne, it's more contagious!)

The most likely origin of the European outbreak is thought to be a fleet of Genoese trading ships that docked in Messina, Italy, in the fall of 1347. By the time the ships reached port, most of the crews were already dead or dying. Some of the ships never even made it to port, running aground along the coast after the last of their crew became too sick to steer the ship. Looters preyed on the wrecks and got a lot more than they bargained for—and so did just about everyone they encountered as they carried the plague to land.

In 1348 a Sicilian notary named Gabriele de' Mussi tells of how the disease spread from ships to the coastal populations and then inward across the continent:

Alas! Our ships enter the port, but of a thousand sailors hardly ten are spared. We reach our homes; our kindred . . . come from all parts to visit us. Woe to us for we cast at them the darts of death! . . . Going back to their homes, they in turn soon infected their whole families, who in three days succumbed, and were buried in one common grave.

Panic rose as the disease spread from town to town. Prayer vigils were held, bonfires were lighted, churches were filled with throngs. Inevitably, people looked for someone to blame. First it was Jews, and then it was witches. But rounding them up and burning them alive did nothing to stop the plague's deadly march.

Interestingly, it's possible that practices related to the observance of Passover helped to protect Jewish neighborhoods from the plague. Passover is a week-long holiday commemorating Jews' escape from slavery in Egypt. As part of its observance, Jews do not eat leavened bread and remove all traces of it from their homes. In many parts of the world, especially Europe, wheat, grain, and even legumes are also forbidden during Passover. Dr. Martin J. Blaser, a professor of internal medicine at New York University Medical Center, thinks this "spring cleaning" of grain stores may have helped to protect Jews from the plague, by decreasing their exposure to rats hunting for food—rats that carried the plague.

Victims and physicians alike had little idea what was causing the disease. Communities were overwhelmed simply by the volume of bodies that needed burying. And that, of course, contributed to the spread of the disease as rats fed on infected corpses, fleas fed on infected rats, and additional humans caught the disease from infected fleas. In 1348 a Sienese named Agnolo di Tura wrote:

Father abandoned child, wife husband, one brother another, for this illness seemed to strike through the breath and sight. And so they died. And none could be found to bury the dead for money or friendship. Members of a household brought their dead to a ditch as best they could, without priest, without divine offices . . . great pits were dug and piled deep with the multitude of dead. And they died by the hundreds both day and night. . . . And as soon as those ditches were filled more were dug. . . . And I, Agnolo di Tura, called the Fat, buried my five children with my own hands. And there were also those who were so sparsely covered with earth that the dogs dragged them forth and devoured many bodies throughout the city. There was no one who wept for any death, for all awaited death. And so many died that all believed it was the end of the world.

As it turned out, it wasn't the end of the world, and it didn't kill everyone on earth or even in Europe. It didn't even kill everyone it infected. Why? Why did some people die and others survive?

The emerging answer may be found in the same place Aran Gordon finally found the answer to his health problem—iron. New research indicates that the more iron in a given population, the more vulnerable that population is to the plague. In the past, healthy adult men were at greater risk than anybody else—children and the elderly tended to be malnourished, with corresponding iron deficiencies, and adult women are regularly iron depleted by menstruation, pregnancy, and breast-feeding. It might be that, as Stephen Ell, a professor at the University of Iowa, wrote, "Iron status mirror[ed] mortality. Adult males were at highest risk on this basis, with women [who lose iron through menstruation], children, and the elderly relatively spared."

There aren't any highly reliable mortality records from the fourteenth century, but many scholars believe that men in their prime were the most vulnerable. More recent—but still long ago—outbreaks of bubonic plague, for which there are reliable mortality records, demonstrate that the perception of heightened vulnerability in healthy adult men is very real. A study of plague in St. Botolph's Parish in 1625 indicates that men between fifteen and forty-four killed by the disease outnumbered women of the same age by a factor of two to one.

So let's get back to hemochromatosis. With all this iron in their systems, people with hemochromatosis should be magnets for infection in general and the plague in particular, right?

Wrong.

Remember the iron-locking response of the body at the onset of illness? It turns out that people who have hemochromatosis have a form of iron locking going on as a permanent condition. The excess iron that the body takes on is distributed throughout the body—but it isn't distributed *everywhere* throughout the body. And while most cells end up with too much iron, one particular type of cell ends up with much *less* iron than normal. The cells that hemochromatosis is stingy with when it comes to iron are a type of white blood cell called *macrophages*. Macrophages are the police wagons of the immune system. They circle our systems looking for trouble; when they find it, they surround it, try to subdue or kill it, and bring it back to the station in our lymph nodes.

In a nonhemochromatic person, macrophages have plenty of iron. Many infectious agents, like tuberculosis, can use that iron within the microphage to feed and multiply (which is exactly what the body is trying to prevent through the iron-locking response). So when a normal macrophage gathers up certain infectious agents to protect the body, it inadvertently is giving those infectious agents a Trojan horse access to the iron they need to grow stronger. By the time those macrophages get to the lymph node, the invaders in the wagon are armed and dangerous and can use the lymphatic system to travel throughout the body. That's exactly what happens with bubonic plague: the swollen and bursting lymph nodes that characterize it are the direct result of the bacteria's subversion of the body's immune system for its own purposes.

Ultimately, the ability to access iron within our macrophages is what makes some intracellular infections deadly and others benign. The longer our immune system is able to prevent an infection from spreading by containing it, the better it can develop other means, like antibodies, to overwhelm it. If your macrophages lack iron, as they do in people who have hemochromatosis, those macrophages have an additional advantage—not only do they isolate infectious agents and cordon them off from the rest of the body, they also starve those infectious agents to death.

New research has demonstrated that iron-deficient macrophages are indeed the Bruce Lees of the immune system. In one set of experiments, macrophages from people who had hemochromatosis and macrophages from people who did not were matched against bacteria in separate dishes to test their killing ability. The hemochromatic macrophages crushed the bacteria—they are thought to be significantly better at combating bacteria by limiting the availability of iron than the nonhemochromatic macrophages.

Which brings us full circle. Why would you take a pill that was guaranteed to kill you in forty years? Because it will save you tomorrow. Why would we select for a gene that will kill us through iron loading by the time we reach what is now middle age? Because it will protect us from a disease that is killing everyone else long before that.

Hemochromatosis is caused by a genetic mutation. It predates the plague, of course. Recent research has suggested that it originated with the Vikings and was spread throughout Northern Europe as the Vikings colonized the European coastline. It may have originally evolved as a mechanism to minimize iron deficiencies in poorly nourished populations living in harsh environments. (If this was the case, you'd expect to find hemochromatosis in all populations living in iron-deficient environments, but you don't.) Some researchers have speculated that women who had hemochromatosis might have benefited from the additional iron absorbed through their diet because it prevented anemia caused by menstruation. This, in turn, led them to have more children, who also carried the hemochromatosis mutation. Even more speculative theories have suggested that Viking men may have offset the negative effects of hemochromatosis because their warrior culture resulted in frequent blood loss.

As the Vikings settled the European coast, the mutation may have grown in frequency through what geneticists call the founder effect. When small populations establish colonies in unpopulated or secluded areas, there is significant inbreeding for generations. This inbreeding virtually guarantees that any mutations that aren't fatal at a very early age will be maintained in large portions of the population.

Then, in 1347, the plague begins its march across Europe. People who have the hemochromatosis mutation are especially resistant to infection because of their iron-starved macrophages. So, though it will kill them decades later, they are much more likely than people without hemochromatosis to survive the plague, reproduce, and pass the mutation on to their children. In a population where most people don't survive until middle age, a genetic trait that will kill you when you get there but increases your chance of arriving is—well, something to ask for.

The pandemic known as the Black Death is the most famous—and deadly—outbreak of bubonic plague, but historians and scientists believe there were recurring outbreaks in

Europe virtually every generation until the eighteenth or nineteenth century. If hemochromatosis helped that first generation of carriers to survive the plague, multiplying its frequency across the population as a result, it's likely that these successive outbreaks compounded that effect, further breeding the mutation into the Northern and Western European populations every time the disease resurfaced over the ensuing three hundred years. The growing percentage of hemochromatosis carriers—potentially able to fend off the plague—may also explain why no subsequent epidemic was as deadly as the pandemic of 1347 to 1350.

This new understanding of hemochromatosis, infection, and iron has provoked a reevaluation of two long-established medical treatments—one very old and all but discredited, the other more recent and all but dogma. The first, bleeding, is back; the second, iron dosing, especially for anemics, is being reconsidered in many circumstances.

Bloodletting is one of the oldest medical practices in history, and nothing has a longer or more complicated record. First recorded three thousand years ago in Egypt, it reached its peak in the nineteenth century only to be roundly discredited as almost savage over the last hundred years. There are records of Syrian doctors using leeches for bloodletting more than two thousand years ago and accounts of the great Jewish scholar Maimonides' employing bloodletting as the physician to the royal court of Saladin, sultan of Egypt, in the twelfth century. Doctors and shamans from Asia to Europe to the Americas used instruments as varied as sharpened sticks, shark's teeth, and miniature bows and arrows to bleed their patients.

In Western medicine, the practice was derived from the thinking of the Greek physician Galen, who practiced the theory of the four humours—blood, black bile, yellow bile, and phlegm. According to Galen and his intellectual descendants, all illness resulted from an imbalance of the four humours, and it was the doctor's job to balance those fluids through fasting, purging, and bloodletting.

Volumes of old medical texts are devoted to how and how much blood should be drawn. An illustration from a 1506 book on medicine points to forty-three different places on the human body that should be used for bleeding—fourteen on the head alone.

For centuries in the West, the place to go for bloodletting was the barber shop. In fact, the barber's pole originated as a symbol for bloodletting—the brass bowl at the top represented the bowl where leeches were kept; the one at the bottom represented the bowl for collecting blood. And the red and white spirals have their origins in the medieval practice of hanging bandages on a pole to dry them after they were washed. The bandages would twist in the wind and wrap themselves in spirals around the pole. As to why barbers were the surgeons of the day? Well, they were the guys with the razor blades.

Bloodletting reached its peak in the eighteenth and nineteenth centuries. According to medical texts of the time, if you presented to your doctor with a fever, hypertension, or dropsy, you would be bled. If you had an inflammation, apoplexy, or a nervous disorder, you would be bled. If you suffered from a cough, dizziness, headache, drunkenness, palsy, rheumatism, or shortness of breath, you would be bled. As crazy as it sounds, even if you were hemorrhaging blood you would be bled.

Modern medical science has been skeptical of bloodletting for many reasons—at least some of them deserved. First of all, eighteenth- and nineteenth-century reliance on bleeding as a treatment for just about everything is reasonably suspect.

When George Washington was ill with a throat infection, doctors treating him conducted at least four bleedings in just twenty-four hours. It's unclear today whether Washington actually died from the infection or from shock caused by blood loss. Doctors in the nineteenth century routinely bled patients until they fainted; they took that as a sign they'd removed just the right amount of blood.

After millennia of practice, bloodletting fell into extreme disfavor at the beginning of the twentieth century. The medical community—even the general public—considered bleeding to be the epitome of everything that was barbaric about prescientific medicine. Now, new research indicates that—like so much else—the broad discrediting of bloodletting may have been a rush to judgment.

First of all, it's now absolutely clear that bloodletting—or phlebotomy, as it's known today—is the treatment of choice for hemochromatosis patients. Regular bleeding of hemochromatosis patients reduces the iron in their systems to normal levels and prevents the iron buildup in the body's organs that is so damaging.

It's not just for hemochromatosis, either—doctors and researchers are examining phlebotomy as an aid in combating heart disease, high blood pressure, and pulmonary edema. And even our complete dismissal of historic bloodletting practices is getting another look. New evidence suggests that, in moderation, bloodletting may have had a beneficial effect.

A Canadian physiologist named Norman Kasting discovered that bleeding animals induces the release of the hormone vasopressin; this reduces their fevers and spurs their immune system into higher gear. The connection isn't unequivocally proven in humans, but there is much correlation between bloodletting and fever reduction in the historic record. Bleeding also may have helped to fight infection by reducing the amount of iron available to feed an invader, providing an assist to the body's natural tendency to hide iron when it recognizes an infection.

When you think about it, the notion that humans across the globe continued to practice phlebotomy for thousands of years probably indicates that it produced *some* positive results. If everyone who was treated with bloodletting died, its practitioners would have been out of business pretty quickly.

One thing is clear—an ancient medical practice that "modern" medical science dismissed out of hand is the only effective treatment for a disease that would otherwise destroy the lives of thousands of people. The lesson for medical science is a simple one—there is much more that the scientific community doesn't understand than there is that it does understand.

Iron is good. Iron is good. Iron is good.

Well, now you know that, like just about every other good thing under the sun, when it comes to iron, it's moderation, moderation, moderation. But until recently, current medical thinking didn't recognize that. Iron was thought to be good, so the more iron the better.

A doctor named John Murray was working with his wife in a Somali refugee camp when he noticed that many of the nomads, despite pervasive anemia and repeated exposure to a range of virulent pathogens, including malaria, tuberculosis, and brucellosis, were free of visible infection. He responded to this anomaly by deciding to treat only part of the population with iron at first. Sure enough, he treated some of the nomads for anemia by giving them iron supplements, and suddenly the infections gained the upper hand. The rate of infection in nomads receiving the extra iron skyrocketed. The Somali nomads weren't withstanding these infections *despite* their anemia: they were withstanding these infections *because of* their anemia. It was iron locking in high gear.

Thirty-five years ago, doctors in New Zealand routinely injected Maori babies with iron supplements. They assumed that the Maori (the indigenous people of New Zealand) had a poor diet, lacking iron, and that their babies would be anemic as a result.

The Maori babies injected with iron were seven times as likely to suffer from potentially deadly infections, including septicemias (blood poisoning) and meningitis. Like all of us, babies have isolated strains of potentially harmful bacteria in their systems, but those strains are normally kept under control by their bodies. When the doctors gave these babies iron boosters, they were giving booster fuel to the bacteria, with tragic results.

It's not just iron dosing through injection that can cause this blossoming of infections; iron-supplemented food can be food for bacteria too. Many infants can have botulism spores in their intestines (the spores can be found in honey, and that's one of the reasons parents are warned not to feed honey to babies, especially before they turn one). If the spores germinate, the results can be fatal. A study of sixty-nine cases of infant botulism in California showed one key difference between fatal and nonfatal cases of botulism in babies. Babies who were fed with iron-supplemented formula instead of breast-fed were much younger when they began to get sick and more vulnerable as a result. Of the ten who died, all had been fed with the iron-enhanced formula.

By the way, hemochromatosis and anemia aren't the only hereditary diseases that have gained pride of place in our gene pool by offering protection from another threat, and they're not all related to iron. The second most common genetic disease in Europeans, after hemochromatosis, is cystic fibrosis. It's a terrible, debilitating disease that affects different parts of the body. Most people with cystic fibrosis die young, usually from lung-related illness. Cystic fibrosis is caused by a mutation in a gene called CFTR; it takes two copies of the mutated gene to cause the disease. Somebody with only one copy of the mutated gene is known as a carrier but does not have cystic fibrosis. It's thought that at least 2 percent of people descended from Europeans are carriers, making the mutation very common indeed from a genetic perspective. New research suggests that, sure enough, carrying a copy of the gene that causes cystic fibrosis seems to offer some protection from tuberculosis. Tuberculosis, which has also been called consumption because of the way it seems to consume its victims from the inside out, caused 20 percent of all the deaths in Europe between 1600 and 1900, making it a very deadly disease. And making anything that helped to protect people from it look pretty attractive while lounging in the gene pool.

Aran Gordon first manifested symptoms of hemochromatosis as he began training for the Marathon des Sables—that grueling 150-mile race across the Sahara Desert. But it would take three years of progressive health problems, frustrating tests, and inaccurate conclusions before he finally learned what was wrong with him. When he did, he was told that untreated he had five years to live.

Today, we know that Aran suffered the effects of the most common genetic disorder in people of European descent—hemochromatosis, a disorder that may very well have helped his ancestors to survive the plague.

Today, Aran's health has been restored through bloodletting, one of the oldest medical practices on earth.

Today, we understand much more about the complex interrelationship of our bodies, iron, infection, and conditions like hemochromatosis and anemia.

What doesn't kill us, makes us stronger.

Which is probably some version of what Aran Gordon was thinking when he finished the Marathon des Sables for the second time in April 2006—just a few months after he was supposed to have died.

Test-Your-Knowledge Form

We encourage you to photocopy and use this page as a tool to assess how the articles in *Annual Editions* expand on the information in your textbook. By reflecting on the articles you will gain enhanced text information. You can also access this useful form on a product's book support website at *http://www.mhcls.com*.

NAME: DATE:

_____

TITLE AND NUMBER OF ARTICLE:

_____

BRIEFLY STATE THE MAIN IDEA OF THIS ARTICLE:

_____

LIST THREE IMPORTANT FACTS THAT THE AUTHOR USES TO SUPPORT THE MAIN IDEA:

_____

WHAT INFORMATION OR IDEAS DISCUSSED IN THIS ARTICLE ARE ALSO DISCUSSED IN YOUR TEXTBOOK OR OTHER READINGS THAT YOU HAVE DONE? LIST THE TEXTBOOK CHAPTERS AND PAGE NUMBERS:

_____

LIST ANY EXAMPLES OF BIAS OR FAULTY REASONING THAT YOU FOUND IN THE ARTICLE:

_____

LIST ANY NEW TERMS/CONCEPTS THAT WERE DISCUSSED IN THE ARTICLE, AND WRITE A SHORT DEFINITION:

We Want Your Advice

ANNUAL EDITIONS revisions depend on two major opinion sources: one is our Advisory Board, listed in the front of this volume, which works with us in scanning the thousands of articles published in the public press each year; the other is you—the person actually using the book. Please help us and the users of the next edition by completing the prepaid article rating form on this page and returning it to us. Thank you for your help!

ANNUAL EDITIONS: Physical Anthropology 10/11

ARTICLE RATING FORM

Here is an opportunity for you to have direct input into the next revision of this volume.
We would like you to rate each of the articles listed below, using the following scale:

1. **Excellent: should definitely be retained**
2. **Above average: should probably be retained**
3. **Below average: should probably be deleted**
4. **Poor: should definitely be deleted**

Your ratings will play a vital part in the next revision.
Please mail this prepaid form to us as soon as possible.
Thanks for your help!

RATING	ARTICLE	RATING	ARTICLE
	1. Charles Darwin Was Born into a World That Today's Scientists Wouldn't Recognize		23. Made in Savannahstan
	2. Was Darwin Wrong?		24. Scavenger Hunt
	3. The Facts of Evolution		25. The Scavenging of "Peking Man"
	4. Evolution in Action		26. Hard Times among the Neanderthals
	5. How the Dog Got Its Curly Tail		27. Rethinking Neanderthals
	6. The Latest Face of Creationism		28. Last of the Neanderthals: A Hunter Retreats
	7. Why Should Students Learn Evolution?		29. The Great Human Migration
	8. The 2% Difference		30. The Littlest Human
	9. The Mind of the Chimpanzee		31. The Gift *of* Gab
	10. Got Culture?		32. The Birth of Childhood
	11. Dim Forest, Bright Chimps		33. The Brain
	12. Thinking Like a Monkey		34. Skin Deep
	13. Why Are Some Animals So Smart?		35. Born Gay?
	14. How Animals Do Business		36. How Real Is Race?: Using Anthropology to Make Sense of Human Diversity
	15. A Telling Difference		37. The Tall and the Short of It
	16. What Are Friends For?		38. The Viral Superhighway
	17. Face-Offs of the Female Kind		39. The Perfect Plague
	18. What's Love Got to Do with It?: Sex among Our Closest Relatives Is a Rather Open Affair		40. The Inuit Paradox
	19. Mothers and Others		41. Dr. Darwin
	20. The Salamander's Tale		42. Curse and Blessing of the Ghetto
	21. The Woman Who Shook up Man's Family Tree		43. Ironing It Out
	22. Hunting the First Hominid		

BUSINESS REPLY MAIL
FIRST CLASS MAIL PERMIT NO. 551 DUBUQUE IA

POSTAGE WILL BE PAID BY ADDRESSEE

McGraw-Hill Contemporary Learning Series
501 BELL STREET
DUBUQUE, IA 52001

NO POSTAGE
NECESSARY
IF MAILED
IN THE
UNITED STATES

ABOUT YOU

Name   Date
_____

Are you a teacher? ☐ A student? ☐
Your school's name
_____

Department
_____

Address   City   State   Zip
_____

School telephone #
_____

YOUR COMMENTS ARE IMPORTANT TO US!

Please fill in the following information:
For which course did you use this book?
_____

Did you use a text with this ANNUAL EDITION? ☐ yes ☐ no
What was the title of the text?
_____

What are your general reactions to the Annual Editions concept?
_____

Have you read any pertinent articles recently that you think should be included in the next edition? Explain.
_____

Are there any articles that you feel should be replaced in the next edition? Why?
_____

Are there any World Wide Websites that you feel should be included in the next edition? Please annotate.
_____

May we contact you for editorial input? ☐ yes ☐ no
May we quote your comments? ☐ yes ☐ no

NOTES

NOTES

NOTES

NOTES

NOTES

NOTES